ROYAL HISTORICAL SOCIETY

STUDIES IN HISTORY

New Series

CHESHIRE AND THE TUDOR STATE
1480–1560

CHESHIRE AND THE TUDOR STATE

1480–1560

Tim Thornton

THE ROYAL HISTORICAL SOCIETY
THE BOYDELL PRESS

First published 2000

A Royal Historical Society publication
Published by The Boydell Press
an imprint of Boydell & Brewer Ltd
PO Box 9, Woodbridge, Suffolk IP12 3DF, UK
and of Boydell & Brewer Inc.
PO Box 41026, Rochester, NY 14604–4126, USA
website: http://www.boydell.co.uk

ISBN 0 86193 248 X

ISSN 0269–2244

A catalogue record for this book is available
from the British Library

Library of Congress Cataloging-in-Publication Data
Thornton, Tim, 1966–
    Cheshire and the Tudor state 1480–1560 / Tim Thornton.
        p.   cm. – (Royal Historical Society studies in history.
    New series, ISSN 0269–2244)
    Includes bibliographical references (p.) and index.
    ISBN 0–86193–248–X
    1. Cheshire (England) – Politics and government.   2. Great
Britain – Politics and government – 1485–1603.   3. Tudor, House of.
I. Title. II. Series.
DA670.C5 T48 2001
942.7'105 – dc21   00–042515

This book is printed on acid-free paper

Printed in Great Britain by
St Edmundsbury Press, Bury St Edmunds, Suffolk

TO SUE JOHNS

A late sixteenth-century representation of Hugh Lupus, 1st earl of Chester
(1071–1101) in his 'parliament' at Chester Castle.
Reproduced from the Pedigree of the Earls of Chester, *c.* 1603,
by kind permission of Chester Archives (ref. CX/2).

Contents

Publication of this volume was aided by a grant from the Scouloudi Foundation, in association with the Institute of Historical Research.

Preface

This book began in the early 1980s, when devolution had disappeared from the Westminster political agenda and elected local and regional government was under serious challenge. It was finished in the week that the first meeting of the Council of the Isles brought together representatives of the Westminster administration with Welsh and Scottish ministers, and those from Eire and Northern Ireland, Jersey, Guernsey and Man. That transformation might obscure the context in which it was initially imagined. Yet even as the Council of the Isles met, regional government remained one of the two pledged reforms for which Tony Blair's government admits actions have not even begun to be taken. The book sprang initially from a determination, originally formed during my A-level years, to examine the centralist assumptions of the vast majority of the scholarly work to which I was exposed, not just on 'British' history but on English. Nick Henshall's teaching supported it. My ambition was further encouraged as I went through undergraduate study, especially by Penry Williams, and it finally took shape as a DPhil. thesis begun in 1989. Chris Haigh was an excellent supervisor, with a deep knowledge of the subject and the willingness to encourage me into the unorthodox. Steve Gunn proved the perfect internal examiner, offering comments that immeasurably improved the work over the last few years; and now as the editor in charge of this book always a friendly source of advice. Cliff Davies's generosity in discussing early Tudor politics and society has been particularly stimulating and helpful.

I have been fortunate to work in some very supportive environments. The sources for this book have their homes in excellent archives and libraries. Whatever one thinks of the Citizen's Charter, the staff of Cheshire County Council Record Office deserve their Charter Mark, and not just for their patience with young researchers. The staff of Chester Archives, the John Rylands University Library Manchester (Special Collections; especially Peter McNiven and Dorothy Clayton), and the Bodleian and Brotherton Libraries in Oxford and Leeds also deserve a special mention. Further, New College, Oxford, and the History Faculty there provided a good place to begin the work. Reading University provided many good colleagues among whom to continue it, especially Professor Michael Biddiss and Professor Donald Matthew who had the courage to invest in me, and Anne Curry, Ralph Houlbrooke and Brian Kemp who helped me in my first months in the profession. I am proud to have finished the book at Huddersfield among colleagues who for sheer concentration of talent and dedication to a transforming vision of higher education cannot be equalled. In particular, Pauline Stafford was a constantly supportive and extremely acute sounding-board for my views, and Bertrand Taithe a room-mate always brimming with ideas and enthusiasm.

I am grateful to E. J. Bourgeois II, Anne A. Cardew, Dorothy Clayton, J. P. D. Cooper, Sean Cunningham, Anne Curry, J. R. Dickinson, Catherine M. F. Ferguson, R. Fritze, R. A. Griffiths, A. M. Johnson, Melanie Lloyd, Patricia J. Marriott, Deborah Marsh, P. T. J. Morgan, P. R. Roberts, R. S. Schofield, Joanna M. Williams and Paul Worthington for permission to quote from their unpublished theses.

It is my good fortune to have parents who value this work and who in so many ways made it possible; and to have as my wife Sue Johns, a woman who, not least in her own writing, is an inspiration and a constant reminder of the responsibilities we have in the work we do. Carys will understand one day how important she was to the completion of the book.

Tim Thornton
December 1999

Abbreviations

APC	*Acts of the privy council of England*, n.s., ed. John Roche Dasent and others, London 1890–
BIHR	*Bulletin of the Institute of Historical Research*
BJRL	*Bulletin of the John Rylands Library*
BL	British Library
Bodl. Lib.	Bodleian Library, Oxford
BRUO	A. B. Emden, *A biographical register of the University of Oxford to AD 1500*, Oxford 1957–9
BRUO, 1501–40	A. B. Emden, *A biographical register of the University of Oxford, AD 1501–1540*, Oxford 1974
CCR	*Calendar of close rolls*, London 1902–
CCRO	Cheshire County Record Office
CChR	*Calendar of charter rolls*, London 1903–16
CCityRO	Chester City Record Office
CDRO	Chester Diocesan Record Office
CFR	*Calendar of fine rolls*, London 1911–
CJ	*Journals of the House of Commons*, London 1803
CP	G. E. C[okayne], *The complete peerage*, rev. Vicary Gibbs and others, London 1910–59
CPR	*Calendar of patent rolls*, London 1901–
CSPD	*Calendar of state papers, domestic series*, London 1856–
DKR	*Annual reports of the deputy keeper of the public records*, London 1840–
DNB	Leslie Stephen and S. Lee (eds), *Dictionary of national biography*, repr. 1949–50
EETS	Early English Text Society
EHR	*English Historical Review*
HBC	E. B. Fryde, D. E. Greenway, S. Porter and I. Roy (eds), *Handbook of British chronology*, 3rd edn, London 1986
HJ	*Historical Journal*
HMC	*Historical Manuscripts Commission*
JRUL	John Rylands University Library, Manchester
L&C Star Chamber	*Lancashire and Cheshire cases in the court of Star Chamber*, i, ed. R. Stewart Brown (RSLC lxxi, 1917 [1916]; no further volumes published)
LJ	*Journals of the House of Lords*, London 1771–
LP	*Letters and papers, foreign and domestic, of the reign of Henry VIII, 1509–47*, ed. J. S. Brewer, J. Gairdner and R. H. Brodie, London 1862–1910; *Addenda*, i, London, 1929–32

NH	*Northern History*
Ormerod, Chester	George Ormerod, *The history of the county palatine and city of Chester*, 2nd edn, rev. and enlarged by Thomas Helsby, London 1882
PRO	Public Record Office, London
RP	*Rotuli parliamentorum*, ed. J. Strachey and others, London 1767–77
RSLC	Record Society of Lancashire and Cheshire
Sheaf	*Cheshire Sheaf*
SR	*Statutes of the realm*, London 1810–28
THSLC	*Transactions of the Historic Society of Lancashire and Cheshire*
TRHS	*Transactions of the Royal Historical Society*
VCH	*Victoria History of the Counties of England*
WHR	*Welsh History Review*

Introduction:
The Historiography of Centralisation and the Palatinate in the Fifteenth Century

[T]he seide comite [of Cheshire] is and hath ben a comite palatyne als well afore the conquest of Englond as sithen distincte & sep[ar]ate from youre coron of Englond[.]¹

Late medieval Cheshire was a palatinate, a strong and vital political entity based upon a potent local identity and community. In judicial, legislative, fiscal and administrative terms the county had considerable autonomy. In the fifteenth century the people of Cheshire were extremely proud and assertive of their privileges.² They rejected the need for involvement with the central institutions of the English monarchy and demanded their exclusion from the shire. It was the palatinate, not Westminster, which was central to political life in late medieval Cheshire. The most striking evidence for this is the petitions which representatives of the county presented in defence of its privileges on at least three occasions in the middle of the fifteenth century, in 1441, 1450 and 1451, uniting as they do the cultural and theoretical foundations of the county's autonomy with its practical implementation.³ It must be admitted immediately that these petitions will be – and where they have been discussed, have been – treated with great scepticism, for they appear to contradict some of the key tenets of English and British historiography. The reasons for this scepticism will be treated in the central section of this introduction; in the meantime, a suspension of disbelief, if only temporarily, will allow the reader to understand something of, at the very least, the potential power of particularist sentiment in late medieval England. It makes sense to take the petitions in turn, for each sets out and demonstrates a key aspect of the palatinate's powers.

The events of 1441 demonstrated the independence and strength of the

---

1 Henry Davies Harrod, 'A defence of the liberties of Chester, 1450', *Archaeologia* 2nd ser. vii (1900), 75–7.
2 Cheshire was intimately connected with neighbouring Flintshire; many privileges were common to both. This was because the palatine earldom of Chester included the county of Flint after its annexation in 1284. However, Cheshire's community tended to deploy and defend its privileges without reference to Flintshire; throughout this study, therefore, the prime emphasis will be on Cheshire alone, although Flintshire is occasionally brought into the discussion.
3 For the context for these petitions, usually taxation demands, see ch. 3.

1

county's fiscal position, as well as its ability to stand aside from legislative and other provisions common throughout the rest of England. During the fifteenth century, the county's form of taxation, the mise, was voted, assessed and collected through local mechanisms; Westminster taxation was not effective in the shire. In 1441 the Cheshire mise was voted only following the redress of a set of grievances.[4] County representatives made several requests associated with the confirmation of their charter. They wanted an acceptance 'that no mon of the Countie of Chester shallbe compellet by the kings priuie seale at the sute of the party for to appeare at London or at any other styde afore the kinges counsell out of the said County', except for offences committed ouside the county. On the same theme, they demanded that all forfeited sureties of the peace, fines for breaches of the statutes of liveries and 'all maner of yssues by the gentils of the shyre afore this tyme forfet by cause the come not to London to take the order of knyghthood' should be pardoned. Further, they required an acknowledgement that the mise would not be levied again, confirming the principle of payment only at the accession or first entry of the earl to his earldom. In response, offences against the Statute of Liveries committed before 10 July 1441 were pardoned, and the law on liveries was eventually changed to exclude Cheshire.[5] The call for an end to privy seals summoning individuals out of the county palatine to the king's council produced on paper a more grudging concession – that none should be issued against anyone from the county for anything done there 'unless it be necessary' – but in practice the already limited number of Cheshire cases in chancery dwindled and disappeared completely.[6] The king also granted pardon, as requested, for all sureties of the peace forfeited before the same date.[7] Finally, the king granted pardon for all trespasses and all sums forfeited for non-appearance by Cheshire gentlemen distrained of knight-

---

[4]   D. J. Clayton, *The administration of the county palatine of Chester, 1442–85* (Chetham Society 3rd ser. xxxv, 1990), 49. On 5 March 1442 3,000 marks were granted to William Aiscough, bishop of Salisbury, and others; on 12 June 1442 collectors for the first tranche of the tax were appointed: *CPR, 1441–6*, 32, 50; CCRO, DSS, Vernon MS 3, fo. 190; *CPR, 1436–41*, 560–1; Tim Thornton, 'Political society in early Tudor Cheshire, 1480–1560', unpubl. DPhil. diss. Oxford 1993.
[5]   The law on livery had been extended to Cheshire in 1429, but the 1468 statute excluded the counties palatine: see p. 120 n. 3 below. See also M. A. Hicks, 'The 1468 Statute of Livery', *Historical Research* lxiv (1991), 15–28 esp. p. 21, although the emphasis on Durham, Lancashire and Cheshire seeking exemption because of a lack of confidence in their own judicial systems should be corrected.
[6]   Developed at pp. 103–6 below.
[7]   With the very limited exception of the surety forfeited by Hamo Massey of Puddington 'and other sureties of the like sort'. Hamo had been the subject of a series of recognizances to keep the peace against Richard de Hokenhull between 1438 and 1440: *Annual reports of the deputy keeper of the public records*, London 1840– , no. 37 (cited hereinafter in the form 37 DKR), 521. A possible reason for this exemption is that the forfeited bond had partly been granted away – the remaining money was granted to John Norreys, esquire, 8 Mar. 1446: ibid. 564.

hood, a process to which the county was not subject in the Tudor period.[8] The document therefore asserted that Cheshire was a semi-autonomous territory and demanded that the king should respect its privileges: its closest parallels are petitions of the Irish parliament, such as that presented in England by Sir Gilbert Debenham in 1474.[9]

Despite the success of the 1441 petition, further confrontation occurred in 1450; this time a Cheshire petition successfully asserted the county's independence of English taxation. On 6 May 1450 the English parliament at Leicester approved a graduated tax on freehold estates, annuities and jointures valued at over £1 *per annum*; lands in Cheshire, Wales and the marches were included. Unpopular generally,[10] in Cheshire the tax provoked particular outrage, since the county had long been exempt from English taxation, and another petition, perhaps the fullest exposition of Cheshire's rights.[11] It claimed that Cheshire had been a county palatine both before and after the Conquest, 'distincte & sep[ar]ate from youre coron of Englond', within which the king had his own parliament, chancery, exchequer and justice for crown and common pleas. The king, as earl, had the right 'by auctoritee of such p[ar]liamentes to make or admitte lawes within the same such as be thoght expedient & behobefull for the will of you and of the enh[er]iters & inh[ab]it[a]nts of the same comitee'; and the inhabitants of the county were

> noght chargeable nor lyable nor have not ben bounden charged nor hurt of thaye londes, godes nor possessions within the same comitee nor the inh[ab]itants of the same comitee of thaye bodies afore this tyme by auctoritee of any p[ar]liamente holden in other places than within the same comitee by any acte but such as that by thaye owen co[mmon]e assent assembled by auctorite within the same comitee have agreet unto.

It was further asserted that the king as earl of Chester had within the county 'Regalem potestatem jura regalia & prerogativa regia', for which reason suits and appeals were said to offend 'contra dignitatem gladii cestri'. The county's representatives, armed with the petition, were successful in asserting the county's freedom from English taxation – and by extension its wider legislative, fiscal, judicial and administrative autonomy. The king granted the petition on 8 March 1451.

Yet although the king accepted Cheshire's fiscal autonomy, Henry VI's government had not properly recognised Cheshire's control over legislation.

---

8 See p. 23 below.

9 Donough Bryan, *Gerald Fitzgerald: the great earl of Kildare*, Dublin 1933, 18–22.

10 Ralph A. Griffiths, *The reign of Henry VI: the exercise of royal authority, 1422–1461*, London 1981, 381, 396; Roger Virgoe, 'The parliamentary subsidy of 1450', *BIHR* lvi (1982), 133; *RP* v. 172–4.

11 Harrod, 'Defence of the liberties of Chester', 75–7; Ormerod, *Chester*, i. 45–6. Key sections are printed in Clayton, *Administration*, 126–7.

This was achieved later in 1451. A writ for resumption of royal grants in Cheshire according to a recently-enacted English statute, passed the palatine seal on 6 September 1451.[12] It produced an outraged response from the gentry of Cheshire which once again set out the tenets of county autonomy. The new petition was in many respects similar to that of 1450, but it did add significantly to the description of the workings of the Cheshire 'parliament'. The 1451 petition thus stated that if the introduction of an act like the resumption was proposed in Cheshire, representatives of its people should be summoned to meet 'Infra Castrum Cestrie in quadam domo ibidem consueta, vel in aliquo alio loco infra dictum Comitatum per Comitem eiusdem Comitatus assignato', where they would then agree to the act.

This episode was also notable for the way the clash between the government and the Cheshire community developed. The events of 1451 demonstrated the breadth and depth of commitment to the county's privileges among Cheshire's inhabitants. Perhaps mindful of the successful 1450 petition, the government consulted the gentry on a hundred-by-hundred basis, presumably to weaken resistance. They also chose much larger groups than before: ninety-three men from areas outside Wirral hundred were consulted, and an initial group of fourteen there, compared to thirty nobles and gentry from the whole county in 1450. The first group to be summoned was that from Macclesfield hundred, which met at Macclesfield on Monday 20 September 1451.[13] The Macclesfield gentry produced an answer which stated quite clearly that the county was not subject to English legislation and that such an act should be considered by a sitting of Cheshire's own parliament. The next hundred to meet was Broxton, on 27 September; they replied as Macclesfield had done. Nantwich followed on 2 November, Eddisbury on 4 November, Northwich the next day and Bucklow on the seventh: all followed Macclesfield's example. Wirral's meeting was arranged for Knutsford, well outside the hundred, in a final effort to break resistance. Even then the failure of representatives to appear drew out the process. The government was not amused by the gentry's refusal: the sheriff of Cheshire handed over the Macclesfield representatives to the keeper of Macclesfield gaol, Richard Hunter. The men of the other hundreds met and continued their defiance under the shadow of imprisonment and duly suffered, being handed over to the deputy constable of Chester Castle, Philip Aldersey. It was perhaps this fate that led to reluctance on the part of the Wirral representatives to appear before the sheriff. Thomas Poole, John Troutbeck and Henry Litherland, three of the most senior men summoned, failed to appear on 1 May and were each fined 1s. The next meeting, arranged for 1 September, saw them joined in their defiance by William Whitmore, and a similar fine was imposed. The

---

[12] BL, MS Harleian 2009, fos 40–1, printed and discussed in Tim Thornton, 'A defence of the liberties of Chester, 1451–2', *Historical Research* lxviii (1995), 338–54.

[13] The strength of royal lordship in the hundred may have suggested it as a weak point at which to begin the persuasion of the county.

summons for 2 November, this time to Northwich, they again ignored. All were fined 1s., but John Troutbeck suffered an additional fine of £100, because, as chamberlain of the county palatine, 'habuit maiorem noticiam de materiis et articulis'. The sheriff had also summoned an additional group of six Wirral gentry to this meeting, headed by William Stanley of Hooton and John Massey of Puddington; they too failed to appear and were fined 1s. each. Yet at this point the administration's will gave out. Nor was it only a few members of the political elite in the county who were willing to defend their privileges. Several were men who played little or no role in the activity of the county's courts; one, John Cryor of Dunham Massey, was described elsewhere as a chapman.[14]

There were, therefore, at least three occasions in the fifteenth century on which Cheshire asserted its privileges: it was not subject to ordinary English taxation or legislation, it was judicially and administratively autonomous, and it possessed a parliament which both legislated for the county and determined what taxation was paid there.[15]

These claims have posed problems for historians, coming as they do from a county in England, allegedly the most centralised political entity in western Europe. The petition of 1450, the best known, has been dismissed as irrelevant, an aberration or even as a misunderstanding of the contemporary constitutional position.[16] This book will argue that this historiography is fundamentally misconceived; it will demonstrate that Cheshire's claimed autonomy was not wishful thinking; and it will examine the ways in which that autonomy was shaped and altered under the early Tudors to emerge adapted but not fundamentally undermined at the accession of Elizabeth I.

An unwillingness to treat Cheshire palatine autonomy seriously runs deep in our major historiographical traditions. Whig history, which tells how English freedoms, of Germanic origin, were oppressed by the Normans but survived and then flourished in the parliamentary monarchy of the Lancastrians, which itself was overthrown by the New Monarchy of the Yorkists and Tudors but revived in the convulsions of the Stuart age,[17] has had a particularly powerful influence on views of the semi-autonomous regions with privi-

---

14 Thornton, 'Defence of the liberties of Chester', 341–2, 352.

15 A possible petition of Edward IV's reign, which may date to c. 1463 when parliament had granted a special levy for war, and a resumption had been agreed, on balance is simply another copy of the 1450 petition, wrongly ascribed: CCRO, DSS, box 22, 2 of 3 (Liber Comitatu' Cestriae 2), fo. 345; BL, MS Harleian 2155, fo. 66r–v. See also C. D. Ross, *Edward IV*, London 1974, 54, 348; *RP* v. 497–9; B. P. Wolffe, *The royal demesne in English history: the crown estate in the governance of the realm from the Conquest to 1509*, London 1971, 143–58.

16 Dorothy Clayton wondered 'why Henry VI, in his reply of 1451, did not deliver a more accurate history lesson to the people of Cheshire than they had to him': *Administration*, 50.

17 See also, especially for its association of the revolutions of 1399 and 1688, George Macaulay Trevelyan, *History of England*, London 1926, 3rd edn with corrections London 1952, 251–7, and also William Stubbs, *The constitutional history of England in its origin and development*, Oxford 1880, iii. 2–6.

leged jurisdictions within the boundaries of England, especially the palatinates of Durham and Chester. Two of the essential pillars of the Whig interpretation are that England differed from its continental neighbours in the Middle Ages first in its strong monarch and second in its lack of compact autonomous fiefs that might have produced a truly exclusive nobility of the blood. Centralisation, fluidity and service were the keynotes.[18] Regional and provincial liberties such as the Cheshire palatinate were therefore atypical and limited in their significance.[19] Although the 'differentness' of these franchises had been reduced by the Angevins and their successors, the Lancastrian constitutional experiment had led to them being tolerated and even encouraged, partly because of its exponents' belief in constitutionalism, but more importantly because behind that political principle lay an utter dependence on the support of major noblemen. Local autonomous jurisdictions, which might be controlled by these nobles, were part of the payment they demanded for supporting the Lancastrian regime.[20] From the perspective of the common Englishman and woman, these were dubious protectors of liberties.[21] One of the greatest Whig historians, George Macaulay Trevelyan, referred directly to Cheshire when he argued that justice was particularly corrupted by the retainers of great men when they could operate from semi-autonomous areas.

> In Cheshire, Lancashire and other franchised places where special local privilege rendered the course of royal justice even more difficult than in the rest of

[18] Trevelyan, *History of England*, 255. See also Stubbs on the palatinate of Chester in *The constitutional history of England*, 5th edn, London 1891, i. 393–4, and the summary of the development of McFarlane's views in the context of Stubbs, Gneist, White, Stenton, Maitland and Denholm-Young in K. B. McFarlane, *The nobility of later medieval England*, Oxford 1973, pp. xxi–xxii. See also David Cannadine, 'British history as a "new subject": politics, perspectives and prospects', in Alexander Grant and Keith J. Stringer (eds), *Uniting the kingdom?: the making of British history*, London 1995, 13–17.

[19] Trevelyan, *History of England*, 122–3. See also Henry Hallam, *The constitutional history of England from the accession of Henry VII. to the death of George II.*, 4th edn, London 1842, i. 7; Edward Creasy, *The rise and progress of the English constitution*, 10th edn, London 1868, 89–91; Edward A. Freeman, *The growth of the English constitution from the earliest times*, 3rd edn, London 1898, 92–3. Cheshire and Shropshire were seen as exceptions that prove the rule by George Burton Adams, *The history of England from the Norman Conquest to the death of John (1066–1216)*, London 1905, 56–7. See also Rudolph Gneist, *The history of the English constitution*, trans. Philip A. Ashworth, 2nd edn, London 1889, i. 139–40; F. W. Maitland, *The constitutional history of England*, Cambridge 1908, 41, 162–4; J. Franck Bright, *A history of England*, 5th edn, London 1897, i. 51.

[20] For example, Dudley Julius Medley, *A student's manual of English constitutional history*, 6th edn, Oxford 1925, 310–14. Only the accession of marcher lords themselves to the throne replaced this phase of development with a return to central power: R. F. Hunnisett, *The medieval coroner*, Cambridge 1961, 140.

[21] C. L. Kingsford, *Prejudice and promise in XVth century England: the Ford lectures, 1923–24*, Oxford 1925, 75, or in more extreme vein, William Denton, *England in the fifteenth century*, ed. Charles A. Denton, London 1888. The territories of Cheshire, Wales and Ireland had, of course, also threatened English liberties in royal hands when Richard II had planned a 'military despotism' based there: Anthony Steel, *Richard II*, Cambridge 1941, 128, 263–4.

England, gentlemen robbers lived in safety, and issued forth at the head of squadrons of cavalry to rob and plunder the midland counties. They murdered men or held them to ransom. They carried off girls to the counties where no constable could follow, married them there by force and extorted extravagant dowries from the unfortunate parents.[22]

'The exclusion of the aristocracy', and by extension the reduction of the liberties from which they flouted the common law of the realm, was, therefore, 'a first principle of Tudor statecraft'.[23] Along with fear of the poor, popular mistrust of the nobility, especially when they operated from franchised lairs, provided some reason for popular acquiescence in Yorkist and Tudor 'absolutism', and for general acceptance of the reduction of local liberties that went with the destruction of the 'over-mighty' subject.[24] When English liberties flowered in the seventeenth century, their defender had clearly become the Westminster parliament; local franchises were now even more clearly revealed as a threat to the people's rights. Their decline was therefore hastened further.[25] The act of the Long Parliament which swept away the Star Chamber was also welcomed by Henry Hallam for its abolition of the Council in the Marches of Wales, the Council in the North, and the jurisdiction of the Chester exchequer, thereby finally ending what he indignantly described as a situation in which one third of the realm had been denied proper recourse to the common law by the 'arbitrary jurisdiction of . . . irregular tribunals'.[26]

The Whig emphasis on remorseless centralisation in the early modern period is echoed in Marxist historiography.[27] Whether it is an interpretation that describes the state as an organ of coercion, or an analysis with a more Gramscian emphasis on the creation and maintenance of consensus, Marxist historiography focuses on the unity of the state and the drive toward centralisation. The transition from feudalism to bourgeois rule entailed, among other things, the creation of a unified economic space, in which capitalism could operate efficiently; it therefore required the eradication of anything that smacked of political disunity. The Yorkists and Tudors were allies of the bourgeoisie and destroyed provincial privilege. Perry Anderson found the absolutist state harnessing the nobility rather than destroying it outright in a doomsday confrontation, but Anderson's absolutist state was still centralising, drawing the nobles to court or to posts responsive to the demands of the centre.[28] Perhaps the most impressively wide-ranging and considered of these interpretations was that of Philip Corrigan and Derek Sayer. For them, the

22 George Macaulay Trevelyan, *England in the age of Wycliffe*, London 1899, 4th edn London 1909, 60.
23 Idem, *History of England*, 275.
24 John Richard Green, *A short history of the English people*, London 1878, 282, 285–6.
25 R. R. Reid, *The king's Council in the North*, London 1921, 54–7.
26 Hallam, *Constitutional history of England*, London 1876 edn, ii. 99 (16 Charles I, c. 10).
27 As in A. L. Morton, *A people's history of England*, London 1938, 61.
28 Perry Anderson, *Lineages of the absolutist state*, London 1974, 118–19.

fundamental truth was that 'state formation is a totalising project, representing people as part of a particular community', at the same time as being a process which 'individualises people in quite definite and specific ways'. The individual and the nation are the only results of this process; local autonomy and regionalism are its enemies. Their account therefore moved from the 'remarkably centralized country' of medieval England, through the revolution of the 1530s and the 'Elizabethan consolidation', to bourgeois revolution and the national machine of the 'old corruption'.[29]

Given the influence of these 'national' historiographies, particularly in the late nineteenth and early twentieth centuries, it is unsurprising that the historiography of Cheshire tended to dismiss the evidence for the richness of the county's political culture and the community it supported in favour of a concentration on the disorder allegedly consequent upon archaic privilege and of a belief in the inevitability of the palatinate's demise.[30] Cheshire's palatinate in the late Middle Ages has therefore been seen as a pale shadow of its former self; for writers of a Whiggish or sub-Marxist outlook it was simply a mask for gross disorder. The debased privileges of this enfeebled constitutional dinosaur allowed the expression of some of the worst excesses of the social system described as bastard feudalism. This had political implications, as social dislocation led rapidly towards civil war. James H. Ramsey described Margaret of Anjou in 1456, engaged in 'nursing a party among the warlike gentry of the Palatinate'.[31] In a career of writing on Cheshire which spanned from the 1920s through the following forty years, H. J. Hewitt emphasised the militarisation of the county's society, the restlessness of its population springing from what he saw as its predominantly pastoral economy and special features such as the avowries which provided sanctuary for the most violent of its own people and the most lawless fugitives from neighbouring shires.[32] A. R. Myers, selecting documents to illustrate disorder for the late medieval volume of *English historical documents*, chose two pieces from Cheshire, more than for any other county but Norfolk. Amongst his documents illustrative of 'the government of the realm' appeared one to illustrate 'the Cheshire institution of avowries', linked by association with disorder.[33]

---

[29] Philip Corrigan and Derek Sayer, *The great arch: English state formation as cultural revolution*, Oxford 1985, 4–5, 14. The authors quoted Foucault with particular approval: 'I'd like to underline the fact that the state's power (and that's one of the reasons for its strength) is both an individualizing and a totalizing form of power.'

[30] For the crucial issue of disorder in Cheshire society see pp. 189–91 below.

[31] James H. Ramsey, *Lancaster and York: a century of English history (AD 1399–1485)*, Oxford 1892, ii. 200.

[32] H. J. Hewitt, *Medieval Cheshire: an economic and social history of Cheshire in the reign of the three Edwards* (Chetham Society n.s. lxxxviii, 1929); *The Black Prince's expedition of 1355–1357*, Manchester 1958; *The organisation of war under Edward III*, Manchester 1966; and *Cheshire under the three Edwards*, Chester 1967.

[33] *English historical documents, 1327–1485*, ed. A. R. Myers, London 1969, items 343, 721, 724. The last, a petition of William, bishop of Coventry and Lichfield to the king in 1449, does not relate to criminal violence but to 'advowers, fornicators, and other misdoers against

Such views have found continued expression, for example in J. A. Tuck's explanation of the Cheshire rebellion of 1393 as the response of a warlike people to the possible peace of that year with France.[34] Paul Booth's writing about Cheshire has the objective of explaining what he sees as a growing separation between Cheshire and the rest of England apparent from the four-teenth century, a separation expressed in increasingly large-scale raiding into neighbouring areas, beginning with poaching in Bromfield in 1355 and an attack on the lordship of High Peak in 1357.[35] Michael Bennett's account of 'Northwest' society, while emphasising the coherence and relative order of county communities, relies on restless militarism as one of the main motors for careerism and the county's reputation as a 'seed-plot of gentility'.[36] Hence also the emphasis on violence and disorder in Cheshire used to explain the Tudor desire to end its privileges, seen in Joan Beck's *Tudor Cheshire* and in some of Eric Ives's work on Cheshire perceived through the lives of Henry VIII's courtiers Sir Ralph Egerton and William Brereton.[37]

Whig and Marxist historiographies of the late Middle Ages and Tudor period have, of course, been criticised. One of the most important of these critiques, that of Geoffrey Elton, in fact represents only a minimal departure from its predecessors in its treatment of provincial liberties.[38] While Elton generally accepted that Henry VII's main challenge was to provide strong leadership, not to reshape social alliances, he believed there was 'only one problem [that] could not be solved by mere restoration or revival, and that was the problem of franchises and feudal courts': the 'untamed passions and disorganised liberties of the Welsh Marches' had been unleashed upon

---

the laws of God'; the bishop desired the right to cite them out of the county and city into any other place in his diocese. See also Peter Heath, 'The medieval archdeaconry and Tudor bishopric of Chester', *Journal of Ecclesiastical History* xx (1969), 245–6, 248.

[34] J. A. Tuck, *Richard II and the English nobility*, London 1973, 165–6. See also Anthony Goodman, *The loyal conspiracy: the lords appellant under Richard II*, London 1971, 31.

[35] P. H. W. Booth, 'Taxation and public order: Cheshire in 1353', *NH* xii (1976), 20, and *The financial administration of the lordship and county of Chester, 1272–1377* (Chetham Society 3rd ser. xxviii, 1981), 7–8. For the importance of the activity of Cheshiremen in the redefinition of 'riot' to cover the activity of gentlemen rather than peasants see John G. Bellamy, *Criminal law and society in late medieval and Tudor England*, Gloucester–New York 1984, 54–6.

[36] Michael Bennett, *Community, class and careerism: Cheshire and Lancashire society in the age of Sir Gawain and the Green Knight*, Cambridge 1983, esp. p. 189.

[37] Joan Beck, *Tudor Cheshire*, Chester 1969; E. W. Ives, 'Patronage at the court of Henry VIII: the case of Sir Ralph Egerton of Ridley', *BJRL* lii (1969–70), 346–74; 'Court and county palatine in the reign of Henry VIII: the career of William Brereton of Malpas', *THSLC* cxxiii (1971), 1–38; 'Faction at the court of Henry VIII: the fall of Anne Boleyn', *History* lvii (1972), 169–88, and 'Crime, sanctuary and royal authority under Henry VIII: the exemplary sufferings of the Savage family', in Morris S. Arnold, Thomas A. Green, Sally A. Scully and Stephen D. White (eds), *Of the laws and customs of England: essays in honour of Samuel E. Thorne*, Chapel Hill, NC 1981, 296–320.

[38] For Elton's account of English constitutional divergence from continental Europe see *England under the Tudors*, London 1955, repr. London 1967, 4.

English politics from the time of Edward II.[39] Elton replaced a historiography of constitutional or class struggle with one focused on institutional change. It was the achievement of the Tudors, and, for Elton, a major element of Thomas Cromwell's 'revolution in government', that they took a country which suffered from the limited remaining disunity and completed its unification.[40] One aspect of the sudden transformation from medieval to modern wrought in the 1530s was the systematic and principled destruction of provincial liberty, backed by an imperial ideology of unity and centralisation, an institutional revolution achieved through parliament and represented above all by the arrival of newly enfranchised representatives in the Commons.[41]

A more fundamental challenge to the Whig and Marxist historiography of liberties like the Cheshire palatinate has come from scholars working in the tradition of K. B. McFarlane, who adopted a more benign view of the activity of gentlemen and nobles. McFarlane replaced Whig and Marxist historians' dismay at bastard feudalism with a belief that it was political weakness and division at the centre – notably the fault of the 'imbecile' Henry VI – which produced the Wars of the Roses, not a collapse of medieval social systems.[42] In work on Cheshire this has led to less emphasis on the county's innate militarism and violence. Philip Morgan, for example, has described the interaction of military activity and county society and concluded that Cheshire's militaristic tradition was a creation of the sixteenth- and seventeenth-century gentry's search to legitimate their status.[43] Interestingly, the powerful influence of McFarlane on late medieval and early modern history, although it did much to undermine the Whig interpretation, resulted in even less attention being paid to the importance of provincial privilege. The predominant spaces occupied by McFarlane's political figures were noble affinities and gentry connections which might be geographically either very localised

---

[39] Ibid. 4, 14–16. Elton does except (p. 15) a little from his strictures about franchises in crown hands.

[40] Ibid. 175–80.

[41] Ibid. 178–9; 'Wales in parliament, 1542–1581', in R. R. Davies and others (eds), *Welsh society and nationhood*, Cardiff 1984, 108–21 (repr. in his *Studies in Tudor and Stuart politics and government*, Cambridge 1974–92, iv. 91–108), and 'Tudor government: the points of contact, I: parliament', *TRHS* 5th ser. xxiv (1974), 183–200. Elton's *The parliament of England, 1559–1581*, Cambridge 1986, unsurprisingly given its title, does not even mention issues raised by the relatively novel presence of Welsh representatives in the Commons. The imperial theme is developed most clearly in the work of Brendan Bradshaw, especially in *The Irish constitutional revolution of the sixteenth century*, Cambridge 1979, and 'The Tudor reformation and revolution in Wales and Ireland: the origins of the British problem', in Brendan Bradshaw and John Morrill (eds), *The British problem, c. 1534–1707: state formation in the Atlantic archipelago*, Basingstoke–London 1996, 39–65.

[42] K. B. McFarlane, 'Bastard feudalism', *BIHR* xx (1945), 179 (repr. in his *England in the fifteenth century*, intro. G. L. Harriss, London 1981, 23–43).

[43] Philip Morgan, *War and society in medieval Cheshire, 1277–1403* (Chetham Society 3rd ser. xxiv, 1987).

or very extended. His most frequently used geographical terms, 'England' and 'English', were elastic in their application.[44] McFarlane's references to provincial privilege were few and often dismissive: in discussing parliament, he agreed that Lancashire's relationship with John of Gaunt might not have been typical of 'the less atavistic south and east'.[45] McFarlane was ready to accept the importance of 'neighbourhood', but this did not rise far above an appreciation that '[f]ourteenth-century society was strongly provincial and men believed that compatriots, those who come from the same "country" as they called each district, should stand together'.[46] Differences of geography, except, interestingly, Ireland and Calais in 1459–60, played little role in McFarlane's Wars of the Roses.[47] Although McFarlane himself held Henry VII's reign to be *sui generis*, his case in opposition to the previous interpretation of bastard feudalism contributed much to an increasing appreciation that the novelty of the new monarchy of Henry VII might have rested more on a forceful implementation of old-fashioned instruments of government than upon new social alliances for the monarchy. It was therefore inevitable that the lessons of his work would be taken up by Tudor historians; McFarlane's influence has meant that the alternative to a Whiggish, Marxist or Eltonian appreciation of the Tudors as destroyers of noble power and provincial privilege would be their recruitment to a world of noble affinities and gentry associations that paid little heed to conventional geographical boundaries.[48] This has been the case in much writing on Cheshire which adopts an ultimately McFarlane-ite approach. Those who have criticised an emphasis on palatine lawlessness and preferred to focus on the coherence and effectiveness of the community of the county have described the palatinate itself as the subject of little sentimental attachment.[49] These historians could draw on the weighty

---

[44] They happily cover activity in Wales, Ireland and even the Isle of Man: McFarlane, *Nobility of later medieval England*, 55.

[45] K. B. McFarlane, 'Parliament and "bastard feudalism" ', *TRHS* 4th ser. xxiv (1944), 56 (repr. in his *England in the fifteenth century*, 1–21).

[46] Idem, 'Bastard feudalism', 32.

[47] Idem, 'The Wars of the Roses', *Proceedings of the British Academy* i (1964), 98 (repr. in his *England in the fifteenth century*, 231–61). A sensitivity to provincial differences is more evident in McFarlane's, *Letters to friends, 1940–1966*, ed. G. L. Hariss with a memoir by Karl Leyser, Oxford 1997.

[48] For example, G. W. Bernard (ed.), *The Tudor nobility*, Manchester 1992; C. S. L. Davies, *Peace, print and Protestantism, 1450–1558*, London 1976. An extreme example of the explicit denial of palatinate significance is David Loades, *Power in Tudor England*, Basingstoke–London 1997: 'more or less inconsequential anachronisms for some time to come' (p. 33).

[49] Especially D. J. Clayton, 'The involvement of the gentry in the political, administrative and judicial affairs of the county palatine of Chester, 1442–85', unpubl. PhD diss. Liverpool 1980, 81–100; 'The "Cheshire parliament" in the fifteenth century', *Cheshire History* vi (Sept. 1980), 13–27; 'Peace bonds and the maintenance of law and order in late medieval England: the example of Cheshire', *BIHR* lviii (1985), 133–48; and *Administration*, 45–67. See also B. E. Harris, 'A Cheshire parliament', *Cheshire Sheaf* 5th ser. i (1976–7), 1–2, and

opinion of Geoffrey Barraclough who asserted that most aspects of the palatinate of Chester were inventions of the lawyers of the late sixteenth and early seventeenth centuries, and that commitment to the late medieval palatinate was minimal.[50] They could also find parallels in the work of revisionists studying the late sixteenth and seventeenth centuries, who relied heavily on similar models when they came to replace Whig and Marxist portrayals of society polarising along ideological or class lines. The Leicester School of Hoskins and Everitt developed a range of interpretations based on the English county community, founded upon the coherence of gentry society.[51] Some of the most important work in this field, notably that by John Morrill, took Cheshire as its subject; all paid little attention to questions of regional autonomy and difference and focused on their counties' essential unity in diversity.[52] The limited signs of palatine vitality, most notably the petitions of the mid-fifteenth century, are, in the analysis of these historians, primarily an indication of unusual royal weakness.[53] Working after McFarlane, historians have therefore concluded that the palatinate finally disappeared, to all intents and purposes, in the early sixteenth century and that this was neither surprising nor likely to have been strongly contested.[54] Franchised provinces and liberties therefore remain, in most historians' eyes, phenomena which do not fit happily into their understanding of late medieval and early modern

'Cover illustration: the Cheshire "parliament" ', *Cheshire History* ii (1978), 57–8; B. E. Harris and D. J. Clayton, 'Criminal procedure in Cheshire in the mid-fifteenth century', *THSLC* cxxviii (1979 [1978]), 161–72, and the volumes of the VCH for Cheshire edited by Brian Harris; Bennett, *Community, class and careerism*.

[50] Geoffrey Barraclough, 'The earldom and county palatine of Chester', *THSLC* ciii (1952 [1951]), 23–57.

[51] Alan Everitt, *The community of Kent and the great rebellion, 1640–1660*, Leicester 1966 (based on his thesis written 1952–7); Thomas G. Barnes, *Somerset, 1625–1640: a county's government during the 'personal rule'*, Cambridge, Mass. 1961; A. Hassell Smith, *County and court: government and politics in Norfolk, 1558–1603*, Oxford 1974; Diarmaid MacCulloch, *Suffolk and the Tudors: politics and religion in an English county, 1500–1600*, Oxford 1986, and many others.

[52] John Morrill, *Cheshire, 1630–1660: county government and society during the English revolution*, London 1974. Historians writing on the shire as such a community have therefore been open to the attack which has recently fallen on those who believe that England was a confederation of gentry republics: Clive Holmes, 'The county community in Stuart historiography', *Journal of British Studies* xix (1980), 54–73; Ann L. Hughes, 'Warwickshire on the eve of the civil war: a "county community"?', *Midland History* vii (1982), 42–72; Christine Carpenter, 'Gentry and community in medieval England', *Journal of British Studies* xxxiii (1995), 340–80.

[53] Barraclough, 'Earldom and county palatine of Chester', esp. p. 27; Clayton, *Administration*, 50–1. For Clayton royal weakness in 1450 was the key ('At this time the king had troubles enough': p. 50). In reality, Henry VI's government was attempting something new in 1450, the imposition of English taxation, something *'strong'* royal government, under Edward III or Henry V for example, had never tried.

[54] Paul Worthington, 'Royal government in the counties palatine of Lancashire and Cheshire, 1460–1509', unpubl. PhD diss. Swansea 1990 (supervised by Ralph Griffiths).

England. Partly as a consequence of McFarlane's insights, many historians have begun to argue that the state might include local governors, broadly defined, and might serve local interests. Any expansion of its role might therefore occur as a result of local demand.[55] There were early signs of this in the examination of the way that central institutions, especially parliament, served local interests.[56] Another more recent consequence has been the introduction into Tudor historiography of the 'over-mighty courtier', a character through whom the centre might be colonised by men from the localities. Cheshire courtiers Sir Ralph Egerton and William Brereton, men backed by court politics and patronage, were able to achieve dominance back in their home area, it has been argued, and this allegedly brought their localities more closely under the control of the centre, possibly even through the destruction of the local liberties from which they had sprung.[57] Centralisation, if on local initiatives, is therefore still the keynote of this historiography.

This study seeks to explore a variety of routes away from these assumptions of centralisation. It attempts to develop the legacy of McFarlane's appreciation of the viability of noble and gentry society by adding to it an understanding that the ideas which shaped this society might include a powerful respect for provincial autonomy. Building on work on other elements of the territories of the English crown, it rejects the idea that autonomy and diversity were doomed in 1500, and it argues for the positive benefits of the system for all concerned, in the locality and at the centre.[58] It argues that such measures as were taken with regard to franchises were limited and intended to operate through existing political structures and systems. Further, the fundamental objectives of the crown and its representatives at the centre never included dramatic change, and the political culture of the time gave little scope for anyone else to push these objectives further. Success and failure depended on limited institutional change and redefinitions of autonomy, not

55 Michael Braddick, 'State formation and social change in early modern England: a problem stated and approaches suggested', Social History xvi (1991), 1–17; Michael Mann, The sources of social power, I: A history of power from the beginning to AD 1760, Cambridge 1986.

56 G. R. Elton, 'Tudor government: the points of contact, I: parliament', TRHS 5th ser. xxiv (1974), 183–200; 'II: council', xxv (1975), 195–211; 'III: court', xxvi (1976), 211–28.

57 Letters and accounts of William Brereton of Malpas, ed. E. W. Ives (RSLC cxvi, 1976); Ives, 'Ralph Egerton'; S. J. Gunn, 'The regime of Charles, duke of Suffolk, in north Wales and the reform of Welsh government, 1509–25', WHR xii (1985), 461–94.

58 In this it draws on the inspiration of some of the recent historiography of Ireland, for example Steven G. Ellis, 'Crown, community and government in the English territories, 1450–1575', History lxxi (1986), 187–204; 'England in the Tudor state', HJ xxvi (1983), 201–12; and 'Tudor state formation and the shaping of the British Isles', in Steven G. Ellis and S. Barber (eds), Conquest and union: fashioning a British state, 1485–1720, London 1995, 40–63. See also Ciaran Brady, The chief governors: the rise and fall of reform government in Tudor Ireland, 1536–1588, Cambridge 1994. The implications are further explored in the conclusion to this book.

subjection or rebellion. The stresses of the sixteenth century, religious, political, social and economic, meant that the Cheshire palatinate of 1500 emerged in 1560 adapted but not radically transformed, still less completely destroyed.

The first section of this book will therefore consider in detail three aspects of palatine vitality and continuity. There is a strong argument for treating Cheshire as a political community 'imagined' by its inhabitants and by outsiders, as discursive.[59] Placing Cheshire in the context of the other territories of the English king, a consideration of political culture will examine the traditions of the county's past and future which supported and were themselves nourished by the county's privileged position. This 'imagined' community was, however, also founded on political and social transactions and institutions, and so the following chapter, an examination of the taxation of the palatinate, will demonstrate the workings of Cheshire's independent fiscal system in the later Middle Ages. This will show how taxation was agreed and collected through local mechanisms. Change occurred in the 1520s with increased application of Wolsey's non-parliamentary grants in the shire, and especially in the 1530s as the English parliamentary subsidy was imposed. During this period, however, the primary form of taxation continued to be the Cheshire mise, and Cheshire remained exempt from the English fifteenth and tenth. The concluding chapter of the first part of the book will consider the activity of the earl's Cheshire council. It will examine the process whereby the chief means for the articulation of the earl's power in the county gradually gave birth to a court of equity, the Chester exchequer. Part two of the book will then consider some of the chief changes that the palatinate underwent in the eighty years from 1480 to 1560, focusing on the role of law courts outside the shire, parliament and office-holding. Jurisdiction and litigation, the first of these topics, provide a contrast between the almost complete absence of Cheshire cases from the courts at Westminster during the fifteenth century and their increasing frequency in the early sixteenth century. The experience of Cheshire's relationship with the English parliament also provides a contrast, with the increased involvement of the county in legislation and the enfranchisement of the county in 1543. Office-holding too suggests a change to a pattern much more analogous with that current in England. In all three cases, however, the adaptation of the palatinate's position did not mean the end of its special place in the polity of the English crown. Finally, questions of local politics will be considered: both how they were conducted in the context of the palatinate and were shaped by it, and their impact on the palatinate as a set of privileged institutions. This will help to emphasise the contingency and *ad hoc* nature of the changes the

---

[59] In the tradition of Benedict R. O'G. Anderson, *Imagined communities: reflections on the origin and spread of nationalism*, London 1983, rev. edn, London 1991; Andrew Hadfield, *Literature, politics and national identity: Reformation to Renaissance*, Cambridge 1994.

palatinate underwent, and the continuing fundamental strength of the palatinate's privileges during the traumatic years of dynastic upheaval and Reformation. First of all, however, it is necessary to establish the *dramatis personae* of this story, the membership of the Cheshire political community.

1

The Aristocracy and Gentry of Cheshire

Investigation of the structure of Cheshire political society must begin with the aristocracy, the traditional leaders of society, and in particular with the most celebrated aristocratic family in late medieval and early modern Cheshire, the Stanleys of Lathom and Knowsley and their connections. Sir John Stanley's successful service to the crown meant he left his origins as a younger son of the Stanley of Storeton family in Cheshire and became established as an important gentleman in Lancashire.[1] Sir John had acquired Lathom in Lancashire following a fortunate marriage to Isabella, the heiress of the Lathom family, about 1385. He died in 1414, and his son John consolidated Stanley power in Cheshire, Lancashire and the Isle of Man.[2] John died in 1437, but his son Thomas was by then well established at the Lancastrian court, with all its opportunities for profit. In 1439 he became controller of the royal household. He was created a baron in 1456, but died in 1459.[3] His successor, Thomas, second lord Stanley, prospered under the new Yorkist regime and was created earl of Derby by Henry VII.[4]

It has been forcefully argued that these men played a key role as brokers between the crown and Cheshire during the period 1480 to 1560.[5] Yet the prevalence of Stanley power there can be questioned. There can be no doubt that the family achieved continuity in the male line over more than two centuries until 1593. The first earl died aged about sixty-nine in July 1504, to be succeeded by his grandson Thomas, the second earl.[6] Thomas died in May

1   Clayton, *Administration*, 69, 145; B. Coward, *The Stanleys, Lords Stanley and earls of Derby, 1395–1672: the origins, wealth and power of a landowning family* (Chetham Society 3rd ser. xxx, 1983), 3–5; Bennett, *Community, class and careerism*, 209–10, 217–18, and ' "Good lords" and "king-makers": the Stanleys of Lathom in English politics, 1385–1485', *History Today* xxxi (July 1981), 12–13; Morgan, *War and society*, 88–91, 171–4, 195–7.
2   Bennett, *Community, class and careerism*, 219–23; Coward, *Stanleys*, 6; Bennett, ' "Good lords" ', 13–14.
3   Clayton, *Administration*, 145–8; Coward, *Stanleys*, 6–9; Bennett, ' "Good lords" ', 13–14; Griffiths, *Henry VI*, 302–10.
4   Clayton, *Administration*, 150–5; *CP* iv. 205–7; Coward, *Stanleys*, 9–15; Bennett, ' "Good lords" ', 14–17; Ross, *Edward IV*, 323, 334; D. A. L. Morgan, 'The king's affinity in the polity of Yorkist England', *TRHS* 5th ser. xxiii (1973), 1–25, esp. p. 19; Rosemary Horrox, *Richard III: a study in service*, Cambridge 1991, 67–70; S. B. Chrimes, *Henry VII*, 2nd edn, London 1977, 28, 39, 44–6, 49, 55, 58–60.
5   See, in particular, Bennett, *Community, class and careerism*, passim and pp. 215–23, where it serves to explain the transition from the centrality of the north-west to political life in the late fourteenth century to its later relative marginality.
6   *CP* iv. 208–9.

1521, and his eldest son Edward, born in May 1509, led the family until his death in October 1572.[7] Edward too was succeeded by his eldest son, Henry, who died in 1593. It was only when Henry's son Ferdinando followed him to the grave a few months later that this continuity was interrupted and contested. The three daughters of Ferdinando and their mother Alice entered into a lengthy dispute with Ferdinando's brother William.[8] Yet, even before this hiatus, Cheshire was not a county dominated by the Stanley family.

First, severe pressures were imposed on the Stanleys by Henry VII and his son. Thomas, first earl of Derby, had close ties to Henry Tudor through his marriage to the king's mother and his support for the king in 1485, but he did not escape the unwelcome attentions of his royal step-son. When he over-stepped the mark in retaining in Warwickshire early in the reign, he was fined heavily.[9] In Cheshire, the earl was the target of the justices in eyre who visited the county in 1499–1500 and was subjected to severe financial penal-ties.[10] Thomas also suffered the loss of his son George, Lord Strange. Strange was already prominent in the politics of Henry VII's reign in the late 1480s, but he died in mysterious circumstances – allegedly by poison – at a banquet on 4 or 5 December 1503.[11] The dynasty therefore lost two key members in the space of eight months. The second earl 'was often tymes hardly intreated and to sore' by Henry VII, who imposed fines which remained unpaid at the king's death.[12] The pressure increased under Henry VIII: outstanding fines imposed under Henry VII were not pardoned, and a further fine of £1,000 was imposed for a riot, to be paid in instalments from November 1515. In 1517 2,500 marks were pardoned, but at the same time the earl had to assign lands for the payment of the 5,000 marks still owing.[13] Second, the limited ability of leading members of the family restricted the role of the Stanleys. This was especially true when the family was headed by young men. The second earl, himself no more than twenty-five when he succeeded in 1504, died in May 1521 when his heir Edward was just twelve. Edward did not receive livery of

---

7 CP iv. 209–10.

8 CP iv. 211–12; Coward, *Stanleys*, ch. iv.

9 Sean Cunningham, 'The Stanley earls of Derby in the early Tudor period, 1485–c. 1536', unpubl. MA diss. Lancaster 1990, and 'The establishment of the Tudor regime: Henry VII, rebellion and the financial control of the aristocracy, 1485–1509', unpubl. PhD diss. Lancaster 1995; Christine Carpenter, *Locality and polity: a study of Warwickshire landed society, 1401–1499*, Cambridge 1992, 566–7.

10 PRO, SC 6/Henry VII/1495 (1505 – on Thomas late earl of Derby, £8,441); BL, MS Lansdowne 644, fo. 21v. In 1499 the vow of chastity taken by his wife Margaret Beaufort emphasised his isolation from the royal family: Michael K. Jones and Malcolm G. Under-wood, *The king's mother: Lady Margaret Beaufort, countess of Richmond and Derby*, Cambridge 1992, 153–4.

11 CP iv. 205–8; *DNB* xviii. 962–5, 937–9 (which gets the date wrong by following Stanley sources). Strange was about 43.

12 C. J. Harrison, 'The petition of Edmund Dudley', *EHR* lxxxvii (1972), 88 (quotation).

13 Helen Miller, *Henry VIII and the English nobility*, Oxford 1986, 107, 208–9

his lands until January 1531, and even then his abilities were questioned: he was described in 1538 as 'a child in wisdom and half a fool'.[14] Third, the Stanleys lacked land in Cheshire and depended on office as the basis for their power there. Stanley power in Lancashire, landed and otherwise, was immense, and was nicely summarised by Sir John Townley of Townley in explaining his refusal to co-operate with the visitation of Thomas Benolt the herald in 1533: 'ther was no more Gentilmen in Lancashire But my Lord of Derbye & Mountegle'.[15] Yet the Stanleys had acquired little property in Cheshire until Richard III's reign, when they received lands taken from the duke of Buckingham and Sir Thomas St Leger. Even then, the accession of Henry VII meant the loss of much that had been gained in 1484, as former rebels came back into favour. Only in 1489 was compensation made, notably in grants of the lands of Francis, Lord Lovell, to Sir William Stanley.[16] Yet it should be noted that Stanley landed power in Cheshire was concentrated in the person of Sir William, and, due to his attainder, all was lost in 1495.[17] Stanley influence could be useful to people and institutions in early sixteenth-century Cheshire, but it was far from indispensable: in the 1530s the third earl held the stewardship of both St Werburgh's abbey and St Mary's nunnery in Chester, but he was an officer of no other Cheshire monastery.[18]

It was the influence derived from the Stanleys' office-holding, therefore, that lay behind their arbitration of many Cheshire disputes.[19] It is, for example, misleading to cite as an example of Stanley dominance a letter written from Liverpool by James Stanley, archdeacon of Chester, to Sir William Stanley, chamberlain of Chester, concerning an arbitration between

---

14 CP iv. 208–10; LP xiii/2, 732. G. W. Bernard questions Anthony Budgegood's judgements: T. B. Pugh, 'Henry VII and the English nobility', in Bernard, Tudor nobility, 97.

15 The visitation of Lancashire and a part of Cheshire made in the twenty-fourth year of the reign of King Henry the eighth, AD 1533, by special commission of Thomas Benalt, Clarencieux, ed. William Langton (Chetham Society xcviii, 1876), 43.

16 Sir William had gained an interest in the barony of Nantwich when he married Joan, widow of John, Lord Lovell, but lost this on her death in 1469.

17 CPR, 1485–94, 263–4; PRO, CHES 3/57 (20 Henry VII, no. 9); Ormerod, Chester, i. 647–50; Joanna M. Williams, 'The Stanley family of Lathom and Knowsley, c. 1450–1504: a political study', unpubl. MA diss. Manchester 1979, 303–21, 133, 182; Michael K. Jones, 'Sir William Stanley of Holt: politics and family allegiance in the late fifteenth century', WHR xiv (1988), 6, 10–12. Barry Coward's over-enthusiastic account (Stanleys, 11–13) is commented upon sceptically by Margaret Condon, 'Ruling elites in the reign of Henry VII', in C. D. Ross (ed.), Patronage, pedigree and power in later medieval England, Gloucester–Totowa, NJ 1979, 136 n. 20.

18 Valor ecclesiasticus, ed. J. Caley and J. Hunter, London 1810–34, v. 205–6, 209, 212, 217.

19 Sir William Stanley retained Piers Warburton on 27 Oct. 1461 and they remained strongly connected: JRUL, Arley charters 9/7, 30/1. Warburton was also employed by Eleanor, first wife of Lord Stanley, in the 1460s: ibid. 30/2. Warburton's son John married Stanley's daughter. Richard Cholmondeley called Sir William Stanley 'my master' when he appointed him his executor before his death in 1489: Lancashire and Cheshire wills and inventories from the ecclesiastical court, Chester, ed. G. J. Piccope (Chetham Society liv, 1861), 41–3.

the Maisterson and Marchomley families.[20] James explained in his letter that he wished to delegate the task because he had been summoned to Lathom by Lord Stanley. This has been presented as the simple reallocation of tasks among the Stanley family. In fact, the letter is addressed to both Sir William Stanley and William Venables. William Stanley is referred to in the letter in the third person, suggesting that the expected recipient was Venables, escheator of Chester until 1467.[21] The text continues after the request 'I pray you will labour to the partyes yff they wyll abyde the dome of my broder chamberlayn . . .', with 'Nedam iustice and me or elles any lernetmon yt wold be egall be twene thaym'. James Stanley's redistribution of arbitration responsibilities took place in the context of local office-holding, for Sir John Needham held the post of deputy justice of Chester.[22] Another example of the involvement of members of the Stanley family in the resolution of disputes as officers of the palatinate resulted from conflict between William Tatton and the city of Chester under Richard III, when Tatton was defending his administration of advowries in the city.[23] In this case William and Thomas Stanley acted explicitly as members of the king's council in Chester, in which they participated as chamberlain and justice of the palatinate.[24] Given this dependence on office to support their influence in Cheshire, it is especially significant that after 1504 the Stanleys held office hardly at all in Cheshire until the accession of Elizabeth, in spite of what they later claimed.[25] In particular, the influence enjoyed by the Stanley family through the lord-lieutenancy of Cheshire has been exaggerated. The commission granted to Edward Stanley in 1536 during the Pilgrimage of Grace did not become in any sense permanent for Cheshire until 1585. In April 1556, for example, he had to appeal to the master of the queen's horse for help in keeping the lieutenancy of Lancashire and Cheshire out of the hands of the earl of Shrewsbury.[26]

[20] Jones, 'Sir William Stanley', 7; BL, MS Add. 34,815, fo. 5 (1476–80).

[21] Clayton, Administration, 185–6; Worthington, 'Royal government', 359.

[22] Needham was first appointed deputy justice on 28 November 1450. He was appointed one of three justices for the county court of 26 May 1461 and sole justice on 28 July 1461. On 1 January 1462 Thomas, Lord Stanley, became justice, and Needham returned to the post of deputy until his death in 1480: Clayton, Administration, 156; Worthington, 'Royal government', 346–7.

[23] JRUL, Tatton of Wythenshawe 444; Jones, 'Sir William Stanley', 9, again cites misleadingly.

[24] See ch. 4 below. The Marchomley–Maisterson arbitration may also have been linked to the council in Cheshire, on which the archdeacon might have sat.

[25] '[S]ince her [i.e. Queen Elizabeth's] grandfather's time': HMC, Calendar of the manuscripts of the most hon. the marquis of Salisbury KG, etc., preserved at Hatfield House, Hertfordshire, London 1883–1976, iv. 378 (26 Sept. 1593).

[26] B. Coward, 'The lieutenancy of Lancashire and Cheshire in the sixteenth and early seventeenth centuries', THSLC cxix (1969 [1968]), 39–64, esp. pp. 46–8; Gladys Scott Thomson, Lords lieutenant in the sixteenth century: a study in Tudor local administration, London 1923, 16–40; HMC, Report on the manuscripts of the late Reginald Rawdon Hastings, esq. of the Manor House, Ashby de la Zouch, London 1928–, ii. 4. Shortly before, in the 1550s,

Other aristocratic families could have provided another pole of authority in the shire: both the Audley and Dudley barons had strong Cheshire connections. Both were, however, experiencing difficulties during this period. The Lords Audley originated from just over the Staffordshire border, but they had gained fame leading Cheshire men to war in the fourteenth century and they continued to hold the Cheshire manors of Tattenhall, Newhall and Buglawton.[27] James Touchet, Lord Audley died leading Cheshire supporters of the Lancastrian regime at Blore Heath in 1459, but his son John married Anne, widow of John Rogers of Bryanston, near Blandford Forum, and daughter and coheir of Sir Thomas Etchingham. Audley activity and interest shifted to the counties of the south coast. John's son and successor, James, led the Cornish rebels of 1497, and suffered attainder.[28] During the attainder, the Audley inheritance was looted, the advowson of Middlewich being transferred to Lenton priory in Nottinghamshire.[29] James's son John was restored in 1512 but, although he lived until 1556, he was penniless and this opened him to manipulation and involvement in violent disputes.[30] Much of the Audleys' Cheshire interest devolved upon the Mainwarings of Over Peover.[31] Tattenhall, Newhall and Buglawton were the subject of recoveries in favour of royal servants in the early years of John Touchet's restoration, and by the reign of Mary the three manors had passed completely out of the family's hands.[32] This loss of land in Cheshire was accompanied by a decline in Newhall Tower, the physical symbol of Audley power, which Leland noted was 'now doune'.[33] There are signs of a return of Audley interests to the north-west after John's death, for his heir George

the Privy Council's arrangements for lieutenancies gave Derby Lancashire, but Cheshire was covered by Pembroke's commission for Wales as Lord President: APC iii. 258–9; iv. 49–50, 276–8.
27 Morgan, *War and society*, 75–6; PRO, CHES 3/52 (6 Henry VII, no. 4); Ormerod, *Chester*, ii. 717; iii. 41, 391. The Lords Audley were descendants of a younger branch of the Touchets of Nether Whitley; a settlement left them with Tattenhall and Buglawton: ibid. i. 660, 662.
28 *DNB* xix. 1003–4.
29 VCH, *Nottinghamshire*, ed. William Page, Oxford 1906– , ii. 93; Ormerod, *Chester*, iii. 180, 185–6; John Thomas Godfrey, *The history of the parish and priory of Lenton in the county of Nottingham*, London 1884, 171–2. Cf. the loss of Tarporley, Rushton and Eyton by the Greys, earls of Kent: PRO, CHES 31/37 (23 Henry VII, 2); C 1/761/45–9; C 1/1221/79–80; Ormerod, *Chester*, ii. 226–7, 235; G. W. Bernard, 'The fortunes of the Greys, earls of Kent, in the early sixteenth century', *HJ* xxv (1982), 674.
30 *LP* iv/3, app. 245; v. 708, 734, 874, 875, 955, 1720.
31 John Mainwaring was appointed constable of Heighley Castle (Staffs.) and seneschal of Nantwich (26 Oct. 1512): JRUL, Mainwaring charters 323–4.
32 Buglawton was granted to Sir Nicholas Bagnall by Edward VI: Ormerod, *Chester*, ii. 717; iii. 41, 391.
33 *The itinerary of John Leland in or about the years 1536–1539*, ed. Lucy Toulmin Smith, London 1964, v. 25; Niklaus Pevsner and Edward Hubbard, *Cheshire*, Harmondsworth 1971, 18.

married his second wife, Joan Flatt, at his oratory in Chester.[34] George's successor Henry married Elizabeth, daughter of Sir William Sneyd of Bradwell, Staffordshire, whose mother was Anne, daughter and heir of Thomas Barrowe of Flookersbrook, Cheshire.[35] Yet this connection to the Sneyds, a successful Cheshire legal and administrative family, is perhaps less significant of local connections than of the nadir of the Audley fortunes at this point.[36] Like the Audleys, the Dudleys were also in severe difficulties during the Tudor period.[37] Their interests around Malpas were a target of their acquisitive relative, Henry VII's minister Edmund Dudley.[38] John Sutton or Dudley, who succeeded to the title in 1532, was never summoned to parliament and was commonly called Lord Quondam, alienated his estates to his rising cousin Sir John Dudley.[39] It was only in 1554–5, after the fall of Sir John from the heights of the presidency of the council and the duchy of Northumberland, and with the accession of Mary to the throne, that the Dudley family estates were restored.

There was therefore no predominant noble dynasty in Cheshire during the early Tudor period, especially during the 1520s and 1530s when the Stanleys suffered minority and incompetence, and other noble families were in crisis. This gave scope for an extension of the influence of the rising magnates of the north midlands, the Talbot earls of Shrewsbury. Military command, especially that exercised by Francis, the fifth earl, in the 1540s, meant that Cheshire men were led to war by Talbots. Randolph More of Nantwich, for example, was one of Earl George's company when he was lieutenant of the vanguard in France in 1513; when he was murdered, his widow went to Shrewsbury for help. Sir William Davenport of Bramhall made Grace, countess of Shrewsbury, recently married second wife of Francis Talbot, one of the overseers of his will in 1553. Talbot political influence made the family a useful patron for

---

[34] CP i. 343.

[35] Elizabeth died in 1609 at Thelwall and was buried at Grappenhall.

[36] Henry was never summoned to parliament; it was left to his son George to rebuild the family's position, being created earl of Castlehaven in 1616: CP i. 343.

[37] PRO, CHES 3/51 (3 Henry VII no. 5); CHES 3/59 (2 Henry VIII no. 59); CP iv. 481–2; DNB vi. 107–9; H. S. Grazebrook, 'The barons of Dudley', *Collections for a History of Staffordshire* ix/2 (1888), 87–8, 94–7, 104–8.

[38] For Dudley purchasing in the Malpas area from John Yonge, alias John Somerset, alleged heir of Sir Thomas Cokesey, see CCRO, DCH B/43 (1506); PRO, C 1/377/16; for leasing lands there see CCRO, DCH B/44 (1507). Although Edward, Lord Dudley, presented to the living at Malpas in 1493 and 1511, in January 1517 he granted the next vacancy to Sir Henry Wyatt, treasurer of the king's chamber: DCH C/454, /442. The patronage passed to Sir Richard Brereton of Tatton and John Harcorte 'of Rauton' in 1543: DCH C/452. Edward, Lord Dudley, wisely made Randal Brereton of Malpas, rising in the king's service, steward of his Malpas properties in April 1497: DCH C/347.

[39] For Sir John's leasing in the Malpas area see CCRO, DCH B/46–47, C/443–45 (1524). Another beneficiary of Dudley weakness was Sir John Port, justice of the King's Bench, who obtained the manor of Church Christleton in spite of the machinations of the Dudleys' stewards, the Egertons: PRO, C 1/1254/51. In 1557 it was sold on to Richard Harpur of Chester: CCRO, DBA 50.

Cheshire monasteries like Combermere: George Talbot had already been steward there for forty years when he wrote asking Cromwell's favour for the abbot in July 1536.[40]

The main beneficiaries of the weakness of Cheshire noble familes were, however, the gentry. The rebels of the Pilgrimage of Grace saw the earl of Derby as the 'ruler' of Lancashire, but considered Sir William Brereton and Sir Piers Dutton to be the 'rulers' in Cheshire.[41] In 1535 the monasteries of Norton and Birkenhead shunned both Derby and Shrewsbury for their stewardships, choosing instead Sir William Brereton and another prominent gentleman, Randal Pole.[42] Studies of the structure of wealth and power in Cheshire society in the later Middle Ages have suffered from a lack of relevant source material, largely because of Cheshire's position as a palatinate.[43] The military summons of 1324 leaves no list of knights for Cheshire;[44] Cheshire was exempt from the poll tax of the later fourteenth century and from subsequent income taxes.[45] No list of gentry required to swear the oath of 1434 exists, and there is no evidence for the distraint of knighthood.[46] Cheshire's own form of taxation, the mise, was based on assessments on townships which had remained constant since the fourteenth century and therefore provides no information on personal wealth or income.[47] It has therefore

[40] *LP* ii/1, 911; xi. 177; CCRO, DDA 1533/1. George was also steward of Vale Royal and of the Derbyshire lands of the abbey of St Werburgh: *Valor ecclesiasticus*, v. 205, 209, 217; G. W. Bernard, *The power of the early Tudor nobility: a study of the fourth and fifth earls of Shrewsbury*, Brighton 1985, 105–36. For the vigorous enforcement of wardship by John Mainwaring, Sr, and Thomas Worall for George, earl of Shrewsbury against Hugh Wickstead, who held by knight service of the Talbots see PRO, STAC 2/20/177 (*L&C Star Chamber*, 137–8).

[41] *LP* xi. 1253.

[42] *Valor ecclesiasticus*, v. 209, 212.

[43] See especially Bennett, *Community, class and careerism*; Morgan, *War and society*; Clayton, *Administration*.

[44] *The parliamentary writs and writs of military summons, together with the writs and muniments relating to the suit and service due and performed to the king's high court of parliament and the councils of the realm, or affording evidence of attendance given at parliaments and councils*, ed. Francis Palgrave, London 1827–34, ii. 437–57.

[45] H. L. Gray, 'Incomes from land in England in 1436', *EHR* xxxxix (1934), 607–39; T. B. Pugh and C. D. Ross, 'The English baronage and the income tax of 1436', *BIHR* xxvi (1953), 1–28; Simon Payling, *Political society in Lancastrian England: the greater gentry of Nottinghamshire*, Oxford 1991, 9–12.

[46] *CPR, 1429–36*, 370–413; the chamberlain was in charge of the Cheshire oath (p. 413). Cheshire made a return for the writs inquiring of holders of more than 40 librates of land, 5 Edward IV (PRO, E 198/4/37) but to none subsequently (E 198/4/16, 19–21, 23–4, 26–7, 35, 38) until the compositions for knighthood, 6–8 Charles I: E 198/4/32.

[47] For the unreliability of inquisitions see C. G. Crump, 'A note on the criticism of records', *BJRL* viii (1924), 140–9; R. F. Hunnisett, 'The reliability of inquisitions as historical evidence', in D. Bullough and R. L. Storey (eds), *The study of medieval records*, Oxford 1971, 206–35; Carpenter, *Locality and polity*, 52–3. No Cheshire records survive from Wolsey's general proscription and taxation: J. C. K. Cornwall, *Wealth and society in early sixteenth-century England*, London 1988; *The county community under Henry VIII: the military survey, 1522, and lay subsidy, 1524–5, for Rutland*, ed. J. C. K. Cornwall (Rutland Record Series i,

proved difficult to do other than to emphasise the great number and importance of the gentry in fourteenth- and fifteenth-century Cheshire.

Our first real insight into the economic structure of the Cheshire community is offered in the subsidy records of the 1540s. Of these, the most informative are those for 1541–2, for the second payment on the subsidy granted in 1540: records survive for Chester, Macclesfield, Wirral, Bucklow, Broxton, Northwich and Eddisbury hundreds.[48] Only Nantwich hundred is missing. The records reveal a society in which wealth was concentrated in land: although about four-fifths of subsidy payers were assessed on goods, the wealthiest payers by far were landowners.[49] The main group of subsidy payers paid 10s. on £20 goods. In Cheshire (excluding Nantwich), 195 (65.66 per cent) paid in this way. In Chester, 32 (68.08 per cent) did so, making the overall total 227 (67.96 per cent).[50] The group of people who paid on land and the group who paid at the highest levels largely coincide. Sixty-four of the seventy who owed more than the mean payment were taxed on land, not goods.[51] If we concentrate on the landed payers, subsidy evidence indicates that only a small proportion of the wealth of the county was held by the highest ranking gentry; men in the income group of £20–39 clearly predominated in terms of numbers. In this, Cheshire's social structure appears similar to that of Cornwall and Staincliffe wapentake in Yorkshire, and unlike that of Norfolk and Berkshire.[52]

1980); C. E. Moreton, *The Townshends and their world: gentry, law, and land in Norfolk, c. 1450–1551*, Oxford 1992, 65.

[48] Chester: PRO, E 179/85/6; Macclesfield: E 179/85/9; others: E 179/85/10.

[49] See Thornton, 'Political society in early Tudor Cheshire', table 2, for these figures in full.

[50] Between these 10s. payers and the 20s. payers were 33 people who paid between 10s. 1d. and 16s., representing 9.59% of the whole sample.

[51] The mean payment was about 17s., an amount at which no-one actually paid. The next highest sum at which people were assessed to pay was 20s., corresponding to an assessment of £20 in land or £40 in goods. Those paying 20s. or more in the subsidy (excluding Nantwich) amounted in Cheshire to 70 people (23.57%) and, if Chester is included, to 83 (24.13%). The majority of these people paid on landed income: outside Chester, only 6 paid on goods (8.57% of the total of higher payers there). Of these men, only 3, John Hammond and Alexander Elcock of Stockport and Richard Grene of Congleton, were successful townsmen, confirming the unimportance of towns in Cheshire (aside, of course, from the city of Chester); these three men can therefore be excluded from this discussion of the gentle county community. See the will of Nicholas Elcock, father of Alexander: PCC 40 Hogen, printed in *Sheaf* 3rd ser. xix (1924), 63–4, no. 4618 (17 June 1536, proved 15 Sept. 1536). The other three who paid at this level on goods, however, William Davenport, Hugh Starkey and Richard Grosvenor, were all members of established gentry families. Only in Chester city did the number of higher payers assessed on goods exceed the number assessed on land, at 7 out of 13.

[52] Thornton, 'Political society in early Tudor Cheshire', table 3; Nantwich is excluded. The comparisons are taken from the 1524–5 subsidy: Cornwall, *Wealth and society*, 33, 45, 48. This impression receives support from the records of the loan of 1542. There was a strong similarity between the loan and tax assessments at the highest levels in the rest of the

The group of landowners worth more than £20 *per annum* were not differentiated from those of lesser means only in economic terms. They represented the main members of the Cheshire political community, and the same families also provided military and administrative leadership in the shire. In 1544–5 seventy-three men were expected to produce ten or more soldiers for service, and another three were given allocations of the same order but not expected to be in readiness. Of these seventy-three men, the majority (forty-eight) were men already recognised as contributors to the loan and to the subsidy at the higher rates.[53] A similar congruence can be observed in the field of administration. The Cheshire community could not be given coherence by office-holding among the elite: the small number of suitable offices and their tenure for life or during pleasure militated against the kind of collective rotation of offices that existed elsewhere. This even applied to the shrievalty, in other English counties open to a new candidate every year, since it was held during pleasure or for life until the 1520s. Many members of the Cheshire elite never held senior offices in the county administration. On the other hand, the administration of Cheshire acted to involve the gentry elite more effectively than office-holding could. Some functions drew on the participation of very large numbers. Commissions for the collection of tax in Cheshire, for example, which involved many gentlemen, were more inclusive than similar commissions in other counties. In spite of the loss of the records for one of the years, when mises were levied in 1442–4, 1463–5 and 1474–6 it is known that 185 individuals were involved as collectors.[54] This is hugely more than the commisioners under the great seal appointed to collect

county. Excluding the inhabitants of Nantwich hundred and the clergy, 71 people advanced money in the loan, while 83 paid 20s. or more in subsidy. These similarly-sized groups overlapped considerably: the majority of loan payers had also paid the subsidy at the higher rates (just 15 out of 71 had not done so). The comparability of the two groups suggests that the loss represented by the lack of subsidy records for Nantwich hundred can partially be recovered: the majority of those who appear on the loan assessment for Nantwich hundred would probably have been rated for the subsidy at the higher level. Comparability is also suggested by examining the proportions of the sums raised in each exercise in the hundreds of Cheshire excluding Nantwich:

	Macclesfield	Wirral	Bucklow	Broxton	Northwich	Eddisbury
Subsidy	26.0%	6.0%	29.0%	10.2%	9.6%	19.3%
Loan	20.2%	7.5%	38.7%	7.5%	11.5%	14.7%

Of the total of £1,002 loaned by Chester and Cheshire, Nantwich provided £190 6s. 8d., 19.0% of the total. Of a total of 90 lenders, 19 (21.1%) came from Nantwich.

53 A list of 1544–5 recorded the names of 159 gentlemen and freeholders with the numbers of men which 'they are able to make for the service of the Kyng H8' in war against the Scots and 67 'not apoynted to be in redynes to serve': CCRO, DSS MS 3, fo. 186, printed, inaccurately, in *Sheaf* 3rd ser. xxxviii (1948), 7, 15, 22, 28, 32, 46, 55–6, 61, 69, 76, 81, 90, 96, 98, 105, 116, 128. The names are analysed in Thornton, 'Political society in early Tudor Cheshire', table 6. The list dates from after May 1544, when Thomas Venables and others were knighted. It was probably compiled soon afterwards, because Sir John Holford died in about 1545 and Thomas Poole in 1546.

54 Clayton, *Administration*, 195–202 (233 appointments).

the subsidies of 1512–15 in other counties of the north-west and midlands, for example. In 1512 twenty-eight men were responsible for Shropshire outside Shrewsbury, twenty-four for Derbyshire and twenty-nine for Staffordshire.[55] Tasks which elsewhere reinforced the powers of a few members of a gentry elite were carried out in Cheshire by a broader selection of gentlemen.

On the other hand, intensive activity in other areas of administrative activity suggests, once again, the dominance of a small group of senior gentry families. Final concords were made at meetings of the Chester county court before the justice and a group of leading county gentry. In 1442–83 seventy-eight concords were drawn up, on which forty-nine different individuals appeared.[56] From the subsequent fifty-five years, 127 different concords show 112 individuals appearing.[57] Although this represents a mean of 4.72 appearances each, thirty-four individuals appeared just once and sixteen twice. A few gentlemen therefore accounted for the majority of the appearances: sixty-two men made three or more appearances, fifty-two four or more, and forty-two five or more. Forty-two men therefore filled three-quarters of all places on final concord panels.[58] The county elite is again illustrated by the close congruence between frequent final concord panellists and those paying the higher rates of subsidy and providing the largest contingents of soldiers for war.

Other aspects of county administration indicate that the emergence of an elite among the gentry was quickening around the beginning of the sixteenth century. This is especially clear in a study of the Cheshire grand jury, and especially the relationship of the jury panel to the final jury selected. The Cheshire county court met eight or nine times a year in Chester; shortly before the start of the session the sheriff was instructed to impanel a sufficient number of men of the county, from whom the inquest or grand jury was selected.[59] The selection of names for the panel, and the selection of people from the panel for the jury itself, did not follow a regular pattern. There is no indication of the names being taken from a book or list of any kind since the order in which names appear varied from session to session. As a rule, however, men of knightly status usually headed the panel, followed by

---

[55] Interestingly, Lancashire is an exception with 67 individuals involved: SR iii. 79–89.

[56] '[M]embers of the Cheshire elite': Clayton, *Administration*, 192–4 (regnal years 20 Henry VI to 22 Edward IV).

[57] Based on those surviving in PRO, CHES 31. There are 538 names on these records: Thornton, 'Political society in early Tudor Cheshire', table 4. As a result of the reform of Cheshire administration, the form of final concords was altered in 1540 to bear only the name of the justice.

[58] 42 men made 74.3% of appearances; 52 81.8%.

[59] The panel list was one of the first items placed on the file. Those chosen to be sworn were marked with the letters 'Jur'. Usually there was one jury; occasionally, two or more. Multiple juries accompanied a high number of presentments and the summoning of more than one panel suggests foreknowledge of a high level of business: cf. the three juries for the justices in eyre in September 1500.

esquires. There does not seem to be any indication of political manipulation of the choice of names: there was a steady continuity in membership over such periods of political trauma as the fall of Sir William Stanley in 1495 and the execution of William Brereton in 1536.[60] Unlike in the period 1625 to 1659, when John Morrill found that obtaining a balance of representation between hundreds from which presentments came was the determining factor in the composition of panel and jury, the fifteenth- and early sixteenth-century material suggests that simple geographical convenience was paramount, with jurors representing, in the main, the area closest to Chester itself.[61]

The panels included many of the most senior members of county society, with usually at least one knight represented on the list, if not the jury actually selected. In the period 1524–33, while these senior figures were frequently listed, they were very rarely selected for service. In fact, those men most frequently selected to appear on the jury were those not accorded status titles in the sessional file panels. They were generally men below the rank of esquire: lesser gentry, lawyers and administrators (although never serving Cheshire palatine officials). Between 1495 and 1504 and 1524 and 1533 a change occurred in the number of people being impanelled. In the period 1495–1504, on average, the panels were little longer than the actual jury, with more than three-quarters of those impanelled being selected.[62] By 1524–33, however, the panels had grown immensely, yet the size of the average jury was no larger. At Epiphany 1532 forty names appeared on a panel from which a jury of just thirteen was selected. Taking the period 1524–33 as a whole, the proportion of the panel actually serving on the jury was 49 per cent. In one sense this represented wider involvement. The total number of individuals serving in a ten-year period rose, and the number of people summoned to each session grew. In particular, there was a much fuller representation of the higher ranks of society: among the seven panels that survive for 1497, the name of only one knight appears, and that only at one

---

60 The following paragraphs are based on two sample ten-year periods, 1495–1504 and 1524–33: PRO, CHES 24/65–71; CHES 24/82–7. Unfortunately, the condition and survival rate of the files deteriorates during the sixteenth century. 49 surviving jury panels represent the business of 43 of a probable total 80 sessions, 1495–1504; just 33 complete panels from a probable 80 sessions survive in 1524–33. This is enough, however, to allow comparison of the participation represented by the panel of those summoned to appear and the jurors who actually served. Unfortunately, the status vocabulary of the lists is limited to 'miles' and 'armiger', apart from a very few men who are designated as 'generosus' or 'gentil-man' in the 1530s. This leaves open the question of whether one or more individuals of the same name are being referred to.

61 This is based on comparison of the material from 1480–1560 with Clayton's work on the mid-fifteenth century: Clayton, *Administration*. See also J. S. Morrill, *The Cheshire grand jury 1625–1659*, Leicester 1976, 13–14.

62 In one case 15 men were impanelled and all were selected to serve on the jury itself (session of the feast of the Holy Trinity, 1497). Considering all the panels, 77% of those summoned were selected for service.

session, yet of five panels from 1533, only one does not have a knight at the head, while the others have one, two, four and seven knights on them.[63] By the 1530s it was virtually automatic that a panel included the most important members of county society. This extra involvement was not one of more extensive service, however. The greater gentry in particular, although summoned more frequently, were very unlikely indeed to be found actually serving as county court inquest jurors. There is no evidence of any Cheshire knight serving as a juror in 1533.[64]

Two contradictory trends can therefore be observed. Those in the county administration compiling the panels seem to have sought wider involvement: a far larger number of people, including a significant representation from the greater gentry, were summoned regularly in the 1520s and 1530s than in the 1490s. At the same time, however, some among the increased numbers summoned failed to attend. This latter phenomenon should not be allowed to overshadow the former. The Cheshire palatine community, expressed in the grand jury, one of its most concrete manifestations, was not in decline before the changes of 1536 and after. If anything, the grand jury came to include more of the ordinary gentry and, in particular, of the greater gentry, and to include them more regularly. On the other hand, the greater gentry were clearly unenthusiastic about the opportunities for involvement that a summons for the grand jury panel represented. The developments of the years between 1490 and 1530 were therefore the start of the trend which saw the end of elite gentry involvement in the Cheshire grand jury; by the early seventeenth century the jury was almost exclusively made up of yeomen or people of lesser status.[65] This is significant in that it implies that the greater gentry of Cheshire had given up – apparently voluntarily – a key role in the county's judicial process before they received an alternative in the form of service on newly-constituted commissions of the peace. This choice may well have been the result of the rise in status of the Cheshire elite and its separation from its inferiors in the local gentry. This was not indicative of a loss of

[63] PRO, CHES 24/68, session of St Martin in winter, 1497 (Sir Thomas Poole); CHES 24/86–7 (the upper sections of only five panels from 1533 are complete).
[64] PRO, CHES 24/86–7. Sir Henry Delves, however, served, judging from a damaged and incomplete panel for the Nativity of the Blessed Virgin 1533 (CHES 24/87). Sometimes this can be shown to have resulted from absenteeism: occasionally the lists show sums of money written after the names of men who did not serve on the jury. The more important the individual, the larger the sum of money, so these were presumably fines for non-attendance. At Epiphany 1525, for example, Sir Piers Dutton of Hatton, Peter Warburton, William Venables of Kinderton, John Glegg, Richard Grosvenor, Thomas Huls and another esquire whose name has been obliterated were all fined 6s. 8d., John Cotton of Lostok was fined 2s. and Robert Smethwick just 1s.: CHES 24/82, panel 2.
[65] Morrill found that the majority of grand jurymen had incomes of not much more than £10 per annum. Of 250 families of knightly rank or with concomitant incomes of £40 or more per annum, only 58 were represented on the jury and all 58 compounded for knighthood in the 1630s at the minimum rate of £10, suggesting incomes of no more than £100 per annum: Morrill, Cheshire grand jury, 15–20.

faith in the palatinate, seen in the commitment of these families to other aspects of its institutional and cultural apparatus, as will be shown below; but elite withdrawal from the grand jury may have been a reason for the local acceptance of the reform that led to the institution of Justices of the Peace for the county in 1536. The commission of the peace represented a new means of involvement in the county administration for men already frequently represented on the inquest panel, in a form that differentiated them from the lesser gentry and yeomanry and gave due recognition to their higher status. This information on wealth, administrative involvement and military contribution can be consolidated in a survey of thirty-nine elite gentry families (see table 1), which illustrates their pre-eminence.

The dominant group in Cheshire society was, therefore, the gentry and in particular a group of between thirty and fifty families. These men, and not the peerage, possessed the wealth of the county, led its men to war and participated in many of the formal aspects of the county's administration. In this sense the gentry fulfilled the 'magnate' role, as Payling described in fifteenth-century Nottinghamshire. [66] This was also apparent in the informal structures of power in the shire, such as arbitration panels. Across the entire period 1480–1560, the gentry acted as arbitrators to the exclusion of the aristocracy. Members of the Stanley of Lathom family appeared in only two of over 120 arbitrations examined, both in the person of George, Lord Strange, in 1488 and 1490.[67] After 1495 they are notable for their complete absence. The only other nobleman to appear was Thomas, duke of Norfolk, who acted as umpire in the dispute among the children and widow of Randal Brereton, chamberlain of Chester. Norfolk was chosen for this role by Randal himself in his will; he passed on the arbitration of the case to John Baker, recorder of London, and John Packyngton. It is interesting that no other Cheshire gentleman chose such an eminent arbitrator, in spite of their contacts at court. So a difficult dispute like Sir John Bromley's differences with John Mainwaring, esquire, was arbitrated by Sir Geoffrey Massey, Sir Robert Fouleshurst, Thomas Poole and Robert Duckenfield in 1483.[68] In 1543 Sir Philip Egerton and Thomas Warburton were chosen to arbitrate between

---

66 Payling, *Political society in Lancastrian England.*
67 JRUL, Rylands charters, 1679; CCRO, DBA 58 (no number, 1 June 1490). There is also the award of 27 July 1485 between Edmund and Margaret Trafford and John Mainwaring of Over Peover, given by Lord Stanley, his son James and Sir William: Lancashire Record Office, DDTr marriages, 2/3/158. To the infrequency of their appearance as witnesses to the transactions of the Cheshire gentry, the grant of an annuity to Hamo Leicester by John Leicester of Nether Tabley on 17 June 1490, when Thomas, George and William Stanley were listed as witnesses (CCRO, DLT A10/1), is a rare exception. A full list of the arbitrations upon which this study is based is to be found in Thornton, 'Political society in early Tudor Cheshire', appendix. Sir William's feoffees included Sir John Savage, Sir Thomas Manley, Piers Warburton, Richard Norris, Edmund Bulkeley and William Tatton (1490): JRUL, Tatton of Wythenshawe 445; Williams, 'Stanley family', 158.
68 CCRO, DCH H/84; DNE, box 5 (award, 5 June 1483).

Table 1
The wealth, administrative involvement and military contribution of thirty-nine elite Cheshire gentry families, 1480–1560

Families	Five or more final concord panels	30 or more men for military service	£30 p.a. or more wealth assessed for taxation
Ashley of Ashley	No	No (20)	Yes
Booth of Dunham Massey	Yes	No	Yes
Brereton of Brereton	Yes	Yes	Yes
Brereton of Shocklach and Malpas	Yes	Yes	Yes
Bruen of Bruen Stapleford	Yes	No (16)	No (£20)
Calveley of the Lea	Yes	Yes	No (£20)
Carrington of Carrington	No	Yes	Yes
Cholmondeley of Cholmondeley	Yes	Yes	No (£20)
Daniel of Tabley	No	No (20)	No (£26)
Davenport of Bramhall	No	Yes	No (50s. on goods)
Davenport of Henbury	No	Yes	No (£26)
Delves of Doddington	Yes	Yes	Yes
Done of Flaxyards	No	Yes	No (£20)
Done of Utkinton	Yes	Yes	Yes
Downes	No	No (20)	Yes
Duckenfield	No	Yes	No (£20)
Dutton of Dutton/ Hatton	Yes	Yes	Yes
Fitton	No	Yes	Yes
Fouleshurst	No	Yes	
Holford	Yes	Yes	Yes
Honford/ Stanley/ Brereton	No	Yes	Yes
Legh of Baguley	No	No (20)	Yes
Legh of Booths	No	Yes	Yes
Leicester of Tabley	No	Yes	No (£26)
Leicester of Toft	No		No (£26)
Mainwaring of Over Peover	Yes	Yes	
Mascy	Yes	Yes	No (?£20)
Poole	Yes	Yes	Yes
Savage	No	Yes	
Smith		Yes	Yes
Sneyd		Yes	Yes
Spurstow	No	No (18)	Yes
Stanley of Hooton	Yes	Yes	Yes
Starkey	Yes	Yes	£4 goods
Tatton		Yes	

Families	Five or more final concord panels	30 or more men for military service	£30 p.a. or more wealth assessed for taxation
Venables	Yes	Yes	Yes
Warburton	No	Yes	Yes
Warren	Yes	Yes	No (£26)
Wilbraham	Yes	No (20)	Yes

Thomas Danyell of Egerton and Peter Leycester of Tabley.[69] Clerical involvement was often important, but the prominence of Randal Poole, head of the Poole of Poole family, suggests that even this could be primarily a sign of the activity of the gentry elite. Even when a contingent of lawyers was involved in the arbitration, senior Cheshire gentlemen were often included.[70] Sir Piers Legh was named at the head of a panel the other members of which were Robert Chauntrell and Otwell Lowe, 'lerned men', in dealing with arbitration between Nicholas Jodrell and Christopher Downes in 1498.[71]

There is more to community, however, than participation in administration. Concentrating on the major families identified above,[72] the family and social connections of the Cheshire gentry seem, on first examination, to support the theory of the 'county community', as espoused by Alan Everitt and others, who have argued that the longevity of families and intermarriage between them demonstrated that the county was the prime focus of identity for the gentry, and that, vice versa, gentry activity was the prime expression of the county community.[73] Further examination of the evidence suggests, however, that a more complex understanding of community and identity is required to explain the experience of Cheshire in the early modern period. There were many motives behind a gentry marriage, for example, from territorial aggrandisement to politics, not forgetting love. In 1504 German Pole of Radbourne in Derbyshire wrote to Sir Robert Plumpton of the affection between his sister Eleanor and Randal Mainwaring of Carincham, Cheshire: 'he beareth great love & favor vnto my sister Ellynor, & she doth likewyse so vnto him the same'.[74] If the county really was the chief focus of identity, these

69 CCRO, DLT A12/24 (bond, 12 Nov. 1545).
70 For legal involvement in arbitration see pp. 91–3 below. Constraints of space prevent the discussion of clerical involvement at length here. For Randal Poole see JRUL, Cornwall-Legh 806; Arley charters 12/7–8; Rylands charters 1361–2; Mainwaring 338; CCRO, DVE B/V/3. George Wilmesley also played a role (JRUL, Tatton of Wythenshawe 864; CCRO, DDS 6/45), as did John Lancaster, prior of Launde (Arley charters 12/27), and more local figures such as James Calveley, master of the college at Bunbury (CCRO, DCH U/12) and Thomas Lewyns (CCRO, DDS 11/2).
71 JRUL, Jodrell 38B (award, 8 Sept. 1498).
72 This excludes the many (perhaps 400) lesser gentry families, partly because of lack of evidence: Clayton, Administration, 134–6.
73 Everitt, Community of Kent, esp. pp. 20–55.
74 The Plumpton letters and papers, ed. Joan Kirby (Camden 5th ser. viii, 1996), 177. See also

motives should have operated within a county context. In fact, approximately two-thirds of Cheshire gentlemen married Cheshire women.[75] Endogamy is particularly striking if we consider the whole of the north-western region of Cheshire and South Lancashire. Between 1374 and 1427 one quarter of papal indulgences for consanguineous marriages in England related to inhabitants of Chester archdeaconry; in 1474–1513 the number of indulgences for inhabitants of the diocese of Lichfield represented 20 per cent of the English total.[76] The thirty-four men who paid the 1540 subsidy on lands worth £30 or more made a total of forty known marriages, and at least twenty-six of their wives were of Cheshire origin.[77] A similar pattern appears when the female children of the Cheshire gentry are considered. Over three-quarters of the daughters of the group of forty-three families who provided most of the troops and had the highest tax assessments in the 1540s appear to have married husbands from Cheshire.[78]

The Cheshire gentry community is also notable for the long history of many of its member families. As Daniel King wrote in the mid seventeenth century, 'there is no County in England more famous for a long continued Succession of Antient Gentry'.[79] All but four of the group of forty-three major families[80] had origins in the county before the fifteenth century.[81] The exceptions were the Booths of Dunham Massey, descended from the Booths of Barton (Lancashire), who arrived in the county in the 1430s; the Sneyds of

Carpenter, *Locality and polity*, 97–116; Susan M. Wright, *The Derbyshire gentry in the fifteenth century* (Derbyshire Record Society viii, 1983), 44; K. R. Dockray, 'Why did fifteenth-century English gentry marry?', in M. Jones (ed.), *Gentry and lesser nobility in later medieval Europe*, Gloucester 1986, 61–80; Colin Richmond, 'The Pastons revisited: marriage and the family in fifteenth-century England', *BIHR* lviii (1985), 25–36.

[75] The genealogies of a group of 121 Cheshire families extracted from the heralds' visitations produce a total of 1,364 males for 711 of whom marriage details are available for the period 1480 to 1560. Of these 471 married Cheshire women: *The visitation of Cheshire in the year 1580, made by Robert Glover, Somerset herald, for William Flower, Norroy King of Arms*, ed. John Paul Rylands (Harleian Society xviii, 1882).

[76] Bennett, *Community, class and careerism*, 11–12. For 1474–1513 (6 out of 30), *Calendar of entries in the papal registers relating to Great Britain and Ireland: papal letters*, XIII: *1471–84*, ed. J. A. Twemlow, London 1955, i. 220; ii. 404–5; XIV: *1484–92*, ed. J. A. Twemlow, London 1960, 6; XV: *1484–92*, ed. M. J. Haren, Dublin 1978; XVI: *1492–1503*, ed. M. J. Haren, Dublin 1986; XVIII: *1503–13, 1503–8*, ed. M. J. Haren, Dublin 1989, 413, 457–8, 479–80.

[77] PRO, E 179/85/9, 10. The missing Nantwich records are replaced by loan records, as above: E 179/85/11. For marriages see Ormerod, *Chester*, passim (the total may be 27). In 1590–1642 three-quarters of the heads of a sample of 92 gentry families or their heirs still married within the county: Morrill, *Cheshire*, 4.

[78] It is possible to identify 304 marriages. Considering only first marriages, for 270 the partner's county of origin can be identified; of these 208 (77.04%) were marriages to Cheshire husbands: Thornton, 'Political society in early Tudor Cheshire', 52–65.

[79] *The vale-royall of England, or the county palatine of Chester illustrated*, publ. Daniel King, London 1656, A3.

[80] Thornton, 'Political society in early Tudor Cheshire', 52–65.

[81] Of the 106 seventeenth-century families studied by Morrill, 50 had origins in the thirteenth century and some went back further: *Cheshire*, 3.

Willaston and Keele who made the move from Staffordshire in the late fifteenth century; Sir John Stanley of Alderley and Wever, the third son of the first Lord Stanley, who married the heiress of Alderley in the mid fifteenth century; and the heirs to the Honford lands, which passed through the hands of another branch of the Stanley family before reaching Urian Brereton early in the sixteenth century.[82] Other families had only been at their place of residence since the early fifteenth century, but were junior branches of other long established Cheshire families. The Davenports of Bramhall and of Henbury established themselves around the turn of the fifteenth century, but did so in the person of younger sons of the Davenport of Wheltrough family, itself sprung from the Davenports of Davenport, 'the best and firste house of the Davenportes', which originated in the reign of William II.[83] The inbred marriage pattern of the county helped ensure that, when a family died out in the main line, there was usually a local junior branch to take on the mantle, or the heiresses were usually married to neighbouring Cheshire families. The struggle over the Dutton inheritance was resolved with a settlement that awarded the bulk of the lands to Sir Piers Dutton, a member of the junior Hatton branch of the family.[84] The Venables barony survived a complex succession dispute to continue in the Venables family. The successful claimant was William Venables, son of Thomas, who was heir and distant cousin of Sir Hugh, who died at Bloreheath in 1459, with a common ancestor in the person of Hugh Venables, who died in the reign of Richard II.[85]

The plundering of church lands in the sixteenth century provided an opportunity for outsiders to establish gentry families in Cheshire, something which had previously been very difficult to achieve.[86] Yet the experience of the shire was remarkable in that the newly established families of the sixteenth century were few and limited in their novelty. If there was a major shift in land-ownership from the Church to the gentry during this period, this did not mean a large influx of new families.[87] The main immediate beneficiaries from the dissolution in Cheshire were the new bishop and cathedral of

---

[82] Ormerod, *Chester*, i. 523–5; iii. 492, 577, 644.

[83] Ibid. iii. 827, 707–8, 721–2; *Itinerary of Leland*, v. 27; *Sheaf* 3rd ser. xviii (1923), 50, no. 4342; *39 DKR*, 266.

[84] Ormerod, *Chester*, i. 650–1; ii. 796; S. T. Bindoff, *The House of Commons, 1509–1558*, London 1982, iii. 334.

[85] Ormerod, *Chester*, iii. 200. For the Dones of Utkinton, whose heiress Ellena married John, the heir of the allied Dones of Flaxyards, see ibid. ii. 248–9.

[86] Bennett, *Community, class and careerism*, 89.

[87] As Beck argued in *Tudor Cheshire*, 96; cf. the sale of crown lands, many of them ex-chantry lands, under Edward VI, which allowed the establishment of many new gentry families. This was not the case in Cheshire: W. K. Jordan, *Edward VI: the young king: the protectorship of the duke of Somerset*, London 1968, 104–17. 263 manors were conveyed to 188 individual purchasers; none was in Cheshire. Two passed by other means, one by exchange and one by gift (of a total of 660 passing by gift and 615 passing by exchange). Of the 668 purchasers of crown lands, only two had a place of residence in Cheshire. In Essex, Glouces-

Chester.[88] Otherwise, the Brookes of Norton abbey were the descendants of the successful soldier son of a local man.[89] Sir Thomas Holcroft, who was granted Vale Royal on advantageous terms in 1544, served Henry VIII, particularly on Scottish affairs, and was an ally of the duke of Somerset, was the son of John Holcroft of Holcroft in Lancashire.[90] The Vale Royal properties of Darnhall and Knight's Grange went to Rowland Hill, a merchant with Shropshire origins, and to Hugh Starkey of Oulton (Cheshire), a royal household servant.[91] Sir Urian Brereton and his son Urian bought the site of St Mary's nunnery in Chester, providing a base in the city for a branch of the Cheshire family that had prospered in the king's privy chamber.[92] Sir George Cotton, who benefited from the dissolution of Combermere abbey, originated from north Shropshire; his mother was Cecily, daughter of Thomas Mainwaring of Ightfield and therefore a close kinswoman of one of the most important Cheshire gentry families. Sir George rose in royal service, holding positions in the households of the duke of Richmond and Prince Edward. Sir Richard, his younger brother, who became controller of Edward VI's household, gained from the weakness of the new chapter of Chester: he received a large grant of manors from the dean and chapter late in the reign of Edward VI and managed to retain them under Mary.[93] Sir Richard Cotton also bought Stanlow, a dependent house of Whalley (Lancashire), and Ince, a manor house of St Werburgh's, Chester.[94] Other families rose to prominence through service in the local administration and courts, but again the disruption to local society they represented was limited. The Sneyds, Birkenheads and Tattons of Wythenshaw are the prime examples of this phenomenon; the last was already a relatively successful local family, and the Sneyds and Birk-

tershire, Kent, Norfolk, Somerset, Wiltshire and Yorkshire about 10% of all manors changed hands.

[88] R. V. H. Burne, *Chester Cathedral from its founding by Henry VIII to the accession of Queen Victoria*, London 1958, 1; VCH, *County of Chester*, ed. B. E. Harris, Oxford 1979– , iii. 144; *LP* xvi. 1135(4)–(6).

[89] Ormerod, *Chester*, i. 680; ii. 454; Beck, *Tudor Cheshire*, 100.

[90] Bindoff, *House of Commons, 1509–1558*, ii. 373–4; Ormerod, *Chester*, ii. 154; HMC, *12th report, appendix, part IV: the manuscripts of his grace the duke of Rutland, GCB, preserved at Belvoir Castle*, London 1888–9, i. 46–8; Jordan, *Edward VI: the young king*, 280, 284, 297–9, and *Edward VI: the threshold of power: the dominance of the duke of Northumberland*, London 1970, 93, 112; *CSPD, addenda 1547–65*, 366, 371–2, 377, 379, 381–3, 395–6. A Scotsman, Sandy Pringle, lived with Thomas Holcroft in 1558, and in 1550 a payment covered his costs in 'espialles' in Scotland over previous years: *APC* iii. 89; vi. 320–1.

[91] Ormerod, *Chester*, ii. 154, 191–2; Beck, *Tudor Cheshire*, 103; VCH, *County of Chester*, iii. 163.

[92] Beck, *Tudor Cheshire*, 100; Ormerod, *Chester*, iii. 644. For the purchase of the house of the Friars Minor in Chester by Richard Hough of Leighton in 1541 see CCRO, DDX 43/57.

[93] Bindoff, *House of Commons, 1509–1558*, i. 711–12; Beck, *Tudor Cheshire*, 103; Burne, *Chester Cathedral*, 24–6. In February 1553 Dean William Cliffe and two canons were committed to the Fleet; soon afterwards the dean granted the bulk of the cathedral's properties (worth £700) to Sir Richard Cotton for £603 17s. *per annum*: *CSPD, addenda 1547–65*, 402, 412; *APC* iii. 230, 237.

[94] Beck, *Tudor Cheshire*, 102–3.

enheads were from neighbouring Staffordshire and Lancashire respectively.[95] Success in the commerce and administration of the city of Chester elevated one family, the Smiths, who achieved knighthood in the person of Sir Thomas.[96]

Longevity of families and an inbred marriage pattern are the classic measures of the cohesion and introversion of a county community. Family heritage and marriage were of course important to the gentry of the county, but qualifications have to be made. Some men married outside the county,[97] and some new gentry families were established, albeit a minority. There is, in fact, much other evidence which suggests that the world in which the Cheshire gentry lived was far from closed. Geographically, the north-west had been relatively isolated: it was on the road only to Ireland and the Isle of Man. It was also commercially isolated from the rest of England: Chester traded little with London, most ships plying to France, Spain and Italy; Liverpool had only thirteen vessels and 200 seamen in 1557 and traded to few ports, mainly Dublin, Bilbao and Lisbon. But this isolation was changing in the sixteenth century. A rapid expansion of population took place; there was considerable growth of trade through Chester, from eighty-six ships in 1542–3, to 117 in 1548–52; and over the Lancashire border Manchester and Bolton acquired their first fulling mills. The strengthening of ties with London was seen in donations from there to Cheshire charities; and there was growing attendance at the Inns of Court and universities, especially St John's, Cambridge, and Brasenose, Oxford.[98] Richard Sutton's activities indicate the developing possibilities and contacts. He was probably the younger son of Sir William Sutton of Sutton in Prestbury, master of the hospital of Burton Lazars, Leicestershire, and he was related to William Sutton, DD, principal of Brasenose Hall in 1468. He was a governor of the Inner Temple in nine years between 1505 and 1523. As steward of the monastery of Sion he paid for the publication of *The orcharde of Syon* in 1519. Sutton is most famous for his patronage of learning in Oxford. As well as his probable contribution to the cost of Corpus Christi College in 1516, he was involved in the foundation of Brasenose College. His will left money to a chantry in Macclesfield, to the

95 Ormerod, *Chester*, iii. 492; ii. 368; iii. 609.

96 Ibid. iii. 503; *Sheaf* 3rd ser. xxxii (1938), 65–6, no. 7163.

97 For out-of-county marriage see Thornton, 'Political society in early Tudor Cheshire', 36–7.

98 This survey is based on Christopher Haigh, *Reformation and resistance in Tudor Lancashire*, Cambridge 1975, ch. vii at pp. 159–63, and the sources cited there. Haigh's belief in sudden and complete change should be moderated slightly in the case of Cheshire. For example, the total given to Lancashire charities was almost twice that given to Cheshire charities; but Jordan's analysis of the birthplaces of great London merchants who died between 1480 and 1660 shows that 14 of the total of 403 were in Cheshire, more than all but Essex, Hertfordshire, Kent, Shropshire, Staffordshire, Yorkshire and London itself: W. K. Jordan, *The charities of London, 1480–1660: the aspirations and the achievements of the urban society*, London 1960, 311–14, 317, 426–7.

Master of the Temple, to the abbess of Sion, to Clements Inn, to Macclesfield Grammar School and the highway around St Giles-in-the-Fields.[99] As Sutton's example suggests, people moved frequently and quickly around the country. The pardon rolls show the varied places of origin of people with a normal domicile in Cheshire. John Moreton was described as of three places in Middlesex, Moreton (Cheshire) and London. Richard Millington was pardoned as late of Pype, Aston, Newborough, Pype Park, and Lyche in Staffordshire, Nantwich in Cheshire, and London. Connections with London were particularly prevalent.[100] Cattle were driven there from Cheshire.[101] On the route to London, connections to Coventry had always been important.[102] Something of the mobility through the marches that was possible is indicated by the frank testimony of Gilbert Godbehere, writing in the early 1530s in Chester:

> Apon an xviij yere agoo, or there apon, I was workyng yn Bramsgrove in Worsytter shyre for iij quarters of a yere and more, and so yt chaunsyd I fyll in fauor with on Johan Standley's wyfe of the same towne, whych was borne in the Myddylst-wyche perech, in so myche that whan her husbande was gon to London with clothe, as was hys vsage yerely, she was content to take such maney as he had laft at home, and to go with me vnto my contre. And so she dyd, untyll we cam vnto Stone in Staffarde shyre, where her husbandy's brother whych persued us and toke us bothe, and sot me in Stafforde castell where I was strayly handlyd[.][103]

Travelling through Towcester towards Daventry in May 1533, Stephen Vaughan encountered Robert Frelove, Richard Woodwarde, a goldsmith of Chester, described as a man who had often been in Ireland, Ralph Pykmer, blacksmith, and Rowland Pykmer, both of Middlewich.[104] William Rede of Oxford, baker, described in February 1537 how, being at Whalley abbey in Lancashire, and intending to go to Oxford, he agreed to carry letters – one to a scholar at Oxford, and another to the abbot of Hailes, whom the abbot of Whalley had seen grow up. He also took another letter for the same scholar, from the proctor of Blackburn. It was a journey with which he was familiar. On the way south, he was accustomed to stop off at the house of the school-

99 *DNB* xix. 181–2; Frank Renaud, 'Memorial brasses of Sir Edward Fitton and Dean Robert Sutton in St Patrick's, Dublin', *Transactions of the Lancashire and Cheshire Antiquarian Society* xi (1893), 46; PRO, PROB 11/21, fos 209v–10v (PCC, 27 Bodfelde) (printed in *Sheaf* 3rd ser. xvii [1922], 89–90, no. 4149).
100 Note also John and Otwell Higginbotham, of Marple, Cheshire, Wigmore, Shropshire, and Beaulieu, Hampshire: *LP* i/1, 438 (pp. 247, 249, 265), and, from early in Edward VI's reign, Robert Wysee, late of Bridge Trafford, Cheshire, or of Graveley, Cambridgeshire, husbandman: *CPR, 1548–9*, 140.
101 Smith, *Vale royal*, 17.
102 Carpenter, *Locality and polity*, 27.
103 Godbehere was prepared to take a position in Calais or Berwick to escape his troubles: *Letters and accounts of William Brereton*, 86–7.
104 *LP* vi. 434 (3 May 1533).

master of Knutsford in Cheshire. On this occasion, the schoolmaster gave him a bundle of letters for delivery to his son Philip at Oriel, Oxford.[105] Those with the necessary resources could move between the county and London, for example, with some speed. During a Star Chamber case, Sir Philip Egerton threatened his opponent Sir Henry Delves that if he refused to amend evidence, 'his horse was as redy in the stable as his was and trusting to be taken with the King's counsell for his truth as well he shuld be'.[106] It was a feasible option for the Davenports of Bramhall 'to seke physyke' in London; Richard Cholmondeley bought at least one of his saddles there before 1490.[107] Religious experience was similarly broadly based geographically, although there were popular religious cults in Cheshire, such as the rood of Chester at St John's and Our Lady of Astbury.[108] John Williams of Malpas, struck dumb, was comforted by a vision sent through the intercession of Henry VI and went to Windsor to seek a cure.[109]

Cheshiremen did not live in a closed world: they simply chose to close their horizons in certain spheres, most notably marriage.[110] Something made it meaningful for Jankyn Leche of Cawarden to be described at the age of eighty-two as 'right well knowen thrugh out all Chestershire for a gode yomon on of the best within the same'.[111] This suggests the need to broaden our concept of political community and society away from simple social mechanics or isolated instances of involvement in specific acts of adminis-tration, so often the case in the historiography, and towards the next theme of this discussion: the political culture of the county.

105 *LP* xii/1, 389: examined 10 Feb. 1537.
106 PRO, STAC 2/30/86.
107 CCRO, DDA 1533 31/19–28b; *Lancashire and Cheshire wills from the ecclesiastical court*, 43. For the use of London tailors in the early seventeenth century see J. T. Cliffe, *The York-shire gentry from the Reformation to the Civil War*, London 1969, 22.
108 PRO, C 1/730/6; C 1/731/1. On the rood see REQ 1/96, discussed in *Sheaf* 3rd ser. xviii (1923), 27–8, no. 4287. William Egwad hoped that its blessing would spread from Chester to Aberystwyth, which also had an image of Christ: H. Elvet Lewis, 'Welsh Catholic poetry of the fifteenth century', *Transactions of the Honorable Society of the Cymmrodorion* (1913 [1911–12]), 31.
109 *The miracles of King Henry VI: being an account and translation of twenty-three miracles taken from the manuscript in the British Museum (Royal 13 c.viii)*, intro. Ronald Knox and Shane Leslie, Cambridge 1923, 210–11.
110 See A. J. Pollard, *North-eastern England during the Wars of the Roses: lay society, war and politics, 1450–1500*, Oxford 1990, 9–27, esp. pp. 21–7, who suggests that although the north-east was clearly recognisable as a region, it was open to the south and west, through landownership, the mobility of service, lawyers and pilgrims and visits by armies and royal progresses.
111 CCRO, DLE 10 (notarial instrument of 30 Mar. 1504).

PART I

THE PALATINATE: ALIVE AND ACTIVE

2

The Political Culture of the Palatinate

Recent accounts of community, especially the county community, in fourteenth-, fifteenth-, and sixteenth-century England place little emphasis on its cultural and ideological background, concentrating instead on its social, administrative or economic foundations.[1] What attention there has been to the culture of community has been restricted to local histories and the portrayal of arms.[2] Yet there are at least two grounds for suggesting that an exploration of this culture in Cheshire might be informative. Study of Brittany in the later medieval period has shown how a sense of community was deliberately bolstered through literature, inquiries into local rights, saints and the display of arms.[3] It is also recognised that there was a distinctive feature of north-western English culture in the later Middle Ages, the continuing popularity of alliterative poetry. Michael Bennett has shown how works such as *Gawain and the Green Knight* were produced for circulation among Richard II's north-western courtiers, and how attachment to this poetry extended from knightly families to relatively minor gentlemen, like Richard Newton. In the late fifteenth and early sixteenth centuries men like Humphrey Newton and Thomas Chetham continued to compose and collect alliterative verse.[4] But this poetic tradition was not specific to Cheshire, and

---

1   See, especially, Michael Bennett, 'A county community: social cohesion amongst the Cheshire gentry, 1400–25', *NH* viii (1973), 24–44, but also Roger Virgoe, 'Aspects of the county community in the fifteenth century', in M. A. Hicks (ed.), *Profit, piety, and the professions in later medieval England*, Gloucester–Wolfeboro, NH 1990, 1–13; J. R. Maddicott, 'The county community and the making of public opinion in fourteenth-century England', *TRHS* 5th ser. xxviii (1978), 27–43. Carpenter's critique of this historiography, 'Gentry and community', will be discussed further below; her *Locality and polity* stresses the importance of collective mentality. Holmes, 'County community in Stuart historiography', 54–73, and Hughes, 'Warwickshire on the eve of the civil war', 42–72, also downplay the significance of cultures of county autonomy.
2   For example, MacCulloch, *Suffolk*, 117–19.
3   Michael Jones, ' "Mon Pais et ma nation": Breton identity in the fourteenth century', in C. T. Allmand (ed.), *War, literature, and politics in the late Middle Ages*, Liverpool 1976, 144–68, esp. pp. 163–5. See also Kathleen Daly, 'Some seigneurial archives and chronicles in fifteenth-century France', *Peritia* ii (1983), 59–73, and 'Mixing business with pleasure: some French royal notaries and secretaries and their histories of France, c. 1459–1509', in Christopher Allmand (ed.), *Power, culture, and religion in France c. 1350–c. 1550*, Woodbridge 1989, 99–115; J. Kerhervé, 'Aux Origines d'un sentiment national: les chroniquers Bretons de la fin du moyen âge', *Bulletin de la société archaéologique du Finistère* cviii (1980), 165–206.
4   Michael Bennett, '*Sir Gawain and the Green Knight* and the literary achievement of the north west midlands: the historical background', *Journal of Medieval History* v (1979),

neither was it directly political.[5] To understand the full significance of the cultural background to autonomy, therefore, we must examine more specifically the way that the palatinate was embedded in the culture of Cheshire. Work on *ethnie* and nations suggests more subtle means to examine the way a community was created, perpetuated itself and could be shaped. This emphasises common myths

> which combine cognitive maps of the community's history and situation with poetic metaphors of its sense of dignity and identity. The fused and elaborated myths provide an overall framework of meaning for the ethnic community, a mythomoteur, which 'makes sense' of its experience and defines its 'essence'.

Cheshire's feeling of distinctiveness was founded in a semi-mythical account of the county's history which can be tested against this model.[6]

Cheshire manuscripts frequently contain local history. Roger Walle (d. 1488), archdeacon of Coventry from 1442 and for a time canon and prebendary of St John's, Chester, included a paraphrase of the earldom's history in one of his manuscripts.[7] The Cheshire gentleman Humphrey Newton of Pownall (d. 1536), the only one of his kind to have left any quantity of evidence for his intellectual interests, wrote a similar account.[8] The most

---

63–88, and *Community, class, and careerism*, 231–5; David A. Lawton, 'Scottish Field: alliterative verse and Stanley encomium in the Percy folio', *Leeds Studies in English* n.s. x (1978), 42–57, esp. pp. 42–3; C. A. Luttrell, 'Three north-west midlands manuscripts', *Neophilologus* xlii (1958), 38–50 (Thomas Ireland of Hale and the Booths of Barton); JRUL, Lyme MS of Scottish Field. See also Deborah Marsh, 'Humphrey Newton of Newton and Pownall (1466–1536): a gentleman of Cheshire and his commonplace book', unpubl. PhD diss. Keele 1995, and ' "I see by sizt of evidence": information gathering in late medieval Cheshire', in Diana E. S. Dunn (ed.), *Courts, counties and the capital in the later Middle Ages*, Stroud 1996, 71–92.

5 It reinforced local difference from the other areas. Contrary to the arguments of Michael Bennett, 'Careerism in late medieval England', in Joel Rosenthal and Colin Richmond (eds), *People, politics and community in the later Middle Ages*, Gloucester–New York 1987, 35–6, rather than enhancing national unity, the particular culture of the king's Cheshire followers alienated many of his English subjects. See also *Mum and the sothsegger*, ed. M. Day and R. Steele (EETS o.s. cxcix, 1936 [1934]), 21–3, lines 317–65.

6 Anthony D. Smith, *The ethnic origin of nations*, Oxford 1986, 24. See also J. G. A. Pocock, 'Time, institutions and action: an essay on traditions and their understanding', in P. King and B. C. Parekh (eds), *Politics and experience*, Cambridge 1968, 209–37; M. I. Finley, 'Myth, memory and history', *History and Theory* iv (1965), 281–302. Anderson, *Imagined communities*, offers useful approaches, but it is here argued that the Cheshire community was founded very securely on an institutional and political structure. See also R. R. Davies, 'The peoples of Britain and Ireland, 1100–1400, IV: language and historical mythology', *TRHS* 6th ser. vii (1997), 1–24, although his theme is the identity of the four peoples and nations of the British Isles.

7 Corpus Christi College, Cambridge, MS 369, fos 1–4; *BRUO*, 1966; Montague Rhodes James, *Catalogue of MSS of Corpus Christi College Cambridge (nos 251–538)*, Cambridge 1911–12, 205.

8 Bodleian Library, Oxford, MS Lat. misc. c.66, fos 9v, 7b (earls of Chester). A Gray's Inn manuscript, usually associated with Dieulacres abbey (Staffs.), includes a chronicle of the

important element of this myth-history was the creation of the palatinate. William I, in granting Hugh [Lupus] of Avranches the earldom of Chester in the conventional manner, by fastening a belt and sword around his waist, gave him, it was believed, the powers of the fifteenth-century palatine earl. The sword was the symbol of his powers, supposedly the same as those wielded by the king in the rest of England. The story was developed by Cheshire writers from the twelfth century, when the Chester monk Lucian referred to the symbol of the earl's powers, the *gladium principis*.[9] Most powerfully, the account of Lupus's creation was deployed in successful defence of Cheshire's exemption from English parliamentary encroachment in 1450–1. In 1450 county representatives used the story of the sword to claim that Cheshire was 'a comite palatyne . . . distincte & sep[ar]ate from youre coron of Englond', the inhabitants of which were not taxable by the English parliament.[10] The exclusive jurisdiction of the archdeaconry of Chester was defended as part of the *dignitas gladii nostri* in 1455.[11] The *Life of St Werburge*, by the monk-antiquarian Henry Bradshaw, illustrates the state of this story's development early in the sixteenth century.[12] This sets out the creation myth with the addition of many unique details. Thus William

abbey based on the history of the earls of Chester: N. R. Ker, *Medieval manuscripts in British libraries*, I: *London*, Oxford 1969, 58–9; M. V. Clarke and V. H. Galbraith, 'The deposition of Richard II', *BJRL* xiv (1930), 125–81 (part II, fos 136–41 at p. 127); Geoffrey Barraclough, 'The annals of Dieulacres abbey', *Sheaf* 3rd ser. lii (1960 [Jan.–Dec. 1957]), 17–27.

9   *Extracts from the manuscript liber Luciani de laude Cestriae*, ed. M. V. Taylor (RSLC lxiv, 1912), 65; David Crouch, 'The administration of the Norman earldom', in A. T. Thacker (ed.), *The earldom of Chester and its charters: a tribute to Geoffrey Barraclough, Journal of the Chester Archaeological Society* lxxi (1991), 71–2. Ranulph Higden did not mention the story in his *Polychronicon*, perhaps because its universal scope made local digressions inadmissible. He mentions the revolt that led to Lupus' creation, but not the creation itself: J. G. Edwards, 'Ranulph, monk of Chester', *EHR* xxxxvii (1932), 94; John Taylor, *The universal chronicle of Ranulph Higden*, Oxford 1966; *Polychronicon Ranulphi Higden monachi cestriensis*, ed. C. Babington and Joseph Rawson Lumby (Rolls Series xli, 1865–86), vii. 266. Neither did the *Annales cestriensis* describe Hugh's creation; they were never intended to be more than a set of annals: *Annales cestriensis*, ed. R. C. Christie (RSLC xiv, 1887), 16. For the presence of traditions about King Harold at Chester see A. J. Thacker, 'The cult of King Harold at Chester', in Tom Scott and Pat Starkey (eds), *The Middle Ages in the north-west*, Oxford 1995, 155–76.

10 See p. 3 above.

11 Heath, 'Medieval archdeaconry and Tudor bishopric of Chester', 248, and 'The medieval church', *VCH*, *Staffordshire*, ed. William Page, M. W. Greenslade and others, Oxford 1908– , iii. 32.

12 *The life of Saint Werburge of Chester*, ed. Carl Horstmann (EETS o.s. lxxxviii, 1887) (from Pynson's 1521 edition). Bradshaw's *De antiquitate et magnificentia urbis Chestriae chronicon*, does not survive, if it ever existed: Bradshaw, *Life of St Werburge*, p. vi. The sole authority for its existence is John Bale, yet he makes no explicit references to the work in his earliest bibliographical catalogue. The only work of Bradshaw's noted there was 'Vitam Werburge virginis', though Bale added 'De caeteris eius scriptis, adhuc nihil reperi, quamvis alia seratur edidisse': *Illustrium maioris Britanniae scriptorum*, Ipswich 1548, fo. 141. The *De antiquitate* is an unjustified inference from Bale's statement that 'Historiam studio

[m]ade a sure chartre to hym [Lupus] and his succession,
By the swerde of dignite to holde it with myght,
And to calle a parlement to his wyll and syght,
To ordre his subiectes after true iustice
As a prepotent prince / and statutes to deuise.[13]

The story of the creation was backed by a concrete symbol: a sword preserved in Chester Castle was supposedly the very weapon with which Hugh was created earl.[14] Its totemic value as late as the Civil War was demonstrated by its removal to London as a trophy.[15] Such symbols helped make the myth more than the currency of monastic chroniclers and made the county more than a lateral community in which only the elite could participate. Ideas of Cheshire's historical coherence and independence pervaded the entire local culture, being present also in the architectural environment. Glass in the choir at Chester Cathedral depicted the earls of Chester, and even more humble displays of heraldry, such as that at Eastham, displayed the earldom's independent history. The windows of Brereton Hall, installed after 1579 by Sir William Brereton, featured nine Saxon earls of Mercia and seven Norman earls of Chester.[16]

The earls of Chester descended from Lupus also provided subjects for an

---

magnopere deditus erat. . . . De antiquitate & magnificentia suae urbis plura susissime narravit'. Bale's *Index Britanniae scriptorum* (ed. R. L. Poole and M. Bateson, Oxford 1902), compiled after 1547, refers only to 'Vitam Werburge virginis. . . . Atque alia nonnulla' (p. 159). By 1557 to the *Vita* was added 'Chronicum quoddam', as well as a note that 'Caetera eius opuscula non vidi': *Scriptorum illustrium maioris Brytanniae*, Basel [1557], 710. Wood then took up Bale's references and attributed to Bradshaw a work called 'De antiquitate & magnificentia Urbis Cestriae Chronicon, &c.': *Athenae Oxoniensis*, ed. P. L. Bliss, London 1813, i, col. 18. Holinshed states that Bradshaw wrote a life of Werburgh and 'a certeine chronicle': Raphael Holinshed, *Chronicles of England, Scotland and Ireland*, London 1807, iii. 864.

[13] Bradshaw, *Life of St Werburge*, 174, lines 1271-5. Interest in Lupus continued, for example his supposed epitaph: JRUL, MS Rylands 202, fo. 76.

[14] 'The rights and jurisdiction of the county palatine of Chester, the earls palatine, the chamberlain, and other officers', ed. J. B. Yates, in *Chetham Miscellanies*, II (Chetham Society xxxvii, 1856), 4; British Museum, *A guide to the medieval antiquities and objects of later date in the department of British and medieval antiquities*, London 1924, 230 (probably twelfth- or thirteenth-century).

[15] As significantly, it was soon returned: R. Stewart Brown, 'The "domesday" roll of Chester', *EHR* xxxvii (1922), 492. Ashmole saw it in Chester in 1663: *Elias Ashmole (1617-1692): his autobiographical and historical notes, his correspondence, and other contemporary sources relating to his life and work*, III: *Texts, 1661-1672*, ed. C. H. Josten, Oxford 1966, 949. By 1692 it was in the Cottonian collection: HMC, *Annual reports*, v, London 1876, i. 383. Cf. the 'relics' of Guy of Warwick kept in Warwick: Emma Mason, 'Legends of the Beauchamps' ancestors: the use of baronial propaganda in medieval England', *Journal of Medieval History* x (1984), 28, 35.

[16] Ormerod, *Chester*, i. 298; iii. 87–8; *Sheaf* 3rd ser. iii (1901), 17–19, no. 378; Owen Salusbury Brereton, 'Exhibition of coloured drawing of a window in Brereton church', *Archaeologia* ix (1789), 368–9; J. H. Cooke, *Bibliotheca cestriensis*, Warrington–Northwich–Winsford 1904, plate facing p. 28.

historical tradition. Ranulph III had acquired a remarkable reputation by the later Middle Ages which was part of the broad-based collective mentality of the county.[17] Like Guy of Warwick, alias Wigod of Wallingford, an ancestor of the D'Oilly family and therefore of the Beauchamps, Ranulph was a real man transmuted into mythical hero.[18] Ranulph's achievements ranged from military exploits in England and on crusade to administrative innovation, and around these grew up apocryphal stories; especially important were those which related to Cheshire and its privileges.[19] The use by Langland of 'rymes of Robin Hode and Ranulf earl of Chester' as an instance of Sloth's pastimes suggests the extensive popularity of stories about the earl among ordinary people. The 'rymes' have not survived, but the tenuous survival of stories about Robin Hood suggests the ease with which even a popular, widespread tradition could be lost. The 'rymes' may have concerned the expedition to Rhuddlan, described by the Cheshire-born historian Raphael Holinshed, when a rabble including many minstrels under the command of the constable of Chester, Roger Lacy, saved the earl from the Welsh,[20] or other events, perhaps his experiences on crusade.[21]

17 Earl Ranulph was part of the general cultural context of popular literature. A good example is his appearance in *Sir Launfal*, a translation of Marie de France's romance by Thomas Chestre, usually dated to the late fourteenth century: *Ancient Engleish metrical romancees*, ed. Joseph Ritson, London 1802, i. 189–90; Mortimer J. Donovan, 'Breton lays', in J. Burke Severs (ed.), *A manual of writings in middle English, 1050–1500*, New Haven 1967, i. 138–9 (Chestre's name suggests a Cheshire origin: Thomas Warton, *History of English poetry from the twelfth to the close of the sixteenth century*, ed. W. C. Hazlitt, London 1871, iii. 96–8; *DNB* iv. 206). This story of the Round Table mentions Ranulph only once, in a passing reference to an incident at a tournament: *Ancient Engleish metrical romancees*, i. 189–90 (at lines 469–72); an indication of its continuing popularity is to be gathered from the presence of the poem Sir Lambewell in the Bishop Percy folio manuscript (i. 142–64). The author felt no need to explain his appearance; Ranulph, like Arthur, was just another of the chivalric worthies whose presence defined the context of the story: J. W. Ashton, ' "Rymes of . . . Randolf, erl of Chestre" ', *English Literary History* v (1938), 205.
18 Mason, 'Legends of the Beauchamps' ancestors', 25–40; DeLloyd J. Guth, 'Richard III, Henry VII and the city: London politics and the "dun cowe" ', in Ralph A. Griffiths and James Sherborne (eds), *Kings and nobles in the later Middle Ages*, Gloucester–New York 1986, 196–9; cf. Godfrey de Bouillon, the Chevalier au Cygne: Maurice Keen, 'Chivalry, heralds, and history', in R. H. C. Davis and J. M. Wallace-Hadrill (eds), *The writing of history in the Middle Ages: essays presented to Richard William Southern*, Oxford 1981, 395–6.
19 B. E. Harris, 'Ranulph III, earl of Chester', *Journal of the Chester Archaeological Society* lviii (1975), 99–114; J. W. Alexander, *Ranulf of Chester: a relic of the Conquest*, Athens, Ga. 1983; Brown, ' "Domesday" roll of Chester', 481–500, esp. pp. 496–7.
20 Holinshed, *Chronicles*, ii. 373; *DNB* ix. 1024–6; May McKisack, *Medieval history in the Tudor age*, Oxford 1971, 116–18. The threat to Ranulph from the Welsh coincided with the annual St Werburgh's fair at Chester, a privilege of which was that no-one should be arrested other than for offences committed there. This drew 'fidlers, players, coblers, debauched persons, both men and women', who, organised by Roger Lacy, alias Hell, rescued Ranulph. Roger was rewarded with a franchise over musicians, players and prostitutes in the county. The original grant of the advowry was, in fact, made to Roger Lacy's son John; and it was he who made the grant to Hugh de Dutton 'magisterium omnium Leccatorum, & Meretricum

Footnote 21 on next page.

The chronicle and more 'popular' verse traditions allow us an insight into the transmission of this local culture. The chronicle accounts were apparently borrowed and copied: the Dieulacres chronicle text, guarded in the monastery where Earl Ranulph's heart was buried,[22] is close to Humphrey Newton's words in his historical and legal collections, and also to the manuscript owned by Roger Walle.[23] For the mass of the population, however, the most effective means of transmission was through the county's minstrels.[24] Minstrels were frequent visitors to the homes of the nobility and greater gentry and to monastic houses, and also visited fairs and other public gatherings.[25] A prominent county figure like the Venables baron of Kinderton retained his own troupe of minstrels, and even such a minor gentry household as that of Humphrey Newton might play host to minstrels, so their influence was extensive.[26] The minstrels of Cheshire were a numerous and varied group. They appear, for example, in taxation records (suggesting that views of minstrels as little more than wondering vagabonds are not always true), and

totius Cestershire ... sicut liberius illum Magisterium teneo de Comite; salvo jure meo, mihi & haeredibus meis': William Dugdale, *The baronage of England*, London 1675, i. 101; Ormerod, *Chester*, i. 36. The terms *leccatorum et meretricum* have caused discussion. By 23 Edward I an inquisition on the death of Hugh Dutton stated he died seized of the advowry 'omnium minestrellorum et meretricum': Daniel Lysons and Samuel Lysons, *Magna Britannia*, London 1810, ii/2, 523. Leycester believed that 'the fidlers' were later included 'as necessary attendant on revellers in bawdy houses and taverns': Ormerod, *Chester*, i. 644. The Lysons suggest *leccator* might be rendered 'a buffoon, or jester': *Magna Britannia*, ii/2, 523. Smith mistook the process whereby the privilege passed first to Lacy and only subsequently to the Duttons. This error originates with St Caradoc of Llancarfan, *The historie of Cambria, now called Wales*, edn 'corrected, augmented and continued' by David Powell, London 1584, 296–7, whom Camden in *Britannia* (London 1586) seems to follow: Ormerod, *Chester*, i. 36. Rauf de Dutton seems not to have existed.
[21] Dugdale's fanciful account of the battle of Lincoln, in which the earl is given a pre-eminent role in forcing Louis to swear to leave England (an event that never occurred), could have been drawn from some kind of verse romance about Ranulph: *Baronage of England*, i. 42; R. M. Wilson, *The lost literature of medieval England*, 2nd rev. edn, London 1970, 117–18; cf. J. H. Round, *Peerage and pedigree: studies in peerage law and family history*, London 1910, ii. 302–6. Ranulph appears frequently in 'Fulk Fitzwarin': M. D. Legge, *Anglo-Norman literature and its background*, Oxford 1963, 171–4; *Fouke Fitz Warin: roman du XIVe siècle*, ed. Louis Brandin, Paris 1930.
[22] Possibly written elsewhere, perhaps at Chester: John Taylor, *English historical literature in the fourteenth century*, Oxford 1987, 190–1; Clarke and Galbraith, 'Deposition of Richard II', 129–31. See also Harris, 'Ranulph III', 113.
[23] Barraclough, 'Annals of Dieulacres', 21–5; Bodl. Lib., MS Lat. misc. c.66, fos 9v, 7b; Corpus Christi College, Cambridge MS 369, fos 1v–3v.
[24] J. C. Holt, *Robin Hood*, London 1982, 109–12, 137–8; J. Southworth, *The English medieval minstrel*, Woodbridge 1989; E. K. Chambers, *The medieval stage*, Oxford 1903.
[25] Holt, *Robin Hood*, 138–9.
[26] Venable's minstrels played for the Chester smiths and shoemakers in 1556–7: *Records of early English drama: Chester*, ed. Lawrence M. Clopper, Manchester 1979, pp. lx, 59–60. Bodl. Lib., MS Lat. misc. c.66, fos 26a v, 34c v (Easter 1499, 1d. for a minstrel; probably 15 Henry VII, 'at Wylmeslowe wakes to mynstrelles', 2d.).

in cases of riots when they helped buoy the morale of participants.[27] They were excellent guardians of the tradition because it was allegedly Earl Ranulph's gratitude for his rescue by them from the Welsh that had given them their privileges, and the jurisdiction which controlled them (and Cheshire's prostitutes) remained clearly part of the structure of palatine authority, even when elsewhere in England minstrelcy became either largely self-policed or subsumed within the general issue of vagrancy. Their organisation, vested in the Dutton family as the steward of the constables of Chester, was uniquely strong. As Rastall has argued, rather than being a gild, this jurisdiction was in origin comparable to the jurisdictions exercised by lords over those who traded in their fairs and markets. It may well be that kings of minstrels had originally controlled players in territorially defined areas of the country, but by the end of the fourteenth century this system had broken down. The initial reaction to the problems of control this posed was a patent to a group of minstrels in 1449 giving them jurisdiction over all the country's minstrels with the exception of those of Chester. This was superseded by a patent of 1469 which gave royal sanction to a national minstrel gild; once again Cheshire was excepted. In this important area of the cultural life of England, there was therefore a clearly divergent pattern of change. In the rest of England, control by royal officers was abandoned in favour of a self-regulating organisation, albeit with royal sanction, in the late fifteenth century. The players of Cheshire, however, remained under the control of a family who drew their authority from a grant to an officer of the earl and his palatinate. When in the following century the Tudor parliaments began to deal with the more disreputable elements among the minstrelcy through the poor laws, an early manifestation of the growing power of the national state to interfere in economy and society, Cheshire's minstrels remained exempt and under the control of the earl's officer.[28]

[27] Henry Ryle 'mynstrell', of Etchells, taxed on goods worth £6 in 1546: PRO, E 179/85/26, m. 1v. An interrogatory to be ministered to Richard Cholmondeley on behalf of Randal Mainwaring in 1537 asked whether Richard 'at his setting forth frome his owne house ... did comande a mynstrell then being there to playe to the felde': STAC 2/24/30.

[28] G. R. Rastall, 'The minstrel court in medieval England', *Proceedings of the Leeds Philosophical and Literary Society (Literary and Historical Section)* xviii (Apr. 1982–Dec. 1982), part 1, 96–105; *CPR, 1446–52*, 262; *CPR, 1467–77*, 153; *English historical documents, 1327–1485*, 1200–1; Chambers, *Medieval stage*, ii. 259; Southworth, *English medieval minstrel*, 121–3. Other examples existed in Newcastle-under-Lyme (Lysons, *Magna Britannia*, ii/2, 524; Chambers, *Medieval stage*, ii. 260; Southworth, *English medieval minstrel*, 123–5; Robert Plott, *The natural history of Stafford-shire*, Oxford 1686, 435–40, repr. in Stebbing Shaw, *The history and antiquities of Staffordshire*, London 1798, i. 52–3) and Beverley, although the latter subsequently became a conventional trade gild. A similar organisation in Shropshire was confirmed during the reign of Henry VI but ignored in 1469: Ormerod, *Chester*, ii. 434–5. For the poor law see 14 Elizabeth I, c.5; 39 Elizabeth I, c.4; 43 Elizabeth I, c.9; 1 James I, c.25; 17 George I, c.5. (SR iv. 590–8, #42 at p. 598; iv/2. 899–902, #10 at p. 901; iv/2. 973–4, #2; iv/2. 1050–2, at p. 1050). In 1572, an attempt to insert a proviso in favour of Welsh minstrels failed: A. H. Dodd, 'Wales's parliamentary apprenticeship

The franchise survived well beyond the sixteenth century, last being exercised in 1756,[29] and the exercise of the lordship appears to have been constant throughout the Middle Ages.[30] In the *quo warranto* enquiry of 1499 Lawrence Dutton claimed privilege on grounds of prescription. At the yearly meeting he received four bottles of wine and a lance, and each minstrel paid 4½d. and each prostitute 4d.[31] The first record of the actual form of the court and associated proceedings, from the start of the Civil War, indicates the impressive nature of the ceremony.[32] First, the lord of Dutton or his deputy rode to a place 'a little above the Eastgate', accompanied by many gentlemen and 'haveing a banner displayed before him, and a drumm and trumpett'. Then proclamation was made that all minstrels should appear before the court. The musicians were further commanded to play before the lord or his deputy and then return to the court house, still playing. There they were to appear to do homage, before continuing to the lord's lodgings, playing once again.[33] After the proclamation, the lord or his deputy rode with the minstrels to St John's Church, where 'a sett of the lowd musique upon their knees playeth a solemn lesson or two'. Thence he returned to the place where the court was held. The minstrels made their appearance one-by-one; then a jury was empanelled. The steward read the charges to the jury: whether they knew of any treason against king or prince, of any performance without licence, of profanation of the sabbath, or of any insult to the heir of Dutton.[34]

The Duttons' jurisdiction over the Cheshire minstrels meant more than the annual court. When in 1539 two of Sir Piers Dutton's daughters were married, the Cheshire minstrels added to the splendour of the occasion. As the procession returned from Dutton Hall it was met at Flookersbrook-bridge by the steward of Dutton, 'attended by the pursuivant and standard bearer of that family, each properly habited and having the insignia used at that Mid-

(1536–1625)', *Transactions of the Honourable Society of the Cymmrodorion* (1944 [1942]), 14; Sir Simonds D'Ewes, *A compleat journal of the votes, speeches and debates, both of the House of Lords and House of Commons throughout the whole reign of Queen Elizabeth, of glorious memory*, London 1693, 220; CJ i. 98.

[29] Ormerod, *Chester*, i. 654. In 1754 21 licences were granted: Lysons, *Magna Britannia*, ii/2,527. Technically the privilege of the minstrels only lapsed in 1822 with the repeal of the Vagrancy Act of 1744.

[30] Ormerod, *Chester*, i. 646. In 1540–2 the arm of the jurisdiction supervising prostitutes came to an end with the suppression of brothels in Chester: Rupert H. Morris, *Chester in the Plantagenet and Tudor reigns*, Chester [1894], 69; Lysons, *Magna Britannia*, ii/2, 524.

[31] By 1642 the payment was 2s. 2d.; in 1666 2s. 6d.: Ormerod, *Chester*, i. 655. See also Lysons, *Magna Britannia*, ii/2, 527 (still 2s. 6d. in 1754).

[32] 24 June 1642: Ormerod, *Chester*, i. 654–5.

[33] A later form of the proclamation is given in Lysons, *Magna Britannia*, ii/2, 525–6.

[34] The involvement of priests in the ceremony was probably reduced during the Reformation when the head of the Dutton family was influenced by the radical Protestant, John Bruen: William Hinde, *A faithfull remonstrance of the holy life and happy death of John Bruen of Bruen-Stapleford in the county of Chester, esquire*, London 1641, 129–31; Patrick Collinson, *The religion of Protestants: the Church in English society, 1559–1625*, Oxford 1982, 167, 169, 230, 243, 268.

summer solemnity, preceded by all the licensed musicians with white scarves across their shoulders, ranked in pairs, and playing on their several instruments'.[35] The jurisdiction also had more sinister uses. Sir Piers Dutton used minstrels assembled for the court to eject Thomas Pyllyn from his house in Chester.[36] Their prevalence meant that they were an integral part of the myth of the palatinate, and at the same time a means of propagating that myth.

It is therefore not surprising that Ranulph, or its corruption Randal, continued to be a popular name among both gentry and lower orders in Cheshire at a time when it had virtually died out elsewhere.[37] Names are a valuable indicator of popular mentality, because naming is no random action but reflects the attitudes and beliefs of the parents.[38] In early modern England children's names tended to echo those of their godparents; in Chester city the level of naming from a godparent stood at over 75 per cent.[39] About half of all cases for which we have sufficient data, however, show children being given names shared by both their same-sex godparents, which implies that although children's names were linked to the names of their godparents, the selection of godparents was undertaken in such a way as to allow the parents to choose the name of their child.[40] This parental choice was often exercised by Cheshire parents in favour of the name Randal. In the period 1480–1560, 4.1 per cent of male children born to a sample of 121 Cheshire gentry families were christened Randal.[41] When a riot took place at Wilmslow in 1494, 5.5

[35] William Cowper, *Collectanea Devana* (CCityRO, COWPER), cited in Ormerod, *Chester*, i. 654.
[36] On midsummer's day Thomas Pynchewar and William Horseman, two priests, came to the house and broke down the doors with iron bars. Dutton made a forced entry accompanied by about 200 others, 'moste parte of theym beynge Mynstrells and of straunge parties': PRO, STAC 2/30/68 (*Sheaf* 3rd ser. xviii [1923], 49, no. 4339). Horseman was a priest of the Fraternity of St Anne: Ormerod, *Chester*, i. 353. See also REQ 1/4/141, discussed in *Sheaf* 3rd ser. xxxv (1948), 17–18, no. 7759.
[37] Morris, *Chester in the Plantagenet and Tudor reigns*, 369.
[38] For example, C. Clark, 'Women's names in post-Conquest England: observations and speculations', *Speculum* lxxx (1978), 223–51; P. Benedict, *Rouen during the wars of religion*, Cambridge 1987, 104–6. A prominent individual could influence the pattern of naming, as Lancelot Lowther did in the lordships of Bromfield and Yale: Gunn, 'Charles, duke of Suffolk, in north Wales', 461–94.
[39] John Bossy, 'Blood and baptism: kinship, community and Christianity in western Europe from the fourteenth to the sixteenth centuries', in Derek Baker (ed.), *Sanctity and secularity: the Church and the world* (Studies in Church History x, 1973), 129–35; Scott Smith-Bannister, *Names and naming patterns in England, 1538–1700*, Oxford–New York 1997. See also BL, MS Harleian 2177.
[40] That this was not pure chance is suggested by the cases of twins such as Margaret and Elizabeth (baptised 24 August 1602), the daughters of Rafe Crosse, yeoman. Margaret's godmothers were Margaret Revington and Margaret Howe; Elizabeth's were Elizabeth Lancashire and Elizabeth Eaton: ibid.
[41] Ormerod, *Chester*, passim. Smith-Bannister, *Names*, 152–3, criticises the idea of Randal as an indicator of interest in the earl of that name, on the basis of his demonstration that godparentage and family influences were predominant in naming patterns (chs ii, iii). He

per cent of the 867 participants indicted at the county court, who ranged in status from knights to labourers, were called Randal.[42]

In the sixteenth and early sevententh centuries, Ranulph remained a prominent symbol of Cheshire honour. Richard Bostock praised the earl in a poem as 'the parragon of all that Ile' (1602–69).[43] This was one element of the mentality of local privilege and identity which made Cheshire distinct from the rest of the country that did not have to be created by self-interested lawyers in the sixteenth century: it was a vigorous inheritance.[44] It is important to note the interplay of the earldom's histories with the growing Stanley tradition, for example in *Lady Bessy* and *Scottish Field*; and even such relatively minor figures as Sir Ralph Egerton could compete in the same arena, as the latter poem shows.[45] This was part of a culture of community which was about more than simply the power of the dominant noble, or in Cheshire's case royal, family; for with the adulation of the great earls of the past went a cultivation of the privileges of the whole shire and many groups and individuals within it.[46]

Cheshire baronies as a focus for cultural identification

Part of the same myth-history were the Cheshire baronies, and they are interesting because they show how the tradition might help support multi-layered identities within the palatinate. The baronies of Cheshire stemmed from the Norman and early Plantagenet earldom. Although some were later in origin than others,[47] they eventually settled into a pattern of eight baronies. Of these, Rhuddlan and Mold in Wales had rapidly become extinct. This left Malpas, Nantwich, Stockport, Dunham Massey, Kinderton and Halton.[48]

---

does not take account of the influence of choice of godparents; his explanation that the prevalence of the name in Cheshire is the result of the proportion of men named Randal, and the proportion of boys named after godparents, does not fully address the differential survival rate of the name.

[42] PRO, CHES 24/65. But note the failure to use other names denoting local cultural identifications, notably Werburgh. An exception is Werburgh, the daughter of John Brereton, son of Sir William (d. 1484–5): Ormerod, *Chester*, iii. 89. The name Otwell is, however, interesting, as it is derived from Brocmail, credited with being a pre-conquest earl of Chester: BL, MS Harleian 2125, fo. 9; 2155, fo. 42; *Venerabilis Baedae historiam ecclesiasticam gentis Anglorum*, ed. Charles Plummer, Oxford 1896, i. 83–4; Holinshed, *Chronicles*, i. 598.

[43] *Bishop Percy's folio manuscript*, ed. J. W. Hales and F. J. Furnivall, London 1868, i. 258, 258–91 (quotation at p. 281, line 252).

[44] Barraclough, 'Earldom and county palatine of Chester', 24.

[45] Lawton, 'Scottish Field', 42–57; Ives, 'Ralph Egerton', 352–5.

[46] Contrary to the argument of Carpenter, 'Gentry and community'; cf. Thornton, 'Defence of the liberties of Chester', 341

[47] Dunham Massey was held *in capite* of the earl, while Stockport was a product of subinfeudation: Ormerod, *Chester*, iii. 788–90.

[48] Ibid. i. 51.

Unlike the majority of honorial baronies, the Cheshire baronies were remarkably long-lasting, and consideration of the foci of authority and identification in Cheshire must take them into account.

In the eleventh and early twelfth centuries not only those who held fiefs in chief of the crown, but also the chief vassals of the more important tenants *in capite* from the king were recognised as barons. By the end of the twelfth century, however, this latter category was generally excluded from the baronage; the only major exceptions were the major vassals of palatine lords such as the bishop of Durham and the earls of Pembroke and Chester, and to a lesser extent the palatinates of Lancaster and Shropshire.[49] The barons of Chester were therefore examples of a very few surviving honorial barons. Rather than being created in their final form by Hugh Lupus, the baronial jurisdictions developed gradually over the first decades of the earldom.[50] As royal government became more sophisticated, it forced ever greater definition in the comital jurisdiction and, in turn, in those of the Cheshire baronies. By the time of the Black Prince they could be expressed in the form of (largely successful) defences against *quo warranto* proceedings.[51]

The power of the Cheshire baronies was expressed through courts which were still active under the early Tudors.[52] These courts should not be confused with the court baron of an individual manor.[53] They were superior jurisdictions covering many manors and townships. The *quo warranto* proceedings of Henry VII's reign reveal extensive powers, at the highest level

[49] Frank Stenton, *The first century of English feudalism, 1066–1166*, 2nd edn, Oxford 1961, 84–114, esp pp. 87–8; Sidney Painter, *Studies in the history of the English feudal baronage*, Baltimore 1943, 15–16; James Tait, *Medieval Manchester and the beginnings of Lancashire*, Manchester 1904, 182–97; Matthew Gregson, *Second part of a portfolio of fragments, relative to the history and antiquities of the county palatine and duchy of Lancaster*, Liverpool 1817, 184. Some historians attempted to distinguish between major and minor barons, while others denied that barons' vassals could themselves ever be barons: John Selden, *Titles of honor*, London 1614, 258–93, esp. p. 275, believed that before the reign of Henry III, both varieties were summoned to 'parliament'. See T. Madox, *Baronia anglica: an history of land-honors and baronies, and of tenure in capite*, London 1741, 133–4: 'the Barones of the Earls and Great Men were styled Barones improperly'.

[50] '[T]hey retained the name of Barons by little and little': Ormerod, *Chester*, i. 51.

[51] Cf. Helen Cam, 'The evolution of the medieval English franchise', in her *Law-finders and law-makers in medieval England: collected studies in legal and constitutional history*, London 1962, 22–43, and 'The decline and fall of English feudalism', in her *Liberties and communities in medieval England: collected studies in local administration and topography*, London 1963, 207–11.

[52] Painter, *English feudal baronage*, 96–106; cf. the barony of Alnwick: M. E. James, *Society, politics and culture: studies in early modern England*, Cambridge 1986, 68, 295ff. William Venables of Kinderton obtained an *inspeximus* of the charter of Cheshire's liberties after the grant of the mise of 1474; it had special relevance to him as one of the barons of Cheshire, to whom the liberties were originally granted: CCRO, DVE CC/I/9.

[53] See Sidney Webb and Beatrice Webb, *English local government from the revolution to the Municipal Corporations Act: the manor and borough*, London 1908, 13–20.

capital jurisdiction of infangthief and outfangthief and gallows.[54] These powers were still being used at the end of the sixteenth century: in 1597 Hugh Stringer was executed for murder after being found guilty by the Kinderton baronial court.[55] These powers were especially formidable when associated with those of the officerships of the county palatine that were attached to the baronies. That of Malpas was linked to the sergeancy of the county, and hence the capital jurisdiction of that office, known as the 'beheading', became associated with the jurisdiction of the baronial court.[56]

The baronies and the families that held them were greatly respected locally. Individual heads of the families were still referred to as 'baron': this was especially true of Baron Venables of Kinderton.[57] National figures took pride in Cheshire baronies: when Sir John Dudley was created Great Admiral of England in January 1543 he was described as viscount Lisle and baron of Malpas; and Sir Robert Cholmondeley was created baron of Nantwich by Charles I in recognition of his services.[58] We should be wary of elaboration due to later sixteenth-century antiquarianism,[59] but for Selden to select the Cheshire baronies as being of particular status required a tradition of esteem that outweighed and outlasted baronies elsewhere.[60] A case in the court of the earl marshal, Thomas Howard, earl of Arundel, in 1626 shows the importance of the baronial tradition for the status of local men. William Brereton stated in his complaint that

> ther weer 8 barons Created and a parl[ia]m[en]t house erected in the Castle of Chester and Seates made on the on syde of the said parl[ia]m[en]t howse for the 8 barons to sitt in parl[ia]m[en]t w[i]th the said earl[.]

At the end of the reign of Elizabeth, vice-chamberlain Glaseor had placed the arms of Eustace, Baron Montalt, in the first seat, in place of those of Robert, son of Hugh, baron of Malpas, 'beeing the first baron that was created by the said Hugh Lupus', and in the fourth place put the arms of 'Davyd

---

[54] For example, Ormerod, *Chester*, i. 526 (Dunham Massey); iii. 426 (Nantwich). See also Stenton, *First century of English feudalism*, 101–5; Painter, *English feudal baronage*, 104.

[55] W. W. Mortimer, 'The Norman earls of Chester', *THSLC* 1st ser. iv (1851–2), 96–7.

[56] Ormerod, *Chester*, iii. 595. Sidney and Beatrice Webb (*English local government*, 32–62, 165–9; cf. Ormerod, *Chester*, i. 530, 537) take as an example the court of the barony of Dunham Massey and its subsidiaries at Altrincham and in Dunham Massey manor itself. These courts continued to confuse feudal and franchisal in a way that Bracton was supposed to have eliminated: Cam, 'Evolution of the medieval English franchise', 40–2.

[57] *Itinerary of Leland*, v. 30; the title 'baron of Stockport' was used (p. 24) for the Warrens. For William Venables see JRUL, Arley charters 27/6 (7 July 1486), 27/60 (24 Apr. 1487). For Sir William see JRUL, Tatton of Wythenshawe 98 (4 Jan. 1536). When Anthony Fitzherbert [Fox in the calendar] wrote to Thomas Cromwell for Sir William Venables, he referred to him simply as the 'baron of Kinderton': *LP* vi. 1096 (7 Sept. 1533).

[58] *LP* xviii/1, 100 (27); Ormerod, *Chester*, iii. 422–5 (1 Sept. 1645).

[59] For complications in Hitchin's courts introduced in the eighteenth century see Webb and Webb, *English local government*, 74.

[60] Ormerod, *Chester*, i. 51.

Malpas al[ia]s Davyd Clerk to the earl of Chester', who 'in deed was never baron of Malpas'.[61] This embarrassed Brereton, whose prestige was enhanced by having his ancestor as premier baron of the county. And as Ranulph III had passed into semi-mythical status, so did the ancestors of the barons of Cheshire. The Venables, for example, were alleged to have freed the Middle-wich area from the attentions of a dragon. In the words of Lawrence Dalton, Norroy King of Arms, making a grant of arms to Sir Thomas Venables in 1560:

> hitt chancyd A terrible dragon to remayne & make his abode in the Lo[rdshi]pp of Moston in the County of Chester where he devoured all such persons as he layd hold on w[hi]ch ye s[ai]d [Thomas] Venables [of Golborne, Sir Thomas's ancestor] hearinge tell of consyderinge the pittyfull & dayly destruction of the people without recouery who in following the example of the Valiant Romaynes & other worthy men not regarding his one life in comparison of the comodity & safegarde of his countrye men did in his one person valiantly & coragiously set on the s[ai]d dragon where first he shott him throw w[i]th A arrow & afterward with othere weapons manfully slewe him at w[hi]ch instant tyme the s[ai]d dragon was devowringe of a child, for the w[hi]ch his worthy & valiant act was given him the Lo[rdshi]pp of Moston in the s[ai]d county by the Auncestors of the thearle of Oxford Lord of the fee their, & also & euer since the s[ai]d Tho[mas] Venables & his heires in remen-brance therof haue vsed to beare as well in his armes & in there crest a dragon[.]

Constant reference to the story was provided for the inhabitants of the area in its celebration in carved ornament on the screen in Middlewich Church. More personal, but none the less powerful, was the testimony of heirlooms, such as the Duttons' sword of Odard, which bears comparison with the earl's sword at Chester.[62]

As well as possessing extensive powers and being sources of prestige for their holders, the baronies were centres for local loyalties and self-identification. They involved many local families in their jurisdiction and function, and therefore in their history.[63] The sergeancy of the county associ-ated with Malpas barony, for example, had attached to it twenty servitors, all

61 BL, MS Harleian 2079, fos 41–2; Kevin Sharpe, 'The earl of Arundel, his circle and the opposition to the duke of Buckingham, 1618–1628', in Kevin Sharpe (ed.), *Faction and parliament: essays on early Stuart history*, paperback edn, London 1985, 209–44, esp. pp. 225, 241–2; P. J. Hardacre, 'The earl marshal, the heralds, and the House of Commons, 1604–1641', *International Review of Social History* ii (1957), 106–25, esp. pp. 112–16.
62 BL, MS Harleian 2119, fo. 40r–v; 'The dragon of Moston', in Egerton Leigh, *Ballads and legends of Cheshire*, London 1867, 223–7. For Odard see *Sheaf* 1st ser. i (1880), 129, 142, nos 419, 453.
63 The jurisdictions subordinate to the prince's lordship in Chester did the same thing for many families. An example is forest administration for which see the records of the Halmote of Mara and Mondrem in PRO, CHES 24/65 (sessional file for county court session of the Conception of Blessed Virgin 1494).

drawn from leading local families.[64] That such families willingly participated in this tradition is demonstrated by the persistence of archaic names linked to the early baronial families in the districts of the baronies. Hence the appearance of the name Urian in the Malpas area, after Urian St Pierre of Malpas, the first man to raise the standard of Prince Edward in the county after the latter's escape from de Montfort;[65] and the name Hamo, the customary first name of the Masseys, around Dunham.[66]

The significance of the baronies should not be over-estimated; but neither should they be ignored, as too often in the past.[67] They were not autonomous foci of identification, since they were closely linked in jurisdiction and history with the paramount court of the county.[68] But the baronies did provide one element in the complex and overlapping patchwork of privilege and jurisdiction through which the self-identification of the local community could be formed.

Cheshire and the Tudor British history

Stories of Lupus' creation, his successors and their barons, remained strong throughout the sixteenth and early seventeenth century, providing clear support for palatine privileges. They were, however, not the only histories on which people in Tudor Cheshire based their view of the county's proper place in the kingdom.[69] Considering the embarrassment of contemporary legal thought at the idea of privileges based on conquest,[70] and the effect of the Reformation,[71] this was perhaps fortunate. In fact the culture of community was growing and developing in the sixteenth century, gaining ever stronger roots at the centre and in the locality.

---

[64] For example, Ormerod, *Chester*, ii. 595; cf. the claim by Hugh Egerton to office under the barony of Nantwich, the history of which is traced back to William Malbank who died *temp.* Henry III: CCRO, DCH/Y/3.

[65] Ormerod, *Chester*, ii. 596; J. R. Studd, 'The Lord Edward's lordship of Chester, 1254–72', *THSLC* cxxviii (1979 [1978]), 15–16.

[66] For example, Ormerod, *Chester*, i. 522; the Ashleys of Ashley, Masseys of Sale, Arderns of Timperley and Carringtons of Carrington: i. 544, 548, 557, 565–6.

[67] VCH, *County of Chester*, ii. 31 ('grandiose' titles).

[68] For example, Ormerod, *Chester*, iii. 790.

[69] For the existence of conceptually distinct, but dialectically related elements of tradition see Pocock, 'Time, institutions and action', 217, and Susan Reynolds, 'Medieval *origines gentium* and the community of the realm', *History* lxviii (1983), 375–7.

[70] J. G. A. Pocock, *The ancient constitution and the feudal law: a study of English historical thought in the seventeenth century: a reissue with a retrospect*, Cambridge 1987, esp. pp. 42–55.

[71] County independence had gained strength from the cult of St Werburgh, now under attack: Bradshaw, *Life of St Werburge*, 12, lines 103–4. Cf. St Edmund: MacCulloch, *Suffolk*, 7, 20, 35–7; St Cuthbert: Pollard, *North-eastern England*, 154; David Marcombe, 'A rude and heady people: the local community and the rebellion of the northern earls', in David Marcombe (ed.), *The last principality: politics, religion and society in the bishopric of Durham, 1494–1660*, Nottingham 1987, 133–4.

The beginning of the sixteenth century saw a revival of interest in British history. This account of how Britain had been founded by Brutus, who, fleeing the siege of Troy, became the ancestor of the Britons, was equivocal. One of its most important components, the Arthur myth, was treated with caution mixed with enthusiasm by many monarchs, because, although potentially supportive of English power, it could provide a charter for Welsh opposition.[72] British history did, however, provide a legitimating link to the Britons and through them to the classical past.[73] With the accession of the Welsh Henry Tudor, whose son was soon christened Arthur, it received new life.[74]

Interest in the British history was readily apparent in Cheshire. Henry Bradshaw drew on its traditions to describe the foundation of the city of Chester by Leon Gauer, a giant, and King Leil:

> The founder of Chestre / as sayth Policronicon
> Was Leon Gauer / a myghty stronge gyaunt,
> Whiche buylded caues and dongions many one,
> No goodly buyldyng / propre ne pleasaunt;
> But the Kynge Leil, a briton sure and valiaunt
> Was founder of Chestre by pleasaunt buyldyng,
> And of Carleil also / named by the kynge.[75]

Although the scepticism felt by the early humanists concerning Brutus and his descendants made some impact on Bradshaw, and he provided a Roman alternative to the British origin of Chester, drawn from Higden, that scepticism was, as Bradshaw's tone implies, limited in its impact.[76] Camden's explanation of Chester's origins was unequivocal in its rejection of the British history and in its support for a Roman foundation, and Webb's account in the

---

72 R. R. Davies, *Conquest, coexistence and change: Wales, 1063–1415*, Oxford–Cardiff 1987, 435–6.

73 Alison Allan, 'Yorkist propaganda: pedigrees, prophecy, and the "British history" in the reign of Edward IV', in C. D. Ross (ed.), *Patronage, pedigree, and power in later medieval England*, Gloucester–Totowa, NJ 1979, 171–92, esp. p. 176.

74 Poetry addressed to the newly-born prince Arthur emphasised links to the legendary Arthur: David Carlson, 'King Arthur and court poems for the birth of Arthur Tudor in 1486', *Humanistica Lovaniensia* xxxvi (1987), 147–83 (Carlson's emphasis on the bourgeois appeal of Arthur is dubious).

75 Bradshaw, *Life of St Werburge*, 144, lines 379–85. Stories about the British foundation of Chester stretched back to Lucian: *Extracts from the liber Luciani*, 41, 45.

76 Bradshaw, *Life of St Werburge*, 144, lines 91–2 ('Obiectyng clere agaynst the britons fundacion, Whiche auctour resteth in his owne opinion'); *Polychronicon*, ii. 76–84. See also T. D. Kendrick, *British antiquity*, London 1950, 35ff.; Sydney Anglo, 'The British history in early Tudor propaganda', *BJRL* xliv (1961–2), 17–48, qualified by Antonia Gransden, 'Antiquarian studies in fifteenth-century England', *The Antiquaries' Journal* lx (1980), 75. Cf. Marjorie Drexler, 'Fluid prejudice: Scottish origin myths in the later Middle Ages', in Rosenthal and Richmond, *People, politics and community*, 60–76.

1620s followed and supported Camden's, dismissing tales of giants.[77] Yet before the very end of the sixteenth century, local writers did not dismiss a British origin for Cheshire out of hand. Holinshed repeated Bradshaw's story, although he tended more towards Higden's scepticism; Smith provided both options.[78] In the pageant celebrated for the creation of Prince Henry in 1610, 'Chester's Triumph', the personification of Chester offered greetings:

> Haile sage Spectators, haile yee reu'rend Sires,
> Haile yonger Brutes, whose worth self Worth admires[.][79]

Interest in the British origins of Cheshire existed at court as well as in the county. The unacceptable nature of Polydore Vergil's attack on the Brutus and Arthur stories was demonstrated by the delay between the completion of his *Anglica historia* and its publication: as a result of Henry VIII's displeasure the treatment of Arthur was moderated. The British history played a prominent part in the justification of the break with Rome. Powerful supporters of the theory included a Welsh associate of Thomas Cromwell, Sir John Price.[80] Some have argued that the British history was recruited by Cromwell and others to provide justification for a political and jurisdictional campaign not only to make the territories of the English crown independent of external authority, primarily the papacy, but also internally more unified and centralised.[81] This is to misinterpret the implications of the British history among those at court: it offered jurisdictional independence but it reaffirmed internal diversity. Sir Thomas Elyot was, in general, one of the early Tudor writers who was most sceptical of it. Yet his *Bibliotheca* gives Neomagus as Chester's original name, derived from the founder, King Magus, son of Samothes, son of Japhet;[82] and the British history of Chester was more fully

---

[77] Camden, *Britannia*, 342; William Webb, 'The vale-royall of England', in *The vale-royall of England*, 8. Samuel Lee in the 1650s expressed scepticism ('I shall lay them [medieval chroniclers] to sleep in their Monkish Cradles.'): 'Chronicon cestrense', ibid. 34.

[78] Holinshed, *Chronicles*, i. 446; Smith, 'Vale-royall', 35.

[79] *Chester's triumph in honor of her prince as it was performed upon St George's day 1610*, ed. T[homas] C[orser] (Chetham Society iii, 1844), vii. Cf. other productions with a British theme, for example 'King Ebranke with all his Sonnes' (1589), about the king who supposedly founded Edinburgh and York: Morris, *Chester in the Plantagenet and Tudor reigns*, 322.

[80] Richard Koebner, ' "The imperial crown of this realm": Henry VIII, Constantine the Great and Polydore Vergil', *BIHR* xxvi (1953), 36–46; Graham Nicholson, 'The Act of Appeals and the English Reformation', in C. Cross, David Loades and J. J. Scarisbrick (eds), *Law and government under the Tudors: essays presented to Sir Geoffrey Elton Regius Professor of Modern History in the University of Cambridge on the occasion of his retirement*, Cambridge 1988, 19–30, esp. pp. 23–4; P. R. Roberts, 'The union with England and the identity of "Anglican" Wales', *TRHS* 5th ser. xxii (1972), 49–70.

[81] The influence of this interpretation of an 'imperial ideal' is especially clear in the work of G. R. Elton and Brendan Bradshaw: see pp. 247–8 below.

[82] McKisack, *Medieval history in the Tudor age*, 102. An example is 'Britania' [sic]) and 'Neomagus', in Thomas Elyot, *Bibliotheca Eliotae: Eliotis librarie*, London 1542.

discussed in a lost Elyot work called *De rebus memorabilibus Angliae*[83] circulating in Cheshire in the sixteenth and seventeenth centuries.[84] The foremost court topographer of the day, John Leland, presented Cheshire material in a British context in a poem on the birth of Prince Edward published in 1543. The *Genethliacon illustrissimi Eaduerdi principis Cambriae, ducis Coriniae, & comitis Palatini* presents pen portraits of Wales, Cornwall and Cheshire.[85] As well as being the traditional landed endowment of the heir to the throne, they are seen as 'western British' territories, distinct from England and yet an integral and specially valued part of the British monarchy.[86] The poem shows how the post-Conquest independent history of Cheshire was celebrated at court and blended with more respectable classical history:

> Hugo Lupus decus admirabile gentis
> Praesidiumque fuit Devanae. Fama loquetur
> Inclyta perpetuo Ranulphi facta, beavit
> Ille quibus gentemque suam nostroque priores
> Profuit & nobis Eduerdi gratia Longi
> Talis erit certe Principis Edoerdus, & urbem
> Aspiciet laetis oculis hanc, omnia fuse
> Elargiturus, quae commoda senserit esse.[87]

Once the break with Rome had occurred, the British heritage attained importance in providing support for the antiquity of the Church of England through the early medieval Celtic Church.[88] The British history was also important at court because the western British territories of Wales, Cheshire and Cornwall, whose importance it emphasised, were the traditional territories of the heir to the throne. The late medieval and early modern period was

---

83 Mentioned as nearing completion in Roger Ascham's *Toxophilus* (1544): *The boke named the gouernour deuised by Sir Thomas Elyot, knight*, ed. Henry H. S. Croft, London 1880, i, p. clxxii. A link to John Twyne's *De rebus albionicis*, London 1590, is speculative, for example the discussion of the etymology of 'Caer' (pp. 108–10) does not refer to Chester: Pearl Hogrefe, *The life and times of Sir Thomas Elyot Englishman*, Ames, Iowa 1967, 102–5.

84 Two of the three references to the work are from Cheshire: in a MS history of Chester (by Chester cleric and antiquarian Robert Rogers [d. 1595]) preserved at Delamere House, Cheshire: HMC, *Annual report*, iv, London 1874, 416 (for Rogers see Ormerod, *Chester*, i, pp. xlii, 115; ii. 828); and, hitherto unnoticed by Elyot scholars, Webb, 'Vale-royall', 7. The other is a mention by Bale probably based purely on Ascham's reference: *Boke named the gouernour*, p. clxxv. See Thornton, 'Political society in early Tudor Cheshire', 77–8.

85 Published in London in 1543, and reprinted in *The itinerary of John Leland the antiquary*, 3rd edn, ed. T. Hearne, Oxford 1769, ix, pp. xxiii–xxvi.

86 This tradition of Chester's British history continued with, for example, Holinshed, *Chronicles*, i. 446; Webb, 'Vale-royall', 7–9; Lee, 'Chronicon cestrense', 34.

87 *Genethliacon illustrissimi Eaduerdi principis Cambriae, ducis Coriniae, & comitis Palatini*, London 1543, repr. in *The itinerary of John Leland the antiquary*, ed. Thomas Hearne, 25, lines 712–19.

88 Cornwall too benefited from this connection: PRO, SP 6/1, fo. 157 (King Donnybalde of Cornwall, who inaugurated sanctuary and was first to own a golden crown, and King 'Licius' [Lucius], first Christian king of Britain).

one in which the succession to the throne was more often than not in some doubt, and this inevitably placed a premium on the prestige of the British past of these territories.

The vale-royall of England

During the sixteenth and early seventeenth centuries, the dynamic blending of British history, with its political and religious connotations, together with the stories of the independent earldom expressed itself in a newly vibrant local culture of autonomy. Cheshire traditions were crystallised in *The vale-royall of England, or the county palatine of Chester illustrated*, a compilation of works written over the previous eighty years published in London by Daniel King in 1656. The earliest was the description of Cheshire by William Smith, written in about 1588; this was followed by a similar work, of the early 1620s, by William Webb.[89]

Smith was a younger son of Randal Smith of Oldhaugh in Warmingham parish. He spent some years in Nuremberg, probably after study at Brasenose College, Oxford. Back in England by 1585, he produced several works of a topographical, historical and genealogical nature and became Rouge Dragon Pursuivant in 1597.[90] His knowledge and experience were therefore highly cosmopolitan, yet he showed a detailed knowledge of Cheshire history. Smith's work begins with a dossier of collected evidences for Cheshire's palatinate status 'as well before the Conquest, as since; whose Priviledges have been confirmed and established by divers and sundry kings of the realm'.[91] He provides a catalogue of Mercian kings, and of Saxon dukes and earls of March 'who were also Palatines of Chester';[92] the 1450 petition for the confirmation of the privilege with Henry VI's acceptance; and Elizabeth I's 'confirmation of privileges'.[93] Some of the more adventurous Cheshire gentry did take measures to deal with the new agenda of the Norman conquest of the Saxons. David Powell wrote to Sir William Brereton of Brereton on 10 January 1591/2 to assure him that a document he had once possessed

> was the Confirmation of certene Armes borne by foure gentlemen of Cheshire whose auncestors weare ther before the Cominge of Hugh Lupus to th[a]t

---

[89] Both works entitled 'The vale-royall of England', in *Vale-royall*. Then came a specially commissioned short history of Cheshire by Samuel Lee ('Chronicon cestrense', 1656), and the book concluded with a 'Short treatise of the Isle of Man' (1653), by James Chaloner.

[90] Elizabeth Berry, 'The vale royal of England, part 1', *Cheshire Round* i/9 (summer 1968), 308, and William Smith, *The particular description of England. 1588*, ed. with introduction by H. B. Wheatley and E. W. Ashbee, London 1879, pp. vi–viii.

[91] Smith, 'Vale-royall', 8.

[92] Ibid. 1–6, 7–8.

[93] Ibid. 9–11, 12–15.

Cuntrie & for that some normans newlie Come with the Conqueror to England vsurped theire armes they Complayned to the king whoe vppon due proffe that the Armes weare thers of Auncient tyme Confirmed the same vnto them.

The arms in question related to the families of Brereton of Brereton, Davenport of Davenport, and Dutton of Dutton. Three of the most important families of sixteenth-century Cheshire were therefore given a direct link back through the conquest to Anglo-Saxon Cheshire. Even here, however, Lupus remains the dominant figure in the historical framework.[94] It has been said that the *Vale-royall* 'belongs to the high Elizabethan period of historical topography', and it does form part of the flood of topographical and historical writing that appeared under Elizabeth.[95] Within this trend, a movement has been defined which has been called the 'discovery of England' in which two strands have been identified: the examination and celebration of the Roman heritage, exemplified by Camden's *Britannia*, and a reassertion of the place of the Anglo-Saxons in English history based on the rediscovery of their language and legislation.[96] These developments, it is claimed, changed the historical context of scholarly thinking. Britain came to be seen in the classical context of the Roman empire, allowing, for example, the *translatio imperii* from Rome necessitated by the Reformation.[97] Society also began to be considered in terms of continuities passing back through the Conquest to a newly-appreciated Saxon heritage,[98] rather than directly to the semi-mythical world of the Britons.[99] This allegedly reinforced a newly intensified English national consciousness, an 'unprecedented effort of national self discovery'.[100] Among county historians, however, Lambarde alone was demonstrably interested in the history of a county in these terms.[101] Smith

---

[94]   BL, MS Harleian 1997, fo. 89v.
[95]   Elizabeth Berry, 'The vale royal of England, part 2', *Cheshire Round* i/10 (summer 1969), 343; Robin Flower, 'Laurence Nowell and the discovery of England in Tudor times', *Proceedings of the British Academy* xxi (1935), 47–73; F. J. Levy, *Tudor historical thought*, San Marino, California 1967, 129–30, 137–50; McKisack, *Medieval history in the Tudor age*, 126–54.
[96]   Levy, *Tudor historical thought*, 125–30, 136–41; S. Piggott, 'William Camden and his Britannia', *Proceedings of the British Academy* xxxvii (1951), 207–8; Flower, 'Laurence Nowell', 54–9, 67–70.
[97]   Levy, *Tudor historical thought*, 125.
[98]   For example, Parker's work establishing a tradition through the Saxons to the early Church: Kendrick, *British antiquity*, 115–20. The reference in Cooke, *Bibiliotheca cestriensis*, 2, to a history of Cheshire collected by Matthew Parker is a confusion over Parker's ownership of the history in Corpus Christi College, Cambridge, MS 369.
[99]   For Lambarde and the law see Levy, *Tudor historical thought*, 137.
[100] Arthur B. Ferguson, *Clio unbound: perception of the social and cultural past in renaissance England*, Durham, NC 1979, 427.
[101] R. M. Warnicke, *William Lambarde: Elizabethan antiquary, 1536–1601*, London–Chichester 1973, esp. chs iv, ix; Levy, *Tudor historical thought*, 159. Ferguson admits, reluctantly, the continuing attraction of the British history: *Clio unbound*, 109. See also his discussion on Coke at p. 272.

demonstrates a complete contrast: his terms of reference were not those of Roman and Saxon Britain. He failed to take the opportunity to look at the Roman past offered by the city of Chester[102] and made no contribution to the study of place names begun by Leland and developed by Nowell. Smith's work cannot be claimed as evidence for a new perception of his county's place, absorbed in England. Instead, it preserved stories reinforcing the historical and constitutional interpretation of autonomy connected with the creation of Hugh Lupus and subsequent earls, not least the baronies and the Duttons' franchise of minstrels, and of Chester's connection with the British history.

The past . . . and the future

All accounts of the past have within them a message about the future. In many cases in the early modern accounts of Cheshire's past, it was a message of continuity within change. In other cases the future was depicted in more direct terms, and nowhere more clearly than in prophecy. Humphrey Newton of Pownall provides a good example of the way the traditions of the earldom, old and new, were blended with myth and prophecy. In a memorandum, probably no later than the mid 1520s, he recorded that 'Thomas Perkynson sang a song of Thomas Ersholedon & the quene of ffeiree Rehersyng the batell of Stoke fild & the batell at Branston of deth of the kynges of Scotts.'[103] The link between popular culture, prophecy and local political culture is demonstrated by what Newton's visitor went on to say after describing the song of Erceldoun, Stoke and Flodden:

> & also rehersyn that a lion shuld come out of walys & also a dragon & lond in werall that eny woman shuld have rowme to milke her cowe w[i]t[h] mony thousands & on a wennysday after to drive don Chester walls & after to feght in the fforest delamar w[i]t[h] a kyng of the southe which shuld have hundreds of m^l & that shu[ld] feght ii or iii days & then ther shuld come a plogh of yew w[i]t[h] clubbez & clot chone & take parte & wyn alle & ther the kyng shuld be kylled w[i]t[h] many an other to the nowmber of lxi m^l & never kyng after bot iiii wardens unto domysday

This prophecy is almost exactly mirrored by the supposed words of the Cheshire prophet, Nixon, suggesting that his prophecy, which had a remarkable and sustained popularity from the sixteenth century, was already current early in the sixteenth century.[104] Cheshire popular culture extended to a

---

102 Smith, 'Vale-royall', 35; cf. Camden's treatment of Chester, categorical about Roman origins: *Britannia*, 342.
103 Bodl. Lib., MS Lat. misc. c.66, fo. 104.
104 The earliest text of this prophecy is in CCRO, DDX 123. See *Nixon's Cheshire prophecies*, ed. W. E. A. Axon, Manchester–London 1873; Tim Thornton, 'Reshaping the local future: the development and uses of provincial political prophecy, 1300–1900', in Bertrand

particular corpus of prophecy. Prophecies were highly important in shaping political action and expressing fears and aspirations, in the 1530s for example.[105] As well as the past, Cheshire viewed the future in a localised context.

Constitutional and political implications of Cheshire's identity

County communities, it is often argued, found their identities late in the sixteenth century through gentry family histories and displays of heraldry.[106] It is clear, however, that the community of Cheshire had earlier founda- tions.[107] In other areas a strong cultural identity associated with a political community is unquestioningly accepted by historians, especially when linguistic differences existed, as in Wales and Ireland.[108] But this strong cultural identity was also to be found in the other palatine county, Durham. There the inhabitants had a clear awareness that they were the people of St Cuthbert, and this had practical application, for example as a basis for their exemption from English taxation and as a rallying point in war.[109]

This has important implications for the interpretation of constitutional and political developments in the period. Politics was not simply about the mechanics of service and patronage. Ideas played a vital part: loyalty could

Taithe and Tim Thornton (eds), *Prophecy: the power of inspired language in history, 1300–2000*, Stroud 1997, 51–67.

[105] Sharon L. Jansen, *Political protest and prophecy under Henry VIII*, Woodbridge 1991; Alistair Fox, 'Prophecies and politics in the reign of Henry VIII', in Alistair Fox and J. A. Guy, *Reassessing the Henrician age: humanism, politics and reform 1500–1550*, Oxford 1986, 77–94; C. S. L. Davies, 'Popular religion and the Pilgrimage of Grace', in A. Fletcher and J. Stevenson (eds), *Order and disorder in early modern England*, Cambridge 1985, 58–91; S. J. Gunn, 'Peers, commons and gentry in the Lincolnshire revolt of 1536', *Past and Present* cxxiii (May 1989), 52–79. Cf. 1485–6, when there were moves to outlaw prophecy: *Plump- ton letters and papers*, 64–5; Michael Bennett, *Lambert Simnel and the battle of Stoke*, Glouces- ter–New York 1987, 35.

[106] For example, MacCulloch, *Suffolk*, 117–19.

[107] Cultural communities elsewhere might be regional in extent, for example Warwick, discussed by John Rous: Kendrick, *British antiquity*, 22–3, 28; Gransden, 'Antiquarian stud- ies in fifteenth-century England', 84–6.

[108] In Ireland a Gaelic identity was more important than and distinct from an Irish identity for those living beyond the Pale: Steven G. Ellis, *Tudor Ireland: crown, community and the conflict of cultures, 1470–1603*, London 1985, 47–8 and ch. ii; Bradshaw, *Irish constitutional revolution*. See also Glanmor Williams, *Recovery, reorientation and reformation: Wales, c. 1415–1642*, Oxford 1987, chs vi, xviii, xix.

[109] Gaillard Thomas Lapsley, *The county palatine of Durham: a study in constitutional history*, London 1900, 296. For the banner of St Cuthbert see John Skelton, *The complete English po- ems*, ed. John Scattergood, Harmondsworth 1983, 360, lines 61–4; Johannis de Fordun, *Chronica gentis Scotorum*, ed. William F. Skene, Edinburgh 1871, i. 224; W. Hylton Dyer Longstaffe, 'The banner and cross of Saint Cuthbert', *Archæologia Æliana*, 2nd ser. ii (1858), 53; *LP* iii. 3481–2, 3506.

carry men on when prudence and the calculation of advantage should have stopped them.[110] Loyalty to the king or to noble and gentry families and concepts of correct behaviour and policy were vital to politics and could be deliberately cultivated.[111] Loyalty to the privileges of the palatinate and its community was just another aspect of this phenomenon.

Where the culture of local identity has been adduced in discussions of politics and institutional change, it has frequently been misused, most obviously in the assumption of oppositionism. Strong local identities did not necessarily mean that localist or even separatist opposition were dominant in politics. For a start, such sentiment always had a regard to the authority of the centre. Cheshire's major origin myth founded the county's position in a monarch's creation, not a separate evolution.[112] When the earl of Derby intervened against the city of Chester to defend the county's privileges, he did so 'for the goodwill I have long tyme borne this Citye, and also neighbourhood sake betwene us, and *mainelye for that I am an Englishman*'.[113] Community feeling could ultimately act against the centre, but in Cheshire the community was willing to adjust to accommodate developments at the centre. The political culture of region and court allowed Cheshire to take a new place within the territories of the English crown, at once closer and at the same time with its identity secured. Local history was more than mere glorification of local characteristics,[114] figures and events, interesting although this might be, for example in the attachment to the Mercian heritage making heroes of Penda and Harold Godwinson:[115] it enabled change by providing a culture which combined the tradition of the Saxon and Norman earldom with the British history, in the locality and at court. Second, this was understood by those at the centre. Their participation in a culture that accepted the validity of palatine autonomy ensured the palatinate's survival.

---

[110] See, for example, Ian Arthurson, 'A question of loyalty', *The Ricardian* vii, no. 97 (June 1987), 401–13; Horrox, *Richard III*, 324–33.

[111] Lawton, 'Scottish Field', 42–57; cf. Mason, 'Legends of the Beauchamps' ancestors', 25–40. It also applied to ecclesiastical institutions, for example the diocese of Lichfield: Thomas Wharton, *Anglia sacra*, London 1691, i. 421–43.

[112] 'Rights and jurisdiction', 14–15.

[113] Ibid. 18–20 (my emphasis); cf. MacCulloch, *Suffolk*, 117–18.

[114] For example 'The [Cheshire] ayr is very wholesome': Smith, 'Vale-royall', 16.

[115] See Bradshaw's glorification of Bede's villain Penda: *Life of St Werburge*, 23, lines 427–8; 25, line 483; Thacker, 'Cult of King Harold', 155–76.

3

The Chester Mise:
Taxation in an Autonomous County

Taxation occupies a sensitive position in the nexus of constitutional, political and social relationships, for it is through taxation that economic resources are mobilized for political ends. . . . [S]ince taxes entail compulsion, the ways in which they are authorized and organized are essentially political matters. A study of taxation, therefore, should throw light . . . on its political and administrative structure and its constitutional concepts of obligation and consent.[1]

'National' taxation of England began early in the thirteenth century, and although Cheshire was intermittently included until 1292, by the crucial period of 1340–60 the shire was not part of the 'national' bargain of taxation and consent that was central to the late medieval English polity.[2] This chapter explores how Cheshire's distinct position continued to be demonstrated in the way that it negotiated and paid tax in the fifteenth and sixteenth centuries.

The incidence of the mise

In place of English parliamentary taxation Cheshire payed a subsidy called the mise, developed in the mid-fourteenth century after English lay taxation was allowed to lapse.[3] The mise was based on two different levies, the common fine for a grant of liberties or pardon, and the *donum* or gift in recognition of a common obligation. The Black Prince concentrated on raising money from the profits of justice after 1346, when a call for £1,000 following Edward III's feudal aid failed: the 1347 and 1357 forest eyres were aimed primarily at this objective; and the general eyre of 1353 was bought off for 5,000 marks. The occasions on which the mise was paid thenceforth varied widely. In 1368 2,500 marks tax was paid to the Black Prince; and in 1373 he received a further 3,000 marks.[4] Under Richard II, 3,000 marks were paid in

---

1   R. S. Schofield, 'Taxation and the political limits of the Tudor state', in Cross, Loades and Scarisbrick, *Law and government*, 227.
2   G. L. Harriss, *King, parliament and public finance in England to 1369*, Oxford 1975.
3   Booth suggests that Cheshire was seen as a military resource and financial returns were ignored: *Financial administration*, 117–25. This supersedes VCH, *County of Chester*, ii. 23–4.
4   Booth, *Financial administration*, 184.

1389 for the confirmation of the liberties of the county.[5] There was a grant at the start of Henry IV's reign in 1401, and another shortly afterwards, in 1403, a communal fine for involvement in the Percy rebellion.[6] By this time the amount of the levy had settled, usually at 3,000 marks collected over three years. The allocation of the burden of the mise within the county was also now fixed.[7] A subsidy of 3,000 marks was paid to Henry V in 1416 and one of 1,000 marks in 1419,[8] and a grant of 1,000 marks was made in 1430 when Henry VI was about to visit France.[9] Another grant of 1,000 marks was made in 1436 in compensation for the county's refusal to pay the income tax of October 1435 for the defence of Calais.[10] In 1441 3,000 marks were paid for the confirmation of the county's liberties and a series of pardons.[11]

In the period between the confirmation of Cheshire's exemption from parliamentary taxation in 1451 and the reorganisation of English parliamentary taxation in the 1530s there was a strong link between mise grants and the advent of a new earl. In 1463 a grant of mise for a confirmation of the county's privileges was made following the accession of Edward IV to the earldom.[12] In 1474 another grant was made after the accession of Edward, prince of Wales, in July 1471, and his establishment at Ludlow in autumn 1473.[13] Henry VII's accession to the earldom resulted in a grant in 1486, with a proviso that if the queen were pregnant with an heir the grant should stand for a subsidy on that heir's creation as earl.[14] This pattern of fifty years of grants on the creation of an earl ended in 1497 when Henry VII won a subsidy of 1,000 marks for war against the Scots.[15] The next grant, in 1500, also represented a change: although the customary 3,000 marks was granted for the creation of Prince Arthur as earl, to it was added a 1,000 mark fine for the redemption of the general eyre, a throw-back to the fourteenth century.[16]

---

[5]   CChR, 1341–1417, 313–15; PRO, CHES 2/62, m. 7v (1), m. 6v. (8); CHES 2/64, m. 2 (1–2) (36 DKR, 95–6). The date (15 Dec. 1389) is misprinted in VCH, County of Chester, ii. 23.

[6]   Anne E. Curry, 'The demesne of the county palatine of Chester in the early fifteenth century', unpubl. MA diss. Manchester 1977, 267; 36 DKR, 43, 103, 411–12.

[7]   The relative size of the sums paid by hundreds in 1352–3 was the same as that in the first surviving mise book (1406): JRUL, Tatton of Wythenshawe 345 (1406); PRO, CHES 38/25/2 (1444.)

[8]   37 DKR, 75, 670; Curry, 'Demesne of the county palatine of Chester', 267–8.

[9]   PRO, CHES 2/100, m. 4(12) (37 DKR, 670).

[10]   PRO, CHES 2/107, m. 6(2) (CFR, 1430–37, 262; 37 DKR, 671, 693; RP iv. 486–7).

[11]   CPR, 1436–41, 560–1; CPR 1441–6, 32, 50. Clayton suggested Henry VI's birthday as the occasion for this grant: ' "Cheshire parliament" ' 19–21.

[12]   PRO, CHES 2/135, m. 2d.(9) (37 DKR, 95, 140, 693; CChR 1427–1516, 202).

[13]   PRO, CHES 2/146, m. 1(1) (37 DKR, 141, 694); Penry Williams, The Council in the Marches of Wales under Elizabeth I, Cardiff 1958, 6–8. For the collectors see Clayton, Administration, 200 (to which can be added Thomas Beston, Richard Spurstow, Thomas Done of Crouton and Ranulph Littlover, Eddisbury, 1475: BL, Additional charter 26,786).

[14]   PRO, CHES 2/158, m. 3 (37 DKR, 201).

[15]   PRO, CHES 2/167, m. 5v. (37 DKR, 694; 26 DKR, 25, no. 36).

[16]   26 DKR, 25 (#55); 37 DKR, 96 (Broxton collectors, 1 June 1501).

There was almost certainly another grant of mise late in Henry VII's reign, probably shortly before 1 March 1508.[17] Under Henry VIII, tradition reasserted itself. The only grant of the reign was made in 1517 following the accession of the king and for confirmation of liberties; it represented the final payment of the mise before the introduction of English parliamentary taxation.[18]

The existence from the fourteenth century of palatine taxation independent of that voted by the English parliament should not surprise us. As taxation developed in the various territories of the English crown from the thirteenth century, not all were subject to decisions made by the English parliament. Most obviously Ireland was not subject to English direct taxation. In the immediate aftermath of the final conquest of Wales, there were attempts to tax that country from Westminster, but these were abandoned after about 1300.[19] Durham had always been exempt from English taxation, its northern neighbours, Cumberland, Westmorland and Northumberland, were withdrawn from the English taxation system in the early fifteenth century, and the French territories ruled by the English crown during this period were not subject to English taxes.[20] Neither were decisions on direct taxation taken at the English parliament relevant to the subjects of the duke of Normandy in the Channel Islands[21] or those of the lord of Man, although from at least the fourteenth century he had an English monarch as his overlord. Instead, these territories developed their own fiscal systems. The Irish subsidy was granted through the Irish parliament to the governor for defence and nominally amounted to 700 marks.[22] In Durham, procedures for determining and allocating common obligations were in existence by 1302, and in 1314 there is evidence of a tax being voted to the bishop.[23] Like Cheshire,

17 Sir William Troutbeck, Sir John Warburton, Sir William Stanley and others were bound to pay 1,000 marks at the following midsummer and 1,000 marks at Michaelmas yearly for two years, 'for their confirmacon of their liberties and their lettres of pardon': PRO, E 36/214, p. 405. Piers Dutton was involved in the negotiation and controversies that arose over the assessment of those not resident in the shire: STAC 2/7/184 (*L&C Star Chamber*, 64).

18 PRO, CHES 2/186, m. 3 (*39 DKR*, 55, 178).

19 J. R. Strayer and George Rudisill, Jr, 'Taxation and community in Wales and Ireland, 1272–1327', *Speculum* xxix (1954), 410–16 (which unfortunately treats Wales and England as unities in the thirteenth and fourteenth centuries).

20 R. S. Schofield, 'Parliamentary lay taxation, 1485–1547', unpubl. PhD diss. Cambridge 1963, 145; B. J. H. Rowe, 'The estates of Normandy under the duke of Bedford, 1422–1435', *EHR* xlvi (1931), 562–8; C. T. Allmand, *Lancastrian Normandy, 1415–1450: the history of a medieval occupation*, Oxford 1983, 21, 172–4, 201–3, 245–62.

21 See Henry VII's memorandum on the taxation of Guernsey in 1497: PRO, E 101/414/6, fo. 129.

22 It in fact only yielded IR£350, until reform in the 1470s: Ellis, *Tudor Ireland*, 60; Art Cosgrove (ed.), *Medieval Ireland, 1169–1534*, Oxford 1987, 371–2; J. F. Lydon, *Ireland in the later Middle Ages*, Dublin 1973, 36–7.

23 In 1344 the community contributed to the bishop's expenses in buying off the Scots and in 1348 for defending the county's privileges: W. Hutchinson, *The history of the county palatine of Durham*, Durham 1823, 153, 375–7, 358; Lapsley, *County palatine of Durham*, 272–3.

the Welsh marcher lordships and the two halves of the principality paid taxes called mises through the later Middle Ages at least into the seventeenth century.[24] In the Isle of Man in the early 1340s, £106 13s. 4d. was levied to pay for a truce with the Scots.[25] As in the case of Cheshire, these territories yielded significant sums in taxation – they were neither ignored, nor expected to provide contributions of another kind, such as military manpower.[26] These taxes were not directly the king's taxes. They were raised in the name of the lord of the territory in question. This lord might be someone who was not a member of the royal family, the most prominent examples of this being the Stanley lords of Man and Welsh marcher lords and their successors after 1543, whose rights were guaranteed by a statute of Mary's reign.[27] The priorities of these lords and their representatives inevitably differed from those of the king. In other territories the lord might be the English king or a member of his family, but this did not mean an identity between English taxes and local taxes. For in these territories the king or his kinsman was lord in their capacity as, for example, earl of Chester or *seigneur* of Jersey or Guernsey.

Negotiation over the mise and the Cheshire parliament

The varying rationale for the payment of tax by Cheshire and its uneven incidence suggest payment did not occur as a matter of course: it resulted either from arbitrary demand or as a result of discussion. Mise was paid in just six years in the period 1450–85: 6,000 marks in thirty-five years. This was followed by payments in ten of the twenty-four years of Henry VII's reign: 10,000 marks. Given that a grant of the mise was approximately equivalent to the grant of a fifteenth and tenth in Shropshire or Staffordshire, Cheshire escaped lightly compared to neighbouring counties, especially in the 1440s and in 1468; yet in the period 1486 to 1509, the county bore a disproportionate burden.[28]

---

[24] R. R. Davies, *Lordship and society in the march of Wales, 1282–1400*, Oxford 1978, 184–7, 219; L. B. Smith, 'The Arundel charters in the lordship of Chirk in the fourteenth century', *Bulletin of the Board for Celtic Studies* xxiii (1969), 153–66. Unfortunately Ralph A. Griffiths, *The principality of Wales in the later Middle Ages: the structure and personnel of government*, I: *South Wales, 1277–1536*, Cardiff 1972, does not mention taxation or the means of agreeing/levying it.

[25] CCR, *1341–3*, 654 (from a total projected tax of 300 marks).

[26] See n. 3 above.

[27] In 1564 the earl of Leicester levied mise in Denbigh, as did Edward, earl of Worcester, in Gower at the very end of the sixteenth century: 1&2 Philip and Mary, c.15 (SR iv. 262); *Calendar of Salusbury correspondence, 1555–c. 1700*, ed. W. J. Smith, Cardiff 1954, 24; T. B. Pugh, *The marcher lordships of south Wales, 1415–1536*, Cardiff 1963, 146.

[28] Booth, 'Taxation and public order', 16–31. Fifteenths and tenths were levied in 1434–5, 1442–3, 1446, 1449–50, 1463, 1468 (two), 1473–4, 1487 (two), 1489, 1491–2 (two), 1496 (two), 1512 (three in two grants) and 1515: Anthony Steel, *The receipt of the exchequer,*

So what determined how much tax Cheshire paid? Community generosity or opposition? Royal pressure or laxity? Cheshire was not a large county: if this were simply a question of the exercise of power, Cheshire could have been compelled to pay tax as the government wished. If we can show that the county was not, this will indicate something of the power of privilege and community in the late medieval polity and the respect for it shown by the crown.

The answer to these questions is to be found in a study of the Cheshire parliament, where the mise was negotiated by members of the earl's council with representatives of the county community. The theory as set out in petitions of 1450 and 1451 is clear: the county's *parliamentum* was empowered to legislate and decide on taxation, and Cheshire was not bound by any decisions made elsewhere.[29] In recent years considerable scepticism has been expressed about the effectiveness of this institution, especially regarding legislation, but the claim over taxation has also been attacked. It was, however, possible for some kind of local representative assembly to 'legislate': the Black Prince held a session of the *parliamentum* that ended the custom of thwertnic, which had originated in the Cheshire 'Magna Carta' granted by Earl Ranulph III.[30] The fact that clearly identifiable examples of the *parliamentum* legislating are few did not stop the community of Cheshire claiming the right, or the crown accepting this without exception in 1451.[31]

One form of redress of grievances on the grant of taxation in the English parliament was legislation in statutes. In Cheshire, there existed no such formalised expression of community will, but even without an adult earl there was scope for legislative-type activity, as the articles presented in 1441 show.[32] Confirmation of palatine privileges allowed grievances to be expressed and remedied, in this case an end to privy seal writs being sent into the county, and the pardon of forfeited sureties of the peace, livery offences and fines on distraint of knighthood. This success demonstrates an active tradition of petitioning for redress of grievances in the mid-fifteenth century, linked to power over taxation.

Recently, the historiographical trend has been to admit some 'parliamentary' power over taxation,[33] and it was in fact very extensive. The short

1377–1485, Cambridge 1954; *SR* ii. 555–6, 642–3; iii. 43–7, 74–91, 195–9; Frederick C. Dietz, *English government finance, 1485–1558*, 2nd edn, London 1964, 53, 55, 56, 58, 93.

[29] Harrod, 'Defence of the liberties of Chester', 75–6. See pp. 3–5 above.

[30] Booth, 'Taxation and public order', 22; R. Stewart Brown, 'Thwert-ut-nay and the custom of "thwertnic" in Cheshire', *EHR* xl (1925), 13–21. Bennett asserts that '[t]he county court, when suitably afforced by the presence of the earl and local notables, could assume parliamentary status': *Community, class and careerism*, 36 (without reference). See also Harris, 'Cover illustration: the Cheshire "parliament" ', 57–8; Clayton, ' "Cheshire parliament" ', 13–27.

[31] Clayton found this 'remarkable': ibid. 18.

[32] CCRO, DSS, Vernon MS 2, p. 190. See pp. 1–3 above.

[33] See especially Harris, 'A Cheshire parliament', 1–2; Clayton, ' "Cheshire parliament" ', 13–27.

interval between issue of the commission to request the mise and the grant itself suggests that after 1450 grants on the accession of an earl were an accepted obligation. Yet there was still opportunity for discussion, even taking account of the time needed to assemble the commission and arrange a meeting with county representatives.[34] Negotiation was a part of the process, for example in 1474: although only two days separate the commission to negotiate from the grant, the occasion for the meeting of the *parliamentum* was a county court session day when many gentlemen would have been present in Chester.[35] In 1436, on 3 March, sheriff Randal Brereton was ordered to summon thirty named men to appear before the 'king's council' in the Chester exchequer on the following Wednesday 7 March, postponed to Friday 9 March. The king's representatives included Robert Frampton, baron of the exchequer, William Chauntrell, deputy justice of Chester, the chamberlain, William Troutbeck, and Richard Bedford, auditor for north Wales jointly with Frampton. After discussion, the county representatives were given until 28 March for consultations in each hundred. The initial demand was for payment of the income tax voted at the 1435 Westminster parliament. A frank exchange of views took place: by 18 March, the crown had been informed that the county would not pay the income tax, and a compromise was worked out.[36] On 28 March the sheriff and ten others were given the power to negotiate by the community, and a grant of 1,000 marks was made. This was a genuine process of consultation involving a wide cross-section of the county gentry. The fact that the group of ten who made the grant included five who were not among the original group specified in the writ suggests that those negotiating on behalf of the county were not royal nominees but were the free choice of the gentry of Cheshire. Similarly, in 1497 negotiation was extended to allow proper discussion. An initial meeting

---

34 In following references the date of the commission to request the mise is given first, the date of the grant second:
1463: 3 Mar. 1463 (PRO, CHES 2/135, m. 2d.(9) [37 *DKR*, 693]); 3 May 1463 (SC 6/779/12, m. 2; SC 6/780/1, m. 2 [Clayton, ' "Cheshire parliament" ', 21]).
1474: 2 Aug. 1474 (PRO, CHES 2/146, m. 1(1) [37 *DKR*, 141]); 4 Aug. 1474 (37 *DKR*, 694).
1486: 20 May 1486 (original appointment of commissioners, 4 Apr. 1486: CPR 1485–94, 86–7; *Calendar of ancient correspondence concerning Wales*, ed. J. G. Edwards, Cardiff 1935, 223–4 [li–111b] [letter to Sir William Stanley as chamberlain of Chester and Flint]); 25 May 1486 (request and grant: PRO, CHES 2/158, m. 3 [37 *DKR*, 201]).
1497: 4 Apr. 1497 (Commission under the palatinate seal: PRO, CHES 2/167, m. 5v [37 *DKR*, 694]. The warrant is dated 1 Apr. (CHES 1/2/36 [26 *DKR*, 25]); 6 Apr. 1497 (CHES 2/167, m. 5v [37 *DKR*, 694]).
1500: 14 Aug. 1500 (warrant: PRO, CHES 1/2/55 [26 *DKR*, 25]); 7 Sept. 1500 (SC 6/Henry VII/1494, m. 1 [39 *DKR*, 178]).
1517: 15 Jan. 1517 (PRO, CHES 2/186, m. 3); 22 Jan. 1517 (39 *DKR*, 55).
35 In 1463, however, the court session of 22 March does not seem to have provided a forum for discussion: Clayton, *Administration of Chester*, 280.
36 Harris, 'A Cheshire parliament'; he fails to consider, however, the events in their national context: PRO, E 28/56/5; cf. p. 74 below.

with county representatives took place on 4 April, when John Challoner (the earl of Derby's lieutenant justice), Robert Chauntrell and others representing the prince were present. Perhaps because something other than the traditional tribute on the accession of a new prince was being considered, the meeting was suspended until 6 April to allow wider consultation. A group of sixteen named gentlemen then came before the commissioners and made the grant.[37] In 1441 and 1508 provision was made for the expenses of those negotiating for the county, and additional sums raised at the collection of the mise to cover them.[38] Unfortunately, only in 1547 do we have an account of the form of debate on these occasions, and this was a standard, relatively uncontroversial, grant on the accession of a new monarch. A certificate was made by the commissioners who requested the mise which illustrates the process of negotiation and, in particular, the role of the sheriff as chief representative of the community. Having received their commission, the king's representatives

> dyd furth with direct o[u]r preceptes vnto the Shyryf of the sayd Countie to gyve Somons and warnynge by open proclamacon to all knyghtes esquiers gentilmen and other greate ffree holders of the sayd countye personally to appere before vs at Chester the sayd xxix[th] day. . . . Whereapon we the aboue named Comissioners together w[i]t[h] a greate and competent nomber of the men of wurshyp and other gentilmen and the inh[ab]itantes beynge the greate ffreholders of the sayd Countye then and there assembled at whiche tyme Immediately after the kynges maiestes plesure by vs the sayd comissioners to the sayd gentilmen and ffreholders set foorth and declared The same gentilmen and inhibitantes by the mowth of S[i]r Thomas Holcroft knyght most humbly knowledged theyre Dutes to o[u]r sayd soueraign lord and liberally and ffrankly graunted to his sayd hyghnes the somne of three thowsand markes for and in the name of the myse forsayd[.][39]

Qualified grants and refusal of supply

Negotiation over taxation was supported by a body of ideas which asserted that the government could not raise tax at will. The author of 'The rights and jurisdiction of the county palatine of Chester' argued early in the seventeenth century that refusal of the mise might be used to defend the autonomy of the county. When the call for the mise came, the chamberlain should summon 'all the gentlemen of the Countrey to mete together and to subscribe to one Petition' for the confirmation of the 'Charter of the Countie Palatyne' and to 'staie the Collection of the saide Mize, till their auntient Liberties bee ratified and confirmed'.[40] We lack similar discussions from an earlier period, but the

[37] PRO, CHES 2/167, m. 5v.
[38] See pp. 2–3 above (John Troutbeck, 50 marks); PRO, STAC 2/7/184 (L&C Star Chamber, 64) (Piers Dutton, more than 20 marks).
[39] PRO, CHES 2/209, m. 1.
[40] 'Rights and jurisdiction', 25–6.

ability of Cheshire not just to negotiate but to refuse or qualify grants of taxation is none the less clear. The demands made in 1441, including opposition to distraint of knighthood in the shire and the sending of privy seals there, were agreed to by the king.[41] In 1486 the representatives of the county won the assurance that they would not be called on to pay again if a male heir were born shortly afterwards. The community desired that as it was 'noysed' that the queen's grace was with child, the commissioners would pray the king that the mise

> myght stonde for the myse which shulde be graunted to the said prince, and
> also for this myse nowe grauntet to the Kyngez Highnez Wherunto they were
> answerd that my seid lordez there present with other Comyssioners wolde send
> to the kyng for there desyrez wheche trust to gete suche answere to theym as
> with reason they shuld be content.[42]

At the same meeting, county negotiators won a more immediate concession from the commissioners: the first payment was put back to Martinmas 1487 'in consideracon of the greet costes & expenses that they haue late made at the filde [of Bosworth] w[i]t[h] the kyngez grace'.[43] There were occasions when a mise might have been expected but was not granted. War produced grants in 1416 and 1497, and yet obvious crises in the late 1440s and early 1450s did not.[44] During this time, however, Flintshire made grants, albeit reluctantly: a grant of 1,000 marks over six years was made in 1447,[45] followed by another grant of 500 marks in 1456–7, later increased to 1,000 marks.[46] It is hard to believe that Cheshire was not being pressed to contribute at the same time. That it did not is likely to be due to successful resistance.

The most interesting example of probable resistance occurs in the 1490s.

---

[41] See pp. 1–3 above.

[42] PRO, CHES 2/158, m. 3; CP iii. 175. This grant was made on 25 May 1486; Prince Arthur was duly born four months later on 20 September.

[43] PRO, CHES 2/158, m. 3. Cf. Flintshire and the Welsh principality, where the first collection was set for Michaelmas 1486: *Calendar of ancient correspondence concerning Wales*, 223–4.

[44] While Henry VI's government, casting round for financial expedients, turned to customary fines from Welsh lordships and shires and managed to get the 1441 grant from Cheshire (Griffiths, *Henry VI*, 385, 398; PRO, CHES 2/100, m. 4), this was the last mise it got.

[45] PRO, SC 6/778/11, m. 2; SC 6/778/12, m. 3; SC 6/778/13, m. 2; SC 6/778/14, m. 3; SC 6/779/1, m. 2; SC 6/779/3, m. 2; SC 6/779/4, m. 2 (*37 DKR*, 284 [11 Oct. 1447]).

[46] By 1458 this had become 1,000 marks over 10 years: PRO SC 6/779/6, m. 2; SC 6/779/7, m. 2 (*37 DKR*, 284, 693). Cf. the offer in May 1457 by the three counties of north Wales of £12,667 over 6 years, which was very poorly paid, only £58 in 1458–9. Nothing was forthcoming in south Wales: Griffiths, *Henry VI*, 788, 836, and 'Royal government in the southern counties of the principality of Wales, 1422–85', unpubl. PhD diss. Bristol 1962, 462–76; Pugh, *Marcher lordships*, 145–7. This suggests Cheshire too was asked and resisted.

On 7 July 1491 a commission was issued to Sir William Stanley, John Arun-
dell, Sir John Savage, Jr, and [John] Ingelby to levy 'assistance' for Henry VII's
intended invasion of France.[47] There are indications that there was an
attempt to levy this as a mise. A warrant exists dated 21 August 1491 for
Thomas, earl of Derby, George, Lord Strange and others to levy an aid in
Cheshire for the king's expedition to France.[48] No mise resulted. At some
point early in the process the attempt was stopped. To say that the payment of
mise in 1500 was made when it was 'belatedly realised' that nothing had been
paid for Prince Arthur's accession is to gloss over a complex negotiation.[49]
The original warrant for negotiation of mise was issued on 14 August 1500;
the grant followed on 7 September 1500.[50] On top of the mise of 3,000 marks,
a further 1,000 marks were granted on the same day representing the fine
made by the county for the dissolution of the sessions in eyre begun in 1499.[51]
The grant by Cheshire in 1500 was hardly likely to be spontaneous, as it
contradicted the proviso extracted by the county that the 1486 grant should
stand as equivalent to that for the king's heir should a son be born. The prince
had been created earl of Chester on 29 November 1489 and invested in
February 1490; if there were traditional grounds for the grant they were the
actual entry of the prince into his earldom for the first time, which took place
when he entered Chester on 4 August 1499.[52] Henry VII and his son's
council was arguing for an extension of the usual grounds for a grant, both on
the accession of a new prince or king and on the first entry of that prince or
king into the county, and its tentativeness shows it knew it. The council
hoped that the six weeks notice required for the eyre meant that 'in the
meane tyme [it] maie be hard how the County taketh it'.[53]

That taxation was agreed not imposed and that the process of agreement
was a genuine negotiation is apparent in other territories of the English
crown. Negotiation allowed the moderation of demands for taxation, redress
of grievances, or even outright refusal of supply. In Normandy agreement to
taxation through representative institutions was not simply that of a rubber
stamp.[54] The estates could moderate tax demands, in 1428 from 200,000 *livres*

[47] *CPR, 1485–94*, 354. Ingelby was also on the commission for Lancashire; he was probably
John Ingleby, prior of Shene and later bishop of Llandaff (1496–9: *HBC*, 294).
[48] PRO, CHES 1/2/7 (*26 DKR*, 21).
[49] VCH, *County of Chester*, ii. 24.
[50] *26 DKR*, 25 (#55); PRO, SC 6/Henry VII/1494, m. 1.
[51] PRO, SC 6/Henry VII/1494, m. 1. Flintshire: commission to survey the earl's properties
and conclude a subsidy, 24 Feb. 1501–2; grant of 1,000 marks over seven years, 4 Mar.: *37
DKR*, 287.
[52] R. Stewart Brown, 'The Cheshire writs of *quo warranto* in 1499', *EHR* xxxxix (1934),
678.
[53] BL, MS Lansdowne 644, fo. 12r–v, discussed at pp. 185–6 below.
[54] Cf. Davies, *Lordship and society*, 184–7, who does not consider the possible involvement
of the communities in the timing and incidence of tax.

tournois to 180,000.[55] In Ireland too the parliament could refuse taxation or make grants that amounted to less than the original demand.[56] Taxation might be in return for what may broadly be described as legislation. Fifteenth-century Norman decrees issued by the duke of Bedford are described as having been made in the estates.[57] The Irish parliament, fortunate in having nationalists as supporters rather than opponents, produced decisions that have achieved recognition as statutes through long-established publication.[58] The charters of the Welsh marcher lordships and principality were produced alongside grants of taxation in negotiation between community and lord. Lists of demands known as Black Books or White Books were put before the marcher lord or officials of the Welsh principality during negotiation.[59] The Manx House of Keys had legislative powers, and the reign of the second Stanley lord was notable for his legal codification; the States of Jersey produced acts which survive from 1524 and probably existed previously. The paucity of 'statutes' results from the limited perceived need to alter their body of custom and law, not the weakness of the institution.[60] Nor should the influence of these 'laws' be under-estimated, for they could compete successfully with statutes of the English parliament.[61]

Those who represented the royal lord of these territories locally themselves had complex interests which meant that local interests strongly influenced what was presented as the royal interest. It is of course true that even at

---

[55] Rowe, 'Estates of Normandy', 562; Allmand, *Lancastrian Normandy*, 172–4, cf. pp. 185–6 for 1446–7.

[56] S. G. Ellis, 'Parliament and community in Yorkist and Tudor Ireland', in Art Cosgrove and J. I. McGuire (eds), *Parliament and community*, Belfast 1983, 43–68, esp. p. 53.

[57] Rowe, 'Estates of Normandy', 570–6, and 'Discipline in the Norman garrisons under Bedford, 1422–1435', *EHR* xlvi (1931), 194–208.

[58] Unlike archetypal English statutes, however, these Irish statutes were often very specific and personal in character and sprang from the judicial and administrative activity of the council: Ellis, 'Parliament and community', 44–8.

[59] J. Beverley Smith, 'Crown and community in the principality of north Wales in the reign of Henry Tudor', *WHR* iii (1966–7), 145–71; Smith, 'Arundel charters', 158; *Calendar of Wynn (of Gwydir) papers, 1515–1690, in the National Library of Wales and elsewhere*, Aberystwyth–Cardiff–London 1926, 116–18; Pugh, *Marcher lordships*, 133.

[60] G. Jefferson, *The lex scripta of the Isle of Man*, Douglas 1819; R. H. Kinvig, *The Isle of Man: a social, cultural and political history*, Liverpool 1975, 96–7; Coward, *Stanleys*, 101; *Actes des états de l'île de Jersey 1524–1596* (12e publication de la société jersiaise, 1897).

[61] For the uncertain power even of the statutes of the English parliament as late as the early sixteenth century see G. R. Elton, 'The English parliament in the sixteenth century: estates and statutes', in Cosgrove and McGuire, *Parliament and community*, 84–6. Irish legislation had remarkable influence, as Pilkington's case and the Waterford Ship case demonstrated. English supremacy was eventually asserted, but not before many English judges and serjeants had asserted that Ireland was a separate entity with legal autonomy: Ellis, 'Parliament and community', 28; Art Cosgrove, 'Parliament and the Anglo-Irish community: the declaration of 1460', in Cosgrove and McGuire, *Parliament and community*, 28–30; J. F. Lydon, *The lordship of Ireland in the Middle Ages*, Dublin 1972, 262–5, and *Ireland in the later Middle Ages*, 144–5; *Select cases in the exchequer chamber before all the justices of England, 1377–1461*, ed. M. Hemmant (Selden Society li, 1933), 81–4.

Westminster what was royal policy was a composite of the interests of those surrounding the monarch, but at least in this case the presence of the monarch, however ineffectual, meant that their personal interests weighed heavily. In the territories in question here, however, the royal interest might be largely composed of the interest of the important nobles, gentry or officials who represented it there. So these levies were taxes, in the sense of being raised for a public or collective purpose, but also in the sense of the late medieval and early modern polity, where collective purpose was identified through the objectives of the monarch, and these the objectives of the monarch in his or her manifestation as sovereign lord of a dependent territory. 'Royal' taxes in these territories might be very similar to royal taxes in the core territory of England. Under Henry VII there was some attempt to co-ordinate levies across all the lands he controlled.[62] Even then, however, responsibility for the actual negotiation of the tax was devolved to local bodies, for example the marcher council; and the independent processes of demand, grant and collection in each territory meant that a complete coincidence was very unlikely.

Attempts to introduce English parliamentary taxation

The power and coherence of the county community and its privileges were clearly seen when central government attempted to extend English parliamentary taxation to Cheshire, as in 1436. These events also show the fluid nature of privilege as it was forged in the debate between the earl and his county, in which both political strength and the context of ideas played their part. There was no wholesale exclusion of financial levies general to all the king's dominions. Loans and benevolences, which reflected the personal lordship of the crown over its subjects and therefore did not impinge on palatine privileges, did extend to Cheshire. Independent lordship was, however, clear from the sending of instructions for the levying of such charges to the chamberlain as intermediary, rather than direct to individual commissioners. Cheshire contributed to the 1481 benevolence through the prince of Wales's council, which operated a completely separate system of assessment and collection.[63] There were, of course, occasions on which the county escaped, such as Edward IV's benevolence of 1474–5.[64] In the early sixteenth century, however, Cheshire men were asked for loans on several occasions, and it may be significant that these introduced Cheshire people to fiscal measures orchestrated and enforced from London and Westminster. Cheshire was

62 BL, MS Cotton, Vitellius 1 C.1, fos 2–5; PRO, E 101/414/6, fo. 129.
63 Roger Virgoe, 'The benevolence of 1481', *EHR* civ (1989), 30.
64 H. L. Gray, 'The first benevolence', in Arthur H. Cole, A. L. Dunham and N. S. B. Gras (eds), *Facts and factors in economic history: articles by former students of Edwin Francis Gay*, Cambridge, Mass. 1932, 96–100.

included in Wolsey's monumental General Proscription of 1522 and in the loans to which it led,[65] and in the Amicable Grant.[66]

Even so, English taxation did not apply to the county until the 1530s. This was not because the crown forgot about Cheshire. The privilege was actively fashioned by repeated attempts to impose taxation. The fifteenths and tenths which were the staple taxation of the later Middle Ages excluded Cheshire. Experiments with new methods of assessment, however, offered the chance to include Cheshire. Cheshire refused to accept the experiments in parliamentary taxation conducted by the Commons in the reign of Richard II, especially the taxes of 1379 and 1383.[67] In the fifteenth century, before the advent of the Tudors, income taxes assessed on individuals were attempted in 1404, 1411, 1427–8, 1431, 1435, 1450 and 1472.[68] Later attempts followed in 1489, 1497, 1504, 1512–15 and 1523. As we have seen, after an attempt to get Cheshire to pay the 1435 tax, a letter from Robert Frampton, baron of the Chester exchequer, and William Troutbeck, chamberlain of Chester, stated that the people of Cheshire 'be not in purpos nor wil that the said leeue shuld be maad amonge hem for asmoch as thei say it shuld be ayenst here ffranchise and libertees'.[69] Nationally, too, this income tax was unsuccessful. It raised sums larger than those garnered by the similar taxes of 1428 and 1431, but still produced no more than £9,000. Chester's mise therefore underlined a lesson of fifteenth-century taxation, that while novel methods might potentially offer greater rewards, the old ways often produced better results. None the less, the county had successfully defended its privileges, and it was the crown which insisted that the payment should not be a precedent: the grant should not stand as 'preiudicial nor deirogatorie in case that we in persone comme into that Comitie but that thanne thei doe to us as it hath be used to doo to oure progenitors commyng thider this graunte not withstondyng'.[70] In 1450, ignoring the setback of 1436, lands in Cheshire, Wales and the marches were included in the subsidy voted by the Leicester parliament, but Cheshire successfully claimed the privileges it had paid to be confirmed in

[65] J. J. Goring, 'The general proscription of 1522', *EHR* lxxxvi (1971), 687; *LP* iii/2, 3683; PRO, E 179/85/1.
[66] PRO, CHES 1/2/134 (Sir Randal Brereton and Sir Ralph Egerton were responsible) (*26 DKR*, 23; *LP* iv/1, 525).
[67] W. H. B. Bird, 'Taxation and representation in the county palatine of Chester', *EHR* xxx (1915), 303; W. M. Ormrod, 'An experiment in taxation: the English parish subsidy of 1371', *Speculum* lxviii (1988), at pp. 77–9 for comments on Durham and Cheshire. I would qualify Ormrod's assumption that these areas were effectively part of the English grants of this period, since they insisted on agreeing their own taxes.
[68] Chrimes, *Henry VII*, 198. Those of 1431 and 1472 were withdrawn.
[69] Gray, 'Incomes from land', 624, 630; VCH, *County of Chester*, ii. 24; PRO, E 28/56/5.
[70] Contrary to the argument of Griffiths, who makes the county demand that the payment not be a precedent. Griffiths is wrong to suggest that Cheshire was subject to the income tax and that its assessment was a huge 10,000 marks: *Henry VI*, 118, 125, misciting PRO, E 28/56/5, 18 Mar. [1436].

1441.[71] The next income tax, voted in 1472, soon produced £31,410 14s. 1½d., but on 18 July 1474 there were still no returns for a group of northern counties including Cheshire. Eventually the counties were exempted in return for a commitment to furnish 590 archers for the king's French expedition, Cheshire's contribution being 60 men; and the prince's council almost immediately instigated the levying of a mise in the county.[72]

The taxation of 1489, based on the act of 1472 and intended to pay for 10,000 archers for one year, met with resistance, most notably the murder of the earl of Northumberland. The subsidy's authors intended the inclusion of Cheshire: the act was to apply to all 'issues and profyttes . . . in England, Wales and the Marches of the same',[73] and there was resistance in Cheshire too.[74] Only £20–27,000 was raised nation-wide, and so the tax was translated into a fifteenth and tenth in January 1490, with the effect that Cheshire was now excluded. From its conception the levy of 1497 had no application in Cheshire: it was based on 'every shire chargeable with the seid xv^{mes} and x^{mes}'.[75] The pattern of acts explicitly excluding Cheshire was continued with the grant in 1504 of a sum of £30,000 in lieu of feudal aids. No commissions were appointed for Cheshire or Durham, although Northumberland, Cumberland and Westmorland were included. This is suggestive, since the tax was linked to Henry VII's desire to survey tenures, a foundation of his policy of exploiting feudal rights. If a latter-day Domesday Book was intended, it was to include the northern counties, but not Cheshire.[76] Cheshire was also still paying a mise originally granted in 1500 for a similar reason, the accession of Prince Arthur to the earldom, with an additional

---

[71] See p. 3 above (and p. 5 for 1463 when an experimental supplement of £6,000 collapsed in the face of widespread opposition in England).

[72] Ross, *Edward IV*, 214–18; Gray, 'First benevolence', 103–4; *RP* vi. 113–15. The provision of men did not replace taxation (see. p. 63, n. 3 above), since a mise was agreed in August 1474. In the benevolence of 1481 the prince's council preferred to enlist military support in Cheshire, forgoing cash although other areas under its control produced £4,000: Virgoe, 'Benevolence of 1481', 32.

[73] For an overview of Tudor taxation to 1534 see Schofield, 'Parliamentary lay taxation'; Penry Williams, *The Tudor regime*, Oxford 1979, 59–62. For 1489 see Schofield, 'Parliamentary lay taxation', 166–80; Chrimes, *Henry VII*, 198–9; *RP* vi. 420–4; M. A. Hicks, 'The Yorkshire rebellion of 1489 reconsidered', *NH* xxii (1986), 39–62.

[74] Morris, *Chester in the Plantagenet and Tudor reigns*, 61, refers to violent opposition, but is unreliable on dates. Ralph Grimesditch, one of William Stanley's servants, was attacked with a pole-axe on Sunday 7 February 1491, he being engaged 'circa leuacionem & distruccionem . . . denariorum . . . domino principi pertinentum': the attack was carried out at Broxton by Thomas Dod of Broxton, yeoman. A larger group of approximately forty, of whom seventeen were specifically indicted, attacked John Sondeford, another of Stanley's servants, at Sale on 4 June 1491: PRO, CHES 25/16, rots 12v, 13v.

[75] *SR* ii. 644–7; Schofield, 'Parliamentary lay taxation', 180–92; Chrimes, *Henry VII*, 199–200. On 1 April, soon after the close of the parliament on 13 March, a commission was issued to negotiate a mise in Cheshire.

[76] *SR* ii. 675–82; Schofield, 'Parliamentary lay taxation', 192–8; Chrimes, *Henry VII*, 200–1.

1,000 marks for the dissolution of the eyre. The antiquarianism of the Westminster grant of 1504 in fact followed experimentation by the prince's administrators in Cheshire and north Wales and by Bishop Richard Fox in Durham.[77]

The reign of Henry VIII opened with a burst of innovation in taxation. In 1512 a grant was made of a fifteenth and tenth, accompanied by a subsidy. This was explicitly intended to cover all counties, 'aswell wythin liberties frauncheses sayntuaries auncient demeane and places exampte as withoute any graunte or use of libertie by letters patentes or prescripcion allowance therof or otherwyse or what somever mater of discharge heretofore to the contrary hadde made or obteyned notwythstondyng'. Commissioners were to be named for 'every Shyre and Ryddyng wythin the seid Realme', yet no commissions were appointed for Cheshire or the northern counties.[78] A similarly inclusive clause was a feature of the 1513–14 act, but this again lacked commissions for Cheshire and the northern counties.[79] By the time the 1514–15 parliament passed its subsidy act, there was an explicit exclusion clause for Cheshire, which was 'utterly acquyted and discharged'.[80] Cheshire had received a confirmation of privileges on 9 May 1511,[81] but the reciprocal grant of the mise – a powerful negotiating tool – was only made on 15 January 1517. This suggests an attempt to include Cheshire during the drafting of the 1512 and 1513–14 acts, but one successfully resisted early enough to prevent commissions being appointed to assess the tax. Cheshire's position was finally accepted in time for it to be written into the 1514–15 act, an acceptance that left the county free to grant the mise. The 1523 subsidy duly included an explicit exemption for Cheshire.[82]

The advent of English parliamentary taxation

English parliamentary taxation first applied to Cheshire in 1534: a book of the subsidy relating to Cheshire was brought into the Westminster exchequer by Randal Lloyd at the end of 1534.[83] The acceptance of this taxation is problematic: there is no evidence of resistance, although the period is marked by

[77] Fox was responsible for a *quo warranto* campaign in the bishopric which strengthened the bishop's position; this offended the Cliffords, and at least one writer in the county believed that his translation to Winchester was due to the devotion of this key minister of the crown to the rights of his bishopric (William de Chambre: 'ratione controversiae ortae … pro jure de Hartilpoole'): *Historiae Dunelmensis scriptores tres, Gaufridus de Coldingham, Robertus de Graystanes, et Willielmus de Chambre*, ed. James Raine (Surtees Society ix, 1839), 150, pp. ccccxlix–ccccliv.
[78] 4 Henry VIII, c.19 (SR iii. 75); Schofield, 'Parliamentary lay taxation', 198–203.
[79] 5 Henry VIII, c.17 (SR iii. 105–19); Schofield, 'Parliamentary lay taxation', 204–9.
[80] 6 Henry VIII, c.26 (SR iii. 156–67).
[81] PRO, C 82/360 (*LP* i/1, 784(15)).
[82] Schofield, 'Parliamentary lay taxation', 213–18. The surviving book of payments does not include any Cheshire contribution: *LP* iv/1, 969(2).
[83] *LP* vii. 1496; cf. PRO, E 179/85/2–3 (certificates relating to non-payment).

the disturbance of the Pilgrimage of Grace. One factor that might have induced Cheshire to accept national taxation is the changing pattern of wealth within the county. The fourteenth-century assessments on which the mise was based were becoming increasingly unrealistic.[84] The tax may have been seen as an isolated phenomenon: it is atypical in its drafting.[85] There are no surviving subsidy rolls listing individual payers, although such evidence survives in plenty for subsequent subsidies. Possibly assessment followed in some way that of the mise, thereby limiting both new administrative machinery and apparent novelty?[86] Even so, the fact that national tax first came to Cheshire in 1534 adds something to the portrayal of Thomas Cromwell as an innovator in taxation.[87] Cromwell had belatedly achieved another stage in the transition from feudal taxation to royal taxation.[88]

Cromwell's ministry also brought English taxation to Wales and Calais. Yet only in the early seventeenth century were Durham, Cumberland, Westmorland and Northumberland also subjected to English taxation. Also, Cromwell's imposition of English taxation was not absolute. Like Cheshire, Wales remained exempt from the fifteenth and tenth, which continued to be levied regularly in the later sixteenth and early seventeenth century, if with an ever-decreasing yield.[89] In terms of taxation, Wales and Cheshire can only be said to have been truly unified with England in the middle of the seventeenth century. And Ireland, Man and the Channel Islands remained outside the purview of Westminster taxation for the remainder of the early modern period, as of course did Scotland after 1603.

The survival of the mise

The mise continued to be levied after 1534. Following the accession of Edward VI, on 8 October 1547 a group led by Richard Sampson, bishop of Coventry and Lichfield, was commissioned to seek a mise. The grant followed

84 Ann Mabrey, 'Two taxations in Wirral', *Cheshire History* vi (Sept. 1980), 28–46. The burden of the 1540 subsidy in Wirral fell differently from that of the mise, probably due to changes in the relative economic prosperity of areas in the hundred.
85 '[F]ar less comprehensive and precise' than 1523: Schofield, 'Parliamentary lay taxation', 215.
86 Cf. confusion over the application of the subsidy at Calais. William Sulyard, asked for legal advice by Lord Lisle, said that if the lords and others at Calais paid, Lisle should likewise: *LP* xii/2, 337 (25 July 1537).
87 Although not in the way intended: G. R. Elton, 'Taxation for war and peace in early Tudor England', in J. M. Winter (ed.), *War and economic development: essays in memory of David Joslin*, Cambridge 1975, 36.
88 G. L. Harriss, 'Theory and practice in royal taxation: some observations', *EHR* lxxxxvii (1982), 819; cf. J. D. Alsop, 'The theory and practice of Tudor taxation', ibid. 1–30.
89 There were grants in 1540 (four), 1544–5 (two), 1553 (two), 1558, 1559 (two), 1563 (two), 1566, etc.: *SR* iii. 812–24, 1019–32; iv. 176–89, 336–48, 384–96, 464–78, 505–19; Dietz, *English government finance, 1485–1558*, 150, 155, 200, 210–11, and *English public finance, 1558–1641*, 2nd edn, London 1964, 22–4.

on 29 October.[90] This long interval may well have been the result of discussion over the implications of the mise now parliamentary subsidies had been introduced. November and December 1547 saw discussion of a bill for the liberties of Chester and worries over the implications of the mise in Monmouthshire and marcher lordships more generally.[91] These difficulties were resolved in some way, for Mary too received a grant of the mise. After the accession of Elizabeth, the chamberlain of Chester was commissioned to assess the mise on 4 January 1560, and, after a protest to the Lords, the collection was allowed to take precedence over the gathering of the first subsidies of Elizabeth's reign.[92] Mises were also raised during this period in Wales, some for the benefit of marcher lords such as the earl of Leicester.[93] The Cheshire mise was levied after the accession of James I, in 1605, and in 1612 and 1617 following the creation of Prince Henry and Prince Charles.[94] It even continued after the Civil War when the last remnants of feudalism had theoretically been abolished.[95] The privileges purchased were real, not least in the field of taxation, with Cheshire's exemption from the fifteenth and tenth. As the relative yield of the subsidy declined, this became ever more valuable.[96]

---

[90] 39 DKR, 57; BL, Additional charter 43,368 (appointment of collectors, Eddisbury, 9 Apr. 1548: Sir Henry Delves, Thomas Wilbraham Esq., Robert Vernon Esq. and Gilbert Walthall gent.).
[91] CJ i. 1–4; PRO, E 314/39/77; APC ii. 545–6 (an affirmation of the king's exclusive right to mise, 19 July 1547).
[92] SR iv. 312, 348; 39 DKR, 196; LJ ii. 549; Dodd, 'Wales's parliamentary apprenticeship', 11; JRUL, Arley charters 15/2 (warrant to collect the Bucklow portion of mise, 7 Jan. 1560).
[93] Suit by inhabitants of Bromfield and Yale, Chirk and Chirkland, Ruthin and Denbigh and Denbighland touching black books for mises, 1553–5: Calendar of Wynn papers, 118. The inhabitants of Denbighshire claimed a discharge of 200 marks supposed to be due from mises there upon payment of the new mise granted to Leicester, 1564: Calendar of Salusbury correspondence, 24, letter no. 4 (Sir John Salusbury to Sir William Norris, 6 Nov. 1564).
[94] Levy of 1605: CCRO, DDX, 43/13; PRO, E 179/369/4; VCH, County of Chester, ii. 36. Levy of 1612: CCRO, DAR I/17, fos 16–17. Levy of 1617: CCRO, DDX 177/1; CCityRO, CR 72/29/21.
[95] Charles II's government tried to levy the mise in 1665, although a year later the chamberlain had done nothing to collect it. The creation of Frederick as prince of Wales in 1729 produced a grant. The prince remitted the money for the building of quarter sessions houses, but in 1733 it was not known what had become of the money: VCH, County of Chester, ii. 36, 65.
[96] Michael Braddick, Parliamentary taxation in seventeenth-century England: local administration and responses, Woodbridge 1994, ch. i, esp. pp. 54–63. The mise also remained an everyday reality as the basis for local rates. Thus, in 1567, for example, a sum equivalent to one year's mise was levied for the repair of bridges: VCH, County of Chester, ii. 53. It was also the basis for national taxation in 1649 and 1665: ii. 65; Braddick, Parliamentary taxation, 148–9. Yet only in late 1821 did the mise breathe its last, when a new rating system was introduced. Differences in burden show how outdated the assessment had become: the Stockport division of Macclesfield hundred saw its share of the county's total burden rising from 6.97% to 13.06%; West Wirral's fell from 6.12% to 3.44%: VCH, County of Chester, ii. 65–9.

Taxation and the crown's attitude to the palatinate

Those who negotiated the mise will be discussed below in connection with the council in Cheshire.[97] It is significant here, however, that successful resistance to the mise was concentrated in periods when the commission to request a grant for the king included powerful local interests. In 1436, in the late 1440s and 1450s, and in the 1480s and early 1490s, those negotiating for the crown had their own reasons for finding a compromise beneficial to the county. In addition, the importance to the crown of their support may have eased the negotiation of an advantageous deal for Cheshire. When the heavy burden of redemption of the eyre combined with a mise was imposed in 1500, local men were significant by their absence from the crown's side of the negotiations.

Taxation is indicative of the general attitude of the crown to the palatinate. The government of Henry VI was eager to get new methods of taxation introduced and in particular to impose national taxation. It was in no position to push these demands through, however. Subsequently, under Edward IV and Richard III the crown was less assertive. Then, after at least one defeat, Henry VII showed that traditional methods could be resurrected and developed to bring impressive results. He used the Council in the Marches to apply local procedures and precedents in the crown's interest. Henry's son chose not to continue this pattern. Those drafting the subsidy acts of 1512–15 may have believed that national taxation might be extended to Cheshire, but this was unsuccessful, and a compromise saw a reversion to the conventional confirmation of privileges in return for a mise in 1517. Henry' government then tried no further innovation until 1534, when national taxation was introduced. This subsidy may have been accepted as an exceptional event, and the continued payment of the mise showed that the county had not been unconditionally absorbed. Wolsey's enforcement of loans and benevolences in the shire in the 1520s may have rung earlier alarm bells, however, and the imposition of the 1540 tax must have made Cheshiremen realise that a new era had begun, and so helped stimulate the county's demand for English parliamentary representation. This, in addition to the imposition of other parliamentary measures in the 1530s,[98] alerted Cheshiremen to the limitations of their *parliamentum* as an instrument for the government of their shire – in a fast changing world, once per reign was too infrequent an occasion for negotiation with their monarch. Inevitably, therefore, English parliamentary taxation, in a limited form, had to be accepted. Yet just as significant was the continuing privilege represented by the Cheshire mise and the exemption from fifteenths and tenths. Cromwellian

97 See ch. 4 below, esp. pp. 87–8.
98 Cf. ch. 6 below.

policies imposed subsidies, but they did not render Cheshire just another English county. Some things were left as they were, because of the advantages local privilege offered to both sides, and because it was so deeply rooted in the ideas of the time.

4

The Chester Council and Exchequer: Powerful Local Institutions

The importance of the palatinate in the day-to-day politics of Cheshire is also demonstrated by a study of the earl of Chester's council operating in Chester and the development from this council of an equity court, the exchequer. The Chester palatinate will be seen to be a vital institution, not just in the background of political ideas or in relatively infrequently-levied taxation, but in the informal flow of lordship in the shire.

The earl and his councils

Potentially the dominant influence on the political life of the county palatine of Chester was its earl. The pattern of his lordship in the county, supported by his property, rights and other powers there, was so dense that his influence might easily exceed that of a lord elsewhere in England. This potential was fulfilled most completely when the earl was an adult, as under the Black Prince or Henry of Monmouth, but at no time during the period of this study was this the case.[1] Edward, son of Edward IV, was invested with the principality of Wales and the earldom of Chester in July 1471, when he was less than one year old. When he succeeded to the throne in 1483 he was just twelve. Edward, the son of Richard III, was born in 1473 and invested in September 1483, only to die in April 1484. The creation of Arthur Tudor occurred in November 1489, when he was just three years old, and his investiture followed late in February 1490. Arthur came closest of all the earls of this period to reaching his majority, but died on 2 April 1502. His brother Henry, born in 1491, was created earl in February 1504. He was nearly eighteen when he became king but was never invested with the lands of his earldom. Although the future Edward VI was widely called prince of Wales and his creation was believed imminent in 1536–7, 1543 and 1546–7, none of Henry VIII's sons (or daughters) was ever created prince or earl, perhaps because of uncertainty over the settlement of Wales until 1543.[2]

---

1   There was no adult earl between the accession to the throne of Henry V in March 1413, and Prince Henry Stuart's elevation in 1610: *CP* iii. 173–6. See Booth, *Financial administration*, and 'Taxation and public order', 16–31; Anne E. Curry, 'Cheshire and the royal demesne, 1399–1422', *THSLC* cxxviii (1979 [1978]), 113–38.
2   *CP* iii. 175; *LP* xii/2, 921, says that Edward was to be created prince on 18 October 1537,

There was, therefore, a titular earl of Chester for only just over twenty-one of the eighty-one years from 1480 to 1560. An earl was invested with the earldom's lands for only sixteen years. These years were concentrated in the twenty-two year period before April 1502. Yet the lack of an adult earl of Chester in the early modern period was not of overwhelming significance. An under-age earl might be vested with his estates and provided with a council to govern his household and manage his lands. Comital counsellors, bureaucrats and servants might be identical with those of the king, but the interests of their two masters did not entirely coincide. The prince's council might be dominated by powerful men with their own interests to further alongside those of the earl. The tenure of Edward, son of Edward IV, provides a clear example. In 1473, the prince's household and council were enlarged, moved to Ludlow and took on wide responsibilities in the marches. The council was integrated with local commissions of the peace, and local nobles entered peace-keeping agreements with the king. This, however, allowed the Woodville family to establish a powerful interest in the area: Earl Rivers used Prince Edward's cofferer as his own agent and paid the prince's bills with his own money.[3]

Even when the king ruled the palatinate, the conditions were in place for autonomous lordship to operate, either through the marcher council or the council in Cheshire. The marcher council ceased to exist on Edward IV's death, and Richard III did not have the chance to develop a settlement for Wales and the marches. After Buckingham's rebellion, power seems to have lapsed to Sir William Stanley and his kinsmen in the north, and to William Herbert, earl of Huntingdon, in the south. Betrothed to Richard's illegitimate daughter, Katherine, and appointed chamberlain to the new prince of Wales, Huntingdon might have become the dominant figure in a new marcher council, but this had not taken place by 1485.[4] Although there was no marcher council in the first years of Henry VII's reign, Prince Arthur's

a date taken up by Grafton and Holinshed, *Chronicles*, iii. 804. See P. R. Roberts, 'The "acts of union" and the Tudor settlement of Wales', unpubl. PhD diss. Cambridge 1966, 271–83; 'Wales and England after the Tudor "union": crown, principality and parliament, 1543–1624', in Cross, Loades and Scarisbrick, *Law and government*, 117; and 'Union with England and the identity of "Anglican" Wales', 58. See also Leland, *Genethliacon illustrissimi Eaduerdi*, and *The chronicle and political papers of King Edward VI*, ed. W. K. Jordan, London 1966, 3. Roberts, ' "Acts of union" and the Tudor settlement of Wales', 273, suggests that the failure to create Edward prince of Wales may have been deliberate, as with the French kings and the title of duke of Brittany. Henri II was never created duke, but François III was crowned at Rennes in a spectacular ceremony in August 1532: Patrick Galliou and Michael Jones, *The Bretons*, Oxford 1991, 282.

3 Griffiths, *Henry VI*, 776–7; Williams, *Council in the Marches*, 6–9; M. A. Hicks, 'The changing role of the Wydevilles in Yorkist politics to 1483', in Ross, *Patronage, pedigree and power*, 75–9; D. E. Lowe, 'The council of the prince of Wales and the decline of the Herbert family during the second reign of Edward IV (1471–1483)', *Bulletin of the Board of Celtic Studies* xxvii/2 (1977), 278–97.

4 Horrox, *Richard III*, 205–12.

council had started to operate by March 1490, almost immediately after his investiture, policing contracts made with marcher officials to suppress felonies.[5] There is, therefore, strong evidence of continuity with the regime of Edward, son of Edward IV. After the death of Jasper Tudor, earl of Pembroke, the leading figure on the marcher council was William Smith, bishop of Lichfield from 1493, and of Lincoln from 1495. Smith was appointed president when the council at Ludlow was formally reconstructed in 1501 following the prince's marriage.[6] The marcher council continued in operation during the interregnum following Arthur's death. Surviving petitions suggest that it was successfully handling a wide range of problems in Cheshire, from the illegal seizure of lands to challenges to the prince's own officers.[7] A specifically judicial role was becoming more defined, and at Arthur's death, while the king retained the prince's lands, it was this function which the marcher council continued to exercise.[8] The marcher council expressed a clearly formulated desire to act independently, demonstrating its ability to achieve an administrative and political momentum independent of the person of a prince.[9]

Under Henry VIII, the marcher council continued to develop its judicial role, again without a prince as nominal head. Bishop Smith was succeeded by Geoffrey Blythe in 1512, and in 1518 the marches generally were included within the council's commission.[10] Wolsey's reform of the marcher council reaffirmed its function as the personal household of a member of the royal family, but still a minor, Princess Mary.[11] The judicial purpose of the reformed

[5]   Williams, *Council in the Marches*, 9–10; Chrimes, *Henry VII*, 250. By 1493, the council had been given powers of oyer and terminer, of array, of inquiry into liberties and the flight of criminals, and many royal marcher lordships were transferred to its control: *CPR, 1485–94,* 438–9, 441.

[6]   *CPR, 1494–1504,* 295.

[7]   Worthington, 'Royal government', 293–301.

[8]   Chrimes, *Henry VII*, 250–1.

[9]   In a set of remonstrances they requested, for example, that all matters at the suit of parties inhabiting within their jurisdiction should be remitted to them, and that no letter or privy seal should be directed at suit of party within their jurisdiction, except in cases touching the king's interest, equity or error. Having first urged the king to remember 'the payne and busynes that the commyssyoners nowe appoynted schall have & susteyne in the marches of Wales', they requested that 'no lettres ne privye Seales only reservyd his owne causes be at the sute of partie directed to any person within thauctoryte of the seid commyssyoners unlesse they have cause or can prove it be in defaute or for lacke of Justice'. They added that they wished to retain control of the revenues of the county palatine of Chester, the earldom of March and the principality of north Wales, with the money being paid 'unto Thomas Lynon [sic] appoynted by the kynges grace for the Resceit of the same and kept by the Commyssoners under thre keys in sundrye handes in a Standard to the behalf of the kynges seid highnes': BL, MS Cotton Vitellius C.1, fos 3–5, 'Remembrances for the Kynges most noble grace to be put in execucion'. See also Roberts, ' "Acts of union" and the Tudor settlement of Wales', 4, 247.

[10] The council retained a role under Henry VIII before 1518, *pace* Williams, *Council in the Marches*, 11: Roberts, ' "Acts of union" and the Tudor settlement of Wales', 10–13.

[11] Williams, *Council in the Marches*, 12–13; Roberts, ' "Acts of union" and the Tudor settlement of Wales', 17.

marcher council was clear: the lord president, John Veysey, had a legal background and was not burdened with household duties. In 1528 the princess was recalled, the household disbanded and the marcher council left functioning simply as a judicial institution. A period of drift then ensued, with growing criticism of Veysey's presidency.[12] By the latter half of 1533, the decision had been taken to send Rowland Lee as bishop of Lichfield to take control of the marcher council. A trusted and worldly agent of Thomas Cromwell, he led the marcher council as the spear-head of a judicial assault on disorder in the region.[13]

The marcher council continued to act in the absence of a prince and achieved more defined powers, in spite of a sometimes rapid change of presidents. Lee was replaced on his death in 1543 first by Richard Sampson, bishop of Chichester and subsequently of Coventry and Lichfield, a conservative ally of Stephen Gardiner,[14] then in 1547 by John Dudley.[15] On Dudley's achievement of the presidency of the council he appointed Sir William Herbert, who was to become earl of Pembroke. On Northumberland's fall, Herbert was replaced by Nicholas Heath, bishop of Worcester, but returned in 1555 when Heath became chancellor. He was again removed, this time for his non-attendance, and replaced by Gilbert Bourne, bishop of Bath and Wells, just before Mary's death.[16] In spite of these changes of presidency, the role of the Council in the Marches was unaffected. A set of instructions from 1553 ordered that the council should hear the suits of the poor, try murder, felony and other cases disturbing the peace, and investigate false verdicts. The council's procedure was to be based on the examination of witnesses, with mesne process for summoning defendants and five principal councillors attending by turns. These instructions therefore enshrined a concentration of the council's role as a formal judicial institution.[17]

There is a danger that conciliar power in the marches is under-estimated because of the lack of formalised institutions and instructions directing their activity. This has been seen in the case of the marcher council, for example from 1502 to 1518, and is particularly true of the king's or prince's council in Cheshire. There is no evidence of formalised structure or membership for this council, no set of instructions. Yet so long as there was a prince or monarch, he had a council in Chester. This is seen in the group of men negotiating the mise with the representatives of the Cheshire community and in judicial

12 For example, *LP* vi. 946, but see Peter Gwyn, *The king's cardinal: the rise and fall of Thomas Wolsey*, London 1990, 254–64, for a defence of the Welsh policy of this period. See also Roberts, ' "Acts of union" and the Tudor settlement of Wales', 24–42.
13 *LP* vi. 1385; Williams, *Council in the Marches*, 14–21; Roberts, ' "Acts of union" and the Tudor settlement of Wales', 45–73, 80–110.
14 Glyn Redworth, *In defence of the Church Catholic: the life of Stephen Gardiner*, Oxford 1990, 109, 111, 116–18; Roberts, ' "Acts of union" and the Tudor settlement of Wales', 290.
15 For signs of impatience with the president in March 1546/47 see *APC* ii. 448.
16 *CSPD, 1547–80*, 106 (*APC* xiii. 63); Williams, *Council in the Marches*, 35–7.
17 Ibid. 27–8.

activity centring on the exchequer in Chester. This Chester 'council' lacked institutional structure because it was defined by its purpose and activity, not membership. Those who represented the prince or king as being of his counsel composed his council. Instructions were the product of special occasions: in Cheshire these crises were absent.[18] Yet this fluidity and informality was qualified by two factors. First, the lack of direct personal attendance, or even distant direction, by the prince or king suggests that being a counsellor was more than simply being a royal minion or advisor. Second, being 'of the council' was almost invariably associated with occupation of certain offices, in the case of judicial activity especially those of justice and chamberlain of Chester. The council could therefore exist independently of the king or prince who theoretically gave it life, and this made the council more of an institution in its own right than a simple expression of royal majesty.

These facts help illuminate the prince's marcher council. Like the Chester council, it was not a formalised institution: under Edward IV, it met at other places than Ludlow, for example in Hereford in 1473 and in Shrewsbury in 1478; and councillors could fulfil specialised functions, such as the prince's council 'Learned in the Law'.[19] If the apparently formless council of the early sixteenth century is considered in this light, the need to search for lost 'instructions' (which probably never existed) is obviated. Without the need for instructions, men acted as king's counsellors in dispensing justice and fulfilling other functions in the marches.

Another argument against the complete formlessness of the prince's or king's council under normal conditions is its specific responsibility for one territory. Wales and the marches were one such area, and so was Chester. The prince's council in Chester represented the prince but was not a sub-committee or delegation from a superior council elsewhere. Under the lordship of Edward, prince of Wales, in the 1480s, for example, 'our counsail there', operating in the Chester exchequer, was ordered to arrest Geoffrey Warburton. Geoffrey 'by force of recognissances' made *coram consilio domini Regis* in the exchequer of Chester, had been imprisoned there pending action 'by *our counsail there*'. His release had been inadvertently ordered; he was to be rearrested 'to abide vnto the tyme he be deliuered by *our counsail there* after the tennor effect and purport of the recognissance'.[20] The marcher councillors were on occasion willing to appeal to the royal council for support but were eager to ensure that punishment was determined by palatine courts: the prince's request in one petition to the king that punishment be imposed by

[18] Margaret Condon, 'An anachronism with intent?: Henry VII's council ordinance of 1491/2', in Ralph A. Griffiths and James Sherborne (eds), *Kings and nobles in the later Middle Ages*, Gloucester 1986, 228–53; J. L. Watts, 'The counsels of King Henry VI, c. 1435–1445', *EHR* cvi (1991), 279–98.

[19] Meeting in London as early as February 1475, the council also considered Cornish matters: Lowe, 'Council of the prince of Wales', 284–9.

[20] PRO, E 28/92 (22 Mar. 1480, my italics). For the form of recognizances see Clayton, *Administration*, 245–6.

the king on the advice of his council was changed to a call for the king's council to make the defendant find surety to appear *in the county palatine of Chester*.[21] When, in 1569, the Council in the Marches lost its jurisdiction over Cheshire, it was partly because of its shift towards a clearer judicial role – the absence of a prince-earl for whom the marcher council could act as personal servants meant that its jurisdiction over the earldom was no longer so obvious.[22] Royal counsel may represent the free flow of royal power, but it was royal power mediated through independent agents and channelled through defined spheres of influence that divided up the royal domains. Cheshire was one such element.

One indication of the potential influence of conciliar power in the marches is provided by the warrants which moved the palatinate seal at Chester. Although many suggest the power of the king to move the seal by warrant or signed bill from wherever he happened to be in the kingdom, half of those in the best preserved class in the Public Record Office for which the place of origin is known stem from the marches or Chester itself.[23] For example, Roger and Richard Downes obtained a warrant for the exchequer to release them from a bond on 15 August 1499 when the council of the prince was at the monastery of St Werburgh in Chester.[24] A grant of custody of the Trussel lands was made to George, earl of Kent, the warrant being dated at Chester on 13 September 1500.[25] Major policy actions could be ordered and supervised from the marches, such as the mise in 1497 and 1500, the appointment of justices in eyre in 1499, and the expulsion of the Scots in 1496.[26] Just as important for the people of Cheshire, if less dramatic in overall implications, were actions like the pardon of William Hulse in 1493, ordered from Wigmore, and the grant of a wardship to Ellen Manley in 1498, ordered from Ludlow.[27] This gave advantages to the prince's officers in the marches. Peter Newton, his secretary, benefited from four of the warrants – for the grant of a wardship, for a lease of Shotwick and for the park-keepership there.[28]

Considering warrants for which we have a firm date, there is no sharp division between periods when warrants originating in the marches predominate and when those from outside do, but their numbers do suggest the importance of the marcher council in the period from 1495 to 1502.[29] The period of

21 PRO, E 28/92 (20 Sept. 1479). The list of 'Petitions relating to Cheshire, to the prince of Wales's Council', given in Worthington, 'Royal government', 411–12, is unreliable. It includes, for instance, this petition, directed by the prince to the king.
22 Williams, *Council in the Marches*, 47.
23 A total of 32 out of 66: PRO, CHES 1/1, calendared in *26 DKR*. The warrants in CHES 1/3 are badly damaged and provide little evidence to support or undermine this conclusion.
24 PRO, CHES 1/1/49.
25 PRO, CHES 1/1/61.
26 PRO, CHES 1/1/36, 55, 48, 30.
27 PRO, CHES 1/1/18, 46.
28 PRO, CHES 1/1/37, 53, 54, 68.
29 While a warrant of 1478 originated from Ludlow, the one surviving warrant from 1485

marcher activity under Arthur after his creation as prince and before his death is the only period when marcher council activity was predominant in directing the affairs of Cheshire.[30]

The patchy survival of these warrants may provide a distorted view. Other aspects of conciliar activity in the marches, however, suggest the continuing vitality of the Chester council. Councillors can be seen operating in Cheshire in commissions negotiating taxation with the representatives of the Cheshire community. The detailed account of the 1436 negotiation shows that the commissioners negotiating for the crown were considered to be 'de consilio dicti domini regis'.[31] During the fifteenth century until 1497 those responsible for negotiating on behalf of the crown were overwhelmingly local men holding local offices.[32] The group usually centred on the chamberlain and justice. The 1463 commission is remarkable in this respect, consisting simply of the Stanley brothers, chamberlain William and justice Thomas. Most of the other commissions do include some outside element in the form of the

---

[30] originated from Guildford and the six from 1487 illustrate Henry VII's movements that year, to York and Newcastle via Kenilworth on the way north and back via Warwick: PRO, CHES 1/3/95, 92, 98, 102. See Rhoda Edwards, *The itinerary of King Richard III, 1483–1485*, London 1983, 40–1. Four warrants (CHES 1/1/6, 10, 14, 18), survive from the early 1490s. Of these only CHES 1/1/18, from 1493, the pardon for William Hulse from Wigmore Castle is from the marches. The heaviest survival of warrants is for the years 1495–1501 and most of these are from the marches. In 1495 the proportion is four out of five, in 1496 five out of five, in 1497 four out of eight, in 1498 six out of seven. The only 1499 warrant is from St Werburgh's monastery in Chester: CHES 1/1/49. In 1500 the four warrants are all from the marches, as are the three from 1501. This was the period of the marcher council's greatest activity and authority: they were responsible for 28 of 33 surviving warrants during these years: CHES 1/1/22–6, 28–30, 34, 36–9, 44–6, 48–9, 52–5, 57, 60–1, 63, 68, and CHES 1/3/19; the other warrants, all from Westminster, are CHES 1/1/31, 33, 35, 40, 51. Subsequently, the proportion declines. Ten warrants survive for the years 1503–6, yet only one, for Christopher Savage from Chester in 1503, is local: CHES 1/3/38. 1507 has six surviving warrants, again only one is marcher: CHES 1/3/54. Although the two 1508 warrants are dated from Chester (CHES 1/3/52–3), from 1503 to the end of Henry VII's reign, marcher council action is far less important than in the years 1495–1501. After this, the survival of warrants is far thinner and therefore the reliability of any conclusions as to the relative significance of places of origin far less. The partial exception to this is before 1513, for which period nine warrants survive. Only one of these (CHES 1/1/78) has a marcher origin. Between then and 1547, 22 warrants survive, but only two are from the marches, CHES 1/1/124 (pardon for Roger Downes, 1518, Chester) and CHES 1/1/130 (Thomas Warburton, 1524, Chester).

[30] Morrill's emphasis ('The fashioning of Britain', in Ellis and Barber, *Conquest and union*, 23–4) on the decline of deliberative councils away from Westminster and the change in their function towards enforcement seems to depend on the lack of royal or princely leadership, itself nothing more than biological accident.

[31] Clayton, *Administration*, 53–4; Harris, 'A Cheshire parliament', 1–2.

[32] Table printed in Tim Thornton, 'Local equity jurisdictions in the territories of the English crown: the palatinate of Chester, 1450–1540', in Dunn, *Courts, counties and the capital*, 50–2; cf. Clayton, *Administration*, 53–7, although she still wishes to show that the council was a delegation of the king's council (conventionally defined) or that appointed for the prince.

auditors for Chester and north Wales, men like John Geryn (1430),[33] Richard Bedford (1436, 1441) and John Brown (1441). The character of the commissions begins to change in 1474, showing the influence of the newly-extended princely household and marcher council. The 1474 commission was headed by the president of the Council in the Marches, and many – but not all – of the other places were filled by important post-holders in the prince's household, his relatives or members of his council.[34] This pattern was not continued. Henry VII's early dependence on the Stanleys, seen at its most complete before the battle of Stoke, and also against the 1489 rebels,[35] meant in 1486 and 1491 that local men again predominated. On the former occasion, the first five names on the commission were either Stanleys or Savages. On the latter, the Stanley presence was balanced but hardly overwhelmed by the prince's chancellor, the deputy justice (another prince's man) and Robert Sherborne, secretary to Cardinal Morton.[36] 1497 signalled a shift from reliance on local magnates, and the Council in the Marches was the leading force on the commissions. Local men continued to appear, especially the first earl of Derby and his son George, but even they disappeared in 1500, and in 1517 the second earl was omitted. Yet this was not to last: in 1547, the commission was led by members of the Council in the Marches, but they were reinforced by a group of local men. Thomas Venables, Henry Delves, John Done and Philip Egerton in fact constituted the majority of those who were actually present when the grant was made. So the evidence provided by records of negotiation over taxation shows that the body of councillors in Cheshire was fluid, never subsumed in the Council in the Marches, and that its membership depended on the function it was intended to fulfil.

The main purpose of this section of the discussion is, however, to explore a second aspect of lordship, arbitration and equity. The activity of the earl's councillors sitting in the exchequer at Chester in a quasi-judicial or judicial capacity before the accession of Elizabeth has barely been discussed and any possibility of such action before the early sixteenth century dismissed.[37] Yet the financial role of the chamberlain of Chester sitting in the exchequer has been extensively examined, and it has long been acknowledged that the

[33] Geryn remembered John Thornton, chaplain of Chester Castle, in his will: PRO, PROB 11/3, fos 190v-1; Ralph A. Griffiths, 'Public and private bureaucracies in England and Wales in the fifteenth century', *TRHS* 5th ser. xxx (1980), 127 (repr. in his *King and country: England and Wales in the fifteenth century*, London–Rio-Grande 1991, 137–59).

[34] Clayton, *Administration*, 54–7; *CPR, 1467–77*, 283, 366. For the king's councillors identified by J. R. Lander for Edward IV's reign see 'Council, administration and councillors, 1461–85', in his *Crown and nobility, 1450–1509*, London 1976, 309–20.

[35] Bennett, *Lambert Simnel*, 82, and 'Henry VII and the northern rising of 1489', *EHR* cv (1990), 44.

[36] *BRUO*, 1685–7: he acted as king's secretary in taking fines from the West Country rebels.

[37] VCH, *County of Chester*, ii. 21; Worthington, 'Royal government', 182–3.

chamberlain had jurisdiction over cases linked to financial administration.[38] The exchequer was also the place where the county's Doomsday Roll and its successors the Enrolments or Recognizance Rolls were kept. The chamberlain in the exchequer therefore had jurisdiction over cases involving production of the rolls, farms, the tallies issued by the chamberlain and similar business. For example, in 1481 he dealt with a dispute over the inquisition *post mortem* of Sir Robert Fouleshurst.[39] Crucially the exchequer was home to the seal of the earldom, and the chamberlain was its guardian. It therefore produced the writs that drove the judicial process of the county; and the chamberlain and those associated with him were in a prime position to intervene in that judicial process.

The Westminster chancery sprang from the action of the king and his council. While other lords' councils had a role in peacekeeping and arbitration, the administrative power of the king's council meant its intervention as arbiter in disputes was especially desirable.[40] Yet equity jurisdiction was still developing at Westminster during the fifteenth century.[41] It is therefore unsurprising to find no developed equity court in Cheshire in the early fifteenth century. By 1484–5, however, a formalised equity jurisdiction was developing from the activity of the earl's council.[42] A petition from John Brigg of Newark, advowryman, to the 'Justice and other of the kynges counsell at Chestre' concludes with the words 'and this in way of charite', a formula characteristic of later Chester exchequer equity bills.[43] By the 1520s the Chester exchequer was operating as an equity court in the form familiar

---

[38] R. Stewart Brown, 'The exchequer of Chester', *EHR* lvii (1942), 294, 296–7.

[39] PRO, SC 8/344/1262, discussed in Worthington, 'Royal government', 296. See also Brown, 'Exchequer of Chester', 294, 296. The fourteen cases in CHES 7 (inventory in *21 DKR*, 44–5), are largely the result of writs of *certiorari* on inquisitions.

[40] Carole Rawcliffe, 'Baronial councils in the later Middle Ages', in Ross , *Patronage, pedigree and power*, 87–108, and 'The great lord as peacekeeper: arbitration by English noblemen and their councils in the later Middle Ages', in J. A. Guy and H. G. Beale (eds), *Law and change in English history*, London 1984, 37–9; J. B. Post, 'Equitable resorts before 1450', in E. W. Ives and A. H. Manchester (eds), *Law, litigants and the legal profession*, London 1983, 68–79.

[41] Action before the council and imprisonment in the Tower could still follow indictment at common law in 1511: Condon, 'Ruling elites', 141.

[42] Was the development of the Chester exchequer's equity jurisdiction linked to periods when the marcher council was weak? The first clear example of Chester 'exchequer' action dates from Richard III's reign, when the marcher council was in eclipse. Another petition to the earl of Derby, from John Cowle of Chester (1491–2), was presented before the full revival of the council under Arthur: PRO, E 163/9/26, m. 1. (The association of this case with m. 2, *Savage and Coton v. Venables*, is suggestive of the forum in which the latter was presented to its addressee, Prince Arthur.)

[43] This is included in a file connected with William Tatton's farm of the Cheshire advowries, the privilege of giving men protection from the law: JRUL, Tatton of Wythenshawe 440–4, petition 443; W. J. Jones, 'The exchequer of Chester in the last years of Elizabeth I', in Arthur J. Slavin (ed.), *Tudor men and institutions: studies in English law and government*, Baton Rouge 1972, 135. See also Thornton, 'Local equity jurisdictions', 37–8.

in Westminster chancery records.[44] A bill presented by David Warburton against Richard Merbury, alleging that the latter had withheld rent, resulted in a writ of *subpoena* on 14 December 1520. Depositions were taken in the exchequer on two occasions, and on 7 August the deputy justice ordered Merbury to pay up, 'unto suche tyme he shewe afore the said Justice a reasonable cause why he ought not so to do', a typical qualification of equitable judgements. That the court's organisation was still relatively rudimentary in the mid-sixteenth century is suggested by the award made by Sir Thomas Wriothesley on 10 March 1543 between the chamberlain, Sir Rees Mansell, and the baron or clerk of the exchequer, Robert Tatton; the chamberlain was ordered to

> at all tymes have readye attendyng within thesaid Exchequier his deputie or Clerke with the kings seale for the sealynge of all processes and other the premysses as reason requyrethe and dothe apperteyne without delaye for the speedie furtherynge of the Kings Ma[jes]ties causes and the causes of his graces subiects within thesaid Countie Palatyne

which suggests that this had not previously been happening.[45] Even so, there can be no doubt that by the second quarter of the sixteenth century the equity court of the Chester exchequer had been born.

The way in which the body of councillors acting in the exchequer might bring a case to a conclusion remained flexible. At Westminster, equity jurisdiction was a specialised role of the chancellor from an early period; in Cheshire, it was still not clear early in the sixteenth century that the chamberlain specifically had assumed this responsibility. In the 1480s justice, chamberlain and possibly others still sat together to decide cases. Of the 196 earliest surviving bills presented to the Chester exchequer, thirty-two are addressed to the justice and chamberlain together, and two are addressed to the justice alone.[46] The chamberlain and other officers might make a decision on the spot,[47] or they might call parties to appear and present evidence, as in 1538, when Richard Kardiff was placed under recognizance to 'appere at Chester from Shier to shier to answer to the bylles of Complaynt' of two plaintiffs, 'and performe such ordre as shalbe taken by the Court her in the sames'.[48] Alternatively, the matter might be put to arbitration. This might be

---

[44] JRUL, Arley charters 15/37 (William Beamont, *Arley charters: a calendar of ancient family charters preserved at Arley Hall, Cheshire*, London 1866, 30); exemplification made during action before the marcher council in 1538.
[45] PRO, CHES 14/3, pp. 510–11; Jones, 'Exchequer of Chester', 130. Soon after, on 1 May 1543, Thomas Pyllyn agreed with Robert Tatton to perform the duties under the terms of the Wriothesley judgment, giving a bond of £100 for their correct execution: JRUL, Tatton of Wythenshawe 414.
[46] Only one group of papers in causes survives from before the accession of Elizabeth, providing evidence for 200 cases, mostly from the late 1530s: PRO, CHES 15/1, bills to justice at CHES 15/1/23, 125. The majority, 152 (77.55%), are to the chamberlain alone.
[47] As in the case concerning land in Vaynoll: see p. 94 below.
[48] PRO, CHES 15/1/24.

made the responsibility of councillors, and the panel might be recorded in the exchequer enrolments. Alternatively, the panel might be semi-official, with ordinary laymen and clerics, possibly alongside officials of the court and palatinate. In the last quarter of the fifteenth century Roger Downes and Thomas Tytherington 'condescendet and agreyd befor my lorde Prynce Councell in thexchequer [sic] of Chester to stande to and abyde the reporte and Certefycathe' of John Worth of Tytherington and Richard Smith, vicar of Prestbury, in a boundary dispute.[49] A land dispute between John Sparrow of Bickley and Urian Rowe was placed in the award of Roger Brereton and Richard Cholmondeley in 1537. In December 1538 Richard Hassall, deputy justice of Chester, William Clayton, 'lyeu[ten]ant of the Countye of fflynt' and John Birkenhead, arbitrators 'indifferently elect & chosen by bothe the sed parties' made an award between Ralph Shipley and Robert More.[50] At other times the arbitration might appear more unofficial. Sometimes, indi- vidual members of the prince's council, explicitly referred to as such, made up the arbitration panel, as in 1531 with Master James Denton, dean of Lich- field, and John Russell, two of the Council of the Marches.[51] Sometimes the prince's council, listed by name or collectively, appeared as umpires or reserve arbitrators in case the first panel failed. In 1517 George Bromley, lieutenant justice of Chester since at least the beginning of Henry VIII's reign, appeared in an initial arbitration panel (with Sir Piers Legh, Sir John Stanley, Sir Richard Bold and Randal Poole) to deal with the dispute between Sir William Booth and Sir John Warburton; if this panel were to fail, the respon- sibility passed to Bishop Geoffrey Blythe, president of the Council in the Marches, Sir William Uvedale, Sir Griffith Rice and Sir Thomas Cornwall and, once again, George Bromley.[52]

More frequently, however, it was the officers of the palatinate adminis- tration at Chester who were involved. In the years around the beginning of the sixteenth century, for example, Edmund Bulkeley, attorney of the earl in Cheshire from 1495 to the early part of Henry VIII's reign, continually took part in arbitrations.[53] George Bromley also appeared frequently, often explic- itly as lieutenant justice of Chester. Sometimes he was the only representa-

---

[49] CCRO, DDS 5/3, datable to the years of Prince Edward after Smith's arrival (1478–83) or of Arthur or Henry (1489–1509).
[50] PRO, CHES 15/1/151, 142, cf. 144.
[51] CCRO, DCH C/66 (award of 6 March 1531, between Randal Brereton of Malpas, Esq., and Thomas Hannell and Joyes his wife).
[52] JRUL, Arley charters 12/7 (bond of 10 Aug. 1517). In 1528, if Edmund Trafford of Traf- ford, Richard Holland of Denton and Robert Hyde of Norbury failed to resolve matters between John Duckinfield of Portwood, John Legh of Baguley and Reginald Holynworth of Mottram, on the one hand, and John Duckenfield on the other, then the arbitration was to be carried out by the prince's council: CCityRO, CR 63/2/578.
[53] Worthington, 'Royal government', 348. Examples of Bulkeley's involvement are CCRO, DAR H/67/1 (1 Nov. 1496); DCH U/6 (11 Aug. 1499, where he is called 'lernet in the lawe'); JRUL, Mainwaring 303 (7 Sept. 1500); CCRO, DCH U/1 (24 Aug. 1501).

tive of the administration;[54] at other times he was joined by others, for example Sir Thomas Englefield, justice of Chester.[55] One of the men with whom he appeared was another lawyer active in the marches of Wales, John Salter.[56] Salter provides a link to the Sneyds, probably the main legal family active in Cheshire during the early Tudor period, since Sir William Sneyd married his daughter, Joan.[57] Sir William's father, Richard, who was appointed earl's attorney in 1522 and acted as lieutenant justice from at least 1523, first appeared in a Cheshire arbitration in 1501, and then in 1505.[58] He then appeared regularly in the years 1511–14.[59] William Sneyd himself appeared in 1533 and 1541–2.[60] In the period after 1530, however, the Sneyds's activity in arbitrations was exceeded by that of the Birkenheads – Ralph Birkenhead, deputy sheriff in 1505 and 1508, had acted together with his fellow officer, the serjeant and escheator Roger Mainwaring, twice in 1500,[61] and in 1505 alone as recorder of Chester.[62] John Birkenhead, who succeeded his father as clerk and prothonotary and was lieutenant justice from 1537, was omnipresent after 1530, appearing no less than ten times before Henry VIII's death.[63] These men, and others like them,[64] were all members of the small Cheshire legal establishment which dominated public office and private practice locally, and they possessed intimate knowledge of the courts of Chester; it is this knowledge which may explain the absence of lawyers from Westminster in Cheshire arbitrations. John Yaxley, Lewes Pollard and Guy Palmes, serjeants-at-law, were involved in the arbitration of a dispute among the heirs of Sir John Bromley in 1505, but they were in a

---

54 JRUL, Rylands charters 194. Bulkeley appeared with Sir William Brereton and Sir George Holford in 1515: Arley charters 12/17.
55 CCRO, DCH U/36 (Englefield to act 'if he be at the next shire'); DLT A/12/14; DLT A/14/46. He also appeared with William Tatton and Adam Birkenhead in 1505: DLT A/12/13.
56 CCRO, DLT A/14/45 (1505); JRUL, Mainwaring 325 (1512).
57 Ormerod, *Chester*, iii. 492.
58 CCRO, DCH U/1, 36. He served as recorder of Chester. Aside from his official posts, in 1515 Richard Sneyd received fees from 53 individuals, totalling £51 13s. 4d.: BL, MS Harleian 2079, fo. 178a: 'ex libro antiquo Ricardi Sneyde de Bradwall armiger'.
59 Eaton Hall, Chester, Eaton charters 538, 543; JRUL, Mainwaring 325; CCRO, DDA 1533/1.
60 CCRO, DLT A/12/19; DAR B/12; DAR D/65/4.
61 CCityRO, CR 63/2/126; JRUL, Mainwaring 303.
62 CCRO, DLE 5/1.
63 JRUL, Mainwaring 338; CCRO, DVE C/III/11; BL, MS Harleian 2022, fo. 93v; CCRO, DLT A/12/19–20; DVE B/V/3; JRUL, Rylands charters 1630; Cornwall-Legh 891; CCRO, DLT A/12/25; DDS 2/2.
64 For example, William Clayton, described as 'lernet in the lawe' (CCRO, DCH U/6; 29 Jan. 1531), controller of Chester and north Wales in 1517, a Cheshire serjeant-at-law from 1524, and lieutenant justice in 1529, who took part in an arbitration in 1535: BL, MS Harleian 2022, fo. 93v (*Sheaf* 3rd ser. xv [1920], 22, no. 3542). Or one of his companions on that occasion, Richard Hassall, serjeant-at-law from 1511 and lieutenant justice in 1540: CCRO, DLT A12/20 (5 Jan. 1536); JRUL, Rylands charters 1630 (10 Oct. 1543).

very small minority.[65] The only other lawyers of their eminence to arbitrate in Cheshire were John Baker, recorder of London, in 1531, and Francis Morgan, serjeant-at-law, in 1555.[66] It is impossible for us to decide whether these men officiated in arbitrations in a strictly private or in a public capacity – in Cheshire the two shaded seamlessly into one another, part of the web of princely lordship that found its clearest expression in the exchequer.

There was a strong connection between equity and one judicial aspect of the exchequer's activity that has been discussed recently, the making of peace bonds.[67] By the fifteenth century the enrolments of the court were dominated by recognizances to keep the peace. It has been suggested that in some way the justice had acquired powers to summon potential law-breakers to the exchequer and cause them to be bound in sums of money.[68] These ranged from £40 to £1,000, either to keep the peace in general or towards specified individuals. Although these bonds usually coincided with sessions of the county court, their subjects were rarely parties to criminal actions there. The bonds were therefore preventative measures, taken to stop gentry disputes leading to violence. It could be that they were entered voluntarily. In many cases, however, a bond was entered by only one party to a dispute. Also, bonds came in several varieties, and a case due to disagreement over the right form, involving John Busshell and Thomas Finlow, priest, demonstrates the absence of consensuality in these obligations.[69] Bonds of good behaviour towards all the king's lieges, rather than against specific individuals, were reserved for the most disreputable elements of society. Busshell objected that Finlow's demand for such a bond was 'ayanst all right and Justice your seid orator beyng of gud name and fame and noo browlyng person but dylygent and loborous to opteyn his lying [sic] by his occupacon and mystery'. Busshell had remained in prison for a long time because he could get 'non of his neyburs to be suretyes to so hie and chargeable boundz'. There were strong connections between the multitude of these bonds that were made in

---

[65] CCRO, DNE, box 2, misc. 1 (award, 10 July 1505). They acted alongside Sir John Savage, Piers Gerard and John Harper.

[66] CCRO, DCH U/30; DCH H/84; DDA 1533/14. The involvement of the royal council in the resolution of the Dutton inheritance dispute in the 1530s does not alter the main point made here: DCH E/106A.

[67] The earliest surviving appearance rolls provide a full day-to-day record of the business of the exchequer as a court and the place of equity within it from 1512. The highest level of business in 1512–13 was on the Tuesday after Michaelmas and Easter (on 5 Oct. 1512, 62 items were transacted, and on 12 Apr. 1513, 115): PRO, CHES 5/1, roll for 4 Henry VIII. Some entries clearly relate to equity cases. The issue of a *subpoena* writ directed to Thomas Huyde on 10 May 1513, returnable on 18 May, appears to be linked to a suit also involving Thomas Warde of Norbury: CHES 5/1, 4 Henry VIII, m.5v. By 1529–30 the court was handling a much increased burden of equity cases: CHES 5/3, roll for 21 Henry VIII. The extant bills of the 1530s cannot be compared with Chester appearance rolls, since none survives for the decade after 1529–30.

[68] Clayton, *Administration*, 266–7, 277 n. 107, and 'Peace bonds', 133–48.

[69] PRO, CHES 15/1/23.

Cheshire in the fifteenth and sixteenth centuries and the issue of *subpoena* writs out of the exchequer during an equity case. An especially good example of the connection between dispute, bill, *subpoena* and recognizance comes in a case during the chamberlainship of William Brereton between Edward ap Hoell ap Tudor, and Rees ap Benet of Vaynoll (Flintshire) and Thomas his son, concerning land in Vaynoll.[70] On 28 June 1534 William Brereton wrote from the Holt to 'my deputie [chamberlain] Rondall Brereton of Chester' on behalf of 'this berer', the plaintiff. Edward had told him how Rees and Thomas forcibly and 'wrangfully haue entred' the premises. William commanded Randal

> that you direct a sub pena agaynst the said Res and Thomas to appere bifore you in the exchequier of Chester at a shorte day by you lymytted and at their apparaunce to take such order and direccion concernynge the premises so that this said pore man may peasably haue occupie and enioye the said lands. . . . And also that they be bounden in recognisaunce to obserue and bere the peace for theym self childer tenants seruants and parte takers vnto the said berer his childer tenants and seruants apon payn of xli.

On the reverse of the letter is a note, dated 29 June, of the issuing of a writ of *subpoena* to Rees and Thomas commanding their presence in the exchequer on the following Friday (3 July). Randal appreciated the urgency and wrote on the letter: 'Make this bearer a sub pena retornable apon fryday next commyng for the persons within named. He hath payd me for the same. Make it in contynent &c.' On 6 July Rees and Thomas, along with three others, entered a recognizance in £40.

There are signs that the Chester exchequer was relatively busy in the early sixteenth century.[71] The growth of its business by 1559 compared advantageously with that of the chancery of the palatinate of Lancaster, which if anything had slightly earlier origins, but only began to sit outside assize weeks in the early seventeenth century.[72] Reasons for the growth in exchequer activity are not hard to find: they lay in the many advantages of equity. The decision in the advowry case brought by William Tatton in 1484–5 demon-

[70] PRO, CHES 15/1/173. Vaynoll is now Bodelwyddan: *List of early chancery proceedings preserved in the Public Record Office*, ix (PRO, Lists and Indexes lii, 1933), 348.
[71] In 75 of the cases in PRO, CHES 15/1, a precise date can be assigned to one or more of the actions of the court. These cases led to exchequer action on 89 definable occasions, concentrated in the years 1537 (26.97%) and 1538 (47.19%). This excludes dated depositions and affidavits, as these may have been taken by commissioners away from the exchequer. In the 1530s action appears to be evenly scattered throughout the year, but there is a clear pattern to the work of the court week by week. Saturday was the busiest day, with 29.21% of recorded actions; apart from Sunday the other days of the week were roughly equally busy: Sunday 4.49%, the other dates ranging from Monday (11.24%) to Tuesday (15.73%); confirmed by dates for the return of the 54 dateable writs issued during these proceedings. Saturday is specified in 57.41% of cases.
[72] Robert Somerville, 'The palatine courts in Lancashire', in Alan Harding (ed.), *Law-making and law-makers in British history*, London 1980, 61.

strates one such attraction of equitable remedies: judgement was not aimed at narrowing the point at issue as much as possible and then awarding an absolute verdict for or against each party, but rather at looking at a problem in the round and producing a balanced, workable solution which did not represent an outright victory for either side. The advowry tenants had their privileges confirmed, but with the pragmatic amendment to the custom of the county that the city sheriffs might regulate their economic activity in Chester. Another advantage was speed. Some bills petitioned for attachments and other common law writs returnable at the sessions of the county court, but most requested a *subpoena* to compel attendance in the exchequer. In forty-seven cases the type of writ and date for return are known, and of these twenty-nine are *subpoenas*, two *subpoenas sicut alias*, and one a *subpoena sicut pluries*.[73] Of the ordinary *subpoena* writs, the modal number of days between the date of the writ and the date for return is just two. The mean interval is 3.79 days. Even an opponent who resisted the first *subpoena* could be brought rapidly to issue. On 12 June 1538 Fulk Lloyd was the victim of a rescue when he attempted to drive away sheep grazing his land at Rhuddlan. He secured a *subpoena* the following day, but this was unsuccessful and he returned to obtain a *subpoena sicut alias*, and, this also being unsuccessful, a *sicut pluries* on 23 June, returnable on 29 June. Depositions were taken on 4 July, just three weeks after the alleged offence.[74] Such examples may be compared with the time permitted for the return of the common law writs of *distringas* and attachment: in the former case the mean number of days is fourteen and in the latter twenty.[75] The Chester exchequer also compared very well with the speed of action in Westminster equity courts which themselves compared very well with central common law courts. To Bayne and Dunham ten days between offence and injunction appeared extreme haste. In many cases this very speed of action made a plaintiff's choice of the Chester exchequer necessary. Jane Thornton prosecuted Peter Asheton of Acton, carrier, in the exchequer because he was allegedly 'fugitive & nowe sellynge suche godes as he hathe and hathe takyn a house in nottyngham shire and thither wolbe gonne within these iii or iiii days comyng'.[76]

Other classic advantages of resort to an equitable remedy were evident in Chester exchequer cases. Detinue of deeds was cited by Thomas Aston against John Dutton of Helsby and Ralph Thomason, his chaplain, after the death of Aston's grandmother, Margaret Vernon. When Henry Helsby of Alvanley took Robert Lloyd's oxen to a place unknown, Lloyd was unable to replevy them and had to resort to the exchequer.[77] The impossibility of

73 There are also two *corpus cum causa* writs and one *certiorari*.
74 PRO, CHES 15/1/100.
75 C. G. Bayne and William Huse Dunham, *Select cases in the council of Henry VII* (Selden Society lxxv, 1958 [1956]), pp. cviii–cx, esp. p. cix.
76 PRO, CHES 15/1/3, 60, 168.
77 PRO, CHES 15/1/5, 102.

getting justice at common law because of the activities of a powerful local gentleman led Peter Corker of Arclid, 'a werey pore man', to take a case against his landlord, John Mainwaring of Nantwich, 'a grett gentilman', to the exchequer.[78] Most obviously, and controversially, the exchequer could be used against the officials and courts of the city of Chester. Thomas Harper prosecuted sheriffs William Glasior and Roger Whitehead for false imprisonment, claiming that a bill exhibited against him in the Pentice by Christopher Waren of Coventry was insufficient.[79] Such superiority could also be used in a supportive manner: the *corpus cum causa* which the abbot of Vale Royal sought against the keeper of his own prison was intended to remove a violent man to the safer prison at Chester from Weaverham gaol where he was causing 'greate dred & cost'.[80] While Philip Egerton could not recover a debt of 13s. 4d. at common law in Chester because it was too small a sum, neither could he act in the hundred court 'by reason of synystre delayes & parcially of thofficers in the same'.[81]

The exchequer was also cheap. The fees of the court were much lower than those levied at Westminster.[82] This advantage was rather similar to those enjoyed by the palatine courts of Lancaster. In the late seventeenth century costs at Lancaster of £7 or £8 compared to £20 to £40 in King's Bench or Common Pleas, or £50–£100 in chancery at Westminster.[83] Just as importantly, costs were saved by the shorter distances to be travelled by participants in cases.

The exchequer also entertained cases springing from its special functions, such as the defence of its advowry men: one of them, Robert ap Day ap David, 'beyng a a woure man and undre your gud mastership proteccon', brought a case to avoid an action for debt in the court of Holywell.[84] Exchequer recognizances produced their own business. Thomas Street and Richard Hewer complained to the chamberlain that they were bound 'in recognizance before your mastership in thexchequier of Chester' in £40 for Thomas Rogerson to keep the peace and leave a form in St Mary's church. They had agreed to this

---

78 PRO, CHES 15/1/31.

79 PRO, CHES 15/1/50. Glasior and Whitehead were chosen sheriffs in 1537: Ormerod, *Chester*, i. 213. Cf. *Thomas Smith v. George Leche and George Lightfote*, late sheriffs of Chester (1536–7), for failure to carry out a writ of execution after he recovered a debt in the Pentice; and *John Trafford chaplain, v. Fulk Dutton* after he recovered 17s. 4d. against John Heyley of Chester, whom Dutton allegedly released, 'your said orator beyng not paid and satisfied': CHES 15/1/50, 145, 169 and also CHES 15/1/68, a case against Glasior from 1538.

80 PRO, CHES 15/1/177, cf. 178.

81 PRO, CHES 15/1/42. The exchequer might also be used against ecclesiastical and local liberties: CHES 15/1/113, 167.

82 CCityRO, CR 63/2/15, pp. 94–7 ('Precedents of the practice in the late exchequer of Chester, *c.* 1770', the first complete list of fees); CCRO, DCH C/954 (expenses dated 1558, showing that a recovery of 63 acres of land cost 37s. 2d.).

83 J. A. Guy, *The cardinal's court: the impact of Thomas Wolsey in Star Chamber*, Hassocks 1977, 114; Somerville, 'Palatine courts in Lancashire', 62.

84 PRO, CHES 15/1/34.

because they thought Rogerson 'gud and reasonable', but it transpired that he 'will not be reformed by eny of his louyng and discrete neyb[our]z thrugh the great beiryng and mayntenance that the seid Thomas hath' and so Street and Hewer wished to be saved harmless for their bond.[85]

Well-represented among exchequer litigants were office-holders seeking to have their authority and actions upheld. Randal Hewett, deputy to Randal Prestland as bailiff of Bucklow hundred, brought the names of fifteen offenders who had been fined for 'ffreys & alehousez', requesting that they be summoned by *subpoena* and ordered to pay.[86] Three cases survive which were brought by Robert Litlover and Randal Ferror, bailiffs of Eddisbury hundred, two for the payment of fines and one for a rescue.[87] The good conduct of a court held by two deputy bailiffs was in question in 1538. Robert Sounde and James Bostok, in Broxton hundred, prosecuted John Puleston, Richard Lawrence of Malpas and Robert Roger for calling a jury 'false harlottes'.[88] A particularly active officer was Roger Brereton, farmer of the casualties of Flintshire: he and his bailiffs were involved in eight surviving cases.[89]

The relationship between the exchequer and potential competitors will be discussed further below, but it is necessary to establish here the respect with which the Chester court was usually treated, because without that respect the court would soon have lost much of its business. The exchequer could play a role supportive of the Council in the Marches, for example entertaining a suit against William Egerton of Hampton for refusing to appear as a witness in a case before the council.[90] On several occasions the Council in the Marches referred suits to the exchequer, which could be an affirmation of the power of the exchequer: an attempt by Rees ap Ithell to challenge his imprisonment after being summoned by an exchequer *subpoena* was referred to Chester and there dismissed.[91] The previous day Roger Lightfoot's bill to the commissioners concerning the theft of a cow in Cheshire had been sent on to Chester.[92] In 1538 some defendants argued that the case against them in the exchequer should be dismissed because 'the cort befor the said Counsaill of the Marches is a superior cort to this honorable cort'. Their arguments were, however, dismissed and the case referred to the next shire court in Chester.[93]

---

85 PRO, CHES 15/1/159.

86 PRO, CHES 15/1/53.

87 PRO, CHES 15/1/97–9. Another rescue, following an attempt to levy 'serten the kyngs dutiez', resulted in a case brought by Nicholas Page, bailiff of Bucklow hundred: CHES 15/1/120.

88 PRO, CHES 15/1/148.

89 PRO, CHES 15/1/15, 18, 57, 62, 64–7. Other officers who used the court were the leave-lookers of salt in Northwich, the deputy constable of Halton Castle and the steward of Saughall and Shotwick defending the deer in his charge: CHES 15/1/196, 12, 108.

90 PRO, CHES 15/1/2.

91 PRO, CHES 15/1/63 (27 Nov. 1538).

92 PRO, CHES 15/1/96.

93 PRO, CHES 15/1/55.

Yet in both these cases sent to Chester from the marcher council, Rowland Legh refers to Richard Hassall not as an officer of the Chester exchequer but as 'oon of this counsaill', a clear implication that the Chester exchequer and other courts were integrated within the judicial system of the marches generally.[94]

The Chester exchequer's advantages were appreciated by a wide range of suitors, from knights and abbots to poor widows. Sir Edward Fitton brought a suit against eleven people for cutting down trees on his manor of Gawsworth in 1538, and another against Henry Stanway, a tenant of his in Betchton, in the parish of Sandbach.[95] John Harware, abbot of Vale Royal, was a particularly frequent plaintiff, for example seeking to have an innkeeper from his lordship of Over bound not to receive fugitives, 'vacabunds, comen Carders and disers' in a disorderly alehouse. He also used the court to gain possession of a messuage in Weaverham from a tenant, and to prosecute a trespass in one of his woods.[96] At the other end of the scale came plaintiffs like Peter Corker of Arclid who described himself as 'a werey pore man'.[97] Margaret Parre described herself as 'a pore wydow and dwellyng in a foreyn Countie' in her bill against William Whiksted and others.[98] The only type of case that appears to be absent is between high status adversaries: a knight or abbot might prosecute a yeoman or husbandman, but would not take on another senior gentleman. The status of plaintiffs can be compared with those using Star Chamber. There over 25 per cent of plaintiffs and over 35 per cent of defendants were of gentry status or above; just over 25 per cent of defendants and plaintiffs and defendants were yeomen or husbandmen, but only 1.5 per cent of plaintiffs and 5.4 per cent of defendants were labourers.[99]

The lordship that provided these solutions to problems in Cheshire still flowed naturally through the medium of the prince's Chester council. If Cheshire's palatinate really was a dinosaur, persisting beyond its time, then the new national courts of equity should have monopolised all potential equity business from Cheshire. Yet they did not. One of the main charges levelled against the palatinates by those who see them as moribund in the fifteenth century is that they were no longer able to innovate; in particular, that they could not respond to new needs with new legal forms. In concluding this section, therefore, it should be noted that Chester was able to adopt and benefit from the most important new writ of the late medieval period, the

---

94 PRO, CHES 15/1/63, 96. The exchequer also took over a case begun when John Weston of Chester and Elizabeth his wife petitioned Dr [Thomas] Lee, 'visitor under the kyngs grace' at St Werburgh's abbey in 1536, although their complaint was against imprisonment in Chester castle: CHES 15/1/188.

95 PRO, CHES 15/1/44–5.

96 PRO, CHES 15/1/174–6.

97 See pp. 95–6 above; PRO, CHES 15/1/31.

98 PRO, CHES 15/1/124.

99 Guy, *Cardinal's court*, 109.

subpoena, from at least 1483–4, and to use it to develop an equity jurisdiction.[100]

The activity of councillors in Chester as an equity court, if in a less developed way than had been achieved by the Westminster chancery, is not unparalleled in other territories ruled by the English king, where a council of some sort existed and dealt with disputes, arbitrating with the backing of the power of its sovereign lord.[101] In some this arbitration was already being delegated to the chancellor or his equivalent, and the beginnings of a formalised equity court were apparent. In the palatinate of Lancaster, created in 1351 without any reference to equity jurisdiction, there had developed the chancery of the duchy at Lancaster which by 1473–4 had equity jurisdiction.[102] In Durham, a closer parallel to Chester in that its palatinate was considered to have existed from time immemorial, the chancery of the bishop was by this time also taking on an equity role.[103] In Ireland from the 1490s the chancery began to take over the equity powers previously wielded by the Irish council and parliament.[104] In Man a separate equity court does not seem to have begun to emerge until the 1560s, although the lord's council was determining equity cases from earlier in the century.[105] Cecil Calvert, the lord of Maryland, his powers based on those of Durham's palatine lord, was from the 1630s able to create the rudiments of such an equity court in his distant lordship.[106]

So Cheshire saw a day-to-day flow of palatine lordship or sovereignty through the equity jurisdiction of the exchequer. This might, however, have been irrelevant when compared to the equity jurisdiction of Westminster and therefore the flows of English lordship. The question of whether Cheshire people chose, or were forced, to use the alternative equity jurisdictions of Westminister, will be examined later, but all the evidence before 1518 is that they did not. This was in spite of the strong motives of self-interest that were

---

[100] W. M. Ormrod, 'The origins of the *sub pena* writ', *Historical Research* lxi (1988), 11–20.

[101] See Reid, *King's Council in the North*, 54–7.

[102] Somerville, 'Palatine courts in Lancashire'; Worthington, 'Royal government', 179–81. This should be distinguished from the duchy chamber.

[103] Christopher Kitching, 'The Durham palatinate and the courts of Westminster under the Tudors', in Marcombe, *Last principality*, 49–70; Kenneth Emsley and C. M. Fraser, *The courts of the county palatine of Durham from the earliest times to 1971*, Durham 1984, 72–90, esp. pp. 74–5.

[104] Ellis, *Tudor Ireland*, 163–4. As elsewhere in these territories, it was often hard to distinguish between what might have been seen in England as a private act of parliament and the decision of the council. See the 'parliamentary' occasion in Cheshire in 1353: Booth, 'Taxation and public order', 22.

[105] Manx National Trust Museum and Library, Douglas, Isle of Man, Liber placitorum 1543–69, *sub* 1568, 26 July; J. R. Dickinson, 'Aspects of the Isle of Man in the seventeenth century', unpubl. PhD diss. Liverpool 1991, 10, 30–1, 54–6, 62, 65–6.

[106] B. C. Steiner, 'Maryland's first courts', *Annual Report of the American Historical Association*, i, Washington 1902 [1901], 213–29; cf. the equity jurisdiction exercised by the warden of the Cinque Ports: K. M. E. Murray, *The constitutional history of the Cinque Ports*, Manchester 1935, 102–19 esp. pp. 112–13.

present to encourage Cheshire men to go to Westminster to exploit the opportunities for parallel actions or use the courts there to challenge a case already decided in Cheshire. After 1518, although alternative jurisdictions in Star Chamber and chancery were more accessible to the people of Cheshire, the exchequer continued to grow. Even in the early seventeenth century the Chester exchequer was a powerful jurisdiction, its position enshrined by a judgement of the Westminster chancery in the controversial case of *Starkey* v. *Starkey*.[107]

In concluding the first part of this book, we should note that Cheshire history in the late medieval and early modern period must be written in terms of the palatinate. The cultural support for palatine liberties was strong. Fiscal resources were still raised through palatine taxation. Lordship and sovereignty flowed overwhelmingly through the earldom of Chester, either in the person of the prince of Wales or of the king. If noblemen had significance, it was as officers of the palatinate. Those who mattered were the princes and their representatives. Westminster and the court mattered far less than we have been led to expect. In fact, royal authority in all of the privileged territories of the English king was less concentrated on the centre, both in terms of Westminster and of the person of the monarch as king of England, and more focused at the local level, supportive of local peculiarity.

107 *CSPD, 1623–5*, 313; Ormerod, *Chester*, ii. 188–90, 192; PRO, C 2/James I/S35/40; BL, MS Lansdowne 163, fos 5, 7, 9, 10, 58–9v, 72–4, 76 (Caesar's notes). The decision was enrolled at Chester on 22 Oct. 1619: CHES 2/287, m. 2 (*39 DKR*, 250).

PART II

DEVELOPMENT AND CHANGE

5

The Westminster and Other External Law Courts

An important element in Cheshire's autonomous position was its judicial independence. In theory, its courts represented a microcosm of the courts at Westminster: there was no need for any Cheshire person to take a case there except in cases of error.[1] The exclusion of Cheshire cases from the central equity courts was less clear, however. A suitor might exploit the opportunities for parallel actions at Westminster or use the courts there to challenge a case already decided in Cheshire. The extent to which such use was made is one measure of the degree to which Cheshire's autonomous institutions were working and accepted by its inhabitants. Strong motives of self-interest existed to encourage Cheshire men to go to Westminster, and it will be interesting to compare respect for autonomy shown here with that exhibited when taxation, for example, was at stake. The way local attitudes to external courts were shaped reveals the centralising consequences of the policies of Cardinal Wolsey, but the strength of palatine institutions in the face of challenges from the city of Chester and the marcher council is also evident.

Chancery

Study of Cheshire cases coming before chancery has been given significance because of its role as a forum for challenges to lesser jurisdictions.[2] Most importantly for Cheshire, chancery represented a resort for suitors foiled in the exclusive jurisdictions of Welsh marches: one suitor under Henry VII stated he had come to chancery because his opponent lived in the marches

---

1 Worthington, 'Royal government', 176–7, 197 (writs of error were customarily referred).
2 The court had an important role in towns, aided by the chancellor's powers over the lesser jurisdictions of staple towns: Nicholas Pronay, 'The chancellor, the chancery and the council at the end of the fifteenth century', in H. Hearder and H. R. Loyn (eds), *British government and administration: studies presented to S. B. Chrimes*, Cardiff 1974, 92–6. The ten staple towns account for two-thirds of the cases in bundle 59 (p. 92). Chancery bills requesting writs of *corpus cum causa* or *certiorari* to be directed to officers of courts in Cheshire are extremely rare: PRO, C 1/421/32 (*John Jenyns, tanner v. the sheriffs of Chester*, 1515–18) is the only early example.

'where the Kynges writtes cannot be served'.[3] In spite of this, however, Cheshire scarcely figured in chancery's proceedings before the reign of Henry VIII.

There are thirteen surviving suits concerning Cheshire in chancery before 1485. Few of them can be accurately dated, but the six or so that can cluster in two periods. The first is in the 1430s. Two cases were brought by Sir John Gresley against Ralph Egerton and Richard Delves, and against Sir Geoffrey Mascy, probably in 1434–5; a case between Alice Hogh and Robert Legh of Adlington belongs to 1432–3 or slightly later; and in about 1440 William Sais brought a case against the sheriff, Ranulph Brereton, which also included criticism of the chamberlain, William Troutbeck.[4] The second cluster is around 1450. Then Ralph Holynshed brought a case against Hugh, John and Roger Browdhurst concerning land in Macclesfield hundred; and most significantly William Denny put in a bill against the chamberlain, John Troutbeck.[5] Both groups of cases had a clear political context. That in the 1430s provided the background for the demand by Cheshire representatives, in negotiating over the mise of 1441, that no further privy seals should be sent into Cheshire – a demand that the crown granted.[6] The cases in the period around 1450 were almost certainly linked to the disgrace of the chamberlain of Chester for his obstinate defence of Cheshire's taxation privileges and resistance to resumption voted by the English parliament.[7] The fact that in two of the cases the chamberlain was specifically criticised by the plaintiffs, and that William Sais attacked sheriff Brereton with a list of (unspecified) 'orrible offenses' 'to mugh to put in a bill to yore said lordeship for thay wold occupie a hole parchement Skyn and more', underlines the fact that these cases were linked to periods of political crisis.

The significance of the very low level of Cheshire cases in the period up to 1518 (by which time Wolsey was firmly established in the post of chancellor) is particularly clear when those from the years 1463–1518, a crucial period in the establishment of chancery's prominent position, are compared with cases from the neighbouring, and in many ways similar, counties of Staffordshire and Derbyshire.[8] The results are given in table 2.

---

3   PRO, C 1/371/40.

4   PRO, C 1/39/87–8; C 1/75/41; C 1/73/117, respectively.

5   PRO, C 1/18/164; C 1/19/133.

6   CCRO, DSS, Vernon MS 3, fo. 190; *CPR, 1436–41*, 560–1.

7   Thornton, 'Defence of the liberties of Chester', 340.

8   Pronay, 'Chancellor, the chancery and the council', 87–103. Figures rely on the allocations to counties by the authors of the calendar. Where a case applies to both Derbyshire and Cheshire, for example, it appears in the statistics for each county. Thus PRO, C 1/220/68, regarding lands in Staffordshire, Cheshire and Shropshire appears twice in the table, in the total for Staffordshire and that for Cheshire. All these and subsequent statistics are based on the class C 1; although some cases in the class C 4 have also been examined, calendaring of these documents is so rudimentary that systematic use has not been possible. These two counties were chosen because of their broadly similar geographical position, population and wealth, and because they do not have within their boundaries any large cities which might

Table 2
Cases in chancery from Cheshire, Staffordshire and Derbyshire, 1463–1518

Bundles	Dates covered	Cheshire	Staffordshire	Derbyshire
30–67	c. 1463–85	3 (0.033%)	61 (0.66%)	46 (0.499%)
76–234, 236–377	1485–1515	24* (0.157%)	322 (2.109%)	164 (1.074%)
378–457	1515–18	27 (1.062%)	166 (2.36%)	95 (1.35%)

* This excludes PRO, C 1/322/20, which does not relate to Malpas, Cheshire, as calendared, but to Malton, Yorkshire.

During Edward IV's reign surviving Cheshire cases represent a negligible proportion of those known to have been heard by the chancellor. There are just three examples. Two are probably in fact datable not to Edward's time but to the reign of Henry VI.[9] The remaining one is only coincidentally a Cheshire case. When John de la Pole, duke of Suffolk, litigated in chancery over his wardship of Francis Lovell, Cheshire was only one minor element in a case that embraced a complex of lands in Shropshire, Yorkshire, Oxfordshire, Wiltshire and Northamptonshire.[10] Even if we go beyond cases listed as concerning Cheshire it is difficult to find examples involving Cheshiremen during the reign of Edward IV. William Nedeham sued Ralph Coton for waste in his manor of Shenton [Shavington?], just over the Cheshire border in Shropshire.[11] Sir Thomas Pilkington sued Sir Piers Legh and his wife Elizabeth, the widow of Thomas's uncle John, over their failure to carry out the award of John [Booth], bishop of Exeter: Sir Piers's main residence was at Bradley in Lancashire, but he did have interests in north-east Cheshire.[12] The three cases allocated to Cheshire, and the tiny penumbra of related cases, only serve to underline the extraordinary absence of Cheshire cases from chancery. This seems to indicate not only a low level of demand for action on Cheshire disputes through chancery, and greater stability within

have produced an atypical concentration of cases. The cases in C 1/1–2, calendared in *Calendars of the proceedings in chancery in the reign of Queen Elizabeth; to which are prefixed examples of earlier proceedings in that court, namely from the reign of Richard the Second to that of Queen Elizabeth, inclusive: from the originals in the Tower,* London 1827–32, i–ii, do not include any Cheshire cases.

9   Sir John Gresley of Derbyshire was brought to a dispute involving Cheshire land through his marriage to the widow of Thomas Massey and the marriage of his daughter to Richard Delves. This produced two suits, both of Henry VI's reign: PRO, C 1/39/87–8. In the latter case, the defendant, Sir Geoffrey Massey, died 4 Oct. 1457: Ormerod, *Chester,* i. 442.

10   PRO, C 1/40/322.

11   PRO, C 1/58/83; cf. C 1/67/263.

12   PRO, C 1/59/118. Cf. *Margaret, widow of Sir Nicholas Langford of Derbyshire v. feoffees* including Cheshiremen William Davenport and Robert Calveley (1483–5): C 1/65/152.

Cheshire than its subsequent reputation for disorder would imply, but also a refusal on the part of the court itself to deal with them.

Comparison with other territories of the English crown suggests that Cheshire's experience was not unique. In the fifteenth century their equity jurisdictions usually excluded those of the Westminster courts (see table 4).[13] Before 1485 thirteen chancery cases are attributed to France outside Calais, seven to Durham, thirty to Wales and four to the Channel Islands. When we come to look in detail at the cases attributed to Ireland, for example, we discover that of the twenty-one cases listed up to 1518, only nine actually concern property or actions in Ireland, or were between two Irish parties. Two cases from the reign of Richard III illustrate the point. The merchants and citizens of Waterford took action to recover their charter from the heirs of a man who had taken it into his safe-keeping in Bristol; and an Irish merchant complained against his agent in Bristol who refused to hand over money he had in his keeping.[14] Before 1515 we are left with just seven cases, two of which brought by foreigners who probably did not understand the judicial system and who cannot be seen as typical litigators.[15] A similar picture could be painted for other peripheral territories. Even when a bill was presented concerning one of these territories, there was no guarantee that it would be accepted by the Westminster jurisdictions; in many cases palatine or other privilege was objected by the defendant. Where chancery action is recorded in one case, concerning lands in Yorkshire, Leicestershire, Nottinghamshire and Durham, the injunction related to land in the first three counties but was silent on the subject of that lying in Durham.[16]

After an absence of thirty years, Cheshire people began to use chancery again under Henry VII. Twenty-four chancery cases relating to Cheshire are to be found from the years 1485–1515, spread fairly evenly across the period at the rate of approximately one per year. There is no concentration of cases

[13] This is calculated from the List and Index Society volumes, the compilers of which allocated cases to these areas with excessive generosity. In this context Ralph A. Griffiths expressed his belief in the long existence of 'imperial' unity in the territories of the English crown: that prerogative courts had long dealt with cases from the full extent of those territories and that this rapidly increased under the Tudors. The evidence he provides, 82 cases from Wales under Wolsey's chancellorship, does not really prove his point: 'The English realm and dominions and the king's subjects in the later Middle Ages', in J. G. Rowe (ed.), *Aspects of late medieval government and society*, Toronto 1986, 99 (repr. in his *King and country*, 33–54). Griffiths sees greater significance in the existence of evidence for a few suits than in its paucity; cf. Franz Metzger, 'The last phase of the medieval chancery', in Harding, *Lawmaking and law-makers in British history*, 82. The organisation of the cases in PRO, C 1/1–2, calendared in *Calendars of the proceedings in chancery in the reign of Queen Elizabeth*, is such as to make inclusion in the analysis difficult, but the bundles contain few relevant cases.
[14] PRO, C 1/65/215; C 1/63/242.
[15] 'Great John', a Prussian, complained against imprisonment in Ireland; some Luccan merchants objected that they could not use English common law over a bond entered into in Dublin: PRO, C 1/69/132; C 1203/5.
[16] PRO, C 1/402/44.

around obvious crises in the palatinate or at the centre. Nor is there any apparent pattern to the type of cases brought. Many were brought by non-Cheshiremen or relate to other counties than Cheshire, such as that brought by Hugh Champyn, a London shearman,[17] or that concerning estates in Shropshire and Staffordshire as well as Cheshire brought by Richard Patryk and his wife.[18] Ralph Massey, as administrator of the goods of Richard Walker, late vicar of Wybunbury, complained against Henry Foljambe, himself the administrator of the goods of Thomas Foljambe, over a debt owed by Thomas for sheep purchased from Walker at Borsall.[19] There were also, however, cases which dealt with exclusively Cheshire matters, such as the Ardern family dispute over the manors of Alvanley and Harden.[20] Thomas, son of Thomas Wilbraham, and Margaret his wife, daughter of Thomas Swettenham, took a case to chancery against George and Rauf Swettenham, bastard sons of the same Thomas Swettenham, over houses and land in Middlewich, Kinderton and Newton.[21] This suggests a change in the policy of the court. There had been a call for its services before, and there was clearly still demand, if at a low level, under Henry VII: now the court was permitting this demand to make itself felt by accepting bills.

Cheshire people were therefore slowly beginning to use chancery. In the years 1515 to 1518, however, the court was suddenly busy with Cheshire cases, a development which was therefore not the culmination of a progressive growth during the previous thirty years. A new factor brought important county figures like Sir John Stanley of Handforth, and John, Henry and William Troutbeck, the sons of Sir William Troutbeck, to use the court in major land disputes.[22] At the other end of the scale it led lesser individuals to chancery: Alice Fletcher complained against Roger, the brother and executor of John Pyke, merchant, over the detention of deeds relating to a messuage and garden in Common Hall Lane, Chester, bequeathed together with one quarter of his ship, the *Margaret*, by John to her and his children by her.[23] Such people, rich and poor, were to be regular litigants in chancery from this

---

17 PRO, C 1/125/23.

18 PRO, C 1/220/68. Three linked cases relating to the lands of the Bradoke or Brook family were caused by the disputed inheritance of John Bradoke: C 1/257/35, C 1/280/79, C 1/290/58. In the latter, the Staffordshire residence of Frances, widow of John Swynnerton, John Bradoke's feoffee, was the reason for taking the case to chancery rather than within the county palatine.

19 PRO, C 1/101/4. John Stanley, esquire, was sued for detention of deeds over seven hays adjoining the forest of Cannock and the lordship of Barrow; his opponent was Thomas Swynnerton of Staffordshire. Cf. London draper, *Thomas Hart v. Henry Riall of Wilmslow*, over a debt: C 1/165/63; C 1/321/16.

20 PRO, C 1/83/27.

21 PRO, C 1/178/26. John, brother and heir of Richard Legh, used the court to allege detention of deeds relating to lands in Altrincham, Prestbury and Heyfeld against Thomas Legh of Adlington: C 1/334/64.

22 PRO, C 1/442/42; C 1/450/41.

23 PRO, C 1/408/3.

Table 3
Cases in chancery from Cheshire, Staffordshire
and Derbyshire, 1518–58

Bundles	Dates covered	*Cheshire*	Staffordshire	Derbyshire
458–600	1518–29	82 (1.717%)	172 (3.601%)	86 (1.801%)
601–94	1529–32	36 (1.526%)	65 (2.755%)	44 (1.865%)
695–712	1532–3	5 (0.936%)	18 (3.371%)	5 (0.936%)
713–934	1533–8	125 (1.745%)	247 (3.448%)	140 (1.954%)
935–1094	1538–1544	163 (2.765%)	314 (5.326%)	167 (2.832%)
1094–1172	1544–7	80 (2.547%)	163 (5.189%)	101 (3.215%)
1174–86	1547	9 (2.113%)	11 (2.582%)	12 (2.817%)
1188–1267, 1269, 1316–1317, 1271–85	1547–51	107 (3.152%)	141 (4.153%)	85 (2.504%)
1286–1315, 1268, 1270, 1318–24	1551–3	53 (4.080%)	64 (4.927%)	41 (3.156%)
1325–97	1553–5	55 (2.110%)	119 (4.566%)	81 (3.108%)
1398–1488	1556–8	90 (2.777%)	155 (4.782%)	106 (3.271%)

point on. Wolsey's chancellorship was clearly of major import in changing the pattern of litigation by Cheshire people.

Comparison with the experience of Staffordshire and Derbyshire confirms the importance of this change. The proportion of cases in chancery relating to Cheshire increased under Henry VII, but still only reached 0.157 per cent in the whole period 1485–1515. In each period Staffordshire cases constituted about twenty times as much of the court's recorded business as did Cheshire suits. Even cases regarding Derbyshire were more than ten times more frequent in their appearance.[24] When Henry VII's reign is compared with that of Edward IV, both Staffordshire and Derbyshire showed considerable increases in the frequency of extant cases: the percentage of Staffordshire cases more than trebled, that of Derbyshire cases doubled. Cheshire's rate of increase was of the same order, but the significant fact remained Cheshire's remarkably low proportion of total extant cases as compared to the other two counties. In the years 1515–18, surviving Derbyshire and Staffordshire cases showed little increase against the previous period in terms of the proportion of all cases which they made up. The percentage of Cheshire cases, however, increased from 0.157 per cent to 1.062 per cent. The absolute number of Cheshire cases was still very low, and this may cast doubt on the significance of the statistic. Yet the fact remains that more Cheshire cases before the chancellor survive from the three years 1515 to 1518 than from

[24] Extant Staffordshire and Derbyshire cases include very few in which the decision of the courts of a town or city are challenged, and so the larger number of surviving cases cannot be explained in this way.

the entire preceding thirty years, an increase at a time when the pattern of litigation in chancery from other counties in the north-west midlands had achieved some stability.

After 1518 Cheshire cases continued to grow in importance as a proportion of all cases in chancery. They never again fell significantly below 1% of the total, and in general an upward trend continued. The proportion of cases with a Staffordshire origin also grew, but the gap between it and the proportion of Cheshire cases narrowed considerably; the gap between the proportion of Derbyshire cases and that of Cheshire cases closed, and during the period 1547–53 Cheshire cases actually outnumbered Derbyshire ones in chancery. (Table 3 indicates the totals of cases originating from the counties of Cheshire, Staffordshire and Derbyshire for which evidence survives, on the same principles as that already given.) In the space of roughly thirty years, between 1515 and 1545, Cheshire had therefore changed from being a county rarely if ever represented in chancery litigation to being relatively typical of the shires of the north-west midlands in this respect. Whether this judicial centralisation was part of a general pattern, however, is questioned by the evidence for other privileged areas ruled by the English crown.

In examining the proportions of cases which relate to Wales, Durham, the Channel Islands, Ireland and Calais (see table 4)[25] it is clear that the experience of some territories was similar to that of Cheshire. Wales showed a rapid rise from a proportion of relevant cases as low if not lower than that of Cheshire to a position whereby under Mary it was touched upon in about 6 per cent of chancery cases. Given its larger population and area, this was a similar experience to that of Cheshire. As with Cheshire, the crucial period was under Wolsey and immediately after his fall; on the other hand, a rapid rise at that time was more clearly sustained in Wales than in Cheshire.[26] The immediate aftermath of the first Act of Union was also obviously important in stimulating cases. In Durham, however, a situation in which the county

[25] On the same principles as the Cheshire figures, with which they are compared. The same qualifications which apply to the Cheshire figures and to the earlier cases from the non-English territories apply here with even greater force. The figures are based on the allocations of cases to counties by the compilers of the list, and these allocations are generous in their willingness to record relevance to one of these territories. The sole 'Irish' chancery case from the period 1533–8, for example PRO, C 1/869/13, was taken by Morgan Phelippe against the mayor and sheriffs of Bristol for a writ of *certiorari* in an action by Richard Duffe and Thomas Sayen, Irishmen, on a bond for the delivery of beans, the export of which was banned by proclamation. Of the two in the subsequent six years, the first (C 1/961/34), again for a *certiorari*, was against the sheriffs of London and related to a dispute between a man from Rutland and a London merchant over a claim for wages while serving in Ireland; the second (C 1/1053/43), between Nicholas Pollerd and William Falander, related to corn delivered at Youghal and was the only true Irish case in more than 10 years. For C 1/1–2 see n. 13 above.
[26] For concern at rising levels of chancery cases from Wales see Roberts, ' "Acts of union" and the Tudor settlement of Wales', 209–10. A chancery litigant in 1528 still argued that north Wales had jurisdictional independence: ibid. 245, citing PRO, C 1/546/88.

Table 4
Cases in chancery from Cheshire, Wales, Durham, the Channel Islands, Ireland and Calais before 1558

Bundles	Dates	Cheshire	Wales	Durham	Channel Is.	Ireland	Calais
3–29	10 Ric. II–5 Ed IV	0.0855%	13 (0.185%)	1 (0.0142%)	2 (0.0285%)	1 (0.0142%)	23 (0.328%)
30–67	1463–85	0.033%	12 (0.130%)	5 (0.0543%)	1 (0.0108%)	5 (0.0543%)	25 (0.271%)
68–75	Uncertain	0.280%	5 (0.350%)	1 (0.0700%)	1 (0.0700%)	4 (0.280%)	6 (0.420%)
76–377	1485–1515	0.157%	39 (0.255%)	19 (0.124%)	6 (0.0393%)	8 (0.524%)	79 (0.517%)
378–457	1515–18	1.062%	27 (1.101%)	3 (0.122%)	2 (0.0815%)	0 (0%)	8 (0.326%)
458–600	1518–29	1.717%	62 (1.298%)	2 (0.0419%)	7 (0.147%)	3 (0.0628%)	11 (0.230%)
601–94	1529–32	1.526%	36 (1.526%)	9 (0.381%)	3 (0.127%)	0 (0%)	7 (0.297%)
695–712	1532–3	0.936%	4 (0.749%)	1 (0.187%)	0 (0%)	0 (0%)	2 (0.374%)
713–934	1533–8	1.745%	200 (2.792%)	9 (0.126%)	10 (0.140%)	1 (0.0140%)	15 (0.209%)
935–1094	1538–44	2.765%	346 (5.868%)	9 (0.153%)	5 (0.0848%)	2 (0.0339%)	11 (0.187%)
1095–1172	1544–7	2.547%	104 (3.311%)	5 (0.159%)	4 (0.127%)	2 (0.0637%)	5 (0.159%)
1174–86	1547	2.113%	23 (5.399%)	1 (0.235%)	0 (0%)	0 (0%)	2 (0.469%)
1188–1267, 1269, 1316–17, 1271–85	1547–51	3.152%	199 (5.862%)	19 (0.560%)	7 (0.206%)	0 (0%)	10 (0.295%)
1286–1315, 1268, 1270, 1318–24	1551–3	4.080%	70 (5.389%)	4 (0.308%)	0 (0%)	0 (0%)	1 (0.0770%)
1325–97	1553–5	2.110%	170 (6.523%)	6 (0.230%)	1 (0.0384%)	0 (0%)	2 (0.0767%)
1398–1488	1556–8	2.777%	192 (5.924%)	11 (0.339%)	5 (0.154%)	0 (0%)	5 (0.154%)

contributed very few cases to chancery continued into the 1540s,[27] and the rise that then occurred was very limited: it was only really in the reign of Edward VI that the county palatine was referred to in more than 0.33 per cent of chancery cases.[28] Cases from the Channel Islands occurred at very low levels throughout the period, and it is hard to discern any real trend. In the two other cases described in table 4, Ireland and in Calais, there was actually a trend away from the use of chancery, a process distinctly in opposition to that seen in Cheshire and Wales. The proportion of cases referring to Calais dropped in the latter part of the reign of Henry VIII to little more than 0.10 per cent; Irish cases almost completely disappeared.

---

[27] During the Pilgrimage of Grace, there were demands that injunctions, *subpoenas* and privy seals should be sent less frequently into the distant counties of the realm, and Durham may have been one centre of this concern: Roberts, ' "Acts of union" and the Tudor settlement of Wales', 246, citing *LP* xi. 1182, 2(7).

[28] Kitching, 'Durham palatinate and the courts of Westminster', 54–9, conceals this slow growth behind a broad statistic for the whole sixteenth century of 'up to' 200 cases; his assertion of the popularity of chancery before 1558 needs to be qualified.

Star Chamber

The record of chancery is comparable with the experience of the king's council in its judicial capacity, which was to become the court of Star Chamber formalised by Thomas Wolsey.[29] The survival of evidence for litigation from the reign of Henry VII is poor,[30] but it is clear that Cheshire matters were very rarely discussed since records of only three cases survive.[31] There is a similar silence when the early years of Henry VIII's reign are considered, apart from a complaint by Piers Dutton about his treatment at the hands of chamberlain Randal Brereton in the previous reign.[32] The difficulties encountered by the plaintiffs in one of the Cheshire cases known from Henry VII's reign suggest why. The dispute over the Venables inheritance, a long-running affair covering half a century, was first seen in Henry's council in 1491 and then reappeared in 1500, when Thomas Venables refused to produce title deeds. His obstinacy eventually led to the cancellation of a recognizance for attendance, and the case went back to common law. Venables was adamant: 'all oder londes & tenementes within the seid Countie be & of the tyme wherof the mynd of man is not to the contrarie, have been enpleaded And the title therof triable & tried withyn the seid Countie [of Cheshire] And in non oder place'. He was ultimately successful.[33]

It was with the arrival of Wolsey on the chancellor's woolsack that, as with chancery cases, there began a growth in Star Chamber cases originating in Cheshire.[34] The chancellor's well-known statements in Star Chamber against

29 On Star Chamber see Guy, *Cardinal's court*, and *The court of Star Chamber and its records to the reign of Elizabeth I* (PRO Handbooks xxi, 1985).
30 Bayne and Dunham, *Cases in the council of Henry VII*. For survival rates see Guy, *Star Chamber and its records*, 24.
31 'Star Chamber proceedings Henry VII' (PRO, STAC 1) include none relating to Cheshire; *List of proceedings in the court of Star Chamber, I: 1485–1558* (PRO, Lists and Indexes xiii, 1901). Two cases remain among the proceedings of the reign of Henry VIII, and transcripts of council proceedings include one closely related case: Guy, *Star Chamber and its records*, 67–73; STAC 2/20/177 (*Wykestede v. Manweryng*); STAC 2/29/188 (*Savage and Cotton v. Venables, Chomley, Grafton and others*, 1500, discussed and printed in Bayne and Dunham, *Cases in the council of Henry VII*, pp. clvii–clviii, 130–4); transcripts, *Cotton v. Venables* (1491): Bayne and Dunham, *Cases in the council of Henry VII*, 24 (MS Ellesmere 2654, fo. 14). There may be other Cheshire cases of the reign of Henry VII among the miscellaneous pieces of the class STAC 10, but even so the total number of cases brought to the notice of the royal council in Henry VII's reign can probably be numbered on the fingers of two hands, at most.
32 PRO, STAC 2/7/182 (*L&C Star Chamber*, 63–4). Two cases apparently dating from the first four years of the reign in fact belong to that of Edward VI. STAC 2/25/302 (*Collections for a History of Staffordshire* [1912], 4–5) relates to an assault between Macclesfield and Swythumley (Staffs.) while soldiers were being conveyed to Scotland in Aug. 1547; STAC 2/12/208 (*L&C Star Chamber*, 84) is in the name of Edward, earl of Derby, and dates from 1550–1.
33 Ormerod, *Chester*, iii. 193, 199. See pp. 180–2 below.
34 Guy, *Star Chamber and its records*, 60–1 gives a regional distribution based on 821 cases

disorder and corruption of the system of justice were not only followed by an increase in the number of cases being brought to the court nationwide: they triggered a remarkable surge in Cheshire cases. In the last years of the 1510s the most important Cheshire gentry were being dragged through a court which had seen very few of their countrymen in the previous thirty years.[35] Soon after Wolsey's accession to the chancellorship, both Sir Piers Dutton[36] and Sir William Brereton, two of the most important members of the Cheshire gentry community, with several others, found themselves humiliated in the Fleet. Sir William Brereton was forced to attend in person on the chancellor in Star Chamber for several months before being fined 500 marks.[37] The previous absence of Cheshire litigation was partly due to the failure of the central authorities to encourage cases. A more significant factor, however, was the unwillingness of potential Cheshire litigants to use courts outside the county, an unwillingness that was only slowly broken down. After a sudden rise in the frequency of Cheshire Star Chamber cases in Wolsey's first years there was an equally rapid decline. Once Wolsey's willingness to encourage cases had abated, he ordered, on 21 June 1521, that 'all matters of Cheshyre dependinge here remitted to the Counsell in the Marches of Wales'.[38] The 1520s saw virtually no activity at all. 1528 witnessed a sudden rise in cases, and the following two years represented a new peak. The number of cases then fell during the 1530s and only after 1536–7 was it restored to a steady, relatively high level. In his eagerness to challenge the unlawful activity of the nobility and gentry of England, Wolsey had opened Star Chamber to Cheshire litigation, and the growth of chancery business may have followed in the wake of this controversial campaign. The cardinal's order of 1521 suggests that it was his antipathy to gentry misbehaviour, and not hostility to local autonomy, that had been uppermost in his mind. Wolsey had, in the long term, changed the pattern of litigation originated by Cheshire people by opening the route to Star Chamber to them, but this was not his conscious intention and the effects were not immediately apparent. In Star Chamber, if not in chancery, the disruption of 1536–43 was required to reinstate a high level of Cheshire litigation.[39]

from the time of Wolsey: cases from the west midlands, which includes Cheshire, are more numerous than those from any other region apart from the south-west, and equal in frequency to those from East Anglia. Guy does not draw any lessons from the totals from individual counties.

[35] For further detail see pp. 188–93 below.

[36] PRO, STAC 2/13/186 (articles v. John Dutton chaplain, printed in L&C Star Chamber, 89–90); STAC 2/24/290; STAC 2/22/329 (Dutton's response); STAC 2/17/227, fo. 5r–v (examination of Sir Piers Dutton, L&C Star Chamber, 22–3).

[37] Guy, Cardinal's court, 64; Gwyn, King's cardinal, 130–1; PRO, STAC 2/3/311; STAC 2/17/185, 227; STAC 2/24/434; STAC 2/26/370 (L&C Star Chamber, 20–3); STAC 2/18/162 (ibid. 120–1); STAC 2/20/175 (ibid. 136–7); STAC 2/19/81; STAC 2/22/113.

[38] Guy, Cardinal's court, 48.

[39] Cf. the Court of Requests: 1.28% of cases related to Cheshire under Henry VII and

When the experience of Cheshire in Star Chamber is set in the broader context, as with the case of chancery, a more complex picture emerges.[40] Among the Star Chamber cases allocated by the Public Record Office to the reign of Henry VII there is only one non-English case, and Durham is as unrepresented as Cheshire.[41] The cases allocated to the reign of Henry VIII include 170 in which Wales is referred to: as in chancery there was clearly a dramatic accession of Welsh business under Wolsey. Yet other territories appear far less frequently: Calais is only referred to in two cases, suggesting that Star Chamber was never a significant resort for disputes arising there, in spite of the importance at certain periods of chancery to the town and its pale. Durham also appears very infrequently, in five cases to be precise;[42] and Ireland only appears twice. Jersey and Guernsey produced nine cases, high by comparison but still reflective of a general trend for Star Chamber not to be concerned with these non-English territories. The pattern remained the same under Edward VI, from whose reign evidence survives for just three Durham cases and one relating to Jersey; and under Philip and Mary, with two Durham cases the only representatives of action relating to these areas.[43]

Cheshire cases also came before the courts of General Surveyors and Augmentations. These courts, dealing essentially with cases arising from the king's landed interests, offered another possible avenue for judicial centralisation in the early sixteenth century. Since the expansion of the king's estate, especially through the dissolution of the monasteries, was one of the most powerful factors in increasing the influence of central authority throughout his territories, it is not surprising that litigants from there began to appear in these courts. It is notable, for example, that although Manx cases are entirely absent from the other central equity courts two cases involving ex-monastic property in the Isle of Man came before the court of Augmentations, both relating to the rectories of St Michael and St Maughold.[44] Although the involvement of Cheshiremen in these courts was limited – cases relating to the

---

Henry VIII, and 1.13% under Edward VI: *List of proceedings in the Court of Requests*, i (List and Index Society xxi, 1906).

40 The organisation and listing of the Star Chamber records allows less precise analysis, but the same broad direction of development is apparent.

41 PRO, STAC 1/65 (Flintshire). There are also three Lancashire cases, STAC 1/23, 81, 116 (*L&C Star Chamber*, 1–5).

42 Kitching, 'Durham palatinate and the courts of Westminster', 58, although again his optimistic account of Durham involvement offers no precise figures.

43 Edward VI: PRO, STAC 3/5/69; STAC 3/6/83; STAC 3/7/82 (Durham); STAC 3/1/40 (Jersey). Mary: STAC 4/1/14; STAC 4/6/63 (Durham). Both reigns saw a continuing high level of Welsh litigation in Star Chamber, evidence surviving for about 16 cases under Edward VI and about 19 under Mary.

44 PRO, E 321/1/96; E 321/3/52 (printed in Mr Owen, ' "Saynt Maholde and Saynt Michell" ', *Proceedings of the Isle of Man Natural History and Antiquarian Society* n.s. ii [1923–6], 257–61). There is also a Channel Islands case (E 321/5/1; E 321/24/82) and several from Calais and its marches: E 321/19/69; E 321/20/23; E 321/25/44; E 321/26/36; E 321/35/36.

county make up just 3 per cent of those listed – the fact that this proportion is towards the top end of the spectrum of involvement suggested by the chancery evidence suggests that the effects of the dissolution drew the people of Cheshire into the orbit of central institutions more effectively than the attractions of equity jurisdiction.[45]

There are clearly comparisons that can be made between the development of chancery and Star Chamber jurisdiction in relation to Cheshire and other privileged areas. While Cheshire and Welsh cases both began to be discussed more frequently in the Westminster equity courts under Henry VIII, other territories had different experiences. A number of possible reasons for this diversity present themselves. Some changes may be due to the influence of particular individuals. Thomas Wolsey's position as bishop of Durham and lord chancellor must have played some part in the number of Durham cases coming to chancery during 1515–18 and more generally to Star Chamber; what is perhaps surprising is that this influence acted to reduce the number of cases, not to increase them. A problem-solver like Wolsey, if he held both local and central office, did not inevitably seek central solutions in a doctrinaire manner.[46] Edward Seymour's influence on the isles of Jersey and Guernsey might have worked the other way in the immediate circumstances of 1547, but with no sustained impact. Another important factor is administrative reform during the period. The reform of Welsh government in 1536 almost certainly led to a rise in chancery cases from the principality.[47] It might be suggested, however, that it was the inadequacies and failures of these reforms that produced the growth in chancery cases, not their success. Several chancery bills of the period after 1536 refer to the failure of the government to institute proper new judicial mechanisms after the destruction wrought in 1536 and especially to the delays in constituting new county administrations and commissions of the peace.[48] There were probably no Welsh commissions of the peace until 1541; sessions began in Caernarfon in October 1541 and the first surviving commission is from May 1542.[49] Once the new Welsh administration was in place, a path to chancery had already been established and litigants continued to use it.[50] Other areas which under-

[45] 107 pieces (2.983%) from the 3,587 in PRO, E 321/1–39, as described in the PRO list.

[46] Kitching, 'Durham palatinate and the courts of Westminster', 49; cf. Wolsey's assertion of his rights to lead and other metals, and to coal, as bishop of Durham: W. Hylton Dyer Longstaffe, 'Cardinal Wolsey's instructions to his officers at Durham', *Archæologia Æliana* 2nd ser. ii (1858), 39–40.

[47] Roberts, ' "Acts of union" and the Tudor settlement of Wales', 180–270.

[48] For example, PRO, C 1/1068/24 (Glamorgan); C 1/1072/69 (Glamorgan and Pembroke); cf. the Montgomery petition, BL, MS Harleian 368, fo. 178 (*LP* x. 1244), discussed by Roberts in ' "Acts of union" and the Tudor settlement of Wales', 205–9

[49] Ibid. 218, 254, 258; *Calendar of the Caernarvonshire quarter sessions records*, I: *1541–1558*, ed. W. Ogwen Williams, Caernarvon 1956, 2.

[50] The disruption caused by the dissolution of the diocese of Durham may have caused the use of Westminster equity courts by its inhabitants: David Loades, 'The dissolution of the diocese of Durham, 1553–4', in Marcombe, *Last principality*, 101–16.

went reform, and where it was more successful, seem as a consequence to have reduced their involvement in chancery. This may be the reason for the decline in the number of times Calais appears in chancery after 1536, when an act of the Reformation Parliament revised the government and jurisdiction of the outpost.[51] The same may be true of the reform of Irish government.[52] If these three assumptions are correct, the lesson of the figures appears to be threefold. First, men with influence over the development of the central equity courts in late medieval and Tudor Westminster were not determined to maximise the number of cases from privileged territories before them. Even a man of such ambition and power as Thomas Wolsey did not do so for Durham. Second, Tudor reform of regional and provincial government did not necessarily lead to centralisation or the weakening of local jurisdiction, and, when it did, this was largely because of the failure of that reform. And third, there were no strong pressures from the inhabitants of privileged territories to open up litigation in Westminster equity courts.

The county courts and the courts of the city of Chester and Council in the Marches

Potential competition for the county's palatine courts also came from the courts of the city of Chester and the Council in the Marches of Wales. The result of this competition was victory for the palatinate's courts, demonstrating that, while Westminster equity courts might have established a role alongside them, they were still very powerful jurisdictions.

The city's claims were based on the 1506 charter, the 1560 patent and the confirmation granted in 1564. A clause had been slipped into the charter granted to Chester early in Elizabeth's reign which removed the city from the jurisdiction of the Chester exchequer, relief in equity being by the Council in the Marches and chancery alone.[53] After a flurry of activity in the early years of the new charter, the relationship settled down to one of quiet coexistence. Tension began to grow, however, in the 1550s, perhaps a sign of the growing prosperity and assertiveness of the city.[54] In 1562, in one manifestation of this assertiveness, the mayor of Chester attempted to enlarge his allowances at

---

[51] P. T. J. Morgan, 'The government of Calais, 1485–1558', unpubl. DPhil. diss. Oxford 1966, 121–4, on the increasing importance of the Calais council. Although the reform of Calais was spasmodic and somewhat ineffective, I would qualify Morgan's emphasis on these failings, especially when they are contrasted with the problems of reform in Wales and Cheshire.

[52] Steven G. Ellis, *Reform and revival: English government in Ireland, 1470–1534*, London 1984, and *Tudor Ireland*, ch. vi.

[53] Jones, 'Exchequer of Chester', 157–9.

[54] Measured by the number of cases on writs of *certiorari* on the Chester enrolments, PRO, CHES 2. There were six such cases in the period before 1515 (39 *DKR*, 55, 92–3, 163, 168, 195, 306), then none until 1540 (p. 278), and then five in the period 1549–58 (pp. 45, 57,

the expense of the exchequer. Fines levied in the city were allocated to the mayor's expenses while other sources of income went to the corporation, so it was in the mayor's interest to ensure that Chester men did not use the county's courts in preference to the city's. Conflict erupted when Fulk Aldersey brought an action for debt against Alderman Thomas Green in the exchequer, a case that Mayor Richard Dutton thought should have stayed within the city courts; acting with the sheriffs, he put Aldersey in ward. William Glaseor, the deputy chamberlain, fined the mayor and sheriffs, who retaliated by disenfranchising Glaseor and Aldersey. The result was a Privy Council enquiry by Francis Walsingham, Walter Mildmay, William Cordell, master of the rolls, and solicitor-general Thomas Bromley that produced orders in 1574 which stated the exemption from the exchequer had been fraudulently obtained. A new mayoral oath included an expression of subordination to chamberlain Leicester and the exchequer.[55]

The trouble was exacerbated by conflict within the city between those who wanted to expand electoral rights and those who wished to close the corporation. In 1572 there was a clash over the election of aldermen and the common council. Mayor Ralph Dutton disenfranchised both the plaintiffs, one of whom was William Aldersey,[56] and vice-chamberlain Glaseor. Aldersey had obtained a charter for the Merchant Adventurers in 1553 which angered the Assembly because he had directly approached the lord chancellor and because it strengthened the gild's control of overseas trade and internal retailing. He had continued in dispute during the whole of the 1560s.[57] In response to the disenfranchisement in 1572 Mayor Dutton was attached by the exchequer. Dutton began an action for false imprisonment, but chamberlain Leicester signalled his unwillingness to see the conflict grow when he refused to consider the petition of those members of the assembly who wanted to reopen the question of popular electoral rights enshrined in the new charter.[58] A similar determination to avoid conflict was seen in the compromise that ended the jurisdictional dispute between city portmote and

---

137, 149, 223). For Chester's assertiveness see David Mills, 'The Chester mystery plays: truth and tradition', in Dunn, *Courts, counties and the capital*, 1–26.

[55] *APC* viii. 223–8; *CSPD, 1547–80*, 476–7; *CSPD, addenda 1566–79*, 460–1; Jones, 'Exchequer of Chester', 157–9; A. L. Browne, 'Sir John Throckmorton of Feckenham, chief justice of Chester', *Journal of the Chester and North Wales Architectural, Archaeological and Historic Society* n.s. xxxi/1 (1935), 61–2; A. M. Johnson, 'Some aspects of the political, constitutional, social, and economic history of the city of Chester, 1550–1662', unpubl. DPhil. diss. Oxford 1970, 167–78; 'Rights and jurisdiction', 15–24.

[56] For Aldersey's disenfranchisement and his petition to Leicester, from the Assembly Book, see Morris, *Chester in the Plantagenet and Tudor reigns*, 184–5.

[57] The charter infringed the rights of all freemen who had previously been entitled to trade. Trouble continued when, after relative peace in the 1580s, a small group tried to monopolise trade in alliance with the London-based Spanish Company. In 1584 this group received a licence for the export of calf skins, but compromise was eventually reached: Johnson, 'Aspects of the history of Chester', 28–9; VCH, *County of Chester*, iii. 110–11.

[58] Ibid. iii. 111.

exchequer in the early 1560s: again probably at the instance of Leicester, it was agreed that no further writs of *certiorari* should be issued against the port-mote.[59] In the city, the result of the affair was understood as compromise: one version of the Chester chronicle emphasised that 'the Maior is not now to appear in the Exchequer for every light matter, except for some great cause'.[60] In a letter of 14 May 1569 Leicester restated his support for a compromise solution when he wrote to Sir Hugh Cholmondeley, vice-president of the Council in the Marches, Sir John Throckmorton, justice of Chester, William Gerrard and Richard Pates, that the city of Chester 'complayne also that many proces sholde be adwarded out of the Courte of the Exchequer by my under officers to the breache of theire Liberties'.[61] None the less, the principle was established in the exchequer's favour.

One external court where Cheshire cases had long been entertained was the Council in the Marches. The way the two councils operated together has already been discussed; it was a relationship that was generally characterised by co-operation. There could equally be tension, but when a crisis occurred in the 1560s the strength of Cheshire institutions won out. Conflict erupted between the county exchequer and the Council in the Marches over the 'right of appeal' from the former after Thomas Radford challenged a sentence of imprisonment imposed by the vice-chamberlain. There was further conflict with the Council in the Marches over the case between William Allen and James Leigh, both of Rostherne, before the justice of Chester in 1568. Leigh petitioned chamberlain Leicester to intervene. The Privy Council referred the matter to a commission of Sir John Dyer, chief justice of Common Pleas, and three other judges. In 1569 they concluded that the chamberlain had all the jurisdiction of the Westminster chancery; that only cases of treason and error could cause a Cheshire person to be summoned to plead outside the county; and that the Council in the Marches was not intended by the 1543 'Act of Union' to cover Cheshire.[62]

The period from the 1510s to the end of the 1570s, therefore, saw a significant new role for Westminster equity courts in Cheshire litigation, largely triggered by the activity of Wolsey and sustained by the problems of the reform legislation of the 1530s and 1540s. For the same reason Welsh involvement in chancery and Star Chamber also grew. But the fact that there

[59] Ibid.

[60] Smith, 'Vale-royall', 86; cf. Webb, 'Vale-royall', 200.

[61] He had earlier in the letter stated his determination to aid the city, 'aswell for that the same ys a Citie of greate antiquitie as also necessarie for many respects to be upholden and mayntaigned': CCRO, DCC 47/1.

[62] Jones, 'Exchequer of Chester', 157–9; Browne, 'Throckmorton', 63–4; CSPD, *addenda 1566–79*, 73–4 (16 Mar. 1569); HMC, *Report on the manuscripts of Lord De L'Isle and Dudley preserved at Penshurst Place*, London 1925–66, i. 344–8; 'Rights and jurisdiction', 24; Roberts, 'Wales and England after the Tudor "union" ', 118. For *Allen* v. *Leigh* see Browne, 'Throckmorton', 66–7.

was no inevitable and general rush to judicial centralisation is suggested by the increasing autonomy of Ireland and Calais and by the Cheshire palatinate's victories elsewhere. The Council in the Marches of Wales found itself excluded from the palatinate, and the courts of the city of Chester failed to undermine the palatinate's courts.

6

Parliament and Legislation

In the fifteenth century Cheshiremen did not consider themselves bound by parliaments outside their territory, as their petitions showed. Yet the English parliament could potentially have a powerful influence on Cheshire. This chapter will demonstrate the initial respect shown by the English parliament for the palatinate's privileges and the limited interest expressed by Cheshiremen in the English parliament. It will then examine the way in which English statutes began to affect the county in the 1530s. This interference was not determined by a considered understanding of local circumstances and needs, nor by local demand, but by the general – and sometimes careless – application of theory. This produced local determination to become involved with the English parliament, largely to prevent further damaging interference. This was done with some success: the legislation in question was in any case never designed to obliterate the Cheshire palatinate.

Before the Acts of Union

The English parliament in the fourteenth and fifteenth centuries had shown remarkable respect for the liberties of Cheshire.[1] For example, an act of 1429 against malicious indictments or appeals of persons in one county who were dwelling in another had attempted a remedy by offering treble damages to those who successfully prosecuted such offences. This was specifically not to apply to indictments or appeals taken within Cheshire.[2] The autonomy of Cheshire was preserved, but the problem of proceedings against a defendant in a county 'in which the said Lieges be not, nor at any time were, conversant nor dwelling' was unhelpfully treated as a problem of criminal intent, not

---

[1]   A 1399 statute stipulated that when certificate of outlawry or exigent in another county was made to the officers of the county palatine the lands and goods of the offender were to be forfeit both in Cheshire and the rest of England. In 1421 the act was continued (while emphasising Lancashire's exclusion from its penalties), but only until Henry V's return from France, which never occurred. The act then lapsed: 1 Henry IV, c.18; 9 Henry V, c.2 (SR ii. 118–19, 204). This was a reaction to the special treatment of Cheshire by Richard II when the deposed king's supporters still represented a military and political threat: Morgan, *War and society*, 185–218; Peter McNiven, 'The Cheshire rising of 1400', *BJRL* lii (1970), 375–96, and 'The men of Cheshire and the rebellion of 1403', *THSLC* cxxix (1980), 1–29. The 1483 Statute of Apparel, 22 Edward IV, c.1, extended to Cheshire, but forfeitures were to go to the prince of Wales as earl of Chester: SR ii. 468–70 at p. 469.
[2]   8 Henry VI, c.10 (SR ii. 246–8).

administrative confusion in an increasingly complex society.[3] The exclusion of the king's writ was still being insisted upon in the early part of Henry VIII's reign when, more constructively, an act provided that notice of such proceedings should be given in any county where a defendant might reasonably be expected to be living, even if this was not the place mentioned in the proceedings. This only applied to places where the king's writ ran, however: in counties like Cheshire where it did not, the proclamation in any action where process of outlawry lay was to be directed to the sheriff of a neighbouring county.[4] Cheshiremen argued confidently about this exemption from statute. As late as the 1520s it was still possible to claim that a statute relating to the liabilities of masters and apprentices did not apply in Chester 'in as moche as the sayd Cytie lies nott within the boundes of the parlement of the realme of Englond by cawse they haue noo knyghts of the shire ner citezens at eny parlement'.[5]

This respect for the palatinate's privileges, and local confidence that it would continue, made it unlikely that Cheshiremen would seek involvement in the English parliament, at least for localist pragmatic reasons. Although there were no seats available in Cheshire, those men who represented the county's community in important negotiations might have sought election elsewhere. Two such groups can be examined to see whether they did: the men who petitioned in 1450 for Cheshire's exemption from English taxation, and those who negotiated the grant of the mise in 1497. In 1450 the list was headed by three ecclesiastics, John Saughall, abbot of Chester, Thomas Kirkham, abbot of Vale Royal, and Richard Norman, prior of Birkenhead, yet no Cheshire abbot or prior was among those regularly summoned to parliament after 1300. After the ecclesiastics appeared Edmund, Lord Grey, and John, Lord Dudley, who could sit in the Lords. Then followed thirty-three other names, mostly members of the Cheshire gentry.[6] Where these men had

---

[3] When in 1468 parliament confirmed existing laws against liveries (extended to cover Cheshire in 1429) it stated that no exigent should be awarded 'by any of the Justices for the Time being, within the said Counties Palatine' of Lancashire and Cheshire: 8 Henry VI, c.4; 8 Edward IV, c.2 (SR ii. 240–1, 426–9).

[4] 6 Henry VIII, c.4, confirming and extending 4 Henry VIII, c.4 (SR iii. 50–1, 126–7).

[5] PRO, C 1/516/23. The agreement between Robert Goodman, merchant adventurer of Chester, who made the claim, and William and Richard Eggerley, on behalf of the apprentice Richard Bekensall, was dated 15 July 1521. The statute is almost certainly the Statute of Apprentices upon which the Commons petitioned Edward IV in 1472–3: RP vi. 8. The word 'lies' is a doubtful reading thanks to damage to the document.

[6] Thomas Stanley, Andrew Ogard, John Mainwaring, John Troutbeck, William Stanley, Thomas Daniell, John Done, Hugh Calveley, Randal Brereton, Richard Cholmondeley, Ranlyn Grosvenor, John of Eggerton, Thomas Beston, Thomas Manley, Ralph Gamull, Thomas Poole, John Dutton of Hatton, William Whitmore, William Holford, Richard Bunbury, Thomas Venables, William Mainwaring, Richard Swinnerton, Richard Spurstowe, Richard Clive, Henry Ravenscroft, Thomas Hough and Jenkyn of Bebyngton subscribed. Those who were to present the petition were to be John Mainwaring (who had appeared as a subscriber), Ranlyn of Eggerton, Robert Legh of Adlington, John Davenport

major interests outside Cheshire, these interests led them to find places in the Commons. Sir Thomas Stanley of Lathom and Knowsley, created first Lord Stanley in 1456 and essentially a Lancashire landowner with Cheshire links, was an experienced parliamentarian, serving as knight of the shire for Lancashire on nine occasions.[7] Sir Andrew Ogard had had a prominent career in France; after returning to England, he shifted his allegiance from the duke of York to Queen Margaret of Anjou. His land-holdings were centred in Hertfordshire and Norfolk; his link with Cheshire was through his marriage to Alice, daughter of Sir Hugh Cokesey, holder of a share in the barony of Malpas.[8] Sir John Needham of Shavington (Shropshire) was at this time deputy justice of Chester and was common sergeant of London in 1449; he was subsequently chief justice of Lancaster, justice of Chester (1461–3) and a justice of assize. Needham remained a Cheshire man at heart: when he died on 25 April 1480 he was buried at Holmes Chapel.[9] Needham had been elected for the duchy of Lancaster borough of Newcastle-under-Lyme in 1442, 1447 and 1449, and served for London in 1449–50; as a judge he was summoned to subsequent parliaments up to 1477.[10] John Troutbeck (d. 1458) of Oxhey, Hertfordshire and Frodsham, Cheshire, the son of William Trout-beck, chancellor of Lancaster, was chamberlain of Chester (1437–57). He was also king's remembrancer of the exchequer from 1447 to 1450, and this and his Oxhey lands meant he could serve as knight of the shire for Hertford-shire in 1442 and 1447, and burgess for Hindon in 1449 and for Weymouth in 1450–1.[11] Thomas Daniell of Frodsham was another Cheshireman who had made good elsewhere. One of the most notorious Lancastrian partisans, he was granted the reversion of the office of chamberlain of Chester in 1445 (in opposition to John Troutbeck), and was king's remembrancer of the exchequer with Troutbeck from 1447 to 1450 and a squire of the body in 1449. This allowed him to achieve a dominant position in Norfolk, where he married Margaret, sister of John Howard, future duke of Norfolk.[12] Daniell sought far and wide – and successfully – for parliamentary seats.[13] The rest of

and John Needham. In the event Robert Fouleshurst took John Davenport's place at the presentation.

[7] In 1427, 1433, 1439–40, 1442, 1447, 1449, 1449–50, 1450–1 and 1455: Josiah C. Wedgewood, *History of parliament: biographies of members of the Commons House, 1439–1509*, London 1936, 800.

[8] Griffiths, *Henry VI*, 262, 273–4, 670; Clayton, *Administration*, 64 n. 11.

[9] Needham was the third son of Robert Needham by Dorothy, daughter of Sir John Savage of Clifton, and he married Margaret, youngest daughter of Randal Mainwaring of Peover and widow of William Bromley of Baddington: Wedgewood, *Biographies*, 624; Clayton, *Administration*, 156–9.

[10] Wedgwood, *Biographies*, 624.

[11] Clayton, *Administration*, 163–4; Wedgewood, *Biographies*, 877.

[12] Wedgewood, *Biographies*, 253–5; Clayton, *Administration*, 165; Griffiths, *Henry VI*, 309, 326, 329, 336–8, 363–5, 369, 428 ('one of the most influential of all the household servants'), 585, 606, 612–13 ('infamous'), 627, 639–41, 651, 683, 706, 824.

[13] In Cornwall in 1445–6; Buckinghamshire and Bedwyn in 1447; Buckinghamshire again

the men representing the county in 1450 were gentry with almost exclusively Cheshire interests. Significantly, none served in parliament.

The group of Cheshire gentry who represented the county in the negotiations over the 1497 mise was more Cheshire-centred than that active in 1450.[14] Their role was to negotiate with the prince's council locally, and therefore there were none among their number of the type of man with extra-county interests called in to help defend Cheshire's privileges at court in 1450. Cheshire used semi-outsiders when it was faced with negotiations at a national level, men conversant with the life of parliament and court. On internal questions its natural representatives had few such ties. The 1497 group, unsurprisingly, does not include anyone with any parliamentary experience either before or after the occasion.

Of course, some people with Cheshire links did sit in parliament before 1543. Yet the members of the Commons for the period 1439–1509, a sample of about 2,600 individuals, include less than fifty with even the most tenuous Cheshire links.[15] Examples include men who had Cheshire ancestry but who had migrated away from the county; men with marriage connections to the shire; men who held office there; Cheshire landowners with significant land-holding elsewhere; and some Cheshiremen who had careers in the service of king or greater nobility. In some cases these links are so tenuous as to make them irrelevant. Thus Sir John Melton (1407–74) of Aston and Kilham in Yorkshire married Cicely, the daughter of Randal Mainwaring of Peover and widow first of Thomas Fouleshurst of Crewe and then of John Curson. He had, apparently, no other Cheshire links.[16] More relevant are those Cheshiremen who made careers that led them to seats in parliament, and they number, at most, fourteen, remarkably few considering the prowess of Cheshiremen when it came to prospering in the royal household and pursuing careers in general. The clearest examples of Cheshire gentry involvement are those of families with landed positions in shires outside Cheshire that made them natural candidates for seats: Sir John Delves of Doddington, Sir Piers Legh of Lyme and Sir John Savage, Jr, of Clifton (d.

---

in 1449; ?Middlesex in 1453–4; Cricklade in 1455–6; ?Buckinghamshire yet again 1459: Wedgwood, *Biographies*, 253.

14 William Troutbeck, William Stanley of Hooton, Thomas Poole, John Done, John Warren, Sir George Holford, William Brereton, Peter Dutton of Hatton, William Bothe, John Mainwaring, Thomas Legh of Adlington, Ralph Delves, Hugh Calveley, William Honford, Robert Duckinfield and Lawrence Dutton, Sr: PRO, CHES 2/167, m. 5v (37 *DKR*, 694).

15 It is unfortunately necessary to use Wedgwood's *Biographies*, notorious for inaccuracies, but the overall picture is, I think, not affected.

16 Ibid. 583–4. The Cheshire ancestry of David Malpas (d. 1497) is dubious and for our purposes irrelevant – he was domiciled at Pickworth (Rutland) and served for Stamford in 1489–90: ibid. 568–9. Cf. William Browning of Melbury Sampford (Dorset, 1439–40, 1450–1, 1455–6), younger son of John Browning who left Nantwich for Leigh (Glos.); William's ties were almost exclusively in the West Country: ibid. 125.

1527).[17] The sons of peers with Cheshire interests, such as Sir Edmund Dudley,[18] occasionally made appearances in the House of Commons, but, as already demonstrated, the peerage was losing its influence in late fifteenth- and early sixteenth-century Cheshire.[19] An excellent example of a Cheshire careerist MP is John Stanley of Battersea. John, the son of Sir William Stanley of Hooton, was captain of Caernarvon (1427–60) and serjeant of the armoury (1431–60). He was usher of the Chamber from 1440 to 1455 and, when the royal household was 'reformed' in 1454, John was one of twelve squires in attendance. John sat for Surrey in 1445–6 and 1447, and Battersea was the adopted home where he decided to be buried, but he served in the household alongside his father and Cheshire ties are likely to have remained strong.[20] On the other hand, there are cases like that of Robert Booth, of Gray's Inn and Stratton, Bedfordshire, Doctor of Laws, who was possibly the brother of Sir Robert Booth of Dunham Massey. He served for Cricklade in 1455–6 and for Westbury in 1459 and was chiefly concerned with Bedford- shire and Buckinghamshire: it is to be doubted whether Cheshire meant much to him.[21]

If it is true that under Henry VII and Wolsey Cheshiremen took a greater part in the national political scene, they barely raised their parliamentary profile after 1509.[22] Men who had made good outside the shire still sought parliamentary careers: Henry Broke of Wrinehill (Staffordshire), son of Thomas Broke of Leighton in Cheshire, married the widow of John Egerton of Wrinehill, served the Audley and Dudley families and sat for Newcastle- under-Lyme in 1542 and 1545.[23] Nicholas Hurleton followed his father and grandfather in the post of surveyor of works in Cheshire and Flintshire. His main interest was his household career: he was Clerk of the Spicery by 1515, and Clerk of the Green Cloth by 1523. He spent his working life in London,

---

17 Ibid. 267 (Delves, Staffs., 1467–8, ?1470–1), 533 (Legh, Lancashire, 1491–2, 1495), 742 (Savage, Staffs., 1491–2).
18 Ibid. 285: MP Staffs., 1472–5.
19 See pp. 17–23 above.
20 Wedgwood, *Biographies*, 797–9; Ralph A. Griffiths, 'Richard of York and the royal house- hold in Wales, 1449–1450', *WHR* viii (1976), 230; *Bodleian Library MS Fairfax 16*, intro. John Norton-Smith, London 1979, esp. p. xiii (commissioned by Stanley).
21 Wedgwood, *Biographies*, 93. The significant thing is that this is a very small group. This is even clearer when it is considered that the total of 50 includes MPs like Thomas de la Pille, coroner of the Marshalsea (Ludgershall, 1442), John a Downe (Guildford, 1449–50) and Richard a Downe (Bodmin, 1497), to whom a Cheshire origin is attributed mainly because of the great number of Cheshiremen in the household: ibid. 685, 278, 279. Wedgwood's logic leads to a circularity of argument when he claims (of de la Pille) 'it may be that this man like so many other royal servants came from the Palatinate' (p. 685). See also Bennett, 'Community, class and careerism', 19–39, and 'Sources and problems in the study of social mobility: Cheshire in the later Middle Ages', *THSLC* cxxviii (1979), 59–95.
22 Evidence from the more reliable Bindoff, *House of Commons, 1509–1558*, considering those men with Cheshire links who sat in the Commons before 1545.
23 Ibid. i. 501–2. His allegations led to investigation of coining at Norton abbey: *LP* ix. 183. See pp. 207–8 below.

and his first marriage brought him property in East Anglia. When he sat for Rochester in 1529, it was probably through the influence of the comptroller of the household, Sir Henry Guildford.[24] Gentry from other shires who had married into Cheshire gentry families naturally sat for their own counties, as did John Corbet of Leigh in Shropshire, who married the daughter of William Booth of Dunham.[25] Men from other shires holding offices that brought them into contact with Cheshire also continued to sit in parliament, and the growing role of the Council in the Marches of Wales increased their number and prominence. Sir Thomas Englefield, Charles and Edmund Foxe, Nicholas Hare and Thomas Holte are good examples.[26] Cheshire gentlemen, however, remained very infrequent parliamentarians.

Even those who represented other places before they became knights of the shire for Cheshire in the early years of enfranchisement, 1543–60, had not started their careers before 1543. Sir Richard Cotton, Sir Thomas Holcroft and Richard Wilbraham had served before they were elected for Cheshire. Cotton, who sat for Cheshire in November 1554, had represented Hampshire in March 1553. He only achieved a significant position in Cheshire with the grant of extensive lands of the dean and chapter of Chester on 14 May 1553.[27] Sir Thomas Holcroft was the son of John Holcroft of Holcroft in Lancashire and sat for that shire in 1545. In 1544 he received the Cheshire monastery of Vale Royal and was returned for Cheshire in March 1553, perhaps due to the influence of duchy of Lancaster contacts like William Cecil.[28] Richard Wilbraham was the second son of William Wilbraham and, although he did eventually succeed to the family estates on the death of his brother in 1558, he was chiefly notable for his service to Mary Tudor. He was Clerk of the Kitchen and of the Spicery in her household in 1525, Clerk Comptroller by 1533 and a gentleman usher in 1536. He was well rewarded when Mary became queen: he sat in the October 1553 parliament for Tavistock, a borough in the patronage of the earl of Bedford who was probably influenced by the queen or Sir Robert Rochester, comptroller of the household. Wilbraham sat again for Cheshire in both the parliaments of 1554 and that of 1555. He was a successful careerist who had a small landed stake in the county but who could not expect the Cheshire inheritance of an eldest son.[29] Cotton and Holcroft were unsurprising carpet-baggers, prominent individuals who arrived in Cheshire late in their careers, having previously represented other shires where they had a substantial landed position. It is possible that the presence in Cheshire of men with parliamentary experience

[24] Bindoff, *House of Commons, 1509–1558*, ii. 418–19.
[25] Ibid. i. 697–8.
[26] Ibid. ii. 103–4, 168–9, 296–7, 381–2.
[27] Cotton's loyalties remained in Warblington (Hants.) where he was buried in 1556: ibid. i. 711–12.
[28] MP for Cheshire, October 1553; for Arundel, April 1554: ibid. ii. 373–5.
[29] Ibid. iii. 614–15; David Loades, *Mary Tudor: a life*, paperback edn, Oxford 1992, 138–9, 141, 191, 336.

and the expectation of a future at Westminster eased the process of enfranchisement for the county by providing potential candidates; since they were not the first to be elected, however, it is unlikely that their arrival in itself resulted in the enfranchisement. The introversion of the community of those who represented Cheshire is underlined by the fact that of these Cheshire members, only Holcroft subsequently sat outside the county.[30]

Our first explicit indication of any interest on the part of Cheshire people in sitting in parliament is therefore the petition that prefaces the act of 1543. Cheshire gentlemen were on the whole only interested in attending parliament as representatives of their own community, once it had been enfranchised. They had not considered it necessary or worthwhile to represent either their county's or their own interests by taking seats outside Cheshire. Parliamentary service was only relevant to them when it was representation explicitly of their shire, and part of the honourable role of the Cheshire gentleman.[31]

Legislation affecting the county palatine, 1530–43

A major reason for the sudden interest in parliament expressed in 1543 lies in the legislative activity of the English parliament over the previous decade: after centuries of non-interference, in the 1530s legislation impinged significantly on Cheshire. It is striking that this interference did not come in the two most prominent areas of Tudor policy in the 1530s. Although legislation relating to religious jurisdiction and doctrine did affect Cheshire, even here there was a sensitivity towards the county's special status. The Mortuaries Act of 1529, for example, included a proviso protecting customary practices in Wales and Cheshire.[32] Neither was there a programme of legislation to deal piecemeal with the apparent causes of disorder, as there was for Wales in the early 1530s.[33] Instead, the incentive for change was largely fiscal. The introduction of Westminster parliamentary taxation in 1534 has already been noted. The other significant interference in Cheshire's privileges during the early 1530s concerned customs, especially those on leather. Leather trades were almost Chester's staple industry: only Northampton surpassed Chester in the importance of leather to a town's economy.[34] The Reformation Parlia-

---

[30] Sir Lawrence Smith also sat for Chester city, where he was mayor: Bindoff, *House of Commons, 1509–1558*, iii. 334–5.

[31] Cf. A. D. K. Hawkyard, 'The enfranchisement of constituencies, 1509–1558', *Parliamentary History* x/1 (1991), 1–26.

[32] 21 Henry VIII, c.6 (SR iii. 288–9).

[33] See pp. 129–30 below.

[34] Leather craftsmen consistently represented 21–4% of admissions to freedom in the years 1540–1662, when in other towns they averaged 8–10% of the labour force: Johnson, 'Aspects of the history of Chester', 22–7; D. M. Woodward, 'The Chester leather industry, 1558–1625', *THSLC* cxix (1968 [1967]), 65–111.

ment produced two acts concerning leather, in 1533 and 1536.[35] When the
first, introducing charges for inspection of the product, was applied in
Chester, Mayor Henry Gee wrote to Cromwell stating that the act had not
been sent to or proclaimed in Cheshire, 'whiche is a Countie palantyne', and
that such statutes had never been enforced there. Gee was willing to put the
act into effect temporarily, but he expected the king to accept the city's
claims 'opon knowlage . . . of our liberties & ffraunchesses'.[36] If the act of
1533 was accepted by the people of Cheshire, it was only on the understanding that Cheshire's liberties would later be vindicated. Yet the following
year saw the introduction of English taxation, and further encroachments
occurred in the 1536 Leather Act, which specifically targeted Cheshire. It
noted that much leather was being exported, 'and in specially out of Wales,
Cheshire and Cornwall, where little or no Custom is paid for same'. A
particular concern was the practice of foreign merchants packing the leather
themselves, which meant that it was impossible to count it. Offical packers
existed to safeguard against this in London and Southampton, but 'not in any
other Ports of this Realm, and specially in Wales, Cheshire and Cornwal', an
omission which, allegedly, produced a high level of exports, dearth and high
prices. London customs rates were to apply in 'any Part of this Realm, Wales,
Cheshire, or other the King's Dominions'.[37] Again there was resistance:
Ralph Waryne, recorder of Chester, wrote to Cromwell supporting a move to
have a confirmation of liberties by the king, in which the mediation of the
duke of Norfolk and Mr Treasurer [Fitzwilliam] was being used.[38] Although
Chester merchants again hoped for success,[39] the lobbying was unsuccessful.
A pardon for various Chester merchants was issued on 24 February 1539,[40]
but further leather exports were being investigated in January 1540,[41] and a

---

35 24 Henry VIII, c.1 (SR iii. 417–19); 27 Henry VIII, c.14 (SR iii. 546–7); VCH, County of Chester, ii. 33.
36 To be communicated by alderman Hugh Aldersey and counsel William Glaseor: PRO, SP 1/76, fos 184–5 (LP vi. 599). It appears that Cromwell wished to antedate the effect of leather legislation to the eighth year of Henry's reign, but it is not clear why this date was chosen: it may be suggested that the minister saw the 1515 Act of Resumption as a point after which Chester privileges were open to attack, or that something connected with the mise of 1517 provided the excuse. The writ for the proclamation in Cheshire of statutes and ordinances passed by parliament, dated Chester 22 May 1534, should be noted: BL, MS Harleian 2046, fo. 31v (LP vii. 700).
37 Customers and comptrollers were to appoint tellers to assess leather exports where no such officials existed, and they were to charge 6d. a dicker from strangers, with 2d. going to the officer and 4d. to the town. Denizens were to pay 4d., freemen of the port just 2d.
38 The mayor, aldermen and citizens petitioned the president of the Council in the Marches that the new custom would lead to the 'Ruyne and destruccon' of the city: PRO, SP 1/142, p. 184 (LP xiv/1, 175); SP 1/113, fos 144v–5 (LP xi. 1453).
39 Two Chester merchants told John Wyate in Bristol that they were free from customs, that Cromwell had their privileges and that the statute was not executed: LP xii/2, 758 (Wyate to Cromwell, 27 Sept. 1537).
40 LP xiv/1, 175, 403(63).
41 PRO, E 314/42/7.

proclamation of 16 February 1541, read in Chester on 2 April, reaffirmed prohibitions on wheat and other products including leather. There then followed a series of attempts by John Massey, the searcher of Chester, to confiscate the goods and ships of merchants breaking the ban.[42]

Massey's activities indicate that some Cheshiremen were willing to aid in the enforcement of what to others were alien statutes. Local men were, however, less important than outsiders in stimulating Cromwell's concern that Chester's privileges were undermining crown revenues. In an undated report, Richard Cowper, a London grocer, claimed that much tanned leather, unmarked, was about to be shipped out of Chester, and that Randal Brereton, the vice-chamberlain, kept a tan house and used a *corpus cum causa* to remove tanners from the custody of the mayor of Chester.[43] Early in 1533 Cowper had brought a quantity of wine to Chester to be retailed at 8*d.* per gallon. The vintners of the city were 'grettely dyspleased and myscontentyd' as they sold the same varieties of wine for a 1*s.* a gallon.[44] Cowper complained to Mayor Henry Gee that William Davyson, William Goodman, Hugh and Robert Aldersey and David Middleton, ex-mayors of the city, all owned taverns and sold wine at 1*s.* a gallon. Cowper attempted to sell his wine, but the 'orthwarde mynde of som persons that agaynst the comyn welthe procuryd myn hynderaunce' resulted in him being unable to sell most of his stock. Cowper stressed the liberties of London and threatened to go to the council if he was not treated properly.[45] The response of Cowper's opponents was to encourage William Lowe to press a false charge of trespass before the sheriffs for an assault on his wife Anne. Cowper was forced to attend court every day, a ruinous burden for a merchant such as him.[46] Given that Cowper was certainly acquainted with Cromwell from at least 1529,[47] his determination to break into the trade of Chester almost certainly helped to bring the implications of Cheshire's privileges to Cromwell's attention; the initiative to challenge them in the 1530s was essentially concerned with the financial needs of the crown and orchestrated from the centre.[48]

---

[42] A large group of separate individuals suffered in February 1542: PRO, STAC 2/28/24. Three others, headed by William Goodman, were prosecuted for an offence on 19 July 1542 (STAC 2/28/1) and several more merchants, including Robert Cotton, William Davidson and William Bennett, were prosecuted for illegal export on 20 July 1542 (STAC 2/24/310: the bill explicitly refers to the 1533 act and the proclamation of 16 February 1541). A proclamation against the illegal export of leather (among other things) was issued on 14 October 1538: *Tudor royal proclamations*, I: *The early Tudors (1485–1553)*, ed. Paul L. Hughes and James F. Larkin, New Haven–London 1964, 268–9 (no. 184).

[43] *LP* vi. 1607. Cowper also alleged that William Sneyd was taking fees from both parties.

[44] PRO, C 1/767/9.

[45] BL, MS Harleian 2091, fos 205–6, 211v–12 (*LP* vi. 202).

[46] PRO, C 1/767/9. Mainwaring and Hanky were sheriffs 1533–4.

[47] *LP* iv/3, 5330; v. 1285(iii); x. 1171.

[48] Economic ties on this occasion may have helped stimulate jurisdictional unification, as argued by Steven Gunn, 'State development in England and the Burgundian dominions, *c.* 1460–*c.* 1560', in *L'Angleterre et les pays bourguignons: relations et comparaisons (XVe–XVIe*

It was not only statutes relating to leather that began to be enforced in the county. In the late fifteenth century, the court at Chester dealt almost exclusively with offences of felony, riot and trespass that were confined to crimes regarding taking small objects or stock, or illegally occupying land and taking from it wood, crops or grass, or various forms of assault. The exceptions were two isolated examples of offences against the statutes on retaining,[49] and more frequent indictments under the statute of 1429–30 regarding entry and forcible holding of land.[50] By the 1530s this had changed: new acts either specifically referred to Cheshire or (more frequently) were proclaimed there for the first time. The statute of 1540 against maintenance and embracery in suits in chancery, Star Chamber, etc., resulted in a prosecution in the Chester courts as early as Easter 1543: William Bromley of Norbury, gentleman, had been indicted before Thomas Venables and John Massey, JPs, on 28 August 1542 for maintaining one Richard Hexteley in a suit.[51] Urian Roo, bailif of Nantwich hundred, was indicted during the county court session of 2 July 1538 for having permitted illegal games to be played in contravention not of a statute but of the king's proclamation, which had been made 'in omnibus villatibus infra comitatis Cestriae'.[52]

All of this legislation had obviously been made without any involvement of Cheshire's representatives. Much of it demonstrated not just disregard for the interests of Cheshire but extreme ignorance of local implications. As a result there was a series of mistakes.[53] Most significantly, the Welsh 'Union' legislation of the period, while it may have responded to the particular needs of, and demands, from Wales, had a confused and unfortunate impact in Cheshire. It was based on the substitution of county administration for

---

s.), Neuchatel 1995, 133–49; I am grateful to Steve Gunn for a copy of this paper. It should be noted, however, that this jurisdictional unification tended to encompass primarily issues related to trade and fiscal matters and not necessarily others; and that on other occasions an overzealous attempt to challenge local economic particularism might be greeted with hostility from the Privy Council: *APC* i. 184 (7 June 1545); cf. i. 499 (29 July 1546).

49 PRO, CHES 25/17, rot. 5: Piers Dutton retained William Ryder on 13 March 1495 at Waverton, for which he was indicted on 6 September 1496; rot. 5v: Sir John Done retained Richard Wright and eight others at Utkinton on 27 September 1496, for which he was indicted on 15 November 1496.

50 PRO, CHES 25/16, rots 3r–v, 4v, 12, 14, 15, 15v (2), 19v, 25v. For the statute, 8 Henry VI, c. 9, see John G. Bellamy, *Bastard feudalism and the law*, London 1989, 16, 22–3, 50, 127. There were also indictments under the statute of 8 Richard II regarding entries: CHES 25/16, rots 4, 19.

51 PRO, CHES 29/247, rot. 16v; 32 Henry VIII, c. 9 (SR iii. 753–4).

52 PRO, CHES 24/89(1); *Tudor royal proclamations*, i. 266–8 (no. 183, 13 Sept. 1538). Two men were alleged to have paid to be allowed to play at 'scalas & bollas & alias illicitas ludas'.

53 For example, the bishopric of Chester spent a short time in the province of Canterbury before finding its (sensible) place under York: 33 Henry VIII, c.31 (SR iii. 870–1). Note the interruption to local structures occasioned by the dissolution of Vale Royal abbey, remedied in 1542 by an act which created the parish of Whitegate: 33 Henry VIII, c.13 (SR iii. 849). These two bills were linked when they were brought from Commons to Lords on 9 March: *LJ* i. 174–7, 183–4, 187–8.

marcher lordships in the context of a revived and expanded territory of Wales, a vision which was never fully accomplished and even in its fullest form never properly accommodated Cheshire.[54]

Welsh legislation, 1534–36

The first Cromwellian campaign of legislation directed at Wales affected Cheshire only incidentally. The first statute was aimed at preventing the victimisation of jurors in marcher courts: the Council in the Marches was given a key role in dealing with misbehaving officers and recalcitrant jurors.[55] The greatest impact of this first wave of legislation on Chester was seen in the introduction of JPs to the existing Welsh shires: this included the lordships of Pembroke and Glamorgan and the palatinate of Chester. It was stated that 'common justice' had not been 'indifferently ministered' as in other places in the realm, and justices were appointed to counter this.[56] The 1536 'first Act of Union' was, however, scrupulous in its refusal to interfere with Cheshire.[57] The marcher lordships were divided into shires. New exchequers and chanceries were set up for the new shires, but the arrangements for north-east Wales did not assume any role for Cheshire: those for Denbighshire and Montgomeryshire were sited at Denbigh.[58] The county was also ignored in the introduction of parliamentary representation for the Welsh shires.

---

[54] Roberts, ' "Acts of union" and the Tudor settlement of Wales', 21–179; ' "A breviat of the effectes devised for Wales", c. 1540–41', ed. P. R. Roberts, in *Camden Miscellany*, XXVI (Camden 4th ser. xiv, 1975), 31–47. This is rather less than the full unification and centralisation believed by Brendan Bradshaw to be the agenda: *Irish constitutional revolution*, esp. pp. 139–46.

[55] 26 Henry VIII, c.4 (SR iii. 499). The supervision of Severn ferrymen, because of felons crossing to the marches or Forest of Dean, was entrusted to JPs in Gloucestershire and Somerset: 26 Henry VIII, c.5 (SR iii. 500). The so-called Statute for Councils in Wales (1534: 26 Henry VIII, c.6 [SR iii. 500–3]) ordered all those summoned to court to honour their obligations, and an end to forced exactions, the committing of people to prison for inadequate reason, the carrying of arms near courts, towns, churches, fairs or markets, the *cymorth* or tenants' ale (mutual aid given within communities, now abused by lords), redemption for murder, and the practice of advowry (*arddel*) by which felons placed themselves under the protection of marcher lords. This provision might have affected the Cheshire advowry-men, but the need for further legislation in 1543 suggests it did not: Rowland Lee and Sir Thomas Englefield asked Cromwell to remember the 'avowrye men of Cheshire' in a letter of 20 February 1536: *LP* x. 330. One went to chancery sometime between 1538 and 1544 to defend his position: PRO, C 1/993/21.

[56] 27 Henry VIII, c.5 (SR iii. 534–5). Fines were to be accounted for by the sheriff to the local exchequers, confirming the role of the Chester exchequer for Chester and Flint. The justices were to be appointed by the lord chancellor or keeper of the privy seal. Caernarfon served the shires of north Wales, Carmarthen the two shires of west Wales, and Pembroke and Cardiff Pembrokeshire and Glamorgan respectively. The £20 *per annum* wealth qualification was waived because of the poverty of the Welsh gentry.

[57] 27 Henry VIII, c.26 (SR iii. 563–9).

[58] Similar institutions were set up at Brecknock for Radnor and Brecknock.

Neither was the instruction that English was to be the language of justice relevant to Cheshire. Earlier legislation had virtually ignored Cheshire while treating it as just another Welsh lordship; the first 'Act of Union' was concerned with Wales and the marcher lordships to the exclusion of Cheshire.

This campaign of Welsh legislation left many questions open, not least concerning Cheshire.[59] Progress towards further settlement was slow. In summer 1540 grants of certain offices for terms of lives were discontinued with the intention of reappointing sheriffs on an annual basis, but this was a measure which had been effective in Cheshire for some years.[60] 28 June 1541 saw the appointment of four justices, one to serve in each of the four judicial circuits to be set up in Wales; by the same year JPs had been appointed. It still seems that Cheshire had not been fully incorporated in a systematic plan however. Sir Nicholas Hare, now created justice in Denbighshire and Montgomeryshire, was already justice of the counties of Chester and Flint, yet this was not explicitly recognised in the new grant. The enrolment was simply endorsed that Hare was justice of Flint.[61] The possibilities being discussed in government circles ranged very widely: there was a proposal that a Welsh court of chancery should replace the Council in the Marches, and that a new, enlarged, principality might be created for Edward.[62]

In the event, the plan for a new principality was not carried through. The 'Act of Union' of 1543[63] placed the Council in the Marches on a vague statutory basis as a delegate of the Privy Council. Cheshire fitted uneasily into this scheme, and many of the county's problems were aggravated. While 'original' seals were created for each of the four groups of Welsh shires, the original seal of Chester 'shalbe and stande for the originall Seale of Flinte for Justice to be mynistred in the saide Shyre of Flinte, and shalbe and remaine in the chardge keaping and custodie of the Chambrelaine of Chestre'.[64] An original seal for Denbighshire and Montgomeryshire was held in Denbigh by the steward and chamberlain of Denbigh. In other spheres, Cheshire was more completely integrated into the arrangements for north-east Wales, if in a rather haphazard fashion. Courts of great sessions were set up, four circuits of three shires each. Each had one justice who was to hold sessions twice a year in each shire, and who had jurisdiction over all pleas in the same way as in

---

[59] The status of Welsh land law was to be examined by a commission after the passage of the act, and the crown was empowered to suspend or repeal the whole act within three years, a right which was reserved for a further three years in 1539. Dignitaries like Walter Devereux, Lord Ferrers and Henry, earl of Worcester (chief justices of Glamorgan and south Wales) continued in position and had their places safeguarded by the act.

[60] See pp. 153–4 below.

[61] *LP* xvi. 947(75). For Hare's appointment as justice of Chester and Flint, 14 Aug. 1540, see *39 DKR*, 143.

[62] ' "A breviat of the effectes devised for Wales" ', 31–47.

[63] 34 & 35 Henry VIII, c.26 (*SR* iii. 926–37).

[64] 34 & 35 Henry VIII, c.26 (*SR* iii. 927 [#7]).

Common Pleas and King's Bench. Cheshire was incorporated into this judicial scheme, since the twice-yearly sessions in Flintshire, Denbighshire and Montgomery were to be held by the justice of Chester.[65] In similar vein, there were to be four prothonotaries, one for each circuit, which in north-east Wales consisted of Flintshire, Denbighshire and Montgomery. So the justice of Chester, depending on which county he was in, presided over great sessions at which writs sealed with two different original seals ran. These inconsistencies are perhaps partly explicable in terms of the ability of Cheshire officials to resist any reduction in their powers during the county's absorption into the new principality: John Birkenhead, prothonotary of Cheshire and Flintshire, defended his position and thereby helped to keep Cheshire out of the clerical arrangements for north-east Wales.[66] They also tell, however, of the lack of system that lay behind the working out of the new arrangements for Wales and, especially, for Cheshire.

It was only in the introduction of JPs that the Welsh legislation of 1534–43 brought truly pronounced change to the political life of Cheshire.[67] Ironically, it caused chaos. A multiplicity of court sessions was produced by the addition of quarter sessions to the existing county court sessions and this imposed impossible strains of attendance on the gentlemen of the county. It was noted that their 'Appearance and Attendance cometh so oftentimes and so thick together, that at many Times they cannot depart from one Court and attend theie Business scarcely one Day, or sometimes less, but they must again ride to serve the other Court, which is too painful, chargeable, intolerable and importune for any Man to sustain and abide.' In 1540, therefore, shire days were reduced from eight or nine to just two.[68] Henceforth the shire court was to meet at Easter and Michaelmas alone, a change which took effect on 18 October 1540.[69] This caused further problems because without regular county court sessions there was no facility for plaints under 40s. and 'there was . . . never sithen the makinge of the saide acte anye exigende of felonye or

---

[65] 34 & 35 Henry VIII, c.26 (SR iii. 926 [#4]). There were therefore to be four 'judiciall Seales', one kept by the justice of Chester to be used in Flint, Denbigh and Montgomery: ibid. 928 (#14).

[66] 34 & 35 Henry VIII, c.26 (SR iii. 929 [#17]); List of the records of the palatinates of Chester, Durham and Lancaster (PRO, Lists and Indexes xl, 1914), pp. v–vi. The prothonotary of Chester, Flintshire, Denbighshire and Montgomeryshire was to be appointed under the great seal of England, but in the event this did not take place and the particular association of Cheshire and Flintshire continued: see p. 233 below. Other provisions of the 1543 act were irrelevant to Cheshire: sheriffs, JPs, coroners, escheators and high and petty constables were created for the new shires. Marcher lords retained jurisdiction only over pleas worth less that 40s., and no new lordships were to be created. Those inheriting land after 24 June 1541 were to obey English inheritance customs. Haverfordwest was given MPs.

[67] Westminster representation was brought to Cheshire by a separate act in 1543: 34 & 35 Henry VIII, c.13 (SR iii. 911).

[68] 32 Henry VIII, c.43 (SR iii. 796).

[69] PRO, CHES 29/242: soon after Nicholas Hare's arrival as justice, m. 1. The last old-style meeting occurred on 16 February 1540: CHES 29/241.

other cause proclaymed within the saide Countie, to the no little hindrance of Justice and to the great boldnes of Offendors'. Another new piece of legislation in 1541 was therefore necessary which instructed the sheriff to keep monthly courts for this purpose, explaining a little sheepishly what an informed government should have known all along, that 'it hath not bene used nor sene that the Sherieff of the same Countie hath kepte any Shire courte for determinacon of playntes and callinge the exigendes, as ys commonly used in other Shires of this Realme'.[70]

Cheshire's recognition of the need for representation

As legislation had an increasing and sometimes disturbing impact on the shire, it became clear to local men that parliamentary representation was needed. This can be examined in detail in the reaction of Chester to the transfer thence from Manchester of the location of one of the newly restricted locations of sanctuary, now towns of refuge, early in 1542, on the grounds that the former city was 'well inhabited having no suche trade of merchaundise [as Manchester's cloth trade] and hath a strong Jayle within the same Cytie for punyschement of Malefactours, and also there is in the same Cytie a Maire Baileffes and other hed Officers'. Chester believed that the new sanctuary would 'not only haue eiduced grete sclander and decaie of credaunce of the merchauntes and inhabytauntes of the same wyth mayny other intollerable inconuenyence which wer lyke to haue ensued to this citie being a port towne and standing so nygh Wales to the grete hinderaunce, daunger, and damage of the same'. Therefore Mayor Hugh Aldersey and Alderman Fulk Dutton, 'by the hole consent of thaldermen and common counsayle', 'rode to the kinges maieste to make sute for the reformacion of the same by whoes diligent labor and profute it pleased his grace vpon certen declarations declarid by them vnto his maieste to remoue the same sanctuary'.[71] The parliamentary session ended on 1 April but, on 30 May following,

---

[70] 33 Henry VIII, c.13 (SR iii. 849). The act also instituted the positions of two county coroners, to 'sytt withe the saide Sherieff at the saide Courtes to geve judgmentes upon outlaries and to do all other thinges as apperteyneth'. It also permitted discretion in the timing of the county sessions, in place of the previous insistence on Easter and Michaelmas. The working out of the implications of Cheshire's partial assimilation into the new Welsh administration continued slowly in some spheres. The chamberlain remained Cheshire's chief financial officer until the year Michaelmas 1548 to Michaelmas 1549; subsequent accounts bear more resemblance to those of Welsh counties than English, including, for example, sheriffs' and escheators' accounts: PRO, SC 6/Edward VI/62–3; *List of ministers' accounts: Edw. VI–18th C. and analogous documents* (PRO, Lists and Indexes, supplementary series ii, repr. New York 1967), 110.

[71] CCityRO, A/B/1, fo. 75 (10 July 1542, which inexplicably dates the journey to 22 June, after the proclamation); I. D. Thornley, 'The destruction of sanctuary', in R. W. Seton-Watson (ed.), *Tudor studies: presented to the Board of Studies in History in the University of London to Albert Frederick Pollard, being the work of twelve of his colleagues and pupils*, London

a royal proclamation declared that Chester was too conveniently placed for escape routes to Wales and overseas. The sanctuary was therefore shifted again, to Stafford.[72] The act itself suggests there had been a certain amount of belated lobbying on Chester's behalf: a proviso was added, annexed to the original act on a separate sheet, to the effect that if it appeared to the king, 'by informacon or otherwyse, that the seid Citie of Chester is not mete to be Seyntuarie nor for a place of priviylege & tuycon for the seyd Offendors & malefactors as ben above remembered, or for such lyke of their condicons', he could alter the act by proclamation.[73]

It is not surprising, therefore, that 1543 saw a fundamental change in Cheshire's relationship to the English parliament. The county and city were each granted the right to elect two members to the parliament in response to a petition. This petition represents an insight into the thinking of local people concerning the integration of their county into England, especially when viewed in the light of dissatisfaction at parliamentary interference. The key motivation behind the request was that through their absence from parliament

> the saide inhabytaunts have hitherto susteyned manifolde disherysons losses and damages . . . [and] have been often tymes touched and greaved with Actes and Statutes made within the saide Courte aswell [derogative] unto the moste auncient jurisdiccons liberties and privileges of your saide Countie [Palantyne], as prejudiciall unto the common wealthe quietnes rest and peace of your Graces moste bounden subjects inhabyting within the same[.][74]

This petition recognised that the absence of representation had damaged the county, causing 'manifolde disherysons losses and damages', but it was the impositions of parliament itself which had undermined the privileges of the shire and been 'prejudiciall unto the common wealthe quietnes rest and peace' of Cheshire people. Parliamentary representation was necessary less because of its positive benefits but in order to prevent negative outcomes, some of which were attributed to parliament itself. The petition was no willing surrender of provincial privilege; rather it sprang from a determination to defend privilege from within parliament.

1924, 203–4 (there were only eight such towns, and the privilege was effectively limited to cases of debt).

72 33 Henry VIII, c.15 (SR iii. 850–1); LP xvii. 357 (30 May 1542); *Tudor royal proclamations*, i. 311–13 (no. 212).

73 Similar lobbying has already been seen regarding the leather legislation of 1533 and 1536: see pp. 125–7 above.

74 34 & 35 Henry VIII, c.13 (SR iii. 911). The readings in brackets are from the original bills and acts, where these differ from those of the parliament roll.

Legislation in the 1540s and afterwards

Once Cheshire's MPs had arrived in the Commons, this defence of Cheshire's privileges faced no serious, considered or determined opposition. Acceptance of Cheshire's position was unquestioned in parliament. The 'Acts of Union' had presented the opportunity to render Cheshire, as they rendered Monmouth, just another English shire. Yet it was not so reduced. Cheshire's position as an uneasy element within a newly-fashioned autonomous entity co-extensive with the land of Wales cannot simply be accounted for by administrative inertia or the resistance of officials: there was clearly some conception of Cheshire's proper autonomy. An example of the effect of this respect for autonomy is to be seen in the act of 1543 for a certificate of convicts to be made to King's Bench, to prevent benefit of clergy being allowed too often because of lack of a record.[75] However much historians may worry about the effects of palatine jurisdiction on the ability of criminals to escape punishment, this act specifically did not apply to Wales, Durham, Lancashire and Cheshire. The timing of this legislation is significant. Having been sent to the House of Commons by the Lords on 21 April, the bill was brought to the Upper House on 30 April, the very same day as the bill for parliamentary representation for Cheshire, often taken as the culmination of the process of integration.[76]

Cheshire's privileges were defended, not abandoned, in subsequent legislation concerning the county, and that defensiveness was confident enough to achieve the successful reshaping of the palatinate. It seems that parliamentary representation for Cheshire first became a fact in 1545, and the opportunities it represented were fulfilled in the act of that year for the maintenance of Huntingdon Lane near Chester. This two-and-a-half-mile stretch was to be cared for by an appointee, selected by Sir William Stanley and Sir Hugh Calveley and their heirs male.[77] Calveley and Stanley were the heads of families based near to the lane, and Calveley was himself a knight of the shire in the parliament. The other knight, Sir Lawrence Smith, had strong connections with Chester, of which he had been mayor in 1540–1. Statutory backing was therefore gained for the solution of local problems by local men.[78] Further positive action of this kind was taken by the city, although with little effect. An act 'concerning the City of Chestre' for weirs in the river Dee was

---

[75] 34 & 35 Henry VIII, c.14 (SR iii. 912–13).

[76] LJ i. 227–8. Kitching has argued that contemporary changes in Durham were similarly limited: Bishop Tunstall 'nodded rather than bowed' to the storm that supposedly blew from Westminster: 'Durham palatinate and the courts of Westminster', 49–70.

[77] 37 Henry VIII, c.3 (SR iii. 987). See Sheaf, 1st ser. ii (1883), 3, no. 974; 3rd ser. xviii (1923), 65, no. 4384. In default, selection was to be made by the city of Chester.

[78] Bindoff, House of Commons, 1509–1558, i. 640; iii. 334. The bill was read in the Lords on 19 December; objections were recorded, for no clear reason, by the earl of Sussex and Lord Cromwell: LJ i. 278–9.

read in January 1550 and passed.[79] An abortive bill called the 'great Bill for the Liberties of Chester', which may have been connected with the grant of mise by Cheshire immediately previously in October 1547, was read in the Commons during November and December 1547.[80]

The vast bulk of the legislation in which Cheshire was involved was concerned with defining the county's liberties and saving them from encroachment. In 1547 an act concerning exigents and proclamations in Wales and Chester clarified Cheshire's privileged position in relationship to Westminster.[81] This, it was alleged in 1547, caused many people to be outlawed in ignorance. The solution was for the sheriff of Cheshire to have a deputy in the courts of King's Bench and Common Pleas, to whom process could be directed for proclamation locally. A clause of the act stipulated that this was not to be prejudicial to other 'Liberties, Franchises or Privileges' of the counties palatine of the county and city of Chester, of Wales, or of the lords marcher. There was a definite attempt to extend the measure to cover Cheshire, although the originators of the idea had not included the county in their plans. Amended to include the county palatine in its title, the bill was read and passed in the Lords on 22 December.[82] The only obvious reason that can be surmised for the success of the second bill as compared to the failure of the first is the addition of Cheshire to the measure – perhaps the expectation of the arrival of the new bill, proposed in the Commons by a Cheshire representative, led the Lords to reject the exclusively Welsh bill that they had already received. The same few days saw the reading of another bill, for fines and proclamations in the county of Chester. This enhanced the status of the actions of Cheshire courts and was proposed with local backing. Like the bill for exigents and proclamations in Wales, however, it failed and, although it was also reintroduced, it disappeared after 21 December.[83] The next parliament saw its successful return, prefaced by a petition from the inhabitants of

---

[79] LJ i. 381–5.

[80] CJ i. 1–4; cf. the city of Chester getting firm statutory backing for recognizances of Statute Merchant or Acton Burnel, which had recently been challenged by 'certain sinister Persons': 2 & 3 Edward VI, c.31 (SR iv. 73). It is slightly misleading to list, as the History of Parliament does, 5 & 6 Edward VI, c.6 (SR iv. 137), as an act concerning Cheshire; it contains a brief reference to Manchester, Lancashire and Cheshire 'cottons', among a huge variety of other textiles: Bindoff, House of Commons, 1509–1558, i. 44.

[81] 1 Edward VI, c.10 (SR iv. 15–16). Previously such legislation respected palatine privilege. See p. 119 above.

[82] The statute originated in a bill relating only to Wales, read in the Commons on 9 November and brought to the Lords on 20 December 1547, but not passed. A second bill, now including the county palatine in its title, had appeared in the Commons on 13 December: LJ i. 310–12; CJ i. 1–3. The earls of Derby and Arundel and Lord Powis objected. All three were marcher lords and probably determined to resist any entry of the king's writ into Wales and the marches. See the proviso for lords marcher attached on a separate schedule: SR iv. 16.

[83] LJ i. 310–12; CJ i. 1–3.

Cheshire.[84] They pointed out that the previous 'beneficial and necessary Statutes do not extend to any Fines to be levied within your said County Palatine of Chester' and therefore requested that all fines levied or acknowledged before the justice, concerning any lands in the county palatine, if they were openly read and proclaimed in the manner used in Common Pleas, were to have the same force as fines levied with proclamations before the Common Pleas.[85]

Provision for the proclamation of exigents in Wales and the county palatine of Chester, and for fines and proclamations there, should be seen in the context of legislation on similar matters in Cheshire and other privileged areas. The issue of exigents was not tackled in Lancashire until the 1552 parliament when a statute provided for proclamations and exigents to be current there.[86] It took even longer, until 1589, for Durham to be included.[87] Regularisation of the position concerning fines with proclamations in Cheshire and Wales did not cover the city of Chester, a county of itself since 1506. This was duly dealt with in 1601, when a statute noted the omission in the Edwardian statute and provided for the fines to be proclaimed in ten city portmotes.[88] Early in Elizabeth's reign, the same provision was made for Durham: although an attempt failed in 1559, by a statute of 1563 fines proclaimed at three sessions in the presence of justices of assize were to have equivalent validity to those proclaimed in Common Pleas.[89]

The enrolment of indentures of bargain and sale was dealt with for Cheshire, Lancashire and Durham in 1562–3.[90] Now enrolments there were to be as valid as those in Westminster. The same parliament extended another piece of judicial legislation to the three counties palatine, and to Wales, making provision to fill up juries *de circumstantibus*.[91] Royal rights to feudal incidents in the palatine counties were regularised and protected, again in just one act, in the statute concerning offices found in the counties palatine of 1576.[92] Transcripts were to be returned to the court of wards and liveries, as they were from petty bag in chancery. The counties palatine were again grouped together, this time with Wales too, in the act for reformation of errors in fines and recoveries in Wales, Haverfordwest and the counties pala-

---

[84] 2 & 3 Edward VI, c.28: SR iv. 71. The bill was brought to the Lords on 15 Jan.: *LJ* i. 331–2, 335, 343.

[85] It was to be proclaimed on three days in open court at the sessions at which it was engrossed, and proclaimed at the two subsequent sessions and on three days in either of the two sessions.

[86] 5 & 6 Edward VI, c.26 (*SR* iv. 158–9).

[87] 31 Elizabeth, c.9 (*SR* iv. 807–8).

[88] 43 Elizabeth, c.15 (*SR* iv. 982–3).

[89] Elton, *Parliament of England*, 286–7; 5 Elizabeth, c.27 (*SR* iv. 456).

[90] Elton, *Parliament of England*, 292; 5 Elizabeth, c.26 (*SR* iv. 456). The previous statute, 27 Henry VIII c.16 (*SR* iii. 549) did not cover them.

[91] 5 Elizabeth, c.25 (*SR* iv. 454–5). 35 Henry VIII, c.16 (*SR* iii. 976) did not apply in Wales, Cheshire, Durham and Lancaster.

[92] 18 Elizabeth, c.13 (*SR* iv. 624).

tine, 1584–5.[93] This provided that false Latin or errors in form would not lead to the effect of the action being reversed.[94]

Three things should be noted from this legislation. The first is that the statutes did not undermine palatine autonomy. In no case was the administration of a palatine county changed so that it became the same as an ordinary English county. Instead the legislation gave palatine courts the same status as the Westminster courts, or provided for ways in which Westminster decisions might be communicated more effectively to the localities, and vice versa. The legislation therefore accommodated the palatinates more clearly alongside the judicial and administrative machinery of Westminster rather than subsuming them within it.

The second point is that, initially at least, this legislation was carried out in piecemeal fashion. Each individual palatine county had its problems with fines and proclamations, and with proclamations upon exigents, dealt with separately and at some distance of years. This piecemeal approach only changed with later acts, after 1560, such as those for enrolment of indentures of bargain and sale, rights to feudal incidents in the palatine counties, and for reformation of errors in fines and recoveries. The apparently co-ordinated series of acts in the parliament of 1563, to which can be added the act for a Welsh Bible, was extremely unusual.[95]

The third significant conclusion is implied by the previous two points: these developments were due to local initiative. The accommodation of Cheshire to the Westminster judicial system was carried out at local instigation to protect local privileges, not by central diktat in the face of local opposition. This seems to be borne out by other evidence, such as the fact that the act for fines and proclamations in Cheshire was prefaced by a petition from the inhabitants of the county. It may be that this action by Cheshire inspired later efforts to clarify the position of the other palatine counties and of Wales in a more systematic way; none the less, Cheshire's parliamentary strategy of involvement to prevent encroachments on its liberties seems clear.

Cheshire's new MPs

It has always been assumed that when parliamentary representation was granted to the people of Cheshire and Wales their MPs immediately began to act like those of other parts of England. Their actual behaviour has been the subject of little detailed study, however. In his piece for the *Victoria County History*, John Morrill demonstrated that Cheshire and Chester MPs were overwhelmingly local men, and that there was no domination of the seats by

93 27 Elizabeth, c.9 (*SR* iv. 715–17).
94 23 Elizabeth, c.3 (*SR* iv. 661–3). See the attempt to address this problem in England in 1581, which did not extend to Wales or the palatine counties.
95 5 Elizabeth, c.28 (*SR* iv. 457).

parliamentary dynasties, but he spent little time on considering their activity.[96] As far as it goes, Morrill's argument is well-founded. The first known members were elected in 1545.[97] There is no sign in the identity of the representatives chosen that the county and city were enfranchised to provide seats for any interest groups, as was apparently the case with boroughs in Lancashire given parliamentary status at the instance of the powerful duchy of Lancaster lobby.[98] There, the grant of representation was followed by the return of individuals linked to duchy servants; in the case of Cheshire, it was not until March 1553 that a member with clear official or court connections was returned, in the person of Sir Thomas Holcroft. Even then, his county landownership credentials were good. Such men could have found places elsewhere with ease if the opportunity of Cheshire seats had not occurred. The new seats simply brought the representatives of the communities of Cheshire and Chester to Westminster. The Cheshire seats were dominated by senior members of the local gentry community, with no sign of intervention by the bishop of Chester or by chamberlain Rees Mansell. If the parliaments of 1545–58 are considered, it will be noted that the sixteen available seats were filled by twelve men. One, Richard Wilbraham, sat three times, and two sat twice (Sir Hugh Calveley and Sir Thomas Holcroft). It was a closely knit group: of the twelve, five were related to the Brereton family, and the rest were related to each other and to the Brereton group. The identity of Cheshire's MPs therefore supports both the theory advanced above of the appearance of an elite group of between thirty and fifty families at the head of the county's society, and the conclusion of the previous section of this chapter, that Cheshire's involvement in parliament was mainly directed at excluding parliamentary interference from the palatinate.[99]

The *History of Parliament* offered a consideration not simply of the identity but of the activity of Cheshire MPs which emphasised that they were active on local matters, and used the occasion of parliament more broadly to approach and influence members of the government. Alastair Hawkyard, however, went further and argued that the enfranchisement of Cheshire was

[96] VCH, *County of Chester*, ii. 98–110; cf. Bindoff, *House of Commons, 1509–1558*, i. 43–5, on the county seats: the 'picture of representation is of a small number of prominent county families, interconnected and often with places at court or in government'.

[97] Ibid. i. 44. The many attestors for this first return suggest it was a novelty, but this does not rule out earlier, even better attended elections.

[98] Jennifer Loach, 'Parliament: a "new air"?', in Christopher Coleman and David Starkey (eds), *Revolution reassessed: revisions in the history of Tudor government and administration*, Oxford 1986, 130–2. See also Hawkyard, 'Enfranchisement of constituencies', 1–26 esp. p. 19.

[99] Bindoff, *House of Commons, 1509–1558*, i. 45; Morris, *Chester in the Plantagenet and Tudor reigns*, 191. Chester city acted in the same autonomous manner (and was therefore atypical as a town): the governing body of about 60 citizens consistently returned its recorder, a prominent lawyer, along with an important local citizen.

part of a deliberate policy of Thomas Wolsey, Thomas Cromwell and their successors: problems involving previously unrepresented peripheral areas under English control were to be solved by their incorporation in parliament.[100] By extension he implied that these areas afterwards played a role in parliament similar to that of English counties and boroughs with a longer established representation. This is therefore to argue that parliament acted as the ultimate institution of unification in early Tudor England, with representatives of Cheshire, Wales, Calais and elsewhere coming together to resolve problems alongside, and generally to behave like, ordinary English gentlemen. As such Hawkyard's argument accords with the dominant interpretation of the Tudor parliament, developed by Geoffrey Elton, as a point of contact between centre and localities in which both government and private business was resolved. Elton himself attempted to apply this thesis to the peripheries in the case of Wales.[101] It is striking, however, that his determination to do so was paralleled by his evident disappointment that Welsh MPs, given the opportunity of being present in parliament, made so little use of it.[102] Welsh MPs did not produce a flood of Welsh legislation as a result of their inclusion in the House of Commons.

The evidence for Cheshire's activity in parliament, in the form of statutes and bills surviving or recorded in the journals of the Houses of Lords and Commons, tends to confirm the picture Elton found for Wales. There was no rush of legislation for Cheshire interests, as there was none for Welsh: it is striking that the act in Cheshire's first parliament, for the maintainance of Huntingdon Lane, which has so many parallels in bills for the improvement of roads, bridges, harbours, lighthouses and the like elsewhere, had virtually no successors. Private acts for Cheshire interests were few and far between. Henry Brereton's blood was restored in 1571; the patronage of Rostherne was assured to Thomas Venables in 1601; and in 1627 John Aldersey and members of his family were naturalised.[103] Meetings of parliament might provide the occasion for representatives of Cheshire to do important business in the capital, but not necessarily as MPs in the Commons chamber. William Aldersey notoriously won a charter for the Merchant Adventurers of Chester during his second term as a Chester MP, and the records of the city of Chester include a stream of commands to their MPs at Westminster to attend to the

---

100 Hawkyard, 'Enfranchisement of constituencies', 1–26.
101 Elton criticised earlier Whig historians' portrayals of parliament as the forum for conflict between the crown and the Commons for Welsh MPs (for example, A. H. Dodd, 'Wales's parliamentary apprenticeship', 8–72) as he had for English. P. R. Roberts has discussed the response of parliament to the uncertainties of the 1536–43 settlement, especially the controversy over the Council in the Marches: 'Wales and England after the Tudor "union" ', 111–38. This was, however, a matter of concern mainly for Worcestershire, Gloucestershire, Herefordshire and Shropshire, determined to cast off conciliar control.
102 Elton, 'Wales in parliament', 91.
103 13 Elizabeth (SR iv. 526); 43 & 44 Elizabeth (SR iv. 959); 3 Charles I (SR v. 53).

interests of the city, virtually none of which resulted in bills or statutes.[104] The comparison with Tournai's representatives coming to Westminster to resolve the details of the city's government under its new English king in 1514, without necessarily thereby becoming full members of the House of Commons in the parliament then sitting, is not too distant.[105]

The other evidence for the impact of Cheshire representatives in parliament from the period immediately after the enfranchisement can be found in provisos for Cheshire in legislation of more general effect. We may assume that these were due to the intervention of Cheshire MPs. The poor relief act of 1552 ordered that bishops should investigate the administration of former cathedral funds allocated to the maintenance of the poor by Henry VIII; a proviso protected the mayor, sheriffs and citizens of Chester and the annuities they had received from Edward VI out of cathedral funds.[106] Cheshire, along with Lancashire and Wales, was exempted from the provisions of the act of 1558 on horse armour and weapons which required the possession of haquebuts; bow and arrows were to be an adequate substitute there.[107] A proviso protective of the interests of Cheshire (as well as Lancashire, Yorkshire, Cumberland and Westmorland) was incorporated in the act for the licensing of badgers of corn and drovers of cattle in 1563. The same parliament also produced a statute for the due execution of the writ *de excommunicato capiendo*, and Cheshire and other places where the writ *capias* did not run were accommodated in its workings.[108] In 1572 the poor law saw the first in the series of provisos protective of the rights of the Dutton family and their franchise of the Cheshire minstrels.[109] Once again, Cheshire was active in the English parliament not for positive reasons but to prevent negative outcomes.

The paucity of legislation relating to Cheshire implies a lack of activity on the part of its representatives which the evidence, thin although it initially is, bears out. There is very little sign of activity by Cheshire MPs in the Commons chamber before the very end of the sixteenth century. The knights

---

[104] Bindoff, *House of Commons, 1509–1558*, i. 302–3. Aldersey also used the opportunity to litigate in Star Chamber against several people, including Ralph Dutton and Piers Tilston; they objected to this, their opponent 'beyng a burges of the parliament & therby havyng his costes borne here at London': PRO, STAC 2/24/256.

[105] C. S. L. Davies, 'Tournai and the English crown, 1513–1519', *HJ* xli (1998), 9–14, especially his criticism of C. G. Cruikshank, 'Parliamentary representation of Tournai', *EHR* lxxxiii (1968), 775–6, and Hawkyard, 'Enfranchisement of constituencies'. Davies also criticises T. F. Mayer's suggestion that Tournai represented a new royal attitude to its power in its dependent territories and, indeed, in general (contained in 'Tournai and tyranny: imperial kingship and critical humanism', *HJ* xxxiv [1991], 257–77, and 'On the road to 1534: the occupation of Tournai and Henry VIII's theory of sovereignty', in Dale Hoak [ed.], *Tudor political culture*, Cambridge 1995, 11–30).

[106] 5 & 6 Edward VI, c.11 (*SR* iv. 131–2: proviso on attached schedule).

[107] 4 & 5 Philip and Mary, c.2 (*SR* iv. 316–20: p. 320 for attached schedule).

[108] 5 Elizabeth, c.12 (*SR* iv. 439–41 at p. 441); 5 Elizabeth, c.23 (*SR* iv. 451–3 at p. 453).

[109] 14 Elizabeth, c.5 (*SR* iv. 590–8 at p. 598 for one of four provisos on a separate schedule); *CJ* i. 99. See pp. 47–8 above (refusal of rights to Welsh minstrels at the same point).

of the shire before 1558 made virtually no impression at all. The one exception is Sir Lawrence Smith, who voted against a government bill in 1555 alongside Sir Anthony Kingston. Although he did not sit again for the county, he was returned twice more for the city of Chester and was active again, in January 1558, when a bill limiting tanners to boroughs and markets was committed to him after its second reading.[110] The only other county member to make an impact on the proceedings of an early Tudor parliament was Sir Richard Cotton, and then only when one of his servants was granted privilege to protect him from arrest in an action for debt.[111] The exceptions to this rule of inactivity are a handful of members for the city of Chester, and the reason for their activity lies in their being, as recorders of the city, prominent members of the legal profession. Thus William Gerard, member for Chester in 1558, was probably appointed as one of four MPs to enquire into a complaint against Walter Ralegh.[112] This was not because Cheshire's MPs were unusually reticent; it was because they did not see the normal debate of the House of Commons as their proper business. When faced by the demand for the subsidy in Elizabeth's first parliament, while a mise was still in process of collection, the representatives of Cheshire and Wales petitioned the Lords rather than raising the matter in the Commons.[113]

The identity of Cheshire's new MPs and their activity therefore suggest two things. First, that the demand for legislation did not cause the enfranchisement, except in the sense that Cheshire's community was determined to prevent further encroachments on their privileges and to set them on a firmer footing; and, second, that once in parliament it was many years before the behaviour of its representatives became similar to that of their longer-standing fellow MPs, a fact which the House as a whole accepted.

Study of the pattern of litigation by Cheshire people has therefore established that the palatinate's position was changed during the period

110 Bindoff, House of Commons, 1509–1558, iii. 334–45; Jennifer Loach, Parliament and the crown in the reign of Mary Tudor, Oxford 1986, 139, 149–58; David Loades, The reign of Mary Tudor, 2nd edn, London 1991, 218.

111 Bindoff, House of Commons, 1509–1558, i. 711–12.

112 Ibid. ii. 205–6; P. W. Hasler, The House of Commons, 1558–1603, London 1981, ii. 186–7. Richard Sneyd may possibly have been the 'Mr Recorder' to whom the bill for Chester city for weirs in the Dee was committed after its second reading on 5 December 1549, although it is far more likely that the reference was to the recorder of London: Bindoff, House of Commons, 1509–1558, iii. 345.

113 LJ ii. 549; Dodd, 'Wales's parliamentary apprenticeship', 11. Elton, Parliament of England, 159–60, suggested this was due to 'slow uptake rather than insolence', neatly offering the reader a choice between Welsh and Cheshire idiocy and truculence. It was only really in the 1580s that members from the county and city began to play a full part in the Commons. In the county it may have been the election in 1584 of Thomas Egerton, already solicitor-general, that brought about the change. Even then, before the Civil War bills did not assume Cheshire's inclusion, which had to be requested; Cheshire MPs might seek exemption, but this was certainly not assumed either: Tim Thornton, 'Dynasty and territory in the early modern period: The princes of Wales and their western British inheritance', WHR xx (2000), 1–33.

1480–1560 but that its distinct position was not destroyed. The same is true of its relationship to the English parliament. Cheshire's privileged position, like that of other semi-autonomous territories, was focused and defined, and the precise nature of the king's sovereignty over his palatinate, and its relationship to Westminster, were clarified. A minimal involvement of palatinate with parliament, and of parliament with palatinate, gave way under Thomas Cromwell to a situation in which English legislation played a more important and, to some, disturbing role. Yet two factors allowed the palatinate to survive. First, there remained a strong commitment among the members of the king's government and his parliaments to the idea of autonomy and privilege, itself springing from a legal and political culture which valued precedent highly; and, second, there occurred an effective adaptation of the palatinate's position, not least the achievement of representation for knights of the shire. This should not cause too much surprise given, for example, the importance placed on particular custom, as the fifth ground of law, by Christopher St German, a key inspiration for the legislative revolution against papal authority. Crucially this was justified on the grounds that 'there is no statute made in this realm but by the assent of the lords spiritual and temporal, and of all the commons, that is to say, by the knights of the shire, citizens and burgesses'; of course, this did not apply to Cheshire, absolutely before 1543 and partially thereafter.[114] Defence of county privileges was a prime concern, as is evident from the nature of the new MPs and their actions. Cheshiremen came to parliament a little unwillingly and primarily to defend their shire. Nothing of what they found there affected this objective.

[114] S. B. Chrimes, *English constitutional ideas in the fifteenth century*, Cambridge 1936, New York 1965, 212–13; Christopher St German, *Doctor and student*, ed. T. F. T. Plucknett and J. L. Barton (Selden Society xci, 1974), 71–3.

7

The Officers of the Palatinate

The officers of justice

Cheshire's judicial system lay outside usual English legal jurisdiction. Those who ran that system were therefore extremely important to the life of the county and in changes to government policy towards the palatinate. The involvement of courtiers or others linked to the central administration was often the subject of controversy in Cheshire and elsewhere.[1] This chapter will consider whether in the early Tudor period local administrative posts were taken by outsiders or by local men with strong interests at court resulting in a diminution in the county's autonomy.[2] It will argue that the officers of the shire remained largely local men; that if they began to represent the influence of any outside body, it was that of the Council in the Marches of Wales as much as the court; and that their influence was neither dramatically new nor disruptive of the privileges and community of the palatinate. In fact, the presence of men with outside interests served to reinforce commitment to the palatinate's traditions and to the rights of elites both in the centre and locality.[3]

[1] For contemporary concern see S. J. Gunn, 'The Act of Resumption of 1515', in Daniel Williams (ed.), *Early Tudor England: proceedings of the 1987 Harlaxton symposium*, Woodbridge 1989, 96, 100. Control through royal servants is emphasised by David Starkey, 'Representation through intimacy: a study in the symbolism of monarchy and court office in early modern England', in I. Lewis (ed.), *Symbols and sentiments: cross cultural studies in symbolism*, London 1977, 187–224. J. A. Guy, 'Wolsey and the Tudor polity', in S. J. Gunn and P. G. Lindley (eds), *Cardinal Wolsey: Church, State and art*, Cambridge 1991, 66–70, argues from analysis of commissions of the peace that it was local influence that brought inclusion in the household.

[2] Worthington argued that 1460–1509 saw encroachment on the autonomy of Cheshire and Lancashire through their officers and that they were drawn into the northern judicial circuit: 'Royal government', 45–6.

[3] All references to appointments are from *31 DKR* (which is organised alphabetically by the surname of the officer), unless otherwise stated. For a full list of Cheshire officers during this period (organised according to office held), with the terms of the grant and references see Thornton, 'Political society in early Tudor Cheshire', 181–93.

The justice and his deputy

The justice of the county palatine was the crucial figure in the judicial adminstration of Cheshire. Although he rarely attended in person, he was responsible for the appointment of the deputy justice.[4] The Stanleys dominated the justiceship during the later fifteenth century. The post was held first by Thomas, second Lord Stanley, and then from 1485 by him as earl of Derby with his son George, Lord Strange. After Thomas's death in 1504, however, the new justice was Sir Thomas Englefield, an appointment prefigured in 1491 when Englefield became deputy justice.[5] Englefield had no personal link with the palatinate. The only son of John Englefield of Englefield (Berkshire), Thomas was a bencher at the Middle Temple by 1500 and a councillor to Henry VII. His national prominence was seen in his speakership of the parliaments of 1497 and 1510, and service as an executor of Henry VII's will.[6] His involvement in the marches is clear from the 1490s; he was a member of the Council in the Marches and to the justiciarship of Chester he added the posts of justice of assize in north Wales in 1506 and in south Wales in 1508.[7]

Apart from justice and deputy justice, Englefield held no other Cheshire posts. In that he was a significant member of the Council in the Marches of Wales, his appointment represents continuity, for both Thomas and George Stanley had also been members. Yet Englefield was first and foremost a lawyer and an outsider member of the Council in the Marches, a potent combination in the future of the justiciarship. While the prominence of their local position qualified the Stanleys for both membership of the Council in the Marches and for the justiciarship, for Englefield it was membership of the council that was a prerequisite of Cheshire office.

There had always been a strong tendency towards heredity in Chester offices. This was even true for an outsider such as Sir Thomas Englefield, for when he died in 1514 he was succeeded by his son, and the Englefields held the justiciarship for a total of thirty-two years, until the death of the second Sir Thomas in 1536.[8] This was, however, heredity within a legal dynasty of the Council in the Marches. In 1536 it was lawyers with connections to the Council in the Marches who contested for the post: George Bromley, John

---

[4] On the powers of the justice see Booth, *Financial administration*, 51–2; Clayton, *Administration*, 142–4; Worthington, 'Royal government', 11–14.

[5] Ibid. 14, 17; Bindoff, *House of Commons, 1509–1558*, ii. 103–4.

[6] During Henry VIII's absence in 1513, he was one of four councillors left in England to advise the queen. He was associated with Reginald Bray, who outbid Giles, Lord Daubeny, for him to have the speakership: J. A. Guy, *Tudor England*, Oxford 1988, 69.

[7] He was JP in Gloucestershire, Herefordshire, Worcestershire and Shropshire from 1493, and in his native Berkshire from 1494; in 1502 he was a commissioner of array for Wales and the marches.

[8] Sir Thomas Englefield II was known by the Welsh as one of two devils, the other being Rowland Lee, president of the council: *LP* xii/2, 896.

Pakyngton and, successfully, William Sulyarde.[9] Sulyarde did not survive long in the job. When he died in 1540, he was succeeded by Sir Nicholas Hare, who was to preside over the transition to the new circuit that also embraced Denbighshire and Montgomeryshire. Hare was the eldest son of John Hare of Homersfield, on the Norfolk–Suffolk border, and after study at Cambridge was admitted to the Inner Temple in 1515.[10] Although knighted in 1539 and speaker in the parliament of 1539–40, he suffered disgrace during that parliament for giving advice on evading the Statute of Uses, and spent time in the Tower. It was soon after his release that he was appointed to the Chester office. In 1545, however, he resigned his marcher posts and returned to court where he was reappointed a master of requests.

Hare was replaced in the justiceship by Sir Robert Townsend, a lawyer with East Anglian origins,[11] who continued in office for a decade, until replaced by Sir John Pollard. Townsend seems to have been an active member of the marcher administration, and his role in Cheshire led to the marriage of his daughter to Ralph Dutton, heir of Sir Piers.[12] Pollard, a lawyer who may have been a bencher at the Middle Temple by 1535, had begun his administrative career in 1536 with a place on the commission of the peace in his adopted home of Oxfordshire.[13] His career took him to the post of under-steward of the duchy of Lancaster in the south parts in 1543, but conservatism in religion may have led him to choose a Welsh judicial post, rather than continue in the uncongenial atmosphere of Edward VI's Westminster. In June 1550 he became a member of the Council in the Marches of Wales and was

---

9 LP xii/2, 770, 775. For Sulyarde see LP iv/3, 6751(12); vi. 890; vii. 94; viii. 24, 66, 119, 422, 708 etc. He advised the Lisles in Calais before his move to the marches. Colin Richmond, 'The Sulyard papers: the rewards of a small family archive', in Daniel Williams (ed.), England in the fifteenth century: proceedings of the 1986 Harlaxton symposium, Woodbridge 1987, 209–10, adds virtually nothing. Expected in the marches in late October 1537, Sulyard was not appointed under the palatinate great seal until 16 January following: LP xii/2, 993.

10 Hare received a life patent under the palatinate seal on 14 August 1540. See Bindoff, House of Commons, 1509–1558, ii. 296–7; DNB viii. 1256–7; Edward Foss, The judges of England, with sketches of their lives, and miscellaneous notices connected with the courts at Westminster, from the time of the Conquest, London 1848–64, v. 374–6; Charles Wriothesley, A chronicle of England during the reigns of the Tudors, from AD 1485 to 1559, ed. William Douglas Hamilton, i (Camden n.s. xi, 1875), 116; S. E. Lehmberg, The later parliaments of Henry VIII, 1536–1547, Cambridge 1977, 56–7, 86–7, 278.

11 Moreton, Townshends, 40–1, 45, 220. The council ordered Townsend to replace Hare on 31 May 1545: APC i. 176.

12 APC ii. 448 (Townsend's riding in the marches, March 1546/7). William Aldersey alleged that Ralph Dutton 'overpresse[d] the kynges ma[jes]ties subiects by Reason that he maryed the doughter of Sir Robert Toneshend knyght': PRO, STAC 2/24/256. Soon after his father's death, Ralph was described by his step-mother as 'a verey younge man gretly gyven to games and pastimes, and verey prodigall in excessyve expences': STAC 2/8/173 (L&C Star Chamber, 86.)

13 This and the following are largely based on Bindoff, House of Commons, 1509–1558, iii. 119–21. For Pollard see also DNB xvi. 59–60.

its vice-president by February 1552. He held the justiceship of Brecknock, Glamorgan and Radnorshire from 23 November 1550 until his death. His tenure at Chester was very short: on 8 April 1557 he added the justiceship to the posts he already held in Wales and the marches but died on 12 August the same year.

Pollard's successor, George Wood, was also a lawyer: he was a bencher at the Inner Temple by 20 November 1552 and a serjeant-at-law in 1555.[14] Unlike his predecessors, however, Wood had some personal interest in the northern Welsh marches. He was probably the son of Humphrey Wood of Balterley in Staffordshire and by 1548 he had married Margaret, daughter of Richard Grosvenor of Eaton in Cheshire, whom he no doubt knew as the widow of Ralph Birkenhead of Crowton, a member of the Cheshire family of lawyers and administrators.[15] He had been involved in property transactions with Robert Tatton in 1546.[16] An interest in Welsh and marcher affairs is therefore not surprising in Wood, and he became justice of Anglesey, Caernarfon and Merioneth on 26 April 1555. He came to the justiceship of Chester and Flint on 2 April 1558, but he was already ill when he made his will on 28 April and he died on 23 June.

There was therefore an active justice of Chester for no more than eight months in the previous fifteen when, on 31 July 1558, not long before the death of Queen Mary in November, John Throckmorton was appointed.[17] Trained at the Middle Temple, he was attorney to the Council in the Marches, under Dudley patronage, from 1550 to 1554. He became a full member of the council in 1558 and was its vice-president from 1565 to 1569. He was a JP of the *quorum* in Cheshire from 1562. He continued in office throughout the early part of Elizabeth's reign, dying in disgrace in 1580, dragged down by a combination of his own partiality, his wife's recusancy and the loss of the earl of Leicester's favour.

From the 1490s, therefore, the justiceship of Chester became a post held by a lawyer from the Council in the Marches, an integration into its power and career structure. The responsibilities of the justice in Cheshire, or at least in the marches generally, were full-time ones. It was not possible to both serve as justice of Chester and pursue an active career at court or in the Westminster courts. Sir Nicholas Hare's appointment (which looks like internal exile under the shadow of the Tower), his resignation in order to return to a court post and Sir John Pollard's move from a career at Westminster to one in the marches suggest that the two were incompatible.

The deputy justice of Chester was appointed by the justice to deal with routine judicial business in his absence.[18] In contrast to the men who were

14 Bindoff, *House of Commons, 1509–1558*, iii. 652.
15 Ormerod, *Chester*, ii. 135.
16 JRUL, Tatton of Wythenshawe 125 (4 Dec. 1546).
17 Bindoff, *House of Commons, 1509–1558*, iii. 455–6; Hasler, *House of Commons, 1558–1603*, iii. 494–5; Browne, 'Throckmorton', 55–71.
18 Booth, *Financial administration*, 51–2; Clayton, *Administration*, 155; Worthington, 'Royal

appointed justice of Chester, those who filled the office of deputy were largely local lawyers, not outsiders from the Council in the Marches. Until 1491 the post was dominated by local men. The only exception after 1450 was John Fyneux, in 1480 and 1481, although this prominent Kent judge was clearly not expected to attend, for he had local men appointed as his deputy simultaneously with his own appointments.[19] Sir John Needham of Shavington (Shropshire) and Holmes Chapel had held the post since November 1450 until his death when he was replaced by Fyneux. Thomas Duncalf, a native of Macclesfield Hundred, held the post during mid-1481 before the reappointment of Fyneux; and in early 1486 John Hawardyn, who had acted as Fyneux's deputy, took on the post himself.

From 9 May 1491 Thomas Englefield held the office of deputy justice, combining it with that of justice from 1504 until 1509.[20] This suggests that his appointment in 1491 was not the usual deputyship, but a declaration of intent, effectively a reversion of the office of justice. This first direct impact of the marcher council on the county palatine continued with the appearance of George Bromley as deputy justice, a position in which he was acting in 1505[21] and to which he was formally appointed on 1 June 1509 and 11 June 1513. Bromley and his successors, however, although they were marcher council men, had stronger local ties. Bromley was a legal officer of the Council in the Marches, but came from Hodnet in north Shropshire.[22] The next deputy justice who can be identified is Richard Sneyd, who appears in 1523 and 1528–9. He was a man with strong local connections. His family originated in Staffordshire at Bradwell and Wolstanton, but his career took him to Chester and by 1512 he was acting in such important private matters as the arrangments for the marriage between Randal, son of Sir Randal Brereton, and Isabel, daughter of Sir Thomas Butler. By 1523 he had married Anne, daughter of Sir Robert Fouleshurst of Crewe.[23] Sneyd too was a functionary of the marcher council: he was appointed attorney to the council under Princess Mary by Wolsey.[24] In the following years the deputy justices

government', 31–3. Appointment by the justice means there is often no record of a formal appointment or the exact period of tenure.

[19] Clayton, *Administration*, 282. His deputies were Randal Billington and John Hawardyn.

[20] Englefield erroneously appears as deputy from 1486 in VCH, *County of Chester*, ii. 13 (noted by Clayton, *Administration*, 206 n. 89.)

[21] For his involvement in arbitrations from 1505 see CCRO, DCH U/36 (bond, 9 June 1505); DLT A14/45 (bond, 16 July 1505); DLT A12/13 (bond, 4 Aug. 1505, in which he is first referred to as justice at Chester). See pp. 89–93 for subsequent arbitrations.

[22] His son George became justice of Chester in May 1580: Bindoff, *House of Commons, 1509–1558*, i. 508.

[23] CCRO, DCH X/12/8. His second son Richard became an alderman of Chester in 1544 and its recorder by 1550 until his death in 1554–5: Bindoff, *House of Commons, 1509–1558*, iii. 345.

[24] He was dismissed by the earl of Wiltshire at William Brereton's instigation: *LP* xii/1, 1110.

remained local men. On 3 February 1529, a joint appointment of William Hassall and William Clayton during pleasure is recorded. On 6 July 1531 Bromley and Sneyd returned, this time jointly during pleasure.[25]

All these local men were appointed during the tenure of Sir Thomas Englefield II as justice. Shortly after his death, there occurred an appointment which parallels those of Fyneux in the 1480s. John Adams was made deputy justice on 10 July 1537, and on the same day John Birkenhead was appointed to act as deputy during his absence. Adams, a prominent administrator with interests elsewhere, was clearly not expected to exercise the post in person. Birkenhead, however, was a local man and a member of one of the most prominent Cheshire legal dynasties.[26] After 1509 the vast majority of deputy justices had been local men who had got on with the job largely undisturbed by changing masters.[27] 1537 was perhaps a sign of things to come, however. Although in 1540, soon after the appointment of Sir Nicholas Hare as justice, another local man, Richard Hassall, was appointed, Sir Robert Townsend's arrival as justice in 1545 coincided exactly with that of James Warnecombe as his deputy. Warnecombe represented to some extent the change in the nature of deputy justices: he had marcher origins, but they were southern rather than northern. He was the second son of Richard Warnecombe of Ivington, Lugwardine and Hereford, and educated at the Inner Temple. He married as his second wife Mary, daughter of John Cornwall of Burford (Shropshire), and besides being deputy justice of Chester he was escheator of Herefordshire and the marches (1548–9) and represented Ludlow in the November 1554 parliament and Leominster in that of 1555.[28] As with the justiceship, membership of the council was now becoming the main reason for appointment; with the justiceship, the process was effected during Henry VII's reign, with the deputyship, only in the 1530s and 1540s.

Other judicial offices

The king or prince was represented in his Chester court by his attorney.[29] Even more than in the case of the deputy justiceship, local domination of the office of attorney continued until the 1540s.[30] However, the exclusive concentration of the office-holder on the job of attorney came to an end:

[25] For Sneyd see PRO, CHES 15/1/63, 95.
[26] See p.160 below.
[27] Emphasis on the role of complete outsiders depends on the atypical examples of 1480–1 and 1537: VCH, *County of Chester*, ii. 13–14. Lack of correlation between the timing of appointment of justices and of their deputies also suggests that different processes were at work behind these two adminstrative actions.
[28] Bindoff, *House of Commons, 1509–1558*, iii. 548.
[29] Booth, *Financial administration*, 55; Clayton, *Administration*, 188–9; Worthington, 'Royal government', 36–9.
[30] Ibid. 34.

instead it became the reward for successful Cheshire crown servants with other posts. Between 1467 and 1495 the post was held by Thomas Wolton, probably the son of Nicholas Wolton of Whalley (Lancashire), a yeoman of the crown to Henry VI and Edward IV. Wolton was succeeded in 1495 by Edmund Bulkeley, member of a family prominent in Cheshire and north Wales. Bulkeley was in turn succeeded by John Porte, whose father was a Chester mercer and mayor there in 1486.[31] Porte became a prominent judge and married Joan, daughter of John Fitzherbert. He acquired Etwall in Derbyshire, the county his son John was to represent in the parliaments of 1539 and October 1553.[32] He was, however, at the time of his appointment still very much a local Cheshire man. The first man appointed as king's attorney under Henry VIII was Richard Sneyd, given a life grant in 1522 and already encountered as deputy justice in 1523 and 1528/29. On 8 July 1538 Urian Brereton and Humphrey Hurleston were appointed for life in survivorship. Brereton was the son of Sir Randal Brereton and brother of the recently executed William Brereton, groom of the privy chamber. Hurleston came from a Cheshire office-holding family that monopolised the post of surveyor of the county for a century. The death of Hurleston led to a new appointment on 16 June 1543, this time with Urian Brereton in combination with Randal Cholmondeley. Randal was a lawyer and member of the rapidly rising family, closely connected to the Breretons, from Malpas parish.[33]

The Cheshire prothonotary fulfilled the duties of clerk to the county court. Once again the pattern of legal office being filled by local men is striking, with one significant exception. Sir William Stanley, the brother of the second Lord Stanley, was appointed in 1464. The next recorded appointment was that of Adam Birkenhead who received the grant of office on 5 July 1507. Receiver to the earl of Derby, Birkenhead came from a family that originated in Wigan. Like the Hurlestons, discussed further below, the Birkenheads were administrators brought to Cheshire in the train of the Stanleys.[34] Adam Birkenhead's family played an important role in administration over a century and more. The exception to the pattern of local men filling this lower judicial position is John Myllet, a Clerk of the Signet, appointed on 4 September 1516. That this was unacceptable seems clear from the appointment just three months later, on 15 December, of Myllet in conjunction with John Birkenhead, in survivorship. John was the son of Adam Birkenhead and

31 Ibid.

32 Bindoff, House of Commons, 1509–1558, iii. 135–6.

33 Hasler, House of Commons, 1558–1603, i. 605 (which calls him Ralph); Ormerod, Chester, ii. 638; W. R. Williams, The history of the great sessions in Wales, 1542–1830, Brecknock 1899, 79. The serjeants-at-law in the county of Chester were also local men and remained so: Thornton, 'Political society in early Tudor Cheshire', 165; Clayton, Administration, 188; Worthington, 'Royal government', 33–9.

34 Sheaf 3rd ser. xviii (1923), 50, no. 4342; Ormerod, Chester, ii. 135, 366–7. Adam was clerk to the halmote court of Macclesfield Forest under Thomas, earl of Derby, and his grandson, from at least 1492 to 1515: CCRO, DDS 9/3; DDS 20/13.

the result was the continuation of that family's domination of the post. This was ensured by the patent to John in conjunction with his son, Ralph, and his brother, Henry, of 8 April 1528; and that to Henry and his sons Henry and Francis of 16 February 1555.

Overall, then, the judicial offices of the county palatine demonstrate the growing importance of the link to the Council in the Marches. This meant the appointment of a new group of outsiders to the county's offices, but since their work in Wales was so important these men had to be present in the area. In addition, the vitality of the courts of Chester meant deputies had to be appointed there; and those deputies had to have local knowledge. The men who did the day-to-day work in the Chester courts therefore continued to come from the local legal community. Indeed, the vitality of the courts meant that the Council in the Marches would in the end lose its role, although the justice himself would retain links to both.

The officers of finance

The chamberlain of Chester was a vital palatine officer: from the fourteenth century his post had grown in importance until he controlled the county's finances and exchequer equity jurisdiction.[35] The post was held between 1461 and 1495 by Sir William Stanley, who was also prothonotary. The crucial importance of the post meant that, as Henry VII's regime attempted to regain control in the palatinate after the fall of Stanley, the chamberlaincy was held by important royal bureaucrats, although the degree of control by outsiders was not as sustained as that experienced in the justiceship. Robert Frost of Ackton (Yorkshire), Prince Arthur's almoner,[36] was chamberlain between 20 February and 10 April 1495, being succeeded by Sir Reginald Bray, arguably the chief financial officer of the regime.[37] In 1500 Bray was succeeded by Sir Richard Pole, chamberlain to Prince Arthur, whose origins lay in Buckinghamshire.[38] In 1504, however, Sir Randal Brereton began to act as chamberlain. Frost and Pole were both members of the Council in the Marches; and Frost, Pole and Bray had all represented a move away from local domination, triggered by Henry VII's mistrust of the local community after the treason of Sir William Stanley, and his determination to place Cheshire's finances under the control of the marcher council. Sir Randal Brereton's position was, however, reinforced by a life grant in 1511, and he continued in

---

[35] Booth, *Financial administration*, 52; Clayton, *Administration*, 161–3; Worthington, 'Royal government', 59–60.

[36] *BRUO*, 731–2.

[37] Guy, *Tudor England*, 54, 56, 67; Condon, 'Ruling elites in the reign of Henry VII', 116, 123, 128, 131.

[38] Pole was knighted in 1499; died November 1504: Hazel Pierce, 'The king's cousin: the life, career and Welch connection of Sir Richard Pole, 1458–1504', *WHR* xix (1998), 187–225; Chrimes, *Henry VII*, 303; *CP* ii. appendix B (p. 546).

office until his death in 1530 when he was succeeded by his son William. Local gentry had regained their grip on the chamberlaincy, but as before they were local gentry with a role at court.

After Brereton's attainder in 1536 Rees Mansell was appointed chamberlain. This was a break from past practice: he was neither a local man nor an imported bureaucrat. Mansell had come to prominence as a military and especially navy man: he served in the navy in 1513 and was in the thick of the fighting in Ireland in 1535, once explaining that he had failed to write to Cromwell because his clerk had been slain.[39] He served under Norfolk in 1542[40] and was vice-admiral of the naval force attacking the French in 1543; he was one of those captains who helped support the campaign in the north in 1544, before moving to the army against Scotland as knight marshal.[41] He then served in the mission of the earl of Lennox before being called south, where he ended the year operating against the French.[42] In 1545 he was again involved in military preparations, this time in south Wales.[43] Mansell also had a career in Welsh administration, being a member of the Council in the Marches from at least 1534 and a JP in Glamorgan from 1536 and Monmouth from 1543.[44] This was the centre of his activity: he sat on the 1546 commissions to survey chantries in the Welsh shires but not in Cheshire and he was sheriff of Glamorgan in 1541.[45] Mansell took an interest in some aspects of the chamberlaincy, but he cannot have been an active local officer.[46] Nevertheless, he held the post until his death, after which Edward, earl of Derby, was appointed on 26 April 1559. This represented a change from the Welsh marcher orientation of the palatine administration and prefigured the exclusion of Cheshire from the influence of the marcher council in 1569.

The absence of Mansell (and many other chamberlains since the late fourteenth century) meant that the post of vice-chamberlain possessed considerable significance.[47] As with the deputy justiceship, local men usually acted in Cheshire. In 1474 John Massey and William Tatton were joint vice-chamberlains; in 1483 John Massey alone; and in 1492 William Tatton. Tatton was still in post in 1497 and 1499, and in 1502 he paid over the product of the mise even though Bray had been appointed deputy in 1500.[48] Sir Randal Brereton became vice-chamberlain in 1504, prior to his appoint-

---

39 *LP* i. 1727, 2304(5); viii. 222, 328, 485 (clerk), 755, 881; ix. 19, 197, 318; xi/1, 1, 103, 934.
40 *LP* xvii. 708(7).
41 *LP* xviii/1, 701, 711, 712, 740, 849, 867; xix/1, 135(ii), 264, 416(2), 643; *Add.* i. 1592.
42 *LP* xix/1, 813; xix/2, 262, 280, 302, 333, 502(4), 601.
43 *LP* xx/1, 1105.
44 *LP* vii. 1455; x. 392(48); xviii/1, 226.
45 *LP* xxi/1, 302(30); xvi. 1391(67).
46 *LP* ix. app. 3; xi, 22.
47 Clayton, *Administration*, 162, 169; Worthington, 'Royal government', 67–72.
48 Ibid. 67–70. Tatton was from Wythenshawe: JRUL, Tatton of Wythenshawe 48, 52, 93 and passim.

ment as chamberlain. The only known vice-chamberlain under Sir Randal was Randal Brereton, in 1527 and again in early 1531.[49] Under William Brereton various local men exercised the deputyship. John Davyas and Robert Vaudray acted in 1532 and 1533. Randal Brereton appears again in 1534 and 1535. Randal was near to death on 25 March 1536, when Randal Lloyd covenanted with William to exercise the office of chamberlain during pleasure.[50] Following Brereton's execution, there was some upheaval in the post. In 1537, in February, John Turbervile was acting as vice-chamberlain; on 16 April Cromwell wrote to Roger Brereton as sheriff of Flintshire and deputy chamberlain of Chester.[51] Yet on 26 May 1537 chancellor Audley was referring to Sir William Brereton as deputy chamberlain, and he continued in post for some years.[52] Sir William was also an absentee, however: he was commanded on 2 October 1539 to serve in Ireland.[53] Even with this exception, the deputy chamberlaincy, like the deputy justiceship, stayed in local hands. When the earl of Derby obtained the chamberlaincy, he appointed William Glaseor of Chester as his deputy.[54]

The barons of the Chester exchequer, whose duties included levying debts, securing payment of arrears and eliciting profits from escheated lands, as well as from pleas, fines, amercements, redemptions, recognizances and other profits of justice,[55] were virtually all local men. Thomas Ferrour was appointed with William Tatton in 1484: Thomas may well have been the son of David Ferrour, who, described as 'of Chester city', was deputy chamberlain to John Troutbeck between 1444 and 1457, and Tatton was already deputy chamberlain when appointed.[56] In 1505 Thomas Lynom and Nicholas Faryngton were appointed, Lynom being the only baron under Henry VII whose main interests were outside Cheshire. He was a national figure, being solicitor-general to Richard III when he famously married Jane Shore, Edward IV's mistress.[57] In 1510, however, a Tatton returned to the post when John was appointed jointly with Faryngton. On 1 March 1509 Thomas Lynom had already agreed with John Tatton that Tatton should exercise the office, take all the fees and perquisites, and seek the surrender of the patent by the king.[58] In 1529 Nicholas Faryngton was replaced by Randal Brereton,

[49] *Letters and accounts of William Brereton*, 30.
[50] *LP* x. 554; cf. PRO, CHES 15/1/175. Randal died on 16 June 1536 (SC 6/HenVIII/360; CHES 3/67 (28 Henry VIII, no. 3)); Lloyd had already received the reversion of the barony.
[51] *LP* xii/1, 950.
[52] *LP* xii/1, 1282.
[53] *LP* xiv/2, 303, 466.
[54] Hasler, *House of Commons, 1558–1603*, ii. 194.
[55] For the relationship between William Brereton, chamberlain, and Randal Brereton, baron, see *Letters and accounts of William Brereton*, 30, and PRO, CHES 15/1/173, quoted in detail at p. 94 above.
[56] Worthington, 'Royal government', 81–2; Clayton, *Administration*, 169–72.
[57] C. D. Ross, *Richard III*, London 1981, 137–8.
[58] JRUL, Rylands charters 839.

a relative of the prominent Malpas clan. On Randal's death, the post was filled by Randal Lloyd and Robert Tatton.[59]

The vice-chamberlainship was therefore sometimes combined with the barony: William Tatton fulfilled both responsibilities in the late fifteenth century. The separation of the post from that of the deputy chamberlain after 1502 seems to show more 'professionalisation'; on the other hand this did not accompany tighter control of the office, for there was a change from grants during pleasure or good behaviour to grants for life. There was also a role for the Council in the Marches of Wales: Lynom was controller of Prince Arthur's household and a member of the conciliar court of audit at least by 1509.[60] But this was very limited: as with the other financial and judicial posts discussed above, local control remained with local men, and even the appointment of Lynom was joint with a local man.

The officers of county administration

The sheriff was responsible for the execution of all judicial and original writs, and the attachment of those summoned by writs. He empanelled jurors and held tourns in Cheshire hundreds. Unlike other sheriffs he was not responsible for holding the county court, although he was still seen as the representative of the county community, and his fee, at £20, was equivalent to that of the chamberlain.[61] Originally, the sheriff was appointed during pleasure or for life, sometimes even in survivorship. The 1520s, however, saw a transition to annual appointment by the king. Although royal control was thus strengthened, this did not loosen the grip of local gentry on the post.

In 1480 the sheriff was Sir William Stanley. He was replaced by his son William in 1489, and he in turn by Thomas Stanley, son of George, Lord Strange. Almost certainly as a result of the loss of royal confidence in the Stanley family after the treason of Sir William Stanley, in 1495 Thomas was replaced by John Warburton. Warburton was a Cheshire man, from Woodhey, but he combined a Stanley connection through marriage to Sir William's daughter, Jane, with royal links as a knight of the body. After Sir John Warburton's death in 1524, the family was immediately involved in controversy thanks to Sir John's relationship with Sibyl Starkey. During his life, John had made provision for Sibyl and his bastard children by her, Thomas, Richard and Geoffrey, with land in Grappenhall and Appleton.[62]

---

59 Thomas Pillyn acted for Robert Tatton, giving a bond for the proper execution of the office on 1 May 1543: JRUL, Tatton of Wythenshawe 414. See also p. 90 above.
60 J. A. Guy, 'A conciliar court of audit at work in the last months of the reign of Henry VII', *BIHR* xlix (1976), 290, 293.
61 Booth, *Financial administration*, 53–4; Clayton, *Administration*, 172–3; Worthington, 'Royal government', 94.
62 JRUL, Arley charters 12/19 (30 Jan. 1522). The trustees included Richard Starkey

On his death, however, John's mistress had withheld deeds relating to the manor of Warburton and other lands from his eldest son Piers, thereby also depriving John's widow Jane of her dower and his daughters Elyn and Dowse of their inheritance.[63] To add insult to injury, it was Thomas Warburton, John's bastard son, who was appointed sheriff on 8 April 1524. Given the disputes that John's relationship produced, it was not surprising that Thomas was replaced as sheriff on 24 September by Sir George Holford. This sudden change of sheriff is striking, and although Holford's was another 'marcher' style appointment, made before the pricking of the next year's sheriffs for the rest of England, he was to be the last sheriff so chosen in Cheshire.[64] The roll for November 1525 carries the first full entry for Cheshire.[65] The Westminster administration was beginning to treat Cheshire more like any other English county, though it had not yet become indistinguishable: the sheriff continued to be appointed under the palatinate seal, some time after the actual pricking. Sir William Stanley of Hooton was appointed at Chester on 20 February 1526. Stanley's appointment was the first in a series of seven annual appointments, all now initiated through the conventional process of pricking. All seven were prominent Cheshire gentlemen: William Venables (1526), Sir William Poole (1527),[66] Thomas Fouleshurst (1528),[67] John Done (1529),[68] Peter Warburton (1530)[69] and Edward Fitton (1531).[70] There then comes a change from the choice of local men, in the appointment of George Poulett, who came from Hampshire.[71] Poulett had an important military and administrative career. He was a captain at Calais in 1515, and was afterwards employed as a commissioner to reform the government, first of Calais under Sir William Fitzwilliam in 1535, and then of Ireland from 1537: it is clear he became a trusted government servant who served in difficult

(Sibyl's brother). John Warburton and Richard Starkey had appeared together previously on 16 January that year, witnessing a grant at Appleton: JRUL, Brooke of Mere, box 1/1/32.
[63] PRO, C 1/590/49–50; C 1/593/44.
[64] The sheriff roll of 10 November 1524 does not include an entry for Cheshire: LP iv/1, 819.
[65] Only two names are legible, Sir William Stanley and Henry Delves: PRO, C 82/572. The calendar omits the Cheshire names (as it does an entire entry for Lancashire) which are only visible under ultraviolet light: LP iv/1, 1795; VCH, County of Chester, ii. 27.
[66] The roll for 1526, PRO, C 82/580 is mutilated, but slightly more can be read than is calendared in LP iv/2, 2672. The other legible name is George ___. Venables was appointed under the palatinate seal on 19 December 1526. The sheriff roll for 1527 is so damaged that it is impossible to determine whether there is an entry for Cheshire, but Sir William Poole, who was subsequently appointed at Chester on 30 November 1527, was almost certainly pricked in the English manner: C 82/594 (LP iv/2, 3581).
[67] Chosen ahead of Sir Henry D[elves?] and George Booth: LP iv/2, 4915.
[68] Chosen ahead of John Talbot and Robert Nedeham: PRO, C 82/621 (LP iv/3, 6072(9), heading mistranscribed as 'Berkshire'.)
[69] Chosen ahead of Edward Littleton and Edward Fitton: LP iv/3, 6721.
[70] No roll is printed in LP.
[71] Chosen ahead of William Davenport of Bramhall and Edward Littleton on 20 November 1532: LP v. 1598.

areas.[72] His main link to Cheshire was his marriage to Jane Larke, Wolsey's mistress, after the death of her husband, George Legh of Adlington.[73] Yet Poulett was the only example of a non-Cheshire gentleman holding the shrievalty in this period. In 1533 there was a return to the appointment of local men, in the person of William Davenport of Bramhall. Sir Piers Dutton was gaining prominence in the county and nationally due to his struggle for the Dutton inheritance when he was pricked in November 1534. The importance of yearly appointment, and perhaps the limited degree to which the principle that sheriffs should only hold office for one year had become established, was demonstrated when in November 1535 Henry VIII took the extraordinary course of rejecting all three candidates offered and writing in the name of Sir Piers Dutton.[74] Dutton therefore served a second consecutive year as sheriff of the county. In November 1536 Sir Piers's name was one of those offered, and he was duly chosen. 1537 saw the end of Dutton's term as sheriff: Sir Henry Delves was preferred. Delves was followed in the post by four men who were either newcomers to the shire or possessed a significant interest elsewhere. This was partly a response to concerns over conflict within the shire, especially between the Brereton and Dutton interests; Sir William Brereton pleaded for an 'indifferent' sheriff on 9 October 1539, just before his departure for Ireland. Although his quarrel with Sir Piers Dutton had been settled, Brereton feared Dutton might take advantage of his absence if a sheriff 'to his mind' was chosen.[75] Sir Robert Needham of Cranage, chosen in 1538, had succeeded his brother early in the century as head of this family with both Shropshire and Cheshire interests.[76] The next year another semi-outsider, Sir Alexander Ratcliffe of Ordsall (Lancashire), was chosen.[77] In 1540 Edmund Trafford of Trafford was selected, a man with Cheshire interests but whose activity was centred on Lancashire;[78] and the relative newcomer John Holcroft was chosen in 1541.[79] November 1542 saw

---

72 *LP* ii/2, 1513–14; ix. 50, 192, 236(3); xii/2, 378–82, 385–6, 388(3), 632, 762; xiii/1, 80, 261. The latter expedition dissolved into recrimination, and Poulett went to the Tower: *LP* xiii/1, 471, 999, 1000, 1021, 1303, 1420.

73 Ormerod, *Chester*, iii. 661–2.

74 *LP* ix. 914(22) (PRO, C 82/704 is now more badly damaged than when it was used for the calendar, although the 'Sir' of the written-in name of Sir Piers Dutton is still extant).

75 *LP* xiv/2, 304. The possible threat posed by a hostile sheriff was behind Richard Cholmondeley's Star Chamber bill of 1536: PRO, STAC 2/8/274 (*L&C Star Chamber*, 72).

76 Ormerod, *Chester*, iii. 128.

77 He married Alice, daughter of Sir John Booth of Barton; his eldest son William married Margaret, daughter of Edmund Trafford (two daughters married John Atherton of Atherton and Richard, heir of Sir William Molyneux): *Visitation of Lancashire and a part of Cheshire made in AD 1533*, 64–5; *Abstracts of inquisitions post mortem, made by Christopher Towneley and Roger Dodsworth, extracted from manuscripts at Towneley*, ed. William Langton, ii (Chetham Society xcix, 1876), 124–5.

78 The Traffords' major Cheshire interest was half the Bollin fee: *Visitation of Lancashire and a part of Cheshire made in AD 1533*, 66–8; *Abstracts of inquisitions post mortem*, ii. 37.

79 Bindoff, *House of Commons, 1509–1558*, ii. 372–3.

the return of the shrievalty to a local gentleman in the shape, once again, of Sir Piers Dutton. Local domination then continued to the end of the reign. In 1543 Sir Edward Fitton of Gawsworth was chosen, for the first time since 1531, despite many appearances on the roll.[80] He was succeeded by Sir Thomas Venables of Kinderton, Sir Henry Delves of Doddington and John Holcroft.

The consequence of the move to the annual appointment of Cheshire's sheriff under Henry VIII was not therefore a significant diminution of local control of the office. The exceptions to this statement are two-fold. The first was the appointment of George Poulett in November 1532, the second the appearance of Needham, Ratcliffe, Trafford and Holcroft in the years 1538–41. Of these, Poulett was the man most clearly a stranger to the county, although even he had a connection through his wife; in the difficult years at the end of the 1530s, the regime's response was to draw on the resource represented by gentlemen with local knowledge but without the intensely partisan local ties of the Cheshire gentry who had held the post in the previous decade.[81] Opening the Cheshire shrievalty to annual pricking therefore had the effect not of introducing outsiders inexperienced in the county's affairs, but of ending the extended domination of the post by single individuals and families. Rhys Robinson has described a similar process in the Welsh marches, with a wider and deeper gentry involvement replacing the domination of office by a small number of (potentially corrupt) individuals.[82] Under Henry VIII, after the short-lived appointment of Thomas Warburton, there were twenty-three Cheshire shrievalties. These were occupied by seventeen individuals: one, Sir Piers Dutton, held office four times, Edward Fitton, Sir Henry Delves and John Holcroft twice. If we take into account those individuals who were named on the sheriff roll but not pricked sheriff, we have a total of fifty places from 1528, when the first full sheriff roll entry occurs, to 1546. Two places were filled by men who are unidentifiable because of damage to the documents. The other places were filled by just nineteen individuals. Edward Fitton and William Davenport appeared eight times, Sir Henry Delves five, Edward Littleton and Sir Piers Dutton four each, John Holcroft three, and Sir William Norris and Sir William Stanley twice each. This represents a remarkable concentration of office. Littleton and Fitton in particular appeared repeatedly, the former without ever actually being pricked. Littleton was a grandson of the famous judge and gained prominence in Staffordshire when he inherited the lands of his father's heiress wife. He held many offices there, including being sheriff three times and MP on five

[80] See n. 69 above.

[81] For the rivalry (obvious to Cromwell and others at the centre) over the appointment to the post of deputy to the sheriff see p. 157 below.

[82] W. R. B. Robinson, 'The Tudor revolution in Welsh government, 1536–1543: its effects on gentry participation', *EHR* ciii (1988), 1–20.

occasions. Yet he did not hold any other office in Cheshire.[83] Edward Fitton and William Davenport appeared as the unsuccessful names together for the four consecutive years 1538–41. They either had a consistently strong but ineffective lobby operating on their behalf, or were deliberately put on to make up the numbers, when the choice of sheriff was already made and simply awaiting the formal approval of the king. That choice, however, allowed the shrievalty of the palatinate, a crucial representative and administrative role, to be shared out among the elite of the shire.

Under Edward VI and Mary, the pattern of annual appointment from a small group of local gentry continued. All but two were knights, and they all had their chief residence in the county. Sir Hugh Cholmondeley, Sir William Brereton (twice), Thomas Aston, Sir John Savage and Sir Lawrence Smith held the position in the six years of Edward's reign. Under Mary there occured the only real discontinuity to this pattern. Sir William Brereton was removed from office, almost certainly for his religious sympathies, and replaced by Sir Peter Legh, who was appointed under the palatinate seal on 26 August 1553, and again on 17 November. He was, however, succeeded by a succession of men whose tenures of office seemed to follow the pattern of control by the Cheshire gentry elite, Sir Hugh Cholmondeley, Richard Wilbraham esquire (the only real exception, as primarily a court favourite), Sir Thomas Venables, Sir Philip Egerton and Sir Edward Fitton. The choice in 1559 was Sir John Savage. The shrievalty after 1524 therefore saw the institutionalisation of the control of the gentry elite identified in respect of wealth, war-leadership and general administration, a phenomenon also observable in the commission of the peace.[84]

The way central government might intervene in the choice of local officials is seen in the case of the deputy sheriff, in spite of the fact that he was appointed by the sheriff himself.[85] The first appointment of which we have record in the sixteenth century is that of Ralph Birkenhead, the local lawyer who was to be the first recorder of Chester. He was appointed during pleasure in 1505 and again in 1508. The next recorded deputy, on 6 December 1527, was Thomas Hurleston (of the local administrative family), who held the post during the shrievalty of Sir William Poole. In 1535–6 Ralph Manning was acting as deputy sheriff to Sir Piers Dutton.[86] Yet the manner in which appointment might be influenced appears when, shortly after his appointment as sheriff in 1537, Sir Henry Delves wrote to Thomas Cromwell objecting to his directions that Thomas Hurleston should be deputy sheriff.

83 Bindoff, *House of Commons, 1509–1558*, ii. 535–7.
84 Patricia J. Marriott, 'The commission of the peace in Cheshire, 1536–1603', unpubl. MA diss. Manchester 1974; VCH, *County of Chester*, ii. 41–4. See pp. 237–9 below.
85 Clayton, *Administration*, 177–81; Worthington, 'Royal government', 106.
86 *LP* viii. 22(2ii); ix. 183, 1106. On 4 April 1541 Ralph Manning received a gold chain from Sir Piers Dutton 'towards the doing of certain great charges to be done': PRO, STAC 2/8/175 (*L&C Star Chamber*, 86–7).

Delves suggested that Thomas Wriothesley and Mr [Richard or Robert?] Southwell should nominate someone less partial.[87] Sir William Brereton then wrote to Cromwell claiming that Delves's objections were due to his favour towards Sir Piers Dutton. Delves had apparently sent one Brook to Brereton, in the latter's capacity as deputy chamberlain, to be admitted as deputy sheriff. If this was Henry Brook, then his partisanship for Dutton's cause would have been obvious.[88] Unfortunately the outcome of this conflict is not clear, but it may well be the cause of the sequence of appointments to the shrievalty itself noted earlier. Needham and his successors were less likely to bring similar problems of partiality.

Such examples demonstrate the power potentially wielded by the king and those with influence around him to appoint the officers of the palatinate. That influence might at times translate itself into the imposition on Cheshire of officers with no interest in the locality beyond the fees they might receive, or who might operate their offices from afar, but through deputies carefully chosen to reflect their interests. These periods are distinct and striking. The first fell in the half dozen years after the fall of Sir William Stanley and mainly affected the chamberlaincy; as has already been shown, it brought closer control from the Council in the Marches of Wales. The second occurred in the first three years of the reign of Henry VIII.[89] The most blatant example of this concerned the constableship of Chester Castle, important because it housed the military, administrative and judicial headquarters of the palatinate.[90] Thomas Fouleshurst, constable from 1483, was a local man. In 1485 Henry Glegge replaced him.[91] In May 1510, however, Christopher Rochester, a groom of the king's chamber, was appointed, a blatant example of the appointment of a courtier exploiting close personal links to the king.[92] Since Rochester was collecting offices across the country, such as a ferry at Datchet and a parkership at Potterspury in Northamptonshire, he can have had little local knowledge and probably no intention of fulfilling the duties in person.[93] Other offices also quickly found themselves filled by members of the king's household. Less than three months after Henry VIII's accession, on 6 July 1509, William Poole, 'unus valectorum honorabilissimi gardi nostri', and household man Edward ap John were given the clerkship of the Dee Mills. Other examples of this trend are to be seen in appointments to the posts of beadle and bailiff of the county's hundreds, which in Cheshire were

---

[87] *LP* xii/2, 1123, 1186.
[88] *LP* xiii/1, 17 (2 Jan. 1538). For Henry Brook's role in Dutton's campaign against the Breretons see pp. 207–8 below.
[89] As in Ireland: Ellis, *Tudor Ireland*, 102.
[90] Worthington, 'Royal government', 155–6.
[91] Despite his local origin Glegge employed a deputy, Hugh Crampton.
[92] Groom of the chamber: *LP* i/1, 20, 82, 228, 500, 640, 772, 877, 1015, 1105; i/2, 2504, 3554. He was also groom of the parliament chamber: *LP* i/1, 1035; i/2, 2555. Henry VIII gave a gilt cup at his child's christening: *LP* i/2, 3336.
[93] *LP* i/1, 94(17), 257(92).

combined.[94] In Northwich hundred James Worsley, 'garcio garderobe robar[um] nostrar[um]', received a life grant in April 1511 confirmed in October 1515. In Nantwich, Thomas Sonde, appointed on 1 October 1511, was one of the king's guard. He had been appointed bailiff of the lordship of Drakelow and Rudheath on the previous 1 January. In Broxton, Edward ap John, 'garcius promptuarii nostri', was appointed on 10 April 1513, also confirmed in 1515.

This was not sustainable, for two reasons. First, it was not in the crown's interests for posts such as these, and especially important ones such as the constableship of Chester Castle, to become sinecures. This became clear very quickly as Rochester stayed in post for less than a year, being replaced on 1 April 1511 by Ralph Egerton. Egerton's local knowledge and interests made him a far more suitable incumbent of the position. It is likely that this aware-ness of the problems in the palatinate caused by patronage decisions early in Henry's reign was one of the reasons behind the Act of Resumption of 1515, which specifically targeted the county.[95] The second reason was that coin-ciding with the crown's desire to appoint officers with more local knowledge were the interests of a group of Cheshiremen with good contacts at court who desired office in the county. In some ways this phenomenon had been already apparent in the years from 1509 to 1513. Although the description in their patents of appointment of men like Sonde, ap John and Worsley as officers of the king's household emphasised their court connections, they were men of the region of north Wales and north-west England. Sonde, for example, appears to have been from Shocklach Oviatt in Cheshire.[96] Ralph Egerton is the exemplar of a man in precisely this position in the early years of Henry's reign, combining a very good relationship with the king with excellent local knowledge and contacts.[97]

There are signs that a tendency toward to the appointment of outsiders to important positions was reappearing in the 1540s, if only in the appointment of William Paget and John Mason (secretary for the French language) to the constableship of Chester Castle. But the far stronger trend throughout the remainder of the early and mid-Tudor period was towards office-holders with both local and court connections. That the dominant factor in the choice of officials was local power, connection and knowledge is clearly indicated by the lack of a rapid change-over of officers, and the frequency with which dynasties of office-holders emerged.

---

94 The former role included accounting for the rents of the hundred, the perquisites of the hundred courts and subsidies granted to the crown; the latter executing royal and palatine writs and commissions: Clayton, *Administration*, 189; Worthington, 'Royal government', 113–18.

95 Gunn, 'Act of Resumption of 1515'; cf. for north Wales his 'Charles, duke of Suffolk, in north Wales', 461–6.

96 Robert Sonde of Shocklach Oviatt was involved in a dispute with Edward Jones of Iscoide, Flints.: CCRO, DCH U/27 (bonds, 20 Oct. 1551).

97 Ives, 'Ralph Egerton'.

The holders of offices such as the escheatorship demonstrate the importance of Cheshiremen with links to court and central government. The post was held in conjunction with that of attorney by Thomas Wolton until 1495.[98] He was then replaced by Edmund Bulkeley as attorney and Roger Mainwaring as escheator. Like Bulkeley, Mainwaring was a serjeant-at-law. These legal professionals probably acted in person as they had no duties elsewhere. At the start of Henry VIII's reign, Roger Mainwaring was reappointed, but a non-legal element was added because the grant was in conjunction with Ralph Egerton in survivorship. On the death of Mainwaring, Egerton served alone until his death. Richard Leftwich was acting as deputy in 1514, a post of increased importance now that the office had come into the hands of a non-lawyer.[99] It was a sign that the post had become a target for courtiers when, with Egerton's position at court coming under challenge from William Brereton, on 1 April 1525 the latter was granted the post in reversion.

Such men with links to the centre can be seen operating in several offices. Like the Birkenheads, discussed above as prothonotaries, the Hurlestons first came to Cheshire office from Lancashire thanks to Stanley patronage: Hugh was described as a servant of Sir William Stanley when he was appointed to the surveyorship in the 1480s.[100] But by the early sixteenth century they had established themselves in the central administration in Westminster and they illustrate the extent to which patronage now operated to give offices to local men with direct court links rather than connections with aristocratic intermediaries. In part this was inevitable, given declining Stanley influence, but it must also have contributed to that decline. Nicholas Hurleston, Hugh's son, became Clerk of the Spicery and Clerk of the Green Cloth, worked in the capital and obtained property in East Anglia through his first marriage.[101] The Hurlestons dominated the position of surveyor of Cheshire until 1531. Hugh was also janitor of Chester Castle and lessee of the Dee Mills. Richard became a serjeant-at-law and constable of Chester Castle. Thomas served as deputy sheriff,[102] and Humphrey was king's attorney in 1538. Yet they were not as active in Cheshire as the Breretons, the best-known example of Cheshire courtiers holding office in the shire. As well as William, whose office-holding is well-known, John became master mason in 1537, and Urian played a part in William's domination before 1536 and carried on the tradition thereafter. In 1528 he succeeded his kinsman Bartholomew as crier of the exchequer[103] and jointly with William became park-keeper of Shotwick.

98 Worthington, 'Royal government', 107–9; Clayton, *Administration*, 181–7.
99 *LP Add.* i/1, 112.
100 *British Library, Harleian MS 433*, ed. Rosemary Horrox and P. W. Hammond, Upminster 1979–83, i. 125; Ormerod, *Chester*, ii. 814–15.
101 *LP* i/2, 3049(10); iv/1, 1610(8); iv/2, 2972; v. 303, 166(37); xiii/1; Bindoff, *House of Commons, 1509–1558*, ii. 418–19.
102 He also acted as clerk to the halmote court of Macclesfield Forest under Edward, earl of Derby, from at least 1545 to 1552: CCRO, DDS 6/6; DDS 19/1.
103 *Lancashire and Cheshire wills and inventories at Chester, with an appendix of abstracts of wills*

After William's fall, he took over the escheatorship, confirming family dominance with an appointment in survivorship with his son in 1550, and he added a joint appointment as king's attorney in 1538.[104]

The period 1480–1560 saw the growth of marcher council influence in the judicial positions of the shire administration. In other fields of responsibility local men continued to be chosen, particularly where the posts demanded local or technical expertise.[105] Although courtier office-holders with no other local stake became prominent for a few years after 1509, the phenomenon was short-lived and mainly true of the county's near-sinecures. The most successful local office-holders were those who achieved a prominent position at court, like Sir Ralph Egerton and William and Urian Brereton; there were also officials at Westminster, like the Hurlestons. Yet this was not without precedent, for in the first half of the fifteenth century the finances of the county had been in the hands of the Troutbecks, father and son, brought into the county from Cumbria, and they had been threatened by the intervention of other Lancastrians from the north-west with links to the heart of the regime, Thomas Daniell and Sir Richard Tunstall.[106] Royal servants had also held minor offices like bailiwicks: a figure like Thomas Sonde might be paralleled with Brian Wager, page of the wardrobe, bailiff of Broxton hundred in 1445.[107] So there was no remarkable new influx of officials, and the key offices of the shire remained in the hands of Cheshire men. Like Wales,[108] Cheshire was part of a wider patronage system, but those who played the system best were local men. Far from undermining the palatinate, these new office-holders with their court links were given a stake in the perpetuation of Cheshire's autonomous jurisdiction.

---

now lost or destroyed, ed. J. P. Earwaker (Chetham Society n.s. iii, 1884), 203; *SR* iii. 929, c.18.

[104] Urian married the heiress Margaret Honford and established a branch of the family at Handforth: Ormerod, *Chester*, iii. 644.

[105] See Thornton, 'Political society in early Tudor Cheshire', 180, for the dynasties which held such posts as the earl's master mason and master carpenter.

[106] B. P. Wolffe, *Henry VI*, London 1981, 109; Clayton, *Administration*, 165–7.

[107] Ibid. 189.

[108] Gunn, 'Charles, duke of Suffolk, in north Wales', 488–92; W. R. B. Robinson, 'Henry VIII's household in the fifteen-twenties: the Welsh connection', *Historical Research* lxviii (1995), 173–90.

PART III

POLITICS AND PROVINCIAL PRIVILEGE

8

Henry VII and the Palatinate

Henry VII has been credited with the instigation of the Tudor policy of centralisation. From Bacon's *History* in the early seventeenth century, Henry's alleged restoration of good government has incorporated an element of the extension of central control. It was Henry, the story runs, who conquered the unruly independence of the barons; it was Henry who enhanced the power and efficiency of the central government. The historiography has taken different directions with the passing of the decades. It is no longer accepted that Henry replaced a dependence on the nobility with a new alliance with the bourgeoisie, or that he 'founded' the court of Star Chamber to effect his attack on the nobles. Yet recent historiography still emphasises the power and intrusiveness of Henry's agents and especially his Council Learned in the Law. This chapter questions whether this intrusiveness altered the pattern of politics in Cheshire in the way that it apparently did in Essex or the Thames Valley.[1] Cheshire's contribution to the victory and survival of Henry Tudor, organised through the Stanley family, meant that palatine privileges were exercised for the county's benefit in the early part of the reign; and, although Henry's destruction of Sir William Stanley ushered in a period during which Cheshire's resources were exploited ruthlessly, this was done through the mechanisms of the palatinate, first through the marcher council and later through men recruited directly from the Cheshire gentry. Under Henry VII, therefore, Cheshire witnessed an intensification of royal lordship through the palatinate, not its destruction by a centralising monarch.

The 1480s saw Cheshire politics heavily influenced by the Stanley family. Sir William Stanley was developing a strong position in the Dee valley lordships and, as chamberlain of the county, occupied a commanding position in Cheshire's administration. Thomas, Lord Stanley, was the justice of Cheshire and a major office-holder in Macclesfield hundred. Sir John Stanley of

---

1 R. Somerville, 'Henry VII's "Council Learned in the Law"', *EHR* liv (1939), 427–42; Chrimes, *Henry VII*; Condon, 'Ruling elites in the reign of Henry VII'; S. J. Gunn, 'Henry Bourchier, earl of Essex (1472–1540)', in G. W. Bernard (ed.), *The Tudor nobility*, Manchester 1992, 134–79; A. Cameron, 'The giving of livery and retaining in Henry VII's reign', *Renaissance and Modern Studies* xviii (1974), 17–35; J. R. Lander, 'Bonds, coercion and fear: Henry VII and the peerage', in J. G. Rowe and W. H. Stockdale (eds), *Florilegium historiale: essays presented to Wallace K. Ferguson*, Toronto 1971, 327–67 (repr. in his *Crown and nobility*, 267–300); M. A. Hicks, 'Attainder, resumption and coercion, 1461–1529', *Parliamentary History* iii (1984), 15–31.

Alderley and Wever, the third son of the first Lord Stanley, had recently established himself in Cheshire.[2] James Stanley was archdeacon of Chester between 1478 and 1485.[3] The Cheshire stock of the family, from Hooton, had held the county shrievalty in the 1460s. If originally challenged by the Council in the Marches of Wales, it therefore seemed that Stanley power might now be accommodated and consolidated by it.[4]

The reign of Richard III ended the influence of the Edwardian Council in the Marches, and more influence devolved upon the Stanleys. The short-lived threat posed by the grants which Richard made to the duke of Buckingham gave the Stanleys good reason to support the king against his rebellion, despite the conflicting commands Lord Strange's secretary knew were flooding the region late in 1483.[5] That support was well rewarded with crown grants to the Stanleys: as early as 10 June 1483 Sir William was granted the wardship of Lawrence, son of Roger Dutton (d. 1476) and heir to the important Dutton inheritance, and significant grants of land and office in the marches followed.[6] Benefits also passed to Stanley followers, and many Cheshire gentlemen profited, for example from the grant of annuities.[7] Yet relations between Richard III and the Stanleys remained tense, in particular due to the activities of Margaret Beaufort, Derby's wife and partisan of her son Henry Tudor.[8] Stanley associates, including some from the north-west, were closely involved in this plotting. Once Reginald Bray informed Margaret of Buckingham's decision to break with Richard III, she sent as a messenger to Henry in Brittany Hugh Conway, a gentleman from north-east Wales with Stanley connections. The conspiracy was master-minded by Margaret from Stanley's London inn. After the collapse of Buckingham's rebellion and Henry's ill-fated attempt to land in the West Country, Humphrey Brereton of Malpas was sent to Brittany with money by Stanley.[9] Their power augmented by Richard himself, the Stanleys were able to lead united Cheshire support to Bosworth Field: the county's military potential in support of the Tudors was immediately obvious. According to the author of

---

2   Ormerod, *Chester*, iii. 577.
3   John le Neve (comp. B. Jones), *Fasti ecclesiae Anglicanae, 1300–1541*, X: *Coventry and Lichfield diocese*, London 1964, 14.
4   Clayton, *Administration*, 175–6; Hicks, 'Changing role of the Wydevilles', 78–9.
5   Ross, *Richard III*, 77; *Plumpton letters and papers*, 60–1; *Harleian MS 433*, i. 4, 8, 10–15, 16–18; Jones, 'Sir William Stanley', 17.
6   See p. 19 above.
7   Life annuities from Lancashire revenues were granted to a group including Sir William Stanley of Hooton, George Booth, William Troutbeck, Thomas Mainwaring, William Davenport and Robert Duckenfield: *Harleian MS 433*, i. 104.
8   Michael K. Jones, 'Richard III and the Stanleys', in Rosemary Horrox (ed.), *Richard III and the north*, Hull 1986, 40–1; Horrox, *Richard III*, 206–7.
9   Ralph A. Griffiths and Roger S. Thomas, *The making of the Tudor dynasty*, Gloucester 1985, 91–6; Jones and Underwood, *The king's mother*, 62–4

Bosworth Feilde, Sir William Stanley led to battle the men of north Wales and 'the fflower of Cheshire'.[10]

Although there was unease about the political situation in December 1485, Cheshire support was again forthcoming for Henry Tudor. George, Lord Strange, kept Easter 1486 with the earl of Oxford at Lavenham; they then both joined the king, who made his way via Nottingham to York. Although the earl of Derby left Nottingham for Lancashire, Sir William Stanley and others joined Henry there, and travelled with the king. Royal forces, albeit relatively small, were enough to make the threat posed by a Yorkist rising around Middleham negligible.[11] Perhaps to consolidate this support, on 23 September 1486 Henry VII retained more than 100 men of Cheshire and Lancashire.[12] Cheshire's role as a prop to the Tudor dynasty was also demonstrated at the battle of Stoke in 1487, when the Stanleys made it all too clear to Henry how important their support was: outside Nottingham, the Cheshire gentry were drawn up for their king's review, but Henry had to leave the town to go to them, and some of his men were initially dismayed to find the Stanley position well fortified.[13] William Troutbeck was knighted after the battle of Stoke, and later that summer John Warren of Poynton was knighted at Ripon.[14] In 1489 the Yorkshire rebellion which began at Ayton in Cleveland on 20 April and culminated in the murder of the earl of Northumberland on 28 April once again saw Henry rely on much north-western support.[15] After this, Henry's need for military support was focused more on continental expeditions. Some Cheshire men continued to contribute practical support: Richard Winnington raised men for service in Brittany in June 1489, and Sir John Savage junior died at the siege of Boulogne in 1492. The county's military role was, however, in general considerably reduced.[16]

The coherence of the county's community meant that military support for

10 'Bosworth Feilde', line 362; *Bishop Percy's folio manuscript*, iii. 248. It should be noted that the main early Tudor accounts do not portray a 'Cheshire' presence at Bosworth: Robert Fabyan, *The new chronicles of England and France*, London 1811, 672–3; Edward Halle, *Chronicle, containing the history of England, during the reign of Henry IV and succeeding monarchs, to the end of the reign of Henry VII*, ed. H. Ellis, London 1809, 411–20.

11 *Plumpton letters and papers*, 63–6 (for December 1485 it is necessary to use the *Plumpton correspondence*, ed. Thomas Stapleton [Camden o.s. iv, 1839], 49 [13 Dec. 1485] because of an omission in the later edition); 'A short and a brief memory . . . of the first progress of our sovereign lord Henry the seventh . . . etc.', in John Leland, *De rebus Britannicis collectanea*, ed. Thomas Hearne, Oxford 1774, iv. 185–92; Bennett, *Lambert Simnel*, 35–8; C. H. Williams, 'The rebellion of Humphrey Stafford in 1486', *EHR* xliii (1928), 181–9.

12 PRO, DL, 42/21, fos 49–50, 108–8a; Bennett, *Lambert Simnel*, 58 (102 men, costing over £1,000 *per annum*, chiefly from the duchy in Lancashire but also from Tutbury and High Peak).

13 'Short and a brief memory . . . of the first progress', 213; Bennett, *Lambert Simnel*, 82.

14 Ibid. 129; J. T. Driver, *Cheshire in the later Middle Ages, 1399–1540*, Chester 1971, 20; Ormerod, *Chester*, iii. 685–6; Edwards, *Itinerary of Richard III*, 41.

15 Bennett, 'Henry VII and the northern rising of 1489', 34–59, esp. pp. 42–4, 56–9; Hicks, 'Yorkshire rebellion of 1489', 39–62.

16 Driver, *Cheshire in the later Middle Ages*, 20

the crown was not simply the achievement of the Stanleys, and neither were the rewards exclusively theirs. Collectively, the county obtained concessions on taxation.[17] Individually, Cheshiremen achieved advancement, in terms of office, grants and careers. This was especially true of families which could show commitment to the Tudors before 1485. Such a record may have helped found the household career of Sir Randal Brereton. There was a Cheshire community in exile in Brittany and France: the author of 'Lady Bessy' tells how, on approaching Tudor's court, he was greeted by a man from his locality. The man refused to take money to allow him entry, explaining

> 'I will none of thy gold', the Porter said, 'nor yett, Humphrey,
> none of thy ffee;
> but I will open the gates wyde,
> & receive thy mules and thee
> ffor a Cheshireman borne am I,
> ffrom the Malpas but miles three'.[18]

Thomas Starkey of Wrenbury received a pension for his service at Henry VII's 'first entry into this his realm', while a group of Stanley associates was protected from the effects of the Act of Resumption of early 1486.[19]

Yet united support for Henry under the Stanleys, even though it produced rewards for Cheshire people, did not bring peace to the county. Admittedly Cheshire did not suffer the upheaval associated with the large-scale confiscations suffered by the Buckingham rebels or the supporters of Richard III. Virtually all Cheshiremen picked the right side on both occasions, and outsiders who did not rarely owned significant land in the shire. So the main sources of disturbance to county society were conflicts between established families, often over succession disputes. Although the Chester county court was not used indiscriminately to bolster Sir William Stanley's position,[20] some were obviously unhappy with Stanley dominance, most notably

---

[17] PRO, CHES 2/158, m. 3.

[18] *Bishop Percy's folio manuscript*, iii. 347, lines 670–6.

[19] *LP* ii/2, 3354; *RP* vi. 352–4.

[20] Examples of men being prosecuted for actions against members of the Stanley family are few. Apart from two incidents when servants of sheriff William Stanley were attacked (see p. 75 above), Richard Cartwright was indicted in April 1486 for taking wood from the earl of Derby's property in Dorfold; John Wade of Wrenbury and Chorley was accused in January 1487 of stealing fish from Sir William Stanley at Ridley; and John Witter allegedly broke into one of Sir William's closes in 1492: PRO, CHES 25/16, rots 1v, 2v, 15v. On the other hand, it was possible for an indictment against John Stanley, bastard son of John Stanley of Wever, to be found a true bill in May 1490 after a large-scale attempt to intimidate the tenants of William Bostock in the Northwich area: CHES 25/16, rot. 9v. See (rot. 10), the indictment of John Griffin of Nantwich, esquire, and many others, including Sir Robert Fouleshurst, John Bromley of Basford and William Venables of Kinderton, at the same session of the court, for intimidation at Newton by Middlewich against William, son of Thomas Bulkeley of Ayton, John Minshull of Church Minshull, and Thomas Massey: both include William Eulowe of Kinderton, gent.

Lawrence Dutton, ward of Sir William, who was repeatedly bound in recognizances to keep the peace towards him beginning on 30 September 1488.[21] Inquisitions on members of the Dutton family held shortly after Sir William's demise suggest that he had abused his position, taking the income from the dower lands of Alice, wife of Thomas de Dutton, 'but by what title, the jury were ignorant'.[22] It is also striking that Sir William does not appear to have played any role in arbitration of disputes in Cheshire between 1480 and 1495,[23] which suggests a lack of trust on the part of the county gentry and, perhaps surprisingly, a lack of power on the part of Sir William when it came to the settlement of their affairs.[24]

It should be remembered that Sir William's position was largely based on his offices. His following seems to have been drawn from lesser office-holders, naturally dependent upon him due to his position of chamberlain, rather than in any independent capacity. Thus those men who were exempted under his aegis from the resumption passed in the first parliament of Henry VII's reign include none more senior than Urian Brereton, then *amobre* of Merionethshire, and, within Cheshire, Henry Glegge, constable of Chester Castle and bailiff of Broxton hundred, and Hugh Hurleston, supervisor of works in Cheshire and Flintshire.[25] The two Sir John Savages, father and son, Thomas and Christopher Savage, had their own exemptions, as might be expected.[26] But so did Thomas Wolton, escheator and attorney-at-law in Cheshire, Robert Henley, clerk of the Dee mills, and Thomas Whiksted and Richard Massey, serjeants-at-law.[27] Perhaps because of its partial nature, Stanley power failed to bring a solution to gentry disputes. One of the most important of these was between the Leghs of Adlington, on the one hand, and the Davenports and Savages. A series of recognizances to keep the peace towards Nicholas Davenport of Woodford and Sir John Savage, Sr, were

---

21 37 *DKR*, 243–4; Williams, 'Stanley family', 133, 182. Soon after Sir William's fall, an inquisition found Lawrence to be of age. He was fortunate that William fell when he did: PRO, CHES 3/54 (11 Henry VII no. 7); Ormerod, *Chester*, i. 647.

22 PRO, CHES 3/54 (11 Henry VII nos 2–6); Ormerod, *Chester*, i. 647–8. See the second inquisition on Sir Thomas Dutton (d. 1459); the first inquisitions on Alice (d. 26 Nov. 1477), widow of Thomas de Dutton; John Dutton, son of Sir Thomas (d. 28 April 1473), and of Margaret, wife of John de Dutton (d. 6 May 1471). In 1504 Lawrence received further lands when Anne, wife of Sir Thomas Dutton, died: CHES 3/56 (19 Henry VII no. 3); Ormerod, *Chester*, i. 648.

23 See p. 29 above.

24 See the demand of John Hanky of Churton in his will (May 1494), that John Calveley, son of Sir Hugh, one of his three executors, should not concern himself with any matter in which Sir William Stanley was involved: PCC 13 Horne, printed in *Sheaf* 3rd ser. xvii (1922), 23, item 3985.

25 Others include Ralph Bruyn, porter of Rhuddlan Castle, Hugh Grymesdiche, vendor of the goods and chattels of felons and fugitives in Cheshire, John Coke, bailiff of Eddisbury hundred, Thomas Braban, bailiff errant in Cheshire, and James Saxton, keeper of Salghall woods: *RP* vi. 353–4.

26 *RP* vi. 339, 355, 383.

27 *RP* vi. 364–78.

entered by Thomas Legh in the Chester exchequer from 1488. A suit was brought by Sir John Savage against Thomas Legh of Adlington and his wife Katherine (Savage's daughter) in 1489–90. The Stanleys of Hooton may have sided with the Leghs in this dispute, for among Legh's sureties in a bond to keep the peace towards Hamo Asheley in April 1489 was Sir William Stanley of Hooton.[28] In 1494 indictments made at the Cheshire county court accused a large number of people, including many gentlemen, of causing disturbances at Wilmslow on 20–1 July. In four separate indictments presented to a county court in December 1494, 403 people were indicted for allegedly having rioted against Nicholas Davenport on 20 July; 200 people were supposedly involved under each indictment. The next day another indictment alleged that 1,000 people including the Nicholas Davenport who had been the target the previous day also rioted; 464 were named in the indictment. The 867 named rioters include several gentlemen. The leaders of those involved in the attack on Nicholas Davenport were the Legh family with its branches based at Adlington, Baguley, Mottram St Andrew and Stockport; those aiding them included members of the Ardern, Bostock, Fitton, Hyde and Venables families. In their response the following day, the Davenports called on the support of branches of their own family from Bram-hall, Woodford and Wilmslow. Alongside them were Savages, Handfords and Wardes, amongst others.[29] Such disputes clearly interacted and had the potential for very significant disorder.

The Wilmslow riot suggests that this potential for disorder was heightened by the ability of other important figures from the Cheshire county commu-nity to exert a powerful influence there and more widely. It was not only the Stanleys who carried weight in Cheshire due to their support for Henry Tudor. The Savages of Clifton were the major rivals to the Stanleys in Cheshire: they had already had an important role before Bosworth, recog-nised by the city of Chester when it created a number of them freemen in 1484. After Bosworth, where Sir John Savage played a far more consistent role in support of Henry than any Stanley, the family was well rewarded and expanded its role in other marcher counties and into the north-west

---

[28] There appear to have been attempts at arbitrating the dispute in 1494–5, perhaps the result of the disturbance referred to below: PRO, CHES 29/190, m. 11v; Ormerod, *Chester*, iii. 658. R. H. Morris's possible references to this (in 'Eaton MSS') are misdated to 1493: *Chester in the Plantagenet and Tudor reigns*, 62.

[29] The dispute concerned 'unam zonam harnesiatam cum argento & deauratam precii sex marcarum, & unum anulum cum uno lapide vocato a dyamonte in dicti anulo infixo precii quadraginta solidos, quos ei injuste detinet': PRO, CHES 24/65 (Conception of the Blessed Virgin Mary 1494). This was just the largest of many riots in the previous few years: exam-ples include those involving Thomas Venables of Kinderton, Ralph Davenport of Daven-port and others to the number of 200; Thomas Bulkeley, Jr, of Eaton and others to the number of 100; and John, bastard son of John Stanley of Wever, again with 100 others and like the others at or near Middlewich in May 1490; and the counter indictments which accused their targets, the Foulehursts and others, in which 166 rioters were actually named: CHES 25/16, rots 9–10.

midlands.[30] Periodically, Savage and Stanley interests came into conflict, as in the dispute over the manor of Mellor, just across the Derbyshire border, between Robert Pilkington and the Aynsworths.[31] While Pilkington relied on his good lords the Stanleys, it was the Savages and especially Bishop Thomas Savage of Rochester, London and later York who supported the Aynsworths. The troubles of the 1490s were therefore at least in part a consequence of Henry VII's own policies, and a realisation that some form of balance was needed in the affairs of the north midlands appears to have come to the king in 1493, following the murder of Thomas Cockayne. This was a particularly heinous crime, but what is more likely to have impressed on Henry the urgency of the situation was the implications of this regional instability for the security of his dynasty; in the same month Humphrey Savage made an initial contact with Perkin Warbeck. There was a *volte-face* in a connected conflict in Derbyshire, that between the Savages and the Vernons of Haddon, at least by March 1494, and Edward Stanley entered a recognizance not to harm Sir John, Christopher and Richard Savage. An even distribution of power in the north midlands was, however, upset by Stanley greed: the most notable example of this was the murder in June 1494 of William Chetwynd by Humphrey Stanley, sheriff of Staffordshire.[32] In April 1494 Robert Aynsworth suffered an attack on his tenants in Mellor; and in July 1494 the riot between the Davenports and the Leghs occurred at Wilmslow.[33]

The post-Bosworth settlement had therefore always been unstable. It had within it the seeds of its own destruction, seen most dramatically in the fall of Sir William Stanley on a charge of treason early in 1495.[34] It will never be known whether Sir William did plan rebellion or whether his fall was simply the result of a palace coup after his behaviour weakened his position with the

---

30 *The rolls of the freemen of the city of Chester, I: 1392–1700*, ed. J. H. E. Bennett (RSLC li, 1906), 8–9. Sir John Savage, Jr, received lordships and manors in Notts., Derbys., Leics. and Salop 'in consideration of his services with a multitude of his brothers, kinsmen, servants and friends at great cost in the conflict and battle against the king's great adversary, Richard III', 7 March 1486: *CPR, 1485–94*, 101–2; Ross, *Richard III*, 236–7; Ives, 'Crime, sanctuary and royal authority', 306–9; Wright, *Derbyshire gentry*, 107. See 'Bosworth Feilde': 'Sir John Savage, that hardy Knight, / deathes dintes he delt that day / with many a white hood in fight, / that sad men were att assay', in *Bishop Percy's folio manuscript*, iii. 255 (lines 549–52), cf. pp. 353, 815.

31 HMC, *Various collections*, ii, London 1903, 28–56.

32 Carpenter, *Locality and polity*, 570–1, 573 (recognizance: PRO, C 244/142/96); Wright, *Derbyshire gentry*, 107–8.

33 HMC, *Various collections*, ii. 34.

34 W. Busch, *England under the Tudors, I: King Henry VII (1485–1509)*, London 1895, 95–6; J. Gairdner, *History of the life and reign of Richard the Third*, new and rev. edn, Cambridge 1898, 286–9; Chrimes, *Henry VII*, 81–6; R. L. Storey, *The reign of Henry VII*, London 1968, 81–4; W. E. Hampton, 'The White Rose under the first Tudors, I', *The Ricardian* vii (97) (June 1987), 414–20.

king. What is certain is that he had grievances and his past suggests that he was never averse to a political gamble.[35]

Twentieth-century historians have tended not to recognise this episode's true import.[36] After 1487, they tell us, Henry had achieved a firm grip on the throne; emphasis therefore shifts to the reform of central and local administration. This is largely because they have accepted the view of the official Tudor historians, who minimised the threats faced by the king, and of the Stanley myth machine, working to make history reflect, however unwillingly, the family motto 'sans changer'. For Vergil, Hall and their fellows, Warbeck was simply 'Perkin', a pathetic deception with little chance of success. Sir William Stanley's involvement in the conspiracy was therefore something they had to explain at length because it was unexpected and apparently irrational. Chroniclers of the Stanley dynasty shared the presumption of the hopelessness of Warbeck's cause but tended to presume in addition Stanley's innocence; for them it was the king's unreasonable behaviour in executing Sir William that had to be explained, or even excused. In the words of the author of the 'Stanley Poem', probably Bishop Stanley of Man, Sir William died simply because of a loose tongue: 'Sir William Standleyes tongue was somewhat ryfe, / For a fonde worde he spake soone after he lost his lyfe.'[37]

Yet Henry himself saw the plot as serious; Warbeck was no story-book joke and Stanley's involvement came as a shock.[38] The view that Henry, informed of the treason well in advance, had the confidence to play his catch before spies gave him enough evidence to reel him in, is based on an opinion of 1521 and relies on the popular view of the king as an all-seeing 'universal spider'.[39] Other evidence argues strongly against it: even Vergil allows Henry to lose his composure when the news is broken by Clifford;[40] and the king's tendency to

---

[35] Leominster believed that Sir William had turned traitor during 1487: Bayne and Dunham, *Cases in the council of Henry VII*, 85–7; Steven Gunn, 'The courtiers of Henry VII', *EHR* cviii (1993), 47.

[36] '[A] fiasco': Chrimes, *Henry VII*, 85.

[37] *Palatine anthology: a collection of poems and ancient ballads relating to Lancashire and Cheshire*, ed. J. O. Halliwell-Phillips, London 1850, 250. See, in the eighteenth century, John Seacombe, 'A shocking Thought! that nothing less than loss of Life could attone for Words, without Action or even evil meanings without a forc'd Construction': *Memoirs, containing a genealogical and historical account of the ancient and honourable house of Stanley*, Liverpool 1737, 41–2 (he gives facts in 'mitigation' of Henry's decision); Jones, 'Richard III and the Stanleys', 32; cf. George Lee Fenwick, *A history of the ancient city of Chester from the earliest times*, Chester 1896, 164 ('grossest ingratitude and cruelty').

[38] For Henry's state of mind see *Calendar of letters, despatches, and state papers, relating to the negotiations between England and Spain, preserved in the archives at Simancas and elsewhere*, ed. G. A. Bergenroth and others, London 1862–1969, i. 99, 104 (no. 136).

[39] Busch, *England under the Tudors*, i. 95; Gairdner, *Richard the Third*, 289; *LP* iii/1, 1283a (p. 490).

[40] 'Ea re cognita, Rex ualde se dolere inprimis aiebat. . . . non poterat adduci, ut Roberti primum dictis crederet': *The anglica historia of Polydore Vergil AD 1485–1537*, ed. with translation by Denys Hay (Camden 3rd ser. lxxiv, 1950), 74, lines 18–23. According to Halle, Henry was 'greatly dismayed and greued' by the revelation: *Chronicle*, 469; cf. Holinshed,

withdraw into his privy chamber may have been accentuated by the shocking revelation that conspiracy had penetrated to the heart of the court.[41]

The reason for this was that the evidence against Stanley went further than the statement, reported by Sir Robert Clifford, that, if Warbeck was truly the son of Edward IV, Stanley would not bear arms against him.[42] This would perhaps have sufficed: as Bacon pointed out it indicated no loyalty to Henry.[43] On its own, however, it was hardly damning evidence. Taken, as it usually is, in isolation, the statement suggests that the main factors behind the execution were simply carelessly revealed hedging on Stanley's part and paranoia on Henry's.[44] The contemporary record of the trial, however, suggests that Stanley himself was responsible for Clifford's mission to Warbeck, after an understanding they came to on 14 March 1493, and that he had agreed to aid Warbeck in war against the king.[45]

Similarly, the motivation of the king's chamberlain was more significant than the crafty trimming usually cited. Vergil implies deep dissatisfaction on Stanley's part.[46] Sir William had given Henry an almost Christ-like gift, at once saving his life and giving him the throne,[47] so although his rewards were great, perhaps an expectation of something more is not incredible. Although Polydore does not detail these further rewards, Hall, who generally follows the Italian's version of events closely, adds that the earldom of Chester was Stanley's chief objective.[48] Support for Hall comes from the late fifteenth-

---

Chronicles, 509. *Bacon's history of the reign of King Henry VII*, with notes by J. R. Lumby, Cambridge 1876, 122, has Clifford forced by an unbelieving king to justify the charge 'upon his soul and life'; cf. Williams, 'Stanley family', 146–8. Ian Arthurson, *The Perkin Warbeck conspiracy, 1491–1499*, Gloucester 1994, 77, 85, is more convinced of the effectiveness of Henry's spy network.

[41] David Starkey, 'Intimacy and innovation: the rise of the privy chamber, 1485–1547', in David Starkey and others (eds), *The English court from the Wars of the Roses to the Civil War*, London–New York 1987, 75–6; Arthurson, *Perkin Warbeck*, 98–9. See also Gunn, 'Courtiers of Henry VII', 38; J. R. Lander, *English justices of the peace 1461–1509*, Gloucester–Wolfeboro, NH 1989, 112–19, 124–7 (but note his comment at p. 124 that this was probably a response to a general atmosphere of suspicion).

[42] Vergil, *Anglica historia*, 72–5; Halle, *Chronicle*, 469; Holinshed, *Chronicles*, 509.

[43] *Bacon's History*, 123–4. A Stanley source admits that Sir William spoke the words alleged: *Palatine anthology*, 250.

[44] J. R. Lander, *Conflict and stability in fifteenth-century England*, 3rd edn, London 1977, 96.

[45] W. A. J. Archbold, 'Sir William Stanley and Perkin Warbeck', *EHR* xiv (1899), 529–31; Arthurson, *Perkin Warbeck*, 62–3, 79.

[46] *Anglica historia*, 76–7: 'Guillermus . . . non aestimabat aequam suis meritis factam esse a Rege remunerationem'; Holinshed, *Chronicles*, 509; 'he did not think he had received good measure from the King, at least not pressing down and running over, as he expected': *Bacon's history*, 125.

[47] '[B]eing like the benefit of Christ, at once to save and to crown': ibid. 124.

[48] '[D]esiryng to be erle of Chestre & therof denyed, began to grudge': Halle, *Chronicle*, 469. See also Holinshed, *Chronicles*, 509; *Bacon's history*, 125; Ormerod, *Chester*, i. 442; Harrod, 'Defence of the liberties of Chester', 81. John Stow, *The annales of England*, London 1601, 1615 edn at pp. 478–9, represents a tradition that does not refer to the earldom.

POLITICS AND PROVINCIAL PRIVILEGE

century decoration of the shrine of St Winifred at Holywell.[49] Among the badges displayed there is Sir William's garter encircling the wolf's head, symbol of the earldom of Chester, implying that Sir William saw himself as a proper claimant to the title.[50] The grant of the earldom of Derby to Thomas Stanley had, after all, alienated a title which was central to the heritage of the royal family and especially the Lancastrian dynasty; perhaps in this context the grant of the earldom of Chester was not totally inconceivable. Rebuffed by Henry, however, Stanley was struck by melancholy.[51] In such a state he became determined to achieve his gaol through a deal to support Warbeck.[52] Strange as such a decision may seem, it fits with what we can gather of Sir William Stanley's character. In a family of cautious men, he was notable for his adventurousness: at Blore Heath in 1459, during the return of Edward IV in 1471 and during the Bosworth campaign, he had gambled with reckless abandon and, winning, reaped remarkable rewards. To such a daring mind, the plan was credible. Strategically, a Warbeck landing in Kent co-ordinated with a Stanley-led rising in Cheshire made sense. It would have caused serious, even fatal, problems to Henry.[53]

It has recently been argued that the fall of Stanley was connected to a coup at court,[54] or to Henry's attempts to clear problems in the midlands and frighten others into submission. Focusing in particular on the apparent involvement of Simon Mountford, Christine Carpenter is sceptical of the reality of the plot, other than as a device to remove troublesome elements in the midland counties.[55] It has also been suggested that lack of landed advancement combined with the tenurial insecurity of a younger son or dynastic sympathy with the House of York lay behind William's decision to rebel.[56]

The causes of Sir William's fall are likely to be complex and may well have included elements represented in some or all of these theories. None is

[49] M. J. C. Lowry, 'Caxton, St Winifrid and the Lady Margaret Beaufort', *The Library* 6th ser. v (1983), 101–17.

[50] Jones, 'Sir William Stanley', 20–1. See also Stanley's attempt to place himself in the tradition of the owners of Holt (Warenne, Fitzalan, Mowbray and Nevill): E. E. Dorling, 'The heraldry of the font at Holt', *THSLC* xxiv (1909 [1908]), 97–104.

[51] Halle, *Chronicle*, 470. This took place immediately before the creation of Arthur as earl of Chester on 29 November 1489: Chrimes, *Henry VII*, 249.

[52] This took perhaps 2½ years to crystallise; it had done so by March 1493 at the latest, when Clifford was sent to Flanders.

[53] Warbeck's believed that, after being foiled in Kent, he might find help in the north-west. His strategy in going to Ireland, Polydore Vergil states, was to try his luck in the west of England: *Anglica historia*, 82–4; Halle, *Chronicle*, 473; Holinshed, *Chronicles*, 511.

[54] Gunn, 'Courtiers of Henry VII', 47.

[55] Carpenter, *Locality and polity*, 584–7.

[56] Jones, 'Sir William Stanley', esp. pp. 20–1; Arthurson, *Perkin Warbeck*, 92–9. Sir William's bastard son Thomas went into exile with de la Pole after Henry VII's death (Arthurson, 'Question of loyalty', 406, citing *LP* ii/2, 3690), but this may have been due more to Sir William's fate than to any Yorkist cause the chamberlain may have espoused.

wholly satisfactory, however, and this suggests that we should look closely at the region of Sir William Stanley's influence. The king's movements suggest there was something of importance in the north-west that demanded his attention at the time of the rebellion. During the summer of 1495 Henry undertook a progress through the Welsh marches and into Cheshire and Lancashire.[57] The usual view is that it was for rest and recuperation in the aftermath of the treason revelations, the family visit of a dutiful son to his mother in Lancashire.[58] As Ian Arthurson has suggested, however, the chronology of the year's events indicates that this is a generous interpretation.[59] Henry began his progress in late spring – on 21 June he was at Wycombe and on 1 July at Chipping Norton[60] – despite the fact that the threat from Warbeck was not yet over; on 3 July the pretender's followers landed in Kent.[61] Although they were repulsed, the episode was still causing concern at Great Yarmouth on 11–12 July,[62] and Warbeck himself survived to return to Flanders. Yet on 3 July Henry paused only briefly at Tewkesbury to dispatch Sir John Pecche into Kent, then resumed his journey.[63] Having visited Worcester on 4 July, he moved north through the marches. He was at Combermere abbey in Cheshire on 16 July; the following day he went to Sir William Stanley's castle at Holt, and then to Chester itself.[64]

The idea that Henry's primary interest in the region was a visit to his parents is a good example of the way the Stanley myth has adapted reality to fit political convenience, presenting a picture of a family with a record of unswerving loyalty.[65] Seacome's work of glorification reduces 1495 to a minor blip, in which the king's bizarre and ungrateful decision to execute the loyal

---

57 *Anglica historia*, 80–1; Halle, *Chronicle*, 471; Storey, *Henry VII*, 83.

58 *Anglica historia*, 80–1: 'animi recreandi causa' (p. 80, line 18); Halle, *Chronicle*, 471: 'to recreate his spirites and solace him selfe with his mother'; Holinshed, *Chronicles*, 510: 'to make merrie with his moother'; *Bacon's history*, 128: 'to confort his mother', to demonstrate his continued trust in the earl of Derby and 'to make merry with his mother and the earl'. See also Jones and Underwood, *The king's mother*, 153.

59 Arthurson, *Perkin Warbeck*, 113.

60 Samuel Bentley, *Excerpta historica, or, illustrations of English history*, London 1831, 103 (Gladys Temperley, *Henry VII*, London 1917, 415, exhibits eccentricities, for example Alnwick [*recte* Winwick, Lancs.], 28 July 1495.)

61 *Anglica historia*, 80–3; BL, MS Cotton Vitellius A xvi, in *Chronicles of London*, ed. C. L. Kingsford, Oxford 1905, 205–6; *The great chronicle of London*, ed. A. H. Thomas and I. D. Thornley, London 1938, 258–9; Anthony Goodman, *The Wars of the Roses: military activity and English society, 1452–97*, London 1981, 110; Chrimes, *Henry VII*, 85; Storey, *Henry VII*, 84.

62 *Paston letters and papers of the fifteenth century*, ed. N. Davis, Oxford 1971–6, ii. 472–4.

63 *Anglica historia*, 82–3. Halle, *Chronicle*, 472, says it was Sir Richard Guildford.

64 Henry VII also visited Hawarden: Webb, 'Vale-royall', 190; Morris, *Chester in Plantagenet and Tudor reigns*, 63; Henry Taylor, *Historic notices, with topographical and other gleanings, descriptive of the borough and county-town of Flint*, London 1883, 102.

65 Alison Hanham, *Richard III and his early historians*, Oxford 1975, 133–4 (on Stanley's arrest and supposed wounding in 1483); Jones, 'Richard III and the Stanleys', 34 (on Lord Strange held 'hostage', 1485).

Sir William Stanley is more than offset by the singular honour of a triumphal affirmation of Henry's trust in his step-father. Building on accounts of the visit by Vergil, Hall and others, Seacome tells of a two-month visit, beginning about 24 June, for which elaborate preparations were made by the earl of Derby.[66] Yet Henry arrived at Lathom only on 30 July, so he spent twelve days in Cheshire as against about eight days in Lancashire, and only about five of the latter at the Stanley houses of Knowsley or Lathom.[67] The privy purse expenses show no presents to the king's mother and step-father, and provide little evidence of festivities during the visit.[68]

Two major problems could have been on Henry's mind when he began his progress in 1495: he was either still pursuing policies for Ireland formulated the previous autumn,[69] or he was responding to a threat revealed in Stanley's treason, or both.[70] There are reasons to believe that there was potential for trouble locally.[71] There were tensions present in the local community, and Stanley was supported by local people, moved by ties of family, interest and community sentiment to risk their lives beside him.

Emphasis tends to be placed on the failure of other members of the Stanley kin to get involved in the conspiracy.[72] The role of the earl of Derby and the other Stanleys is indeed one of apparent loyalty. Others from the region, however, were deeply implicated. Two of the four or five clerics arrested for conspiracy originally came from the area of south Lancashire and north Cheshire.[73] William Worseley, dean of St Paul's, was probably a member of

---

[66] Seacome, *Memoirs*, 41–3; Gregson, *Second part of a portfolio of fragments*, 230 (building of Warrington bridge). Henry is supposed to have worshipped in the 'king's chancel', Ormskirk: J. Bromley, 'The heraldry of Ormskirk church', *THSLC* xxii (1907 [1906]), 74.

[67] Bentley, *Excerpta historica*, 103–4.

[68] Payments were made to 'the women that songe before the king and the queen, in rewarde, 6s. 8d.' on 2 August. In addition a reward was paid to a French herald: Bentley, *Excerpta historica*, 104; cf. BL, MS Add. 7099, fos 27–30.

[69] Bentley, *Excerpta historica*, 103–4; Agnes Conway, *Henry VII's relations with Scotland and Ireland, 1485–1498*, Cambridge 1932, 78–84; *CPR, 1485–94*, 12; Steven G. Ellis, 'Henry VII and Ireland, 1491–1496', in J. F. Lydon (ed.), *England and Ireland in the later Middle Ages: essays in honour of Jocelyn Otway-Ruthven*, Blackrock, Co. Dublin 1981, 237–54; Arthurson, *Perkin Warbeck*, 104–6.

[70] He cannot have been thinking of an immediate threat from Warbeck in Ireland: this would have required foreknowledge of the debacle at Deal. (This casts doubt on Henry's intelligence, since, had he known of it, the projected Deal invasion was serious enough to have kept him in the south-east.)

[71] *Pace* Jones, 'Sir William Stanley', 13–18 at p. 21. Arthurson, *Perkin Warbeck*, 95, suggests connections with neighbours in the conspiracy.

[72] Coward, *Stanleys*, 15; cf. *CPR, 1494–1509*, 24, 29. Potential opponents, however, were forced to display their loyalty, for example the marquess of Exeter and his wife at the baptism of Princess Elizabeth in 1533: E. W. Ives, *Anne Boleyn*, Oxford 1986, 231.

[73] *Great chronicle*, 256–7; *Chronicles of London*, 203; *Anglica historia*, 72–3. The other clerics were William Rochford, provincial of the Dominicans; Thomas Poyntz, another Dominican; Richard Lessy, dean of Cicely, duchess of York (*BRUO*, 1136) and Thomas Powys, prior of King's Langley, Herts.

the family of Worseley of Booths, Eccles, south Lancashire.[74] William Sutton, formerly principal of Brasenose Hall, Oxford, and rector of St Stephen's Walbrook, London, 'a ffamous dyvyne', was possibly a relative of Sir Richard Sutton, founder of Brasenose College.[75] Both may have partly owed their promotion to Stanley influence.[76] Particularly interesting are the accusations of treason made against a prominent Cheshire knight, Sir Humphrey Savage. As the son of Sir John Savage (d. 1495) and his wife Catherine, daughter of Thomas Stanley, he was nephew to Sir William Stanley.[77] On 20 May 1493, shortly after Sir William Stanley's meeting with Clifford, Sir Humphrey allegedly met with one John Burton, described as late of Westminster, and others, and they plotted to destroy King Henry; he had been involved in similar activities with Sir Gilbert Debenham and others on 10 February 1493.[78] Sir Humphrey was a senior member of one of the most important families of Cheshire gentry, whose conspicuous support for the Tudors, beginning before Bosworth, had been well rewarded.[79] The Bulkeleys of Cheadle and Beaumaris, growing all the time in prominence in Cheshire and north Wales, were also involved.[80] William Bulkeley, yeoman of the crown, was hanged at Tyburn on 26 February 1494, along with three men accused of spreading seditious libels.[81] Rowland Bulkeley too may have been under suspicion.[82] Several other Cheshire gentlemen were bound in recognizances or sought general pardons in the period around the discovery of Sir William Stanley's treason. Some of this may have been due to a natural desire for insurance against malicious prosecution, but the suspicion remains that it may have been based on well-grounded feelings of vulnerability. Sir John Warren, knighted only a few years before by Henry, gave a bond in 500 marks for his allegiance on 10 November 1494, and received a pardon for all actions

---

74 Ibid. 2089; Arthurson, *Perkin Warbeck*, 85. See also, in connection with Eccles chantries, *CPR, 1467–77*, 86.

75 *BRUO*, 1826; *Chronicles of London*, 203; Arthurson, *Perkin Warbeck*, 85, 90.

76 Bennett, ' "Good lords" ', 17. As Bennett has pointed out, however, careerism created complex webs of patronage that cannot invariably be traced back to a single prime mover: 'Community, class and careerism', 28–32. Worseley was related to the Bothe family which produced several senior ecclesiastics in the fifteenth and sixteenth centuries: *BRUO*, 2089.

77 Ormerod, *Chester*, i. 713–16.

78 Archbold, 'Sir William Stanley and Perkin Warbeck', 532–3; Arthurson, *Perkin Warbeck*, 62, 66, 74, 95; cf. 11 Henry VII, c. 64 (*SR* ii. 632–3).

79 See Ives, 'Crime, sanctuary and royal authority', 304–10. Christopher Savage, Sir Humphrey's brother, had been involved in the trouble at Wilmslow in July 1494: PRO, CHES 24/65.

80 D. Cyril Jones, 'The Bulkeleys of Beaumaris 1440–1547', *Transactions of the Anglesey Antiquarian Society and Field Club* (1961), 1–20. For their connections with Sir William Stanley see Jones, 'Sir William Stanley', 16–20.

81 Arthurson, *Perkin Warbeck*, 74–5, 95; *Great chronicle*, 250; Fabyan, *New chronicles*, 685; Hampton, 'White Rose', 416 (John Stow, *Annales*, London 1601, 799: 'Robert Bikley').

82 *CCR, 1485–1500*, 270 (bond in £500 not to go further than ten miles from London, 5 Dec. 1495); Jones, 'Sir William Stanley', 21; Jones, 'Bulkeleys of Beaumaris', 7.

up to 25 November 1494 (associating the act with Warbeck's conspiracy) on 5 February 1495.[83] On 17 February 1495, Sir Piers Legh, Richard Delves of Doddington, and Thomas Agar of Broughton in Northamptonshire entered a bond in 500 marks for the loyalty and appearance of Thomas Venables.[84] The involvement of people such as Sir Humphrey Savage and the Bulkeleys in an intended Stanley rising, and the potential for support from a volatile county, suggest that the threat from Stanley was real. In the aftermath of the execution of Sir William, the appointment by Henry of complete outsiders to a string of important offices forfeited by Sir William does not suggest a belief in the unquestioning loyalty of the local community.[85]

In particular, we should set the alleged treason of Sir William Stanley and the suspected involvement of Cheshire gentlemen in the context of the approach to palatine liberties adopted by Henry VII. Not only was Sir William possibly disappointed in a desire for the earldom of Chester, but that earldom was already being used by Henry in a way that might concern Sir William and his neighbours. The influence of the Council in the Marches in the closer financial supervision of the palatinate quickly made itself felt. Arrears had risen to £468 8s. 6d. by 1488–9, but they fell to £225 1s. 1d. in 1489–90, and £133 19s. in 1490–1.[86] In 1491 Thomas Englefield had been appointed deputy justice of Chester, and, although the earl of Derby continued to hold the justiceship itself, Englefield's appointment was clearly a grant of the reversion of the post to an outsider and close royal servant.[87] In 1489 there had been an attempt to impose English taxation on the shire which may have met with resistance, and in 1491 an attempt to levy a mise for Henry's French war does not seem to have produced a positive response.[88] Both personally as a Stanley,[89] and as chamberlain and chief financial officer of the county palatine, Sir William had cause for immense concern. The gentry of Cheshire no doubt shared these concerns, and it may only have

---

[83] CCR, 1485–1500, 240; CPR, 1494–1509, 24; Arthurson, Perkin Warbeck, 95.

[84] CCR, 1485–1500, 246. Sir George Holford had been bound in 1494; PRO, C 255/8/4, nos 48, 50; Sean Cunningham, 'Henry VII, Sir Thomas Butler and the Stanley family: political control and the assertion of crown authority in north-western England, 1471–1521', in Tim Thornton (ed.), Social Attitudes and Political Structures in the Fifteenth Century, Stroud 2001, forthcoming. In addition, on Deal beach Warbeck's supporters included Thomas Baryngton, groom, of Sandbach, and Ralph Carden, yeoman, of Carden: Arthurson, Perkin Warbeck, 220–1.

[85] See p. 150.

[86] PRO, SC 6/Henry VII/1482–5.

[87] See pp. 144–5.

[88] See p. 71.

[89] Shortly before the meeting of Savage and Debenham on 10 February and that of Clifford and Stanley on 14 March 1493, William had been replaced as sheriff of Cheshire by Thomas Stanley, son of Lord Strange (20 January 1493). Thomas was born after his parents' marriage sometime before February 1481, and before 1485, and was therefore eleven at the most (he was made a knight of the Bath on 31 October 1494): CP iv. 208–9. This may have been an attempt to undermine Sir William's position, albeit through the appointment of a minor of the main Stanley line.

been their mistrust of Sir William that prevented them from supporting him more whole-heartedly. The choice between Earl Arthur and Earl William was not a palatable one.

This suggests that the continuing potential power of the earldom, both in material terms and in its emotional hold over the people of the county, was great enough to make Stanley's treason more threatening than many accounts suggest. It also suggests that Henry's regime was far more fragile than is usually allowed,[90] vulnerable to rebellion by even the most prominent of the political nation.[91]

Sir William Stanley was replaced by the king's closest servants, a shift which emphasised the role of the Council in the Marches. Robert Frost took on the chamberlainship, succeeded a few days later by Reginald Bray. Some of Sir William's successors, however, were household men from Cheshire. Henry recruited key figures from the Cheshire community to replace Stanley influence in the shire. The new sheriff was Sir John Warburton of Warburton and Arley, whose royal and Stanley connections underlined continuities in the change of the next few years.[92] Sir Randal Brereton, chamberlain of the county after Sir Richard Pole, was a similar figure. Brereton had been granted the receivership of Denbigh in 1493, for service in the king's wars. In 1498, as a king's knight, he was one of those who benefited directly from the confiscation of Sir William Stanley's lands.[93] Meanwhile, the surviving Stanleys came under increasing pressure. The justiceship of the earl and his heir was rendered more of a cypher than usual by the reduction in royal trust; financial pressure built; and George, Lord Strange, died a mysterious death in 1503, allegedly by poison at the hands of his enemies or even of the agents of the king himself.[94]

More intense management of Cheshire's affairs by his combination of trusted royal servants, often from the Council in the Marches of Wales, and men with ties in the county and at court changed the political life of Cheshire in the last fifteen years of Henry's reign. If the removal of Sir William Stanley had been intended to bring order to Cheshire, it failed.[95]

---

90 See Condon, 'Ruling elites in the reign of Henry VII', 134.

91 Arthurson, 'Question of loyalty', 401–13, emphasises loyalty as the key factor denying Henry lasting stability, but disappointed ambition, the failure of Henry's man-management and concern for palatine privileges seem more important causes.

92 Ormerod, Chester, i. 574.

93 Ives, 'Court and county palatine', 4.

94 For pressure on the Stanleys see p. 18 above. See also Condon, 'Ruling elites in the reign of Henry VII', 113–14; CP iv. 208, citing Stow, Annales, 484 (Stow, Annales, 1601 edn, 811), does not mention the manner of Strange's death; nor does the 1615 edition [p. 485]). In the Great chronicle, 327, the episode passes without comment: 'Upon the iiiith day of december or nere abowth dyed the lord Strange'; it is not even mentioned by Fabyan, New chronicles, or Halle, Chronicle.

95 There is a possibility that Henry's policy was deliberately designed to cause maximum disruption, although this would have been a risky strategy.

The involvement of prominent royal servants, notably Edmund Dudley,[96] caused continuing disruption. The way such intervention occurred varied. Sometimes parties to disputes with connections outside Cheshire sought arbitration. In 1490 Elena Delves, widow of Sir John, Sr, was in dispute with Sir James Blount and Robert Sheffield, who had married the two heiresses of Sir John Delves, Jr. Henry's attorney-general James Hobart was one of three arbiters appointed to resolve difficulties over the dowry of the daughters in the manor of Doddington, and it was later alleged that he deliberately prolonged the dispute and obstructed judgement.[97] Intervention might also come through the action of the courts: the insolubility of the Venables of Kinderton inheritance dispute was due in part to the involvement of such royal servants. The inheritance was the subject of prolonged action by Sir John Savage and Richard Cotton against Hugh and Thomas Venables, the male heirs of Hugh Venables. Savage's wife, Anne Bostock, was Hugh's coheir through her grandmother Elizabeth, one of Hugh's daughters; Cotton was another coheir, descended from Elizabeth's sister Joan. Sir Hugh, son of Hugh, had died at Blore Heath in 1459, and ever since the coheirs had been struggling with the heirs male. Inquisitions found both sides possessed of the barony and lands.[98] Some time before autumn 1492, Sir John Savage entered a bill before the council to recover possession of the property, alleging that William Venables had deforced him. The court found for Savage. Venables refused to obey, entered the Westminster sanctuary and there died, on 14 September 1492, to be succeeded by his son Thomas. A memorandum on the case of 1 October 1495 noted that the lands in variance and profits had to be answered for until livery was given; that Venables had forfeited 500 marks, and Cotton £80.[99] In 1500 Thomas was examined in Star Chamber. He obstinately refused to produce title deeds and eventually, in July 1501, the recognizance for his appearance was cancelled and the case remitted to common

---

[96] Dudley had an interest in the area through his kinship with the Dudley barons, and this he exploited through purchases and leasing around Malpas: see above ch. 1 nn. 38–9. It should be noted that Richard Empson was absent, despite activity in other parts of the midlands and north: *Plumpton letters and papers*, 88, 116–17, 140, 143, 149–50, 154–5, 159–60, 165–6, 185–8, 282–3.

[97] In 1513–15 Richard Delves claimed that, as the heir of his brother Ralph, he was the inheritor of lands including the manors of Doddington and Weston, but that, in connection with the arbitration, Ralph had given certain evidence relating to the properties to Sir James Hobart, who now refused to return it: *CCR, 1485–1500*, 136 (28 Feb. 1490); PRO, C 1/303/25 (1513–15?). Both Ralph and Richard were brothers of Sir John Delves, Jr. Ralph (who himself had three daughters) died on 2 March 1513 and was succeeded by his brother, a canon of Lichfield: Ormerod, *Chester*, iii. 522; Mill Stephenson, *List*, 70. In early 1490 the Plumptons had been concerned over the dispute because of its connection with the manor of Crakemarsh in Staffordshire, still held by the dowager Lady Delves, but eventually to pass to Sir James Blount: *Plumpton letters and papers*, 90–1.

[98] Ormerod, *Chester*, iii. 192–4.

[99] PRO, E 101/414/6, fo. 120.

law.[100] On 3 June 1505 a deal came to fruition, but the main beneficiary is not clear: two fines were made in favour of Sir Thomas Lovell and Edmund Dudley regarding the advowson of Rostherne, the first by Thomas Venables and the second by Sir John Savage, Anne his wife, Thomas Cotton and Katherine his wife.[101] In 1491 James Legh was succeeded as rector of Rostherne by Thomas Savage, the future bishop of Rochester; the collation took place on 15 December, soon after the case had been heard in council.[102] When Savage was succeeded by Giovanni Gigli, Henry VII's diplomatic agent at Rome and later bishop of Worcester, the patron *hac vice* was Richard Fox, keeper of the privy seal: this was a royal presentation when Rostherne was under crown control.[103] In September 1498 James Stanley, the future bishop of Ely, was presented by Thomas Venables, yet in March 1506, when Stanley moved to Ely, his succesor Hugh Hyll was presented by Sir Thomas Lovell and Edmund Dudley. Lovell and Dudley received licence to grant the advowson to the priory of Launde in February 1507.[104] The choice of Launde as recipient is significant: the house had strong court connections: its prior, John Lancaster, was a royal chaplain,[105] and in the period before the appropriation of Rostherne it received grants from a group of close royal servants, including Thomas Kebell, serjeant-at-law, William Smyth, John Skevyngton, William Bolte, Robert Brudenell, Gilbert Smyth, Henry Sotehill, Thomas Smyth and William King.[106] The disruption caused by court intervention

---

[100] Bayne and Dunham, *Cases in the council of Henry VII*, pp. clvii–clviii, 24, 130–4 (the introduction is not reliable, for example it erroneously has *Hugh* Venables for *William*); Ormerod, *Chester*, iii. 194.

[101] PRO, CHES 31/37 (20 Henry VII, 1; 21 Henry VII, 2); Ormerod, *Chester*, iii. 194. The Venables family had held the advowson since Edward III's reign: CHES 31/37 (20 Henry VII, 1; 22 Henry VII, 1); Ormerod, *Chester*, i. 438. In Michaelmas 1504, Sir Thomas Butler, Sir John Warburton, Thomas Savage (then archbishop of York) and two priests signed an agreement to pay 500 marks within forty days after Sir John Savage and Anne his wife occupied the manor of Kinderton: BL, MS Add. 21,480, fo. 115.

[102] *The register of John Morton, archbishop of Canterbury, 1486–1500*, ed. Christopher Harper-Bill (Canterbury and York Society lxxv, pt cxlviii, 1987), 144 (no. 512); Bayne and Dunham, *Cases in the council of Henry VII*, 24. Legh had been presented to the living of Rostherne in 1456 by Robert Grosvenor of Holme, Hugh Venables's trustee: Ormerod, *Chester*, iii. 193.

[103] Papal provision, 3 Dec. 1492; consecration 28 Apr. 1493: *BRUO*, 1646; *DNB* vii. 1190.

[104] *CPR, 1494–1509*, 535.

[105] Ibid. 353.

[106] *CPR, 1485–94*, 343; *CPR, 1494–1509*, 156, 318, 518; Sybil Jack, 'Monastic lands in Leicestershire and their administration on the eve of the dissolution', *Transactions of the Leicestershire Archaeological and Historical Society* xli (1965–6), 16; VCH, *Leicestershire*, ed. William Page and W. G. Hoskins, Oxford 1907– , ii. 10–13; *LP Add.*, i/1, 574; iii/1, 657; iv/3, 6799; Chrimes, *Henry VII*, 150–1. Brudenell became a serjeant-at-law the following year and was Smyth's colleague on the Council Learned in the Law; Sotehill had a distinguished duchy career, including the posts of deputy steward in the north parts and king's attorney, and his grandson married Joan, daughter of Richard Empson: Eric Acheson, *A gentry community: Leicestershire in the fifteenth century, c. 1422–c. 1485*, Cambridge 1992, 250–1. For the Skeffingtons see ibid. 249–50.

under Henry VII meant that the benefice was still the cause of dispute in Henry VIII's reign.[107] Even seven years after the fall of Sir William Stanley, serious tensions remained in Cheshire which might manifest themselves in violence, as a major riot between the Venables and the Mainwarings early in 1502 shows.[108]

There were, therefore, interventions in Cheshire by close servants of Henry VII. This is unsurprising given their vital role in the polity of his kingdom. What is more surprising, and suggests reasons for its occasionally disruptive effect, is that the involvement in Cheshire of, for example, the Council Learned, far from being large-scale and systematic as it may have been elsewhere, was very limited. William Smyth, page or groom of the wardrobe of robes and probably page of the privy chamber, rapidly accumulated offices in the shire after the fall of Sir William Stanley, and he has been described as the chief agent of the Council Learned in the area. When there was a personal royal mission to be carried out into the north-west, Smyth was invariably given the task. It was in relation to Smyth that the most important intervention by the Council Learned in Cheshire occurred. Thomas Legh of Adlington was bound by a recognizance in £100 on 17 July 1501 to keep the peace towards William Smyth esquire and all household servants to the feast of the Nativity of St John the Baptist following. On his appearance shortly after that date, he showed that he had been bound in recognizance before the chancellor in Star Chamber in 1494, and was therefore allowed to depart.[109] Legh appeared again in 1503, following the issue of a privy seal to attend and pay a fine for not having taken up knighthood although qualified to do so. That said, it is noticeable that Smyth, based in Staffordshire, could not achieve the standing of a Cheshire gentleman – he did not, for example, feature as a county court juror or as a final concord panellist – and he made relatively few significant interventions in local political life.[110] At the same time in 1503, Peter Dutton, Sr, of Hatton was also summoned before the Council Learned to pay a fine for not having taken up knighthood,[111] but this was typical of the otherwise minor involvement of the council. In 1504 the resolution of the affairs of Lord Audley led to other individuals with a role in Cheshire being dealt with, for example Hugh Egerton of Wrinehill, Stafford-

---

[107] Philip Legh of Booths was forced to disclaim an interest in the benefice: Ormerod, *Chester*, i. 432; PRO, STAC 2/17/80, 146, 245; STAC 2/23/311. For the divorce of the advowson of Middlewich from the Audley inheritance see VCH, *Nottinghamshire*, ii. 93; Ormerod, *Chester*, iii. 180, 185; Godfrey, *Priory of Lenton*, 171–2.

[108] PRO, CHES 24/70 (St Hillary, 1502); cf. *Sheaf* 3rd ser. xviii (1923), 63, item 4376.

[109] This may well have been linked to a dispute between Thomas Legh of Adlington and his wife Elena and the brothers and sisters of Thomas, put to arbitration before Edmund Chadderton and Geoffrey Downes, with a bond in 1,000 marks (later reduced to 100 marks) of 5 July 1489 to abide the award being enrolled on the Close Rolls: CCR, *1485–1500*, 107, 129.

[110] Gunn, 'Courtiers of Henry VII', 31–3; Ives, 'Ralph Egerton', 350.

[111] PRO, DL 5/2, fos 39, 47; CCR, *1500–9*, 10.

shire.[112] Disputes between Thomas Mainwaring and Thomas Gerard, gentleman, and over Winnington led to the appearance of Mainwaring and Philip Egerton in 1505.[113] John Dawne appeared in 1508 in relation to a dispute with Sir John Bothe.[114] It therefore appears that it was only Legh who got seriously entangled with Smyth and Henry's Council Learned in the Law.

It is only by spreading the net wider, to include men whose primary interests did not lie in Cheshire, that we find other examples, connected with actions against retainers in 1504–5.[115] In 1507 Sir Edward Savage, Edward Savage, Richard Savage and Christopher Throgmorton paid £30 'for Reteyndors'.[116] The accounts of the treasurer of the chamber show how other offences were brought to fines, as in 1495 when the abbot of Chester offended against the statue of praemunire and therefore became liable to pay a fine, an affair in which Bishop Smith probably played a leading role.[117] An indirect impression of the impact of the Council Learned's policies in Cheshire is gathered through an examination of payments under obligations received by the treasurer of the chamber. Senior members of the Cheshire gentry are represented – Thomas Venables makes four appearances in these records,[118] as does Randal Brereton.[119] Lawrence and Piers Dutton[120] appear twice each; there are also two appearances for Ralph Ravenscroft,[121] and two each for John and Roger Mainwaring.[122]

This involvement was therefore not general and systematic intervention in justice, but was focused on supporting rather than challenging the work-

112 PRO, DL 5/2, fo. 73, cf. fo. 83v.

113 PRO, DL 5/2, fos 92, 94v, 97–v, 101; DL 5/4, fo. 28.

114 PRO, DL 5/2, fo. 136v.

115 PRO, DL 5/4, fo. 53 (information from Piers Newton, secretary to the Council in the Marches, against Lord Dudley, Sir John Savage and Sir Robert Throgmorton).

116 PRO, E 36/214, fo. 535 (12 Dec.).

117 PRO, E 101/414/6, fo. 120 ('my lorde of Chester knoweth all the mater').

118 PRO, E 101/414/6, fo. 90; E 101/414/16, fo. 95; E 36/214, pp. 393, 521; cf. CCR, 1500–9, 231.

119 PRO, E 101/414/16, fo. 101; E 101/413/2/3, p. 235; E 36/214, pp. 462, 517.

120 Lawrence: PRO, E 101/414/6, fo. 90; E 101/414/16, fo. 95. Piers: E 36/214, pp. 462, 472.

121 PRO, E 36/214, pp. 397, 408; cf. CCR, 1500–9, 251, 356.

122 John: PRO, E 36/214, pp. 478, 487. Roger: E 36/214, pp. 461, 514. There are also single appearances for Sir John (E 101/414/16, fo. 90v) and Lawrence Warren (E 36/214, p. 396; cf. CCR, 1500–9, 218), Robert Duckinfield (E 36/214, p. 440), Ralph Delves (E 36/214, p. 477), Robert Fouleshurst (E 36/214, p. 540), Sir John Warburton (E 36/214, p. 462), Sir George Holford (E 36/214, p. 408; cf. CCR 1500–9, 251, 356), Robert Massey (E 101/414/16, fo. 101), and John Donnes [Done] (E 101/414/16, fo. 101), Ranulph Pole (E 36/214, p. 502), Thomas Glegge of Gayton (1 Oct. 1505: he 'hath frely yeven to the kinges grace by way of transporte whiche Thomas late Erle of Derby ought vnto him the somme of' £800: E 36/214, p. 457), Thomas Liversage (E 36/214, p. 408; cf. CCR, 1500–9, 356), and John and Richard Bulkeley (E 36/214, p. 514). Other Cheshire gentlemen can be added to the list from the Close Rolls: William Brereton of Brereton, Robert Needham of Cranage, Ralph Birkenhead, Nicholas Faryngdon and Roger Brereton of Sandbach: CCR, 1500–9, 199, 346, 360.

ings of the palatinate and, in spite of the undoubted disruption occasionally caused, it is this which was the most important feature of Henry VII's government in Cheshire after 1495. As in other spheres, royal government worked through rather than against the Chester palatinate. In particular, the Council Learned acted to support – and discipline – the actions of Cheshire officers in their fiscal and especially taxation responsibilities. In 1506 the collectors of clerical subsidy in the diocese of Lichfield were to command those who refused to pay 'to apper bifor the kinges counsell lerned'; two Cheshire churchmen were involved in obligations before the king's council for 'mony due to the kinges grace of and for the subsidie', and the bonds were passed to William Smyth for action in 1507.[123] When Randal Brereton became deputy chamberlain of Chester, he entered a recognizance to the king in £1,000 that he would pay the king or Prince Henry 400 marks *per annum*.[124] On his promotion to chamberlain, he was to pay forty marks *per annum* for the post to John Heron.[125] The sum of 400 marks was to exclude revenue from mises, and royal officers kept memoranda of local taxation grants, for example in March 1497 that 'my lorde princes Counsell hath taken in Charge to levy a certayn ayde & subsidie in the principalite of Wales & Chisshir towardes the werres of Scotland'.[126] Late in 1507 the council was acting to ensure that the Cheshire mise was paid by the chamberlain, Sir Randal Brereton.[127] On 1 March 1508 Sir William Troutbeck, Sir John Warburton, Sir William Stanley and other Cheshire gentlemen were bound to pay 1,000 marks at the following midsummer, and 1,000 marks at Michaelmas yearly during the following two years, 'for their confirmacon of their liberties and their lettres of pardon'.[128] The management of royal lands in Cheshire was also considered by the council, with Sir John Warburton being summoned in 1509 for alleged waste in Northwich.[129] The receipt books of the treasurer of the Chamber show the result of this supervision, for example in a payment by Sir Richard Pole, chamberlain of Chester, of arrears of the mise granted to Arthur, on 29 October 1502, and payments by William Smyth of £67 2s. 4d. as receiver of Cheshire and of Ridley, and of £86 11s. as receiver of the

---

[123] PRO, DL 5/4, fo. 81; DL 5/2, fo. 117v (the abbot of Vale Royal and the prior of Norton.)

[124] CCR, *1500–9*, 132 (10 Apr. 1504).

[125] Ibid. 190 (5 Apr. 1505).

[126] Also in 1505, to the effect that 'Chesshir owe of suche money as they promysed the kinges grace [in 1497] towardes his werres in Scotland the some of xlviii li. xv s. viii d.': PRO, E 101/414/6, fo. 129; E 36/214, p. 616 (1 Oct. 1505). For Denbigh and Chirkland, 1506, see ibid. 619–20.

[127] Sir Richard Cholmondeley and others were bound in an obligation of forty marks that Brereton should appear and pay £18 of the 'subside graunted within the Countie of Chestre', and he duly handed the money to John Heron: PRO, DL 5/4, fo. 112.

[128] PRO, E 36/214, p. 405. This may be the grant in which Piers Dutton was involved, which produced disputes over the rating of 'foreigners' not inhabiting in the shire: STAC 2/7/184 (*L&C Star Chamber*, 184).

[129] PRO, DL 5/4, fo. 155v.

Cheshire lands of Lord Audley.[130] The accounts of the treasurer of the Chamber also show the way the council managed the prerogative rights of the king in Cheshire. On 2 November 1495 Sir Piers Legh, Sir William Stanley, Randal Brereton, Thomas Legh, Thomas Venables and Ralph Ravenscroft were bound to pay 100 marks for the wardship of Piers Gerrard. A month before the earl of Derby had offered £500 'for a forfeiture of one Mainwaring'.[131] Among the wards listed in October 1505 was that of Cotton of Cheshire.[132] This management helped ensure that the finances of the palatinate remained extremely sound. Arrears were only £61 13s. 7d. in 1494–5, and just £26 12s. in 1495–6.[133] Although they rose as high as £458 9s. 9d. in 1501–2 this was because of the huge increase in revenues that resulted from the grants of mise and fines in 1497 and the following twelve years. The arrears did not mean that the money available for use outside the county was negligible. In 1501–2 the total delivered exceeded £1,050; the following year, it was higher still, exceeding £1,100.[134]

Turning to consider the activity of the Council in the Marches,[135] we find increased financial, judicial and political oversight, especially at the visit by justices in eyre in 1499; Thomas Kebell presided along with John Mordaunt, who was in charge of the campaign to enforce royal lordship in Wales.[136] Prince Arthur visited Chester from 4 August to 9 September 1499, and the *quo warranto* writs were issued on 12 August.[137] The intention behind the eyre was clearly financial and political gain.[138] A mise was to be sought; considering taxation had already been paid, it was hoped that the six weeks' notice required for the eyre meant that 'in the meane tyme [it] maie be hard how the County taketh it'. '[T]he putting in of the princes reuenewes in suretie' was intended.[139] Another concern was that 'many pretended ffranchises are usurped uppon the prince w[i]thout tytle or ground, but upon a long

---

130 Pole: PRO, E 101/413/2/3, pp. 9, cf. 59, 208. Smith: ibid. 55–6, cf. 141, 209.

131 PRO, E 101/414/6, fos 116, 120v.

132 PRO, E 36/214, p. 635.

133 PRO, SC 6/HenryVII/1488–9.

134 PRO, SC 6/HenryVII/1518–19; E 36/213, fos 11v–11.

135 For north Wales see Smith, 'Crown and community in the principality of north Wales', 159–68.

136 Brown, 'Cheshire writs of *quo warranto*', 676–84. Reginald Bray, chamberlain of Chester 1495–1500, was also an associate of Mordaunt. Smith, 'Crown and community in the principality of North Wales', 157–9, 168–71, describes intensive investigation of finances, customs and charters in 1504, 1506 and 1507.

137 Brown, 'Cheshire writs of *quo warranto*', 676–84.

138 BL, MS Lansdowne 644, fo. 21r–v ('Remembrances for the Prince against his being at Chester'). The remembrances indicate the merging of policy-making for Chester and the marches, suggesting that 'the ordering of Northwales & Merion Marsh to be at Chester first, & then att Denbigh for suretie takeing of the bondes'.

139 The chamberlain was to be required to 'putt in his suretie, & his accomptes to be seene & such thinges to be allowed therein as are to be allowed & the others dampned, & soe to followe yerely'.

contynewed wronge', and this was to be addressed by the *quo warrantos*.[140] It has been argued that the *quo warranto* enquiries begun in 1499 were motivated by the hope of financial gain, and to the extent that this was the objective rather than the destruction of local privileges, this cannot be questioned. The very action of investigating franchises, however, demonstrated the prince's political dominance expressed through his council, and this was a greater imperative.[141] The political objective was clear in the intention to 'know how my lord of Derby occupieth' Overmarsh and Northwich, and in the way the Black Prince's eyre of 1353 was recalled as a conscious model: 'he reteyned & bound the whole Countie to himselfe & every man knewe his owne thing and did there duties many yeares after'. The prince was to 'shewe himselfe there to his subiectes and the cause of his comeing for the weale of them and the County and to reform wronges done'; it was, however, not decided 'whether the Prince shall retaine all the Countie to himselfe onely or not'. The redemption of the sessions in eyre in 1500 also served to emphasise the power of the council, since it drew on precedents from south Wales rather than from north Wales or Cheshire, where redemption had not been attempted for many years.[142]

Henry VII's policy in Cheshire was therefore to use the palatinate to his own purposes, not to destroy it and replace it with subjection to central institutions. In the same way, the powers of other palatinates were emphasised around this time through *quo warranto* inquiries in Durham and Lancaster.[143] Under Edward IV it had been local power-brokers from Cheshire who took places on the Council in the Marches; now it was outsiders who increased their influence in Cheshire on the back of combined council and Cheshire office-holding. Their exploitation of the county's resources, especially its financial resources, was highly effective. If there was a threat of a Cheshire palatine rebellion under Sir William Stanley, Henry Tudor's response was not to dismantle the palatinate but to tighten his grip upon it. The reign of Henry VII saw the most intensive and active period of palatine lordship in Cheshire since the days of Henry V.

---

[140] There was also to be a strict examination of, for example, encroachments on the forests. Specific quarrels were also addressed, including the matter between the prince and the city of Chester, which encompassed such issues as the making of craftsmen, forfeitures there, the city boundaries, the murage, the Dee and its fish garths and mills and the fee farm. There was also mention of the 'ordering' of Middlewich and Macclesfield.

[141] Brown, 'Cheshire writs of *quo warranto*', 681–2; cf. Harold Garrett-Goodyear, 'The Tudor revival of *quo warranto* and local contributions to state building', in Arnold, Green, Scully and White, *On the laws and customs of England*, 231–95. The determination of the prince's council to retain its autonomy, was expressed, for example in BL, MS Cotton Vitellius C.1, fos 3–5.

[142] Pugh, *Marcher lordships*, 36–42.

[143] Garrett-Goodyer, 'Tudor revival of *quo warranto*', 236–7.

9

Wolsey, Cromwell and Cheshire Politics, 1509–1536

During the ministries of Thomas Wolsey and Thomas Cromwell, the palatinate of Chester underwent unprecedented change. This chapter examines how Wolsey's lust for power and determination to achieve glory for his master led him to intervene in Cheshire with lasting, if not necessarily intentional, results; and how more urgent pressures, the need for religious uniformity, fears of civil war and treason, and the urgency of raising revenue, compelled Cromwell to attempt greater systematisation and to integrate the palatinate more fully into the king's dominions. Behind these practical imperatives, at least in Cromwell's mind, there operated an ideology of 'imperial' government which sought the unification of authority. Alongside the plans of ministers worked the brokerage of courtiers who acted as a link between the county and the king and his ministers. Sir Ralph Egerton and William Brereton have been seen as 'over-mighty courtiers' whose rise and fall increased central control over Cheshire, and even brought palatine autonomy to an end. The argument here will be that the influence of Wolsey and Cromwell, Egerton and Brereton, was not so dominating or so catastrophic for the palatinate community as might have been expected.

The impact of Thomas Wolsey

While Henry VII concentrated on making the palatinate work for him, and not undermining it, Wolsey subjected the major Cheshire gentry to unprecedented concerted persecution in courts directly under his control as chancellor and brought the administration of the county further into line with that of the rest of England. In so doing he opened the county to the influence of his agents, both royal servants and his own.

The end of Henry VII's reign saw the disappearance from Cheshire politics of William Smyth, one of the men most closely identified with the king's tough financial policies. Sir Randal Brereton continued as chamberlain of Chester, yet the general atmosphere of recrimination over the policies of Henry VII's last years opened him to at least one complaint, from Piers Dutton, and his stewardship of the county's finances was noticeably lax, with arrears as high as £1,359 6s. in 1514.[1] Something of a political vacuum,

---

1   For Dutton see PRO, STAC 2/7/182 (*L&C Star Chamber*, 63–4); cf. ch. 6 above. Arrears

reflecting the sudden disappearance of the intensive regime of Henry VII's last years, was apparent, for example in patronage policy for the offices of the shire.[2] Rapidly, however, a new power emerged in Cheshire: Sir Ralph Egerton benefited particularly from Smyth's fall and he did so because he combined a local base in the palatinate with the ability to capitalise on the courtly and military emphasis of Henry VIII's first years. Egerton took over as keeper of Ridley lordship and, as he showed himself a brilliant jouster and soldier, he added other offices. In the 1513 war in France he took an enemy standard; in January 1514 he was made standard bearer for life and, soon afterwards, received an outright grant of Ridley.[3]

Egerton's success was particularly notable given the problems experienced by the Cheshire gentry community in the first few years of Henry VIII's reign. In 1513 most of the Cheshire gentry campaigned not in France but in Scotland. Although Flodden was a remarkable triumph for the English, Cheshire forces acquitted themselves badly. Ralph Brereton [recte Ranulph], Sir John Booth and Richard Done served on the right of the foreward under Sir Edmund Howard, with the remainder of the Cheshire forces commanded on the left wing by Sir Edward Stanley. Howard's men suffered heavily: Thomas Venables, baron of Kinderton, and William Honford were killed, and Sir John Fitton was captured.[4] The contingent from Macclesfield took especially heavy casualties, which included the mayor, Christopher Savage.[5] The author of 'Scottish Field' explained that the failure of Cheshire forces was due to their being placed under the command of Sir Edward Howard, when they were used to the command of the Stanleys;[6] whatever the reason, their performance did the county no credit, even if the king did not believe reports of the Cheshire men's cowardice.[7]

Against this background of failure, Wolsey launched a campaign of law enforcement through Star Chamber that was to have long-term effects on the

---

fell to about 1,000 marks in 1518–20, then climbed again to exceed £700 in the 1520s: SC 6/Henry VIII/337–53 (1514: SC 6/Henry VIII/343, m. 1). Brereton was deprived of the receivership of Denbigh in 1517 for accounting arrears: Ives, 'Court and county palatine', 4–6.

[2] See pp. 158–9 above.

[3] Egerton was receiver of the forfeited lands of Lord Audley and Lord Lovell, lessee of Aldford, Etchells and Alderley, constable of Chester, and had a reversion on a lease of the manor of Shotwick: Ives, 'Ralph Egerton', 351–8; Driver, Cheshire in the later Middle Ages, 21; Ormerod, Chester, i. 482.

[4] Halle, Chronicle, 557–64; Holinshed, Chronicles, iii. 592, 596, 598; CCRO, DVE P/10; PRO, CHES 3/61 (7 Henry VIII, 4). For contrasts between accounts of Flodden in Halle and Holinshed see p. 233 below.

[5] Driver, Cheshire in the later Middle Ages, 21; Morris, Chester in the Plantagenet and Tudor reigns, 66.

[6] Bishop Percy's folio manuscript, i. 225–6, lines 264–9.

[7] '[T]he kynge had a secrete letter that the Cheshyre men fledde from Syr Edmond Hawarde, whyche letter caused great harte burninge and many woordes': Halle, Chronicle, 564.

political life of the county.[8] On 2 May 1516 Wolsey made an oration in the Star Chamber for indifferent justice, a message reinforced in council on 14 May 1517 and 27–8 October 1519. The central courts of equity had previously made little impact on Cheshire, yet suddenly in the late 1510s there occurred a judicial offensive against the major Cheshire gentry. Many historians have seen these events as indicative of high levels of crime in Cheshire, one element of the historiographical tradition which sees Cheshire's privileges as by the fifteenth century little more than a mask for disorder and a spur to radical constitutional reform. It has contributed to the misleading portrayal of leading gentry as gangster-like figures abusing their power. Sir Ralph Egerton's career illustrates the point. Importance has been attached to Egerton's involvement in a dispute over land in Peckforton which produced litigation in the Chester exchequer, the Council in the Marches and Star Chamber: his servant Ralph Shipley resisted occupation by Robert More, who claimed a grant by Sir John Dudley. The Peckforton dispute has been presented as the issue which demonstrated that Egerton's influence was based on violence and therefore led to his downfall, yet it did not fatally injure Egerton's reputation, for it preceded and therefore obviously did not prevent his appointment to the Council in the Marches, the culmination of his career.[9] The violence in the case was limited, and Egerton is most usefully seen as primarily an administrator after 1523, involved as a member of the Council in Marches in such measures as the repair of Wrexham courthouse.[10]

Cheshire cases in Wolsey's Star Chamber should not be interpreted as a sign of Cheshire's lawlessness implying that changes to its jurisdictional status were inevitable.[11] Fluctuations in the pattern of prosecution and the

8 Gwyn, *King's cardinal*, 116–20.

9 Ives, 'Ralph Egerton', 363. More's bill to the Chester exchequer refers to an order by the Chester council on 6 Apr. 1525: PRO, CHES 15/1/114. The accounts of Morgan Broughton, bailiff of Peckforton, for 1521–3 are CCityRO, CR 63/2/495/1.

10 Gunn, 'Charles, duke of Suffolk, in north Wales', 488. As late as 12 December 1538 an order was made in the Chester exchequer: PRO, CHES 15/1/142. On 23 August 1525 Sir Ralph also became steward of Holt, Yale, Chirk, Chirkland, Cynllaith and Owen, and of Haverfordwest: *LP* iv. 1610. Compare Ives, 'Ralph Egerton', 358–63, with Gunn, 'Charles, duke of Suffolk, in north Wales', 488. Egerton is seen acting as councillor at Shrewsbury in 1521: Hereford Record Office, BG 11/29 (references I owe to the kindness of Dr S. J. Gunn.)

11 See the discussion of this issue in the historiography in the introduction at pp. 6–13 above. Geoffrey Barraclough depicted disorder, resulting from a recently and artificially created palatinate, as the inspiration for change, and Paul Booth agreed with him: Barraclough, 'Earldom and county palatinate of Chester', 23–57, esp. pp. 42–7; Booth, *Financial administration*, 6–7. See also Geoffrey Chesters, 'Power politics in Cheshire', *Cheshire Round* i/1 (Dec. 1961), 25–6, and 'Power politics and roguery in Tudor Cheshire', ibid. i/2 (Oct. 1962), 45–7, 57, for emphasis on disorder and crime. R. H. Morris's example of the 'need for repression' in early Tudor Cheshire actually refers to Chester-le-Street: *Chester in the Plantagenet and Tudor reigns*, 66 (*LP* also errs at ii. 4258). Beck alleged an improvement in conditions upon comparison with Michael Drayton's description of the battle of Blore Heath, a dubious source: *Tudor Cheshire*, 1.

language of allegations reflect factors other than the real level of crime in the county. The issue of violence in late medieval and early Tudor England is dogged by problems of evidence. Philippa Maddern has recently shown that the allegedly violent landscape of East Anglia in the 1420s and 1430s was in fact remarkably free from acts of criminal violence and has suggested that this model might be applied to England more widely at this period.[12] Although the evidence must be treated with extreme caution – it represents prosecution rather than 'actual crime', if such a phenomenon can be discerned – it may well be that Cheshire society was not significantly more violent under the palatinate than in the century and a half after the reforms of the 1530s; and it may well be that Cheshire was in general not a significantly more violent society than other parts of England. Although virtually all Cheshire gentlemen were accustomed, on occasion, to the application of force to help resolve disputes, there is no sign that this was atypical of early Tudor society in general, as in the case, for example, of the West Riding of Yorkshire.[13] Unpublished work by Dorothy Clayton suggests that in the period 1461–83 homicide represented 20 per cent of all felony indictments, just under 10 per cent of all indictments.[14] Considering the period 1580–1709, J. A. Sharpe's figures suggest that homicide and infanticide represented about 16 per cent of indictments for felony in Cheshire's sessions.[15] Using these figures, Sharpe argued that the county's pattern of crime was not starkly different from that in counties of the south-east; if there was a difference it was possibly only in experiencing a more dramatic rise and fall in crime before and after the Civil War respectively.[16] The proportion of homicide among the felony indictments in Cheshire, 16 per cent, was the highest but one of the eight samples given by Sharpe, but not startlingly higher than the others.[17] Considering homicide alone, Sharpe suggests that in Cheshire this rose slightly from the 1580s towards the atypically violent 1620s, then adopted a downward trend

---

[12] Philippa C. Maddern, *Violence and social order: East Anglia, 1422–1442*, Oxford 1992. She does, however, cite Morgan as saying that Cheshire's militarism and the small size of its military community cause us interesting and exciting problems when thinking about the impact of war on levels of violence in society: ibid. 17.

[13] R. B. Smith, *Land and politics in the England of Henry VIII: the West Riding of Yorkshire, 1530–46*, Oxford 1970, esp. pp. 144–51. For the situation in fifteenth-century Derbyshire see Wright, *Derbyshire gentry*, 127–42.

[14] Assault represented over 50% of the trespass indictments. Overall felony represented 44% of indictments, trespass 56%.

[15] Sharpe also suggested that, at least in the seventeenth century, levels of crime on the Scottish borders were not distinctly higher than those in the south east of England: J. A. Sharpe, *Crime in early modern England, 1550–1750*, London 1984, 56–7, citing Catherine M. F. Ferguson, 'Law and order on the Scottish borders, 1603–1707', unpubl. PhD diss. St Andrews 1980.

[16] Sharpe, *Crime in early modern England*, 57.

[17] Ibid. 55. Devon assizes, 1700–9, 15%; Cornwall, 1700–49, 13%; Essex assizes 1620–80, 11%; Sussex assizes, 1559–1625, 10%. The starkest contrast would be with Middlesex assizes, 1550–1625, and Hertfordshire, 1559–1625, at 5%.

which was typical of England as a whole.[18] Bearing in mind Maddern's argument that the moral context of violent actions was important in the way they were viewed, it might be that criminal and especially violent criminal activity in Cheshire appeared the more shocking, especially to outsiders, because it was often accompanied by sexual immorality. The reports of Adam Beconsall on Cheshire, as also for north Wales, would seem to confirm this.[19] There is also little evidence to suggest a direct link between prosecution of Cheshire crime and constitutional change. In any case, it is hard to see Wolsey's attentions as indicative of lawlessness characteristic of autonomous provinces when less exclusive jurisdictions (such as the home counties, to which the cardinal referred when he threatened to enforce the 'new law of the star chamber') were also targeted.[20]

What is significant about the 1510s is the extent to which criminal activity resulted in prosecution at Westminster. The murder of Thomas Huchyns, probably in 1518, involved Sir Piers Dutton.[21] Sir Piers allegedly

[18] Ibid. 60–1. This figure in particular lacks comparisons from other counties, and in all this material it is proportions of indictments rather than absolute numbers which are being discussed, so it is hard to tell whether Cheshire's apparently fairly average proportion of violent felony to other crime actually represents a fairly average number of violent offences per 100,000 of population. It is worthy of note, however, that Sharpe's agenda may affect his treatment of these figures: he wishes to use Cheshire figures as typifying English experiences, and therefore to point out contrasts in the experience of the prosecution of crime would undermine his further arguments. An intriguing line of investigation might be suggested by the fact that church courts studied by R. A. Marchant seem to show higher proportions of sexual immorality among the reported delinquency in the two northern counties considered there, Yorkshire and Cheshire, than in Somerset and Suffolk: Ronald A. Marchant, *The church under the law: justice, administration and discipline in the diocese of York, 1560–1640*, Cambridge 1969, 219. Marchant compares Doncaster and Frodsham deaneries with those of Sudbury, Crewkerne and Dunster. This should be considered in the light of Martin Ingram's criticisms of Marchant's methodology which led him to generally pessimistic conclusions about the process of church discipline: *Church courts, sex and marriage, 1570–1640*, Cambridge 1987, 345, 352.

[19] Beconsall's report to Cromwell (c. 1535) failed to reveal serious violence but recounted numerous tales of fornication and adultery: *LP* viii. 496. See also the petition of Bishop Booth in 1449 referring to 'advowers, fornicators, and other misdoers against the laws of God', indirectly associated with disorder and maintenance: *English historical documents, 1327–1485*, item 724, discussed in Heath, 'Medieval archdeaconry and Tudor bishopric of Chester', 245–6, 248.

[20] *LP* ii. app., no. 38 (the dispute involving serjeant Pygot and Sir Andrew Windsor). It is probably the case, however, as suggested above, that Cheshire's poor performance at Flodden and difficulties over the agreement of the mise in the 1510s meant that the palatinate community was less able to resist such challenges when they came.

[21] Prosecution before 2 April 1520 when a pardon was granted to 'John Dutton, chaplain, of Chester, of Hatton (Cheshire), of London, of Weston (Oxfordshire), and of Holt': *LP* iii/1, 779(2). John stated that he had been kept in London since the first day of the previous Hilary Term. His first imprisonment may therefore be placed in early 1518 or 1519: PRO, STAC 2/22/329. An examination of Sir Piers Dutton is dated 26 June: STAC 2/24/434 (*L&C Star Chamber*, 22–3). Dutton was pardoned for unspecified offences on 28 April 1519: *LP* iii/1,206(28). Piers' examination is therefore datable to 1518.

ordered a priest and near kinsman, John Dutton,[22] to convey the murderers from Cheshire to Oxfordshire and other shires and back again.[23] Dutton's spell in the Fleet allowed further disputes to come to the attention of Star Chamber. One of Richard Done's servants, Hugh, was murdered by Ralph Dutton with the alleged connivance of Piers; the latter responded that while he was in the Fleet, Done had ordered that his servants should assault John Fletcher, one of Dutton's servants.[24] The plaintiff in the Huchyns case was John Stringer, a cousin of the Breretons of Malpas,[25] yet this was not a one-sided intervention in Cheshire politics on behalf of the Breretons, because Sir Randal Brereton himself was also one of Wolsey's targets. Alice, widow of Richard Tilston, alleged that Edward Brereton, servant to Sir Randal, and Roger, Randal's son, had murdered him with a sword 'afore the holy sacrement of the aulter' in the chapel of Our Lady of Rouncivall, Westminster. The main target of the prosecution was Sir Randal himself, the chamberlain of Chester.[26] In November 1518 Sir William Brereton of Brereton was fined for his involvement in the murder of Lawrence Swettenham of Swettenham while playing bowls at Brereton Green in 1516.[27] Also prosecuted for their role in murders were Thomas Starkey, William Davenport, Sr, of Bramhall and John Massey of Puddington.[28]

It could be that Wolsey had in mind a deliberate policy of subjecting

---

22 PRO, STAC 2/13/186 (L&C Star Chamber, 89–90). This is the same John Dutton who was pardoned: Hatton (Cheshire) was Dutton's main seat before the 1530s, and Weston, Oxfordshire, is mentioned in the articles as an alleged scene of the crime. John replied to the articles against him on 28 November, probably in 1519: STAC 2/24/290.

23 John Dutton admitted that he had brought money to Oxfordshire from Sir Piers in the Fleet prison. Four of the murderers, Robert Massey of Nantwich, Nicholas Lightfote of Barrow, Richard Kirfote of Halton or Hatton and Randal Fletcher, had gone into sanctuary at Durham; the other two, Thomas and John Molyneux of Tattenhall, had gone he knew not where. It was also alleged that Dutton had sent money to Massey via his feoffees since the murder, with the implication that the enfeoffment was intended to defraud the king: PRO, STAC 2/13/186 (L&C Star Chamber, 90).

24 The murder must have occurred before 2 August 1516, when Done died: PRO, STAC 2/7/185; STAC 2/12/165–6 (L&C Star Chamber, 64, 83); STAC 2/24/354.

25 L&C Star Chamber, 22–3. John Stringer of Crewe married Anne, daughter of Humphrey Brereton, son of Bartholemew, brother of Randal Brereton, chamberlain Randal's father: Ormerod, Chester, ii. 686–7. Dating this is difficult: the marriage may be subsequent to the incident, yet it still seems that Stringer had Brereton links. Crewe is in the parish of Farndon, close to the heart of Brereton influence: Lancashire and Cheshire wills and inventories at Chester, 22–4.

26 LP iii/1, 779(25); PRO, STAC 2/18/287. This was the former hospital of Rouncivall, a cell of the priory of Rouncivall in Spain, replaced in 1475 by a fraternity. It was situated next to Charing Cross: John Stow, A survey of London: reprinted from the text of 1603, intro. and notes Charles Lethbridge Kingsford, Oxford 1908, repr. 1971, i. 73; ii. 100, 144, 374; CPR, 1467–77, 542.

27 PRO, STAC 2/26/370; Guy, Cardinal's court, 121; Gwyn, King's cardinal, 130–1.

28 PRO, STAC 2/18/256, STAC 2/24/266 (Starkey); STAC 2/5/135, 164–5 (L&C Star Chamber, 20–1, 47–8), STAC 2/21/229, 239, STAC 2/24/235 (Davenport); STAC 2/7/210 (L&C Star Chamber, 65–6) (Massey). Further details are to be found in Tim Thornton, 'The

Cheshire and its gentry to his personal control in his courts at Westminster. All the signs are, however, that this was not the case. The first of the important Cheshire gentry to be affected by the new policy was Sir John Savage, and it was his activities in Worcestershire, not Cheshire, that led Wolsey to be receptive to complaints against him.[29] Once Wolsey had demonstrated that a Cheshire gentleman might suffer speedy retribution in one of his courts, however, other potential plaintiffs realised that they might follow a similar route. Some of the cases which then came before him may well have been welcome to him, as his interest in Sir William Brereton testifies. Yet on 21 June 1521, after the initial rush of Cheshire cases to Star Chamber, Wolsey ordered 'all matters of Cheshyre dependinge here remitted to the Counsell in the Marches of Wales'.[30] In part this may have reflected a realisation that prosecution did not have a lasting effect in the locality; perhaps Wolsey also simply got bored with the pursuit. More importantly, it represented a return to a reliance on the local administration and the Council in the Marches for much of Cheshire's government, as under Henry VII. Henceforth, Cheshire cases involving senior members of the gentry elite appeared in Star Chamber far less often. Although Cheshire people litigated in Star Chamber with greater frequency than before 1515, they did so without the focus on such prominent malefactors. Wolsey was interested in a few high-profile targets in the short term, not in changing the constitutional position of the palatinate.

Wolsey's involvement in Cheshire also affected the monastic houses of the shire. The experience of Abbot John Birchenshawe of Chester illustrates again that the impact of Wolsey on Cheshire could be impressive in the short term, but also confused and strictly limited. It shows Wolsey challenging a major bastion of political power in the palatinate, but it also demonstrates that this challenge and the response to it were focused on specific problems and that the centre did not intend ultimately to destroy provincial privilege. The first significant conclusion from the evidence is that Wolsey was very slow to get involved and, when he did, acted without extreme partiality. Birchenshawe came into conflict with Bishop Blythe of Coventry and Lichfield over the abbot's use of the mitre, ring and pontificals. The abbot refused to co-operate with the case at Rome and, during 1516, the pope invoked

integration of Cheshire into the Tudor nation state in the early sixteenth century', *NH* xxix (1993), 42–3.

[29] There were links between Savage's murder of Paunsfote and his interests in the northern Welsh marches: PRO, STAC 2/34/23 (*Collections for a History of Staffordshire* [1912], 9–13); Guy, *Cardinal's court*, 31–3; Ives, 'Crime, sanctuary and royal authority', 296–320. The policy was already in action in the £1,000 fine imposed upon Thomas, earl of Derby, for a riot, the first payment due in November 1515: Miller, *Henry VIII and the English nobility*, 107. In 1516 the earl of Shrewsbury was worried about Wolsey and his policies: Bernard, *Power of the early Tudor nobility*, 18–25.

[30] Guy, *Cardinal's court*, 48.

Wolsey's assistance allowing the cardinal to become involved.[31] This dispute interacted with conflict over the lease of Prestbury made by Chester abbey. In 1515–16, due to financial difficulties caused by the dispute with Bishop Blythe, the abbot broke an agreement with Thomas Legh of Adlington and leased the tithes to Sir John Stanley of Handforth.[32] Yet only in 1524 did Wolsey act decisively. On 14 March a *congé d'élire* was granted to the Chester monks to replace Birchenshawe, and a month later they elected Thomas Highfield, sub-prior of the monastery, at the nomination of the cardinal.[33] Even then Chester's immunities were not undermined in the long term, for soon after, on 19 July 1524, letters of exemption from the jurisdiction of Lichfield and Canterbury were issued in the abbey's favour.[34] Only with the removal of Birchenshawe was a judgement brought in the Prestbury dispute. It went in favour of George, heir of Thomas Legh.[35] There were contemporary allegations of bias, due to the fact that George Legh's wife was Jane Larke, Wolsey's mistress.[36] Yet the fact that there was no conclusive end to the chancery suit for such a long period and the evidence for Birchenshawe's sharp dealing with Stanley suggests Wolsey was not acting in an outrageously partial way. Unfortunately for Wolsey, on 25 June 1528, Sir John Stanley and his wife Margaret were released from their marriage vows, and Sir John ended his life as a monk of Westminster, allegedly broken by the cardinal's harsh dealing.[37]

Second, if Wolsey's intervention was neither rapid nor outrageously partial, neither was it lasting. Birchenshawe undoubtedly benefited from the fall of Wolsey, for he was back in position in Chester soon afterwards.[38] Third, Wolsey's failure to challenge the county's jurisdiction was in spite of the most direct provocation so to do: Birchenshawe lost no time in wrapping himself, as it were, in the flag of the palatinate's privileges. One response to earlier strife between the abbey and city of Chester in 1510 was monk Henry Brad-

---

31 R. V. H. Burne, *The monks of Chester: the history of St Werburgh's abbey*, London 1962, 149. See Gwyn's view of Birchenshaw as aggressor in this case: *King's cardinal*, 324.

32 Burne, *Monks of Chester*, 152. The Leghs had long held the Prestbury lease. First recorded in 1448, it was renewed in 1461 and 1492–3, the latter due to expire in 1523–4: Ormerod, *Chester*, iii. 647; Frank Renaud, *Contributions towards a history of the parish of Prestbury in Cheshire* (Chetham Society xcvii, 1876), 49. Legh had already paid £106 of a total fine of £200.

33 *LP* iv/1, 160, 390(14).

34 *LP* iv/1, 546(19); Burne, *Monks of Chester*, 151–2.

35 Ibid. 152.

36 Ormerod, *Chester*, iii. 658. The marriage occurred before 29 November 1523, the date of a post-nuptial agreement in which Thomas and Peter Larke acted as trustees. In March 1527 Thomas Legh was born (aged 2½ at his father's inquisition on 2 September 1529): PRO, CHES 3/65/12. Legh may have been in Wolsey's household, but does not appear in its subsidy assessment: 15 Henry VIII; E 179/69/9.

37 Burne, *Monks of Chester*, 153; Ormerod, *Chester*, iii. 641. Highfield died in October 1527 and was replaced by Thomas Marshall, prior of Wallingford: Burne, *Monks of Chester*, 154.

38 Ibid. 155. Marshall was charged with misdemeanours at his election and in the summer of 1528: BL, MS Stowe 141, fo. 10r–v.

shaw's *Life of Saint Werburge*. This work powerfully combined the local political culture of the palatinate, as has already been discussed, with a more particular emphasis on the saint's role as patroness of the monastery and city. Having been thoroughly informed of the history of the palatinate, the audience, and especially those who 'haue be, parauenture on late,/ Studious to disquiet the place, the company,/ And diuers libertes haue alienate', were enjoined to 'be neuer vnkynde' to the monastery.[39] Later, faced with the two challenges over the Prestbury lease and the jurisdiction of the bishop of Coventry and Lichfield, Birchenshawe sponsored the publication in 1521 of the *Life* as propaganda in support of the privileges of the abbey and his own position.[40]

Under Wolsey, therefore, a route was opened for litigation in the central courts of equity, and experiments with loans and benevolences meant that Cheshiremen experienced relatively novel fiscal demands from the centre – but without any systematic or forceful purpose.[41]

The rise of William Brereton

The extent of Wolsey's interference in the palatinate also had consequences for the politics of the palatinate in the prominence it gave to his agents. The rise to prominence in Cheshire of William Brereton, son of the chamberlain of Chester and a groom of the privy chamber, was the result of a combination of his close proximity to the king, and the interventionist policy adopted by Wolsey. During the 1520s William and Urian Brereton, younger sons of chamberlain Sir Randal Brereton, rose to take prominent positions in the king's privy chamber. By 1521 William was at court; in 1526 he was one of the

---

[39] Bradshaw, *Life of St Werburge*, 190–5, esp. lines 1874–6. For Bradshaw on palatine traditions see above pp. 43–4. The dating is supported by the description of Alexander Barclay as 'now beyng religious' (p. 199, line 2025). Barclay moved to Ely and became a Benedictine monk *c.* 1509–11: *DNB*, 1078 [1885 edn; iii. 156–64]; *The ecologues of Alexander Barclay, from the original edition by John Caward*, ed. Beatrice White (EETS o.s. clxxv, 1928 [1927]), p. xx.

[40] A poem appended to the printed edition of the *Life* conceals an acrostic, the name 'BULKELEYC', possibly Charles Bulkeley, master of the works in the monastery and supporter of Birchenshawe. He and Prior Highfield were told by the abbot to 'boldely geve unsware' against Legh. See Curt F. Buhler, 'A note on the "balade to Saynt Werburge" ', *Modern Language Notes* lxviii (1953), 538–9, who suggests the name of the Bulkeleys of Cheadle; PRO, C 1/535/45. As has been seen before, the refrain at the end of the poem is 'Wherfore to the monasterie be neuer vnkynde': Bradshaw, *Life of St Werburge*, 191, for example at line 1785. Another work probably by Bradshaw, *The lyfe of Saynt Radegunde* (ed. F. Brittain, Cambridge 1926, esp. pp. vi–viii), printed by Pynson 1508–29, was also inspired by a challenge to a religious house, the conversion of the nunnery to a college by Bishop Alcock: F. Brittain, *Saint Radegunde, patroness of Jesus College, Cambridge*, Cambridge 1925, 72; VCH, *Cambridge and the Isle of Ely*, ii. 219; Arthur Gray, *The priory of Saint Radegunde, Cambridge* (Cambridge Antiquarian Society octavo publications xxxi, 1898), 40–4.

[41] For the amicable grant etc. see pp. 73–4, 76 above.

four grooms of the privy chamber, with a crucial part in manoeuvres surrounding Henry's 'divorce', for example taking the petition addressed to Clement VII supporting the king's divorce to Wolsey himself.[42] The flow of patronage into William Brereton's hands was relatively free between Sir Ralph Egerton's fall from grace in 1525–6[43] and about 1530. The first reward for Brereton's service at court had come less than a year after he arrived there. On 1 March 1522 he received a grant of the salt tolls of Northwich, in the king's hands during the minority of the earl of Derby. This was followed just over a year later, on 20 April 1523, by the controllership of Chester and Flint but the office was already occupied by Ralph Wryne and William Clayton.[44] It was only the following year, after his admission to the privy chamber,[45] that Brereton was able to make good his possession of it.[46] His first major office was acquired almost immediately after his elevation to the privy chamber: the stewardship of the duchy of Lancaster honour of Halton on 20 April 1524.[47] Grants flowed in plenty from 16 March 1525, as Brereton used his position close to the king to challenge Sir Ralph Egerton's power in Cheshire. On that date two important reversions were granted to William, both of offices relating to former Lovell properties then exercised by Ralph Egerton. The farm of Etchells, Aldford and Alderley was granted in reversion for twenty years from 1530 and the stewardship of Longdendale was to be held for life from the death or surrender of Egerton.[48] October 1525 brought an annuity of 10 marks from Denbigh.[49] As page of the privy chamber, on 12 November 1526 Brereton was made serjeant of the peace in the lordship of Bromfield and Yale.[50] A further reversion at the expense of Ralph Egerton was granted on 1 April 1527: Brereton was to exercise the escheatorship of Chester and

---

[42] Ives, 'Court and county palatine', 4–5. Brereton and his companion received only four sovereigns as a tip from Wolsey and were not happy: George Cavendish, *The life and death of Cardinal Wolsey*, ed. Richard S. Sylvester (EETS ccxliii, 1959), 139–46. The letter of authority he carried to the first earl of Cumberland, dated 13 June 1530, is printed as letter 6 in 'Letters of the Cliffords, Lords Clifford and earls of Cumberland, *c.* 1500–*c.* 1565', ed. R. W. Hoyle, in *Camden Miscellany*, XXXI (Camden 4th ser. xliv, 1992), 38. Brereton's expenses for this mission are *LP* iv. 6489, placed May 1530.

[43] Ives, 'Ralph Egerton', 365–8.

[44] *Letters and accounts of William Brereton*, 12, 99; *39 DKR*, 29. Wryne in particular was later fiercely opposed by Sir Piers Dutton and his allies in the mid-1530s: *LP* xi. 1497.

[45] On 23 March 1524, as groom, he received an annuity of £10: *LP* iv. 213(23). *Letters and accounts of William Brereton*, 12, has 23 April; the date is correctly given at p. 99.

[46] Initially, Brereton had to be satisfied with purchasing the office from Clayton on 6 November 1524: ibid. 99. On 1 April 1525 the controllership of Chester and Flint was confirmed to William Brereton to be held for life on the surrender of Ralph Wryne and William Clayton: ibid. 12, 99.

[47] Ibid. 12; *LP* i. 511.

[48] *Letters and accounts of William Brereton*, 12; *39 DKR*, 29.

[49] 10 October 1525: *LP* iv. 772; *Letters and accounts of William Brereton*, 12, 99.

[50] *LP* iv. 2673; *Letters and accounts of William Brereton*, 12 (the reference on p. 57 to 'D.10' is incorrect), 100.

rangership of Delamere forest for life on the death or surrender of Egerton.[51] April 1527 also brought Brereton his first outright fee simple grant of a substantial amount of land – as groom of the chamber he received 200 acres of land in Chorlton, Hampton and Shotwick, part of the lands of the attainted Sir William Stanley.[52] The reversion of the farm of Etchells, Aldford and Alderley was re-granted on different terms on 30 May 1527, as was that of the stewardship of Longdendale.[53] Brereton's dominance in the northern Welsh marches was confirmed later in the year by the grant on 15 November 1527 of the stewardship of the Holt, of Bromfield and Yale, of Chirk and Chirkland, of Cynllaith and Owen; and the receivership of the Holt, Bromfield and Yale, and Chirk.[54] Again this was in reversion for life from the death or surrender of Ralph Egerton. Brereton complemented these Welsh grants with the farm of the mills of 'Pentrich' and Dyserth on 1 March 1528, and the shrievalty of Flint was granted to Anthony Knyvet on 1 April, with Knyvet already bound to Brereton to allow him to exercise the office and draw the fee.[55] One of his most important acquisitions of landed influence in Cheshire came on Lady Day 1528, in the form of the farm of the lands of Sir John Savage; as Eric Ives has shown, these accounted for more than half of Brereton's income in 1536.[56] On 8 June 1528, with his brother Urian, William Brereton received the keepership of the park at Shotwick, the mastership of the hunt and the farm of the lordship there.[57] Two weeks later William received the shrievalty and escheatorship of Merioneth for life.[58]

[51] Ibid. 12; 39 DKR, 29. Shortly afterwards, another reversion, this time bought from Richard Gifford, promised the farm of the Menai ferries for twenty-one years: Letters and accounts of William Brereton, 12 (the reference on p. 57 to 'D.9' is also incorrect), 100.

[52] This occurred on 26 April 1527: LP iv. 3087(26); Letters and accounts of William Brereton, 13.

[53] As page of the privy chamber; Aldford, Etchells and Alderley, then still currently held by Ralph Egerton at an annual rent of £100; also steward of Longdendale, with an annuity of 100s., also held by Egerton: LP iv. 3142(30); Letters and accounts of William Brereton, 13, 100. An apparent draft grant of the farm of Aldford, Etchells and Alderley to Edmund Peckham, king's cofferer, also bearing the date 30 May 1527, LP iv. 3139, is in fact a miscalendaring of a copy of the grant of this date to Brereton, amended as a basis for the later grant to Peckham: PRO, SP 1/42, pp. 33–6.

[54] LP iv. 3622(15); Letters and accounts of William Brereton, 13 (the reference on p. 57 to 'D.11' is again incorrect), 100–1. The same period may also have seen Brereton granted the offices of master forester of and improver of Bromfield and Yale: Letters and accounts of William Brereton, 13.

[55] For 21 years from Michaelmas 1531: ibid. 13; 39 DKR, 29. For Knyvet see Letters and accounts of William Brereton, 26.

[56] Ibid. 13, 75–6.

[57] Ibid. 13; 39 DKR, 29. This was on the surrender of the park-keepership by John Southall and the cancellation of Ralph Egerton's grant of the other two offices.

[58] Letters and accounts of William Brereton, 14. Around this time William Brereton and William Almer were granted the keepership of Merseley Park in the lordship of Bromfield; this was to be re-granted to William alone on 20 August 1529: LP iv. 5906(20); Letters and accounts of William Brereton, 14, 101.

1529 saw the acquisition of the wardship of John Savage, and the farm of the lands of Sir John Savage in the right of Lady Savage after Brereton's marriage to her.[59]

That Brereton was able to seize a role in Cheshire was due not only to royal favour but to the disturbance created by Wolsey's interventions. At the abbey of Vale Royal, for example, Wolsey took an interest in the election of Abbot Butler in c. 1517; Butler later alleged that the cardinal had 'manassyd & threatenyd . . . that he shuld be as lowe as he was hye onlesse he wolde agree to gyve cccc marks sterlyng'.[60] Twelve years later, in September 1529, the cardinal ordered an investigation of Vale Royal under Dr [Rowland?] Lee and John Paslew, abbot of Whalley, and Oliver Adams, abbot of Combe.[61] As a result Butler was deprived in or before November 1529. There was, however, apparently sharp practice on Lee's part, and by 29 May Butler was back in position.[62] It was this sequence of events which allowed Brereton to take a bond for £1,000 from Butler on 2 December 1529 which bound him to resign at Brereton's command in favour of a nominee of Brereton's at any time.[63] William Brereton also benefited from the confusion surrounding Abbot Birchenshawe's deprivation and restoration. Brereton held his audit at Chester abbey in 1531, received a pension on 11 October in the same year, 'for his gode counsell laufull favor ayde & help in all & euery the causez & busynez of the said house', and got the advowson of Astbury for his kinsman John Brereton.[64] Brereton's rise to power in the locality must be seen in the context of Wolsey's activities, and of the vacuum left by his fall.

---

[59] Ibid. 14; *LP* vi. 179; xii/1, 795(38). In October 1529 Brereton also received the wardship of Godfrey Fuljambe: *Letters and accounts of William Brereton*, 14, 103.

[60] PRO, C 1/685/10: the case came to court not because the abbot dared challenge Wolsey, but because one of Wolsey's minions (Davy Vincent) took a subsidiary extortion too far after his master's fall. Allegation: October 1529 to May 1532. Butler appears in the records of Vale Royal from 1517: VCH, *County of Chester*, iii. 164.

[61] After the investigators' visit the abbot was 'contentyd to submytt hym sellff to my Lorde Cardinall his owne personall correction', but by the time the letter was written, Lee claimed the abbot of Vale Royal had admitted guilt.

[62] In a letter to Roger Wigston, recorder of Coventry, Abbot Adams complained of Lee's actions. For Adams see VCH, *Warwickshire*, ed. H. Arthur Doubleday and William Page, Oxford 1904–, ii. 75. Wigston was linked to many midlands monasteries and became a member of the Council in the Marches on the appointment of Rowland Lee in 1533: *The register of the guild of the Holy Trinity, St Mary, St John the Baptist and St Katherine of Coventry*, ed. Mary Dormer Harris (Dugdale Society xiii, 1935), 108 n. 7; *The records of the guild of the Holy Trinity, St Mary, St John the Baptist and St Katherine of Coventry*, ii, ed. Geoffrey Templeman (Dugdale Society xix, 1944), 170; Bindoff, *House of Commons, 1509–1558*, iii. 611–13. See BL, MS Stowe 141, fo. 12. Convocation, 8 Nov.–3 Dec. 1529, was attended by an Abbot William: *LP* iv/3, 6047 (p. 2700), 6411.

[63] The bond (PRO, E 326/10693) is correctly listed in *Letters and accounts of William Brereton*, 103, no. 32, but misattributed elsewhere in Ives's work to 1535, as noted by A. J. Kettle, 'The abbey of Vale Royal', in VCH, *County of Chester*, iii. 162. See further pp. 206–7 below.

[64] VCH, *County of Chester*, iii. 143; PRO, C 1/1070/4. Wolsey also took an interest in the other two great Cheshire monasteries, Norton and Combermere. Cromwell is later

Thomas Cromwell and the fall of William Brereton

In the event, the fall of Wolsey was to damage William Brereton's position. The following year another crucial event changed his political fortunes. Soon after the death of his father, William was appointed chamberlain of the county on 11 June 1530.[65] Henceforth, William was to exercise perhaps the most important palatine office, and to do so under a chief minister with a different approach to that of Wolsey, Thomas Cromwell. Brereton's relations with others at court, especially Cromwell, deteriorated steadily. In fact, Brereton was on bad terms with Cromwell from soon after the fall of Wolsey, which limited his ability to rely absolutely on support from court. From about 1530 the flood of office and reward seems to have dried up. The last grant that William Brereton received in Cheshire, apart from one receivership of properties of which he was, in the main, already the farmer, was the manor of Longdendale, granted to him jointly with Lady Savage for life in survivorship, at an annual rent of 1d., on 2 August 1530.[66] Further grants in the marches were few and far between: jointly with his brother Roger, he was made sheriff of Flint on 30 September 1532; and on 25 May 1533 with John Puleston he became sheriff of Merioneth.[67] It is not true that this was because there was nothing left to receive, as has been suggested.[68] Even in Cheshire itself, royal patronage was extensive enough for important grants to be made to others in 1529 and after. The wardship of Richard, son and heir of Ralph Egerton, was granted on 27 April 1529 to William Wilbraham, clerk; Egerton soon received special livery to himself and a group of trustees. Sir Anthony Browne and his wife Alice received Sir William Stanley's lordship of Nantwich and neighbouring manors, confirmed on 23 June 1529, partly

---

recorded as having a paper concerning a murder done by the abbot of Combermere (the abbot's servant, John Jenyns, killed a monk, Otwell Huncote, on 11 Feb. 1520): *LP* vii. 923(xxi); VCH, *County of Chester*, iii. 154; STAC 2/19/158 (*L&C Star Chamber*, 129–30), STAC 2/26/18. Cromwell also possessed a memorial of the life of William Merton, abbot of Norton, who was elected in 1507 and is last mentioned in 1524, before being replaced by Thomas Birkenhead, who first occurs in 1525: *LP* vi. 228(ix) (placed 1533); VCH, *County of Chester*, iii. 171.

65 *LP* iv. 6490(11); *Letters and accounts of William Brereton*, 14, 104.

66 *LP* iv. 6600(2); *Letters and accounts of William Brereton*, 14 (Ives refers to this as a grant of the stewardship). Brereton was appointed receiver of Catherine of Aragon, now again called princess of Wales, in her properties in Chester and Flint (which included Longdendale and other properties of Sir William Stanley). He was acting in this role at least by Michaelmas 1533, when he accounted for the first time: PRO, SC 6/Henry VIII/400–1; *Letters and accounts of William Brereton*, 15.

67 Ibid. 14–15.

68 Ives describes the flow of patronage as continuous for the next eight or ten years after 1523, i.e. admitting a possible check in about 1531: 'Court and county palatine', 11. *LP* reveals nothing after the grant of Longdendale in 1530, apart from confirmation of Lesnes priory in Kent of which he was already in possession by 1530: *LP* vii. 419(6). For palatinate material see 26 *DKR*, 18; 30 *DKR*, 145–52; 39 *DKR*, 29–30: the latest grant recorded here is that of the lordship of Shotwick with Urian on 8 June 1528.

through exchanges of manors with Sir John Gage. It was Sir Richard Rich who became attorney general in Wales and the counties palatine of Chester and Flint in May 1532, and William Legh, gentleman usher of the king's chamber, who received the reversion of the office of controller of all pleas of fines, amercements, etc. before the justice of north Wales in September of that year.[69] Grants of office and reward continued to flow; but William Brereton ceased to be a considerable beneficiary.

Brereton's management of the finances of Cheshire may have been one reason for this. Following a dramatic improvement in the finances of the county in the last years of his father's chamberlaincy, with arrears at their lowest since Henry VIII's accession, William Brereton continued to reduce arrears, until they reached just £486 10s. 5d. in 1535–6. The amounts of money transferred to the king's use declined just as dramatically, however. In the period before 1530, they had never been lower than £300 and usually exceeded £400. In the years of William Brereton's control, however, they averaged about £230–40.[70] There can be no doubt that this decline was noticed at court: the revenues dealt with by the chamberlain of Chester were included in the 'memorial for the King's highness, declaring the kind of things wherein riseth yearly as well his certain revenues as his casual revenues'.[71] Even more serious grounds for antipathy are seen in Brereton's obstruction of the collection of the revenues of the vacant bishopric of Lichfield in Cheshire in 1532, following the death of Geoffrey Blythe on 19 February 1532.[72] This had major ramifications because the bishopric played a part in policy on the king's 'divorce' when it was in a precarious state, with both an independent English solution and the case at Rome being pursued. Early in 1532 the case was removed from the Rota to the papal consistory, where the case would be decided by the (more bribable) body of cardinals.[73] From at least March 1532 the revenues of the vacant bishopric of Lichfield were intended as an inducement to Cardinal Benedict de Accoltis of Ravenna to win him to Henry's side.[74] Benedict was the nephew of Pietro de Accoltis of Ancona, the chief lawyer in the consistory and a potential English

---

[69] *LP* iv. 5510, 6490(23); v. 627(6), 1065(21), 1370(6).

[70] PRO, SC 6/Henry VIII/355–61. A major reason for the reduction was a dramatic rise in the level of annuities paid at Chester, which roughly doubled from £65 19s. 2d. in the mid-1520s to £123 5s. 10d., mainly due to the grant of a £40 annuity to Sir William Gage.

[71] *LP* v. 397 (placed Michaelmas 1531).

[72] For the date see PRO, CHES 3/66 (23 Henry VIII, no. 3); *Letters and accounts of William Brereton*, 35; *LP* v. 277, 332, 848; vi. 373, 389, 479, 586.

[73] Geoffrey de C. Parmiter, *The king's great matter: a study in anglo-papal relations, 1527–1534*, London 1967, 176–7. See also W. E. Wilkie, *The cardinal protectors of England: Rome and the Tudors before the reformation*, Cambridge 1974, 207–8. Earlier, in mid-1530, the English government had been in a state described by one authority as panic, for fear that the judges might give way to imperial pressure, and Brereton's activity regarding the Lichfield estates must be viewed in this light: Nicholson, 'Act of Appeals', 19.

[74] *LP* v. 887, 974, 1493.

ally.[75] During such delicate negotiations, Cromwell's exasperation at the dis-
obedience of the local administration in Cheshire is understandable.[76] Brereton's role in the divorce campaign was not in policy formation but as a
hard-working servant; when the chance to make some money from his local
position arose, the king's policy could take a back seat. Cromwell's need to
secure compliance with religious change, to ensure the security of the realm
and to win acceptance for a new royal marriage – and the possible difficulties
of doing so in the Chester palatinate – must have been highlighted by this
episode.

Brereton's difficulties with the king and his minister were exacerbated by
the existence of alternative power centres in Cheshire: Brereton's control
was never absolute.[77] Cromwell was considered a source of help by anti-
Brereton petitioners from early in his ministry. On 18 September 1531 Ralph
Sneyd, rector of Woodchurch and canon of Lichfield, and a member of a
family notable for its opposition to Brereton, wrote asking Cromwell to inter-
vene against Brereton over the benefice of Astbury.[78] Sneyd's rival was John
Brereton, William's relative, who had also prospered in the king's service. By
September 1532 he was canon and prebendary of St Paul's, London, and St
Stephen's, Westminster, rector of Malpas and Christleton, and chaplain to
Henry VIII.[79] John Brereton's nomination to Astbury, ultimately in the gift of
St Werburgh's, may even have been part of the price of Brereton's support in
achieving Birchenshawe's reinstatement. Ralph Sneyd had an earlier grant.[80]
John Brereton was ultimately successful, but only in the face of local resis-
tance that continued at least until 1533 and through presentation, on 24
September 1535, by the king himself, when it was stated that the benefice
was in royal hands *hac vice* by the grant of William Brereton.[81] Sneyd's influ-

---

[75] As cardinal protector of Scotland, Pietro had been useful to the English; his judgement
that the marriage of Henry's sister Margaret of Scotland was invalid had given cause for
hope, if temporarily. At this time, however, he was noted for his support for Catherine:
Wilkie, *Cardinal protectors*, 91, 93, 98–103, 169, 172–4, 179–80; Parmiter, *The king's great
matter*, 178. Pietro was to die in December 1532, so the bid for Benedict's support might have
been well-timed.

[76] On 2 November 1532 the offer of nomination to Lichfield was replaced by that to Ely: *LP*
v. 1507. Hence perhaps the more friendly tone of Brereton's letter to Cromwell on 14
December 1532: *Letters and accounts of William Brereton*, letter 29, p. 91 (*LP* v. 1631).

[77] *Pace* Ives's description of Brereton as a 'proconsul': *Letters and accounts of William
Brereton*, 34.

[78] Ives, 'Court and county palatine', 26; *Letters and accounts of William Brereton*, letter 24, p.
87 (*LP* v. 426)

[79] *LP* v. 627(20), 1370(13). In 1531 he was also rector of Hatford, Berks. and dean of
Astley, Warks.; he was elected master of St Bartholomew's Hospital in Smithfield, London,
in 1532, became rector of St Mary-on-the-Hill in Chester and Longstanton, Cambs., in
1534, and was appointed vicar of Buckland, Berks., and rector of Compton Bassett, Wilts.,
in 1535. In addition, he was a canon of St Asaph and prebend of Venall: *BRUO, 1501–40*,
67–8.

[80] Presumably from Abbot Highfield or Abbot Marshall: *LP* v. 426 (18 Sept. 1531).

[81] John Brereton was in Cromwell's favour early in 1534, when one of Cromwell's remem-

ence and powerful connections, who included Sir Anthony Fitzherbert and William Venables, had already been displayed in his clash with the prior of Launde over the rectory of Rostherne. This dispute also saw him defeating the Brereton interest. On 1 May 1529, Randal Brereton, with George Booth of Dunham and twenty others, threatened the prior after he refused to give a lease of the rectory to Booth. On 5 May, however, William Venables, along with Ralph Sneyd, whom he had presented to the rectory, and Richard Legh, tricked William Hardwyche, who held the benefice by the nomination of Launde, into leaving the church and then barred the door. That day it was Ralph Sneyd who sang high mass; according to one Matthew Barnes, Sneyd said that no vicar would say mass there who was not his servant, and that the impropriation, for which Sir Thomas Lovell and Edmund Dudley had been responsible, was not legal.[82]

Royal and ministerial will was, however, obviously deployed in favour of one of Brereton's rivals in the dispute over the Dutton inheritance in the late 1520s and early 1530s: at stake were eight manors and land in a further ten places worth 4,000 marks a year.[83] Lawrence Dutton died in 1527; he was the sole issue and heir of Roger Dutton (d. 1476), himself the heir of John, his nephew, who had died in 1473. This perilous descent had already been the occasion for a good deal of trouble.[84] Despite a prodigious array of bastards, Lawrence had no legitimate children; his heirs general were the daughters of Sir Thomas Dutton, Lawrence's uncle, and their descendants. These daughters were Anne, who married Sir Thomas Molyneux of Sefton; Isabell, who married Sir Christopher Southworth of Southworth; Elizabeth, who married Ralph Bostock of Bostock; Margaret, who married Thomas Aston of Aston-iuxta-Sutton, and after his death Ralph Vernon of Haslington; and Eleanor, who married Richard Cholmondeley of Cholmondeley.[85] Elizabeth's daughter and heiress, Anne Bostock, married Sir John Savage of Clifton. Savage interests were under Brereton's control by 1529, and he was closely associated with the two other Cheshire heirs general, Thomas Aston and Richard Cholmondeley.[86] Lawrence did not, however, wish his lands to pass to his heirs general.

brances suggested the need to find 'Dr Brereton' some promotion: *LP* vii. 257. For resistance to Brereton see PRO, C 1/730/6; C 1/731/1; for the presentation see *LP* ix. 504(13); also presentation 24 Feb. 1536, *LP* x. 392(50). See also Ives, 'Court and county palatine', 10.
[82] PRO, STAC 2/17/146 (*L&C Star Chamber*, 109–10); STAC 2/17/245; STAC 2/22/280 (*L&C Star Chamber*, 110–12); STAC 2/30/42. For Lovell and Dudley's role see pp. 180–2 above.
[83] Ives: 'Court and county palatine, 27; *Letters and accounts of William Brereton*, 32–3; Ormerod, *Chester*, i. 648. The value is Lawrence Dutton's estimate shortly before he died: PRO, STAC 2/18/181 (*L&C Star Chamber*, 91).
[84] Ormerod, *Chester*, i. 646–9. See pp. 166, 169 above.
[85] These heirs are set out as at 11 Henry VII in, for example, the inquisition for Alice, wife of Thomas de Dutton: Ormerod, *Chester*, i. 647.
[86] Ives, 'Crime, sanctuary and royal authority', 319. For Aston see *Letters and accounts of William Brereton*, 31. Cholmondeley was Brereton's nephew: Ives, 'Court and county palatine', 3–4; *LP* x. 849 (letter to William annotated 'Rychard Cholmundeley').

Even in old age he hoped for a child, but if this hope should not be fulfilled, he wished that his inheritance should pass to Sir Piers Dutton. He knew, however, that this would not be easily encompassed. During a conversation two years before his death, after his recovery from a severe illness, Lawrence had said to his wife, 'if I hadd dyed now ye mowght have hapned to have hadd some busyness', and then turned to Robert Massey and said

> thou art an olde man, and I will tell there be many that pretendith title to my lande, and to have yt after my decese, as my cosen Savage he pretendith to have it, my cosens Sir Pierce a Legh, Warberton and Aston . . . but for as moche as his lande hadd ben of long tyme entaylid to the heires masles, he [Lawrence] wolde never putt it from the heir masle, but as he found it, so wolde he leave it.[87]

Lawrence Dutton made his will on 4 October 1527; he was dead by 20 January 1528. His will described Sir Piers Dutton as his 'next ryght heyer male, in default off issue, as appereth by my old evydences'.[88] Sir Piers had had an active career in local politics, and as Lawrence's preferred candidate was in a strong position.[89] The initiative locally was taken by Dutton's opponents. On 15 January 1528, at night, John Bostok and William Groves, at the instigation of Sir John Savage and Richard Aston, came to the manor of Dutton and set up a pavilion. Dutton alleged that they behaved in a riotous manner, and also that the Brereton connection in the palatine administration had been used to harass him and his allies. Sir John Savage and his associates defended their actions by claiming that Dutton had made no certain title to the lands, and that the rightful heirs were the sisters of John Dutton.[90] On 13 February 1528 the court ordered that the property should be placed in the hands of Justice Sir John Porte and Sir William Leyland; this was a success for Dutton, as it was Porte whom Lawrence had chosen as overseer of his will.[91] On 13 November 1528 Richard Leftwich wrote to William Brereton, perhaps because the news was bad for him and his associates in the case, saying 'I doute howe my Lorde Cardynalle's Grace will accepte the fyndyng of Dutton's londes; it is misdone, ye loke therunto, consideryng his decre.'[92]

---

87 Hoping for a child of his own, he commented that his wife was younger than Sir Piers Dutton's wife, who had had a child the year before: PRO, STAC 2/18/181 (*L&C Star Chamber*, 91).
88 Ormerod, *Chester*, iii. 647.
89 For earlier examples of the Dutton–Brereton conflict see *Letters and accounts of William Brereton*, letter 18 (pp. 82–3), letter 20 (pp. 83–4).
90 PRO, STAC 2/13/178–81; STAC 2/13/183–5 (*L&C Star Chamber*, 87–92).
91 PRO, STAC 2/17/398 (*L&C Star Chamber*, 115); cf. C 1/677/28, C 1/706/7–8; *Lancashire and Cheshire wills. . . from the ecclesiastical court*, 29.
92 *Letters and accounts of William Brereton*, 80–1. There are no surviving inquisitions on any members of the Dutton family between those on Ralph and others in 9 Henry VIII and that on Sir Piers in 37 Henry VIII.

Sir Piers was in contact with Cromwell at least as early as June 1529, when he was listed as one of those who owed money to him.[93] The relationship seems to have continued and improved: Dutton was enjoying Cromwell's favour well before 1533, when he was recommended to the minister by Rowland Lee, who wrote 'it is better for a man to lesse hys ryght than seue, but only for your good help where unto hee only trusteth and as hee promesseyd to you hee wyll kepe as knowyth J[es]hu'.[94] In 1533, Sir Piers was on the point of victory: a resolution of the council in the dispute between him and Thomas Aston on 12 July 1533 determined Dutton to be right heir male.[95] The case concluded when the royal judgement was enacted by parliament. All Brereton could achieve was the exclusion of the Savage interest from the ruling, to be decided upon later when the heir came of age.[96]

As a result, at least as early as 1533 Cromwell's potential as an influential force in opposition to Brereton power had become very clear. In February Sir Richard Bulkeley wrote to Cromwell on behalf of his brother, John Bulkeley MA, to ask for the benefice of Davenham. This was in the gift of John Savage, the ward of William Brereton. With a rumour abroad that Edmund Bonner, illegitimate scion of the Savages, was to be the new bishop of Lichfield, Bulkeley offered the first year's value of the benefice and one third of subsequent revenues as an incentive.[97] Although Bulkeley was unsuccessful and George Savage received the benefice,[98] on 13 June 1534 Brereton's deputy as escheator, Richard Leftwich, suffered the indignity of having his wife evicted from her favourite pew in Davenham church by Cromwell's agent Adam Beconsall; at the family living of the Savage family, this was a grave affront to Brereton's power.[99] The judicial murder of John ap Gryffith

---

[93] *LP* iv. 5330. Was the connection through Dutton's wife Juliana, well connected in Lollard/Lutheran circles?

[94] *Letters and accounts of William Brereton*, letter 26 (p. 89): Paulet writes to Randolph Brereton of Chester for Dutton and restraining payment of annuities from Savage revenues, except to 'Master Snede', 10 Mar. 1532. For Lee's recommendation see PRO, SP 1/77, fo. 80 (*LP* vi. 700, 25 June 1533). This mission is referred to in a later letter at fo. 89 (*LP* vi. 715).

[95] PRO, SP 1/77, fo. 198 (*LP* vi. 818). Aston not long after complained against Dutton: *Memorials of the Duttons of Dutton in Cheshire, with notes respecting the Sherborne branch of the family*, London–Chester 1901, 123–6.

[96] This was passed in the parliament, 4 Feb.–14 Apr. 1536: *LP* x, p. 87 (printed in *Memorials of the Duttons*, 113–21). The Cholmondeleys had a copy of the agreement: CCRO, DCH H/96. The enmities of the Dutton succession dispute continued through the 1530s. In 1536, for example, Richard Cholmondeley complained that he could do nothing against trespassing cattle in pasture at Acton because the sheriff, Sir Piers Dutton, 'beyreth hym no good will': PRO, STAC 2/8/274 (*L&C Star Chamber*, 72).

[97] *LP* vi. 179.

[98] George Savage was a bastard son of Sir John Savage (d. 1492) and therefore Bonner's half-brother: Ormerod, *Chester*, iii. 237; C. A. Haigh, 'A mid-Tudor ecclesiastical official: the curious career of George Wilmesley', *THSLC* cxxii (1971 [1970]), 2. Bonner asked Cromwell to be remembered to Brereton: *LP* v. 1658 (24 Dec. 1532). It is perhaps significant that Bonner did not get the bishopric.

[99] PRO, SP 1/84, fo. 173 (*LP* vii. 835). The bill provides only the date, Saturday 13 June.

Eyton in the summer of 1534, made famous by George Cavendish's *Metrical visions*, alienated Brereton further from Cromwell. Eyton, a Flintshire gentleman, was taken from London by Brereton and hanged in defiance of Cromwell's orders.[100] This episode reflected not Brereton power but impotence. He could no longer expect the verdict he desired in the capital, so he took the matter into his own hands – and, unfortunately but inevitably, worsened yet further his standing at court. A major reason for the significance of the Eyton incident was its coincidence with the arrival in the marches of Rowland Lee after his nomination to the bishopric of Lichfield. Brereton had never secured power over the operation of the Council in the Marches, and now it had a vigorous new royal servant at its head. Lee had arrived at Beaudesert in Staffordshire on 3 June, and it was from there on 10 July that he wrote to Cromwell reporting 'grett porte and solemnites' at the Holt.[101] Only Sir Piers Dutton, Sir Henry Delves and a few other Cheshire gentry were absent. It is not clear where Dutton was at this point, but Delves's absence from the Holt was due to his being among the nobles and gentry who entertained the newly arrived bishop and his charge, Cromwell's son Gregory, on the 10th.[102] In Chester on 6 September, Henry Dowes reported the further kindness of Sir John Done, Sir Henry Delves, Mr Massey and Randal Brereton, baron of the exchequer.[103] At least two of these men, Brereton and Done, were close supporters of William Brereton; they were now present to greet the president of the marches, although William remained notable by his absence.[104] The earthquake that hit Chester at 5 a.m. on 15 September 1534 was slight, but it was symbolic of the new forces that were moving into the politics of the marches.[105] Brereton's waning influence was confirmed by the choice on 14 November 1534 of Sir Piers Dutton as sheriff.[106]

The politics of the city of Chester were affected by the power of Dutton, who was beginning to use his connections there to make life difficult for Brereton's associates. Philip Constantine, merchant of Chester, found himself imprisoned and his goods arrested by the sheriffs of the city, 'by the

---

Ives's dating to 1535 (*Letters and accounts of William Brereton*, 39) is unnecessary – 13 June was a Saturday in 1534, a Sunday in 1535 – and may be influenced by his determination to date Brereton's decline from after the summer of 1534. For Beconsall see Haigh, *Reformation and resistance*, 2–4.

100 Ives, *Anne Boleyn*, 395–6, and 'Court and county palatine', 28–30; *Letters and accounts of William Brereton*, 37–8; *Metrical visions by George Cavendish*, ed. A. S. G. Edwards (Renaissance English Text Society 5th ser. ix, 1980), 46–7. Cavendish depended (at pp. 9–11) on Lydgate's *Fall of princes*, especially for lines 477–83, the most damning for Brereton.

101 *LP* vii. 967–8; *Letters and accounts of William Brereton*, 38.

102 *LP* vii. 967: entertainment at Beaudesert by Lord Stafford, Mr Asheden, Mr Hercott, Mr Delves, Mr Ardern and others.

103 *LP* vii. 1135.

104 Richard Done, Sir John's father, was already associated with Sir Randal Brereton in his rivalry with Dutton early in the reign of Henry VIII: see pp. 188, 192 above.

105 *LP* vii. 1151.

106 *LP* vii. 1498(13).

procurement of Sir Peers Dytton knyght sheref of the Countie of Chester'.[107] The concern felt in the city at the introduction of charges for the inspection of leather by means of a Westminster statute in 1533 (and the subsequent introduction of English taxation) may well have increased antipathy there to Brereton as the most prominent representative of the county at court.[108] Another area of potential trouble for William Brereton was the dispute over the goods of Henry Standish, bishop of St Asaph, who died in July 1535.[109] They were pursued for the crown by Adam Beconsall, but resistance from Sir Randal Poole, 'the grett factor vn to Master Wylliam Brerton in our partes', meant that even in March 1536 Beconsall had still only raised 20 marks.[110] Early in 1535 Abbot Birchenshawe of Chester, probably an early beneficiary of Brereton's power, lost faith in him: he 'requyred the said William Brereton laufully to yele hym counsell fauor & help in a matyr betwene hym & one Gilbert Arrosmyth[, a Brereton connection,] for & consernyng the ferme of an house & landes in Irby nowe in the holdyng of John Legh . . . wherin the said William Brereton wold then in no wise so do', and his pension was cancelled.[111] By this point the abbot was clearly under the influence of Brereton's enemies, including the Sneyds, and those who remained true to William at the monastery were very concerned for their futures.[112] In mid-1535 Brereton experienced serious problems following the death of Abbot John Butler of Vale Royal.[113] Brereton failed to win the appointment of his preferred successor, Ralph Goldsmith, a monk of Vale Royal: the king granted free election to the monks, and they felt able to ignore the chamberlain.[114] Goldsmith had several rivals: Sir Piers Dutton wrote to Cromwell from

---

[107] PRO, C 1/757/42. The case is dated to 1534–5, for the sheriffs in question were John Thornton and Thomas Martyn and they were still in office when the bill was put in.
[108] See pp. 76–7, 125–7 above.
[109] 9 July 1535: HBC, 296.
[110] LP ix. 34, 35 (quotation from Letters and accounts of William Brereton, 39, citing PRO, SP 1/95/35); x. 522.
[111] The annuity was paid at Christmas 1534, but not in June 1535 or thereafter: PRO, C 1/1070/4–8. Ranulph Arrowsmith was the second individual to be remembered in the will of Ranulph Poole in 1538, receiving his black trotting gelding with a bald face: B 11/27, fo. 130.
[112] Gilbert Godbehere told Brereton no later than 16 June 1535 that 'my sayde Lorde [the abbot], that was very good vnto me at my fyrst commyng, [was caused] to be heuy lorde vnto me now and all be cause I sende that letter vnto yow that I dyd, besechyng yow to be good master vnto me', this disfavour being at the instance of the marshal of the abbey, who has not been identified but was an ally of the Sneyds: Letters and accounts of William Brereton, 86–8 at p. 86.
[113] It has been claimed that Brereton made the succesful candidate, John Harware, enter a £1,000 bond, to resign at Brereton's command in favour of his nominee at any time. For Ives, this demonstrated that Brereton 'brooked no challenge in his own back yard': 'Court and county palatine', 23–4; Letters and accounts of William Brereton, 31. But the bond has been misattributed. It actually relates to the readmission of an abbot whose standing was under serious question from central government: see n. 63 above.
[114] VCH, County of Chester, iii. 162.

Hatton on 21 June to recommend Randal Wilmslow, a monk of the same house;[115] and on 18 July Anne Boleyn herself wrote to Cromwell asking for favour for the unnamed candidate favoured by Robert Power.[116] On 6 August Adam Beconsall wrote to him from Whatcroft, near Vale Royal, asking him to be good to a further candidate, John Harware, abbot of Hulton.[117] It was Harware who was successful, with the additional support of Cromwell's monastic visitor, Dr Legh.[118] Although Harware had Brereton connections,[119] and although William Brereton took a £100 bribe and a pension of £20 *per annum* from the new abbot, the real victor was Cromwell, who in 1536 became steward of the house and used this position to press for advantageous leases. The chamberlain's negotiations with the newly-elected abbot for a bond of 200 marks contrast starkly with his obtaining £1,000 in security from Harware's predecessor and seem, at worst, the petulant action of a defeated man.[120]

In the summer of 1535 Brereton also faced difficulties at Norton Abbey. On 3 August, in the same letter as he recommended Randal Wilmslow for Vale Royal, Sir Piers Dutton reported to Cromwell the arrest of the abbot of Norton and Robert Jannons, one of his bailiffs, for illegal coining: another Brereton client had found his patron unable to protect him.[121] Perhaps scenting Brereton's blood, Dutton left for London about Michaelmas 1535.[122] His journey may also have been intended to secure his reappointment as sheriff; in this he was successful, the king's determination to re-appoint him being indicated by the fact that his name was written into the list by Henry himself.[123] In addition to the group of coiners, other criminals played parts in this complex story. Robert Hale, a goldsmith, and Piers Felday, his servant, were involved in a series of crimes in Thame, Oxfordshire, and in Chester, where they exchanged false coin with the aid of Thomas Cotgrave of Barrow.

115 PRO, SP 1/84, fo. 197 (*LP* vii. 868 [misdated to 1534]). On 3 August Dutton again wrote on his behalf: *LP* vii. 1037 (misdated 1534).
116 *LP* viii. 1056. This letter locates the episode in 1535. Power was later gentleman usher and waiter to Princess Elizabeth: *LP* x. 1187(3).
117 *LP* ix. 34. For Harware and Hulton see VCH, *Staffordshire*, iii. 236–7 (which suffers from dating the Vale Royal election to 1534).
118 The election produced an allegation that Dr Legh had taken a bribe of £15: *LP* ix. 622. The resulting vacancy at Hulton also caused controversy: *LP* vii. 1094.
119 *Staffordshire Historical Collections* n.s. x/1, 174; ibid. 1912, 25–6.
120 PRO, C 1/902/16–18 (c. 1540).
121 *LP* vii. 1037. Sir Piers was responding to information from Henry Broke, who had observed false coin in connection with canons and employees of Norton over the previous two years: *LP* ix. 183 (26 Aug. 1535).
122 *LP* ix. 1106: undated, but linked to the order of the Council in the Marches, 4 Feb. 1536: *LP* x. 259.
123 *LP* ix. 914(22). Was Audley trying to exclude him deliberately on Brereton's behalf? There were signs of tension between Cromwell and Audley over Cheshire affairs in 1536: see pp. 211, 216 below. Dutton used his third successive appointment as sheriff as evidence of his especially high favour with king and council: *LP* xii/2, 58(2) (p. 20).

The robbery involved the abbot of Valle Crucis. Hale was captured and offered information about his accomplices. This reached Cromwell, who passed it on to Sir Piers Dutton and Adam Beconsall. By 6 July 1535 Hale, Philip Constantine, a Chester leather merchant already harassed by Dutton, Thomas Cotgrave of Barrow and Stephen Sumner, a Tarporley smith and tenant of Sir John Done, were in the Tower of London for illegal coining.[124] Dutton also arrested Piers Felday, Hale's servant. Dutton orchestrated the accusations to damage Brereton, offering Felday a pardon if he would implicate his enemies. These included Randal Brereton of Chester (an old friend of the father of goldsmith Robert Hale), Sir John Done, Randal Poole, Sir William Poole, Ralph Rogerson, alderman of Chester and others. By 3 August 1535 Randal Brereton, deputy chamberlain of Chester, was under arrest; Randal took this seriously enough to make his will.[125] Robert Salusbery, abbot of Valle Crucis, was arrested on 1 September. About this time the men taken prisoner in Cheshire were moved to London; Dutton probably accompanied them. Dutton returned home for Christmas 1535 but probably went south again early the following year.[126] He may even have been in London to witness the execution of William Brereton in May 1536. Soon after, on 20 June 1536, Felday confessed crimes committed at Thame and Aylesbury two years before;[127] Dutton directed Felday's evidence before the council.[128] Although neither Randal Brereton nor the abbot of Norton appear to have been taken to London,[129] William Brereton's fall came against the background of his closest associates being tried before the council.[130]

The Brereton brothers have provided a crucial case study for the relationship between centre and locality: William is the exemplar of the local impact of court faction. According to this interpretation, William achieved nearly complete dominance in Cheshire due to his influence at court, an influence

---

[124] *LP* viii. 1001. It is tempting to link Philip Constantine with Brereton's friend George Constantine. They had been preceded by one William Wright of Nantwich, held for coining by 10 June 1535. At about the same time in Cheshire John Wreygth, who had passed false coin to Henry Broke in 1533, was arrested; a few days later the abbot of Norton's smith fled the country.

[125] The will was dated 15 Aug. 1535, and the overseer named was 'my master' William Brereton: PRO, PROB 11/27, fo. 62v.

[126] *LP* ix. 1106.

[127] *LP* x. 1170.

[128] As a result Piers Bruen of Tarvin, Richard Barker of Chester, John Hale of Chester, John Wryce [Wreygth?], smith of Nantwich, Thomas Holfe, and Robert Jannons joined Robert Hale, Cotgrave, Constantine and Sumner in the Tower.

[129] Both were back in Cheshire in 1536: Chesters, 'Power politics and roguery, part II', 47.

[130] The episode fizzled out once Brereton was dead: Bruen was released after eighteen weeks; others such as Robert Jannons and Philip Constantine were back in Cheshire by 1538 at the latest. Felday was kept in Newgate until June 1537 when he was brought to Cheshire by Sir William Brereton, who had been in Ireland between October 1534 and May 1536. Brereton extracted from Felday a confession of Dutton's attempt to make false allegations against Brereton followers, on which much of this account is based: *LP* xii/2, 58.

ensured in turn by his powerful local following. The king and his ministers were happy to augment the local influence of a man they knew personally and trusted.[131] Brereton was destroyed by factional conflict at court; the manner of that destruction – sudden execution on trumped-up charges – showed how court politicians depended on, and feared, both the support of the king and local power. The decline and fall of William Brereton has been dated from autumn 1534, following the execution of Eyton, making it a sudden response to this particular event.[132] Seen in this light, the 1536 Welsh legislation was closely linked to the destruction of Brereton and his colleagues. According to Ives, Brereton's execution of Eyton made it 'imperative to curb his power. The passage of marcher lordships into the hands of the crown had not brought increased royal control – *pace* historians; in some ways the royal servant appointed steward was more powerful than the previous marcher lord because he was a royal servant.'[133] Yet the truth is that Brereton's relative powerlessness, both to deploy the influence of the court interest in the county and to defend the county's privileges at court, had been the keynote of the 1530s. The king and Cromwell had not given him their support after the fall of Wolsey; instead they had increased the instability of the shire by building up Brereton's rivals while never actually fatally undermining him until the sudden dramatic crisis of 1536. Not since the worst disturbances early in Henry VII's reign had the political society of the palatinate been so disrupted. Even so, the worst was yet to come, for in 1536 Thomas Cromwell's meddling in the privileges of the shire, evident since 1533, culminated in the Welsh reform legislation with its transformation of the judicial and administrative structures of the shire. Interference, without system, followed by an attempt to introduce a new system in ignorance of the local conditions: such was Cheshire's experience under Thomas Cromwell.

Given this, it is important to emphasise that the allegation against William of adultery with Anne Boleyn, which led to his execution, is not so absurd as to be worthy of abrupt dismissal as no more than the pretext for his removal from the political scene. Of all those accused, Brereton seems least guilty, especially as no evidence was apparently presented against him at the trial.[134] His schoolfriend, George Constantine, said Brereton confessed in his cell that he could not understand the charges.[135] Constantine was, however, not the most reliable witness: he had his own point to make (and skin to

131 Ives, 'Court and county palatine', 8–12, 18–31.
132 Ives, *Anne Boleyn*, 395–6, and 'Court and county palatine', 28–30; *Letters and accounts of William Brereton*, 37–8. This linkage is more deterministic in the writing of Peter Roberts than in that of Eric Ives: see, for example, his review of Ives's work in the *Times Literary Supplement*, 18 Mar. 1988.
133 *Letters and accounts of William Brereton*, 38.
134 Ives, *Anne Boleyn*, 394, and 'Court and county palatine', 31–2.
135 T. Amyot, 'A memorial from George Constantine', *Archaeologia* xxiii (1831), 50–78; Ives, *Anne Boleyn*, 391.

save), and circumstantial evidence linked the Breretons with Anne.[136] William led the mission to collect signatures for the papal petition on Henry's 'divorce', and may have been present at the king's wedding.[137] Urian's contacts were even more personal. His dogs with Anne's savaged a cow to death when they were hunting together;[138] Anne's lap dog was allegedly called Urian after him.[139]

There is also a chronological objection to a direct connection between the 1536 legislation and the fall of William Brereton. Although the absence of journals for this parliament means the chronology of its legislation concerning Wales and Cheshire is uncertain, the first 'Act of Union' received the royal assent at the dissolution on 14 April 1536 – before the first signs of trouble over the queen's behaviour.[140] In addition, the act's contents do not support the argument that William Brereton was their target. The legislation did nothing to limit the power of chamberlain Brereton – indeed, it guaranteed his position.[141] The greatest legislative challenges to the palatinate and the chamberlain had occurred many months earlier, in the imposition of English subsidies and customs on leather. If William's guilt towards Boleyn is at least arguable, and the 1536 legislation was not part of his destruction, it is worth examining Brereton's career without the assumption that local activity must have prompted his execution.

William Brereton's associates in Cheshire did not suffer alongside him. The theory of faction would suggest that destruction of a faction leader should affect others in his connection. Instead, Urian continued at court,[142] and in Cheshire the influence of the Breretons remained and even grew. Almost immediately after the executions, Sir William Brereton was among those who were on Cromwell's list of candidates to succeed to William's offices in Bromfield and Yale, and the Brereton ally Sir John Done was

---

[136] G. W. Bernard, 'The fall of Anne Boleyn', *EHR* cvi (1991), 584–610; Retha M. Warnicke, 'Sexual heresy at the court of Henry VIII', *HJ* xxx (1987), 247–68; E. W. Ives, 'Stress, faction and ideology in early Tudor England', ibid. xxxiv (1991), 193–202.

[137] Idem, *Anne Boleyn*, 164, 211, and 'Court and county palatine', 7–8.

[138] *LP* v, p. 752 (Sept. 1530). In 1528 Urian was one of those members of the privy chamber of whose recovery from the sweat Henry VIII informed Anne Boleyn: *LP* iv. 4477 (placed 7 July 1528).

[139] Fortunatus Dwarris, 'Observations on the history of one of the old Cheshire families', *Archaeologia* xxxiii (1849), 74, where he observes 'Trifles light as air, are to the jealous confirmations strong as proofs of Holy writ'; R. Brooke, 'On Handford hall, in Cheshire . . .', *THSLC* ii (1849–50), 43; R. Stewart Brown, 'The royal manor and park of Shotwick', ibid. lxiv (1913 [1912]), 115. None adds a source. It is not in William Latimer's account of Boleyn in Bodl. Lib., MS Don. C. 42 ('William Latymer's Chronickille of Anne Bulleyne', ed. Maria Dowling, in *Camden Miscellany*, XXX [Camden 4th ser. xxxix, 1990], 23–65). On Anne Boleyn's affection for dogs see *LP* ix. 991.

[140] *LJ* i, pp. ccxlv–ccxlvii; Bernard, 'Fall of Anne Boleyn', 589–91.

[141] E. W. Ives, 'Faction at the court of Henry VIII: the fall of Anne Boleyn', *History* lvii (1972), 171. New stewards were appointed to Holt, Bromfield etc. after Brereton's execution: Roberts, ' "Acts of union" and the Tudor settlement of Wales', 200–2.

[142] He proved useful to William Brereton's widow: *LP* xi. 1024.

proposed for forester of Delamere.[143] As this might imply, support at court for either 'faction' in the locality also reflected no rigid division. Responses to trouble during the dissolution of Norton abbey suggest most clearly what other episodes hint at: that Secretary Cromwell and Chancellor Audley favoured different sides in the dispute.[144] It was Sir William Brereton who reported events to the former, Dutton to the latter; and when Audley instructed Roland Lee, a Cromwell man, to appoint Dutton a member of the Council in the Marches, Lee wrote to Cromwell questioning the decision.[145] Cromwell, destroyer of William Brereton, was now the Breretons' main hope against Sir Piers Dutton, the minister's most powerful instrument against Brereton. Coming in the immediate aftermath of the death of the chamberlain, this was hardly the action of a minister implacably opposed to 'the Brereton faction'. If this was faction, it was faction so fluid as to be meaningless as an analytical device.

Quite apart from problems with the view of centralisation through faction discussed above, study of William Brereton suggests two other limitations on the control that might be exercised through such a man. William obtained the site of the priory of Lesnes in Kent, near to London, and an excellent site for the house of a courtier gentleman.[146] Cheshire was never good at accommodating its successful sons: men pursuing careers left home and settled in estates all over the south-east and beyond, giving the county its reputation as a 'seed plot of gentility', but denuding it of resident agents of the crown.[147] In addition, it was Brereton's agents who were prominent and notorious in the locality. Alleged 'minions' like Leftwich, Poole and the rest had considerable freedom of action.[148] Brereton's influence over John Puleston has been emphasised but in 1532 Brereton disposed of the offices of sheriff and escheator of Merioneth to him, obtaining a joint grant of the shrievalty in the following year.[149] Going to court did not necessarily mean combining the

---

[143] This is in a note on the back of a letter dated 20 May: *LP* x. 929(iii). The dispersal of offices following Brereton's fall is discussed in ch. 10, and by Ives, 'Court and county palatine', 33–4.

[144] For the Norton incident see p. 216 below. S. E. Lehmberg detected differences over patronage and jurisdiction in 1535–6: 'Sir Thomas Audley: a soul as black as marble?', in Slavin, *Tudor men and institutions*, 11–14.

[145] *LP* xii/2, 985, 993.

[146] *Letters and accounts of William Brereton*, 21. Another grant in the early part of 1530, that of the farm of the manor of Finchley, during the minority of Peter Compton, indicated the importance of Brereton's interests in the court: ibid. 14, 104.

[147] Morgan, *War and society*, 169.

[148] For Brereton's agents see Ives, 'Court and county palatine', 22–3. Although admittedly it was in Brereton's interests to show it thus, much of the Eyton episode comes across in this way: ibid. 28–30 (PRO, STAC 2/14/194–5).

[149] See Ives, 'Court and county palatine', 29–30 (for Brereton's influence), 26 (for the sale). Puleston's biography in Bindoff, *House of Commons, 1509–1558*, iii. 160–1, does not even mention Brereton.

worlds of centre and locality; it could mean crossing the divide between those worlds, a divide that could not be frequently traversed.

Another possible means of centralisation, along with the use of courtiers like Brereton, circular letters, and the like, was the employment by Cromwell of servants without the important county vested interests represented by William Brereton's chamberlaincy.[150] As an example we might take the Holcrofts. Thomas Holcroft first appeared in Cheshire in March 1532, carrying an important commission; William Holcroft had a horse at pasture at Shotwick thanks to William Brereton's kindness in 1531–2; and by 1536 Thomas was sufficiently powerful for Robert Tatton to worry that he might discharge him from his position in the exchequer at Chester soon after he and the new chamberlain, Rees Mansell, had taken possession of their offices there.[151] The influence of such ministerial agents did not always imply greater central control, however. Such an agent was Richard Hough of Leighton and Thornton Hough, a 'sage and sober person' and a man to be reckoned with.[152] The link with the minister was strong – Hough's son William married Cromwell's bastard daughter, Jane – but it again fails to provide evidence of closer centre–locality ties.[153] Instead the evidence confirms the picture of local officers pursuing ministerial policy without subordinating their own interests. Hough was not expected to be in daily attendance on the secretary, and spent only part of the year in Cromwell's household.[154] For the rest of the year his time at home might be expected to be spent promoting Cromwell's interests, with the minister's support flowing in return to promote the servant's. Hough's activities included touring Cheshire monasteries collecting fees for his master; carrying messages to and from Ireland and to the earl of Derby; and bringing prisoners from Winchester to London.[155] Yet although he served the ultimate modernising bureaucrat minister, Hough's impact hardly represented a bureaucratic, centralising alternative to provincial privilege. When he was implicated in the murder near Chester of Randal Davenport, a servant of John Massey of Puddington, early in 1532,[156] his attempts to use local Wirral gentry connec-

---

[150] Such a policy is typical of Sir Geoffrey Elton's centralisation thesis as expounded in *Policy and police: the enforcement of the Reformation in the age of Thomas Cromwell*, Cambridge 1972, and developed by those writing in his tradition, such as Mary L. Robertson, ' "The art of the possible": Thomas Cromwell's management of west country government', *HJ* xxxii (1989), 793–816.

[151] *Letters and accounts of William Brereton*, 89, 160; *LP* xi. 22 (3 July 1536).

[152] Bindoff, *House of Commons, 1509–1558*, ii. 397–8; *LP* xii/1, 622.

[153] Ormerod, *Chester*, ii. 552; *Visitation of Cheshire in the year 1580*, 128.

[154] *LP* xiii/2, 1184.

[155] *LP* xiv/2, 782; xii/1, 622; xi. 1066; xi. 381; Hough correspondence, University of Wales Bangor, Mostyn Collection, 7773–4.

[156] PRO, STAC 2/17/188; STAC 2/18/222 (*L&C Star Chamber*, 113–14, 122–3); STAC 2/29/145; STAC 2/32/10; STAC 2/34/96; Bangor, Mostyn Collection, 585. Wrongly attributed to 1543 in Bindoff, *House of Commons, 1509–1558*, ii. 397–8, the incident can be dated by the examinations of Thomas Pyllyn, Henry Hokenhull, Richard Grosvenor and Edward

tions to protect himself did not stop the case coming to Star Chamber, and embarrassing revelations ensued. Hough was pardoned for the murder early in 1533, and Cromwell and Rowland Lee made an arbitration which ended the dispute on payment by Hough of just £20.[157] Hough's opponent, John Massey, is also significant in this context. As searcher of Chester, Massey was responsible for the enforcement of centrally-imposed customs duties, one of Cromwell's most intrusive innovations in the palatinate.[158]

Hough and Brereton used court links to increase their power in the county, as men had done since the thirteenth century, without doing so in such a way as to bring Cheshire more closely under the management of the centre. They pursued their self-interest in the context of general acceptance of Cheshire's privileges. This was accepted by the crown and its ministers, so long as any resulting disorder did not get too far out of hand. Brereton served his masters relatively obediently but exploited his position on occasion, as was the case with the bond and pension extracted from the abbots of Vale Royal, or the estates of the bishopric of Lichfield. In no case, however, did their power become so all-embracing as to mean that the palatinate stood and fell with them. The crown's interests and contacts in Cheshire were always varied and varying.

During the years 1509–36 the palatinate of Chester witnessed dramatic upheavals. Wolsey and Cromwell had Cheshire gentry dragged into Star Chamber and Cheshire abbots dismissed and reinstated. Yet this activity took place in the context of continued acceptance of Cheshire's special palatine position. Gentry like Sir Ralph Egerton and William Brereton held – and sometimes abused – palatine offices, but it was they and not their offices that were attacked by government actions. In 1536, however, Thomas Cromwell decided to sweep away much of the previous structure of government in Wales and Cheshire. This was partly motivated by specific concern at the disorder and potential disloyalty of parts of the region, especially some marcher lordships, but not primarily Cheshire. Partly, as the discussion of legislation showed, it was motivated by the cavalier application of a theoretical model of systematisation. Initially the result of these actions was chaos. That the palatinate ultimately emerged strengthened and renewed was due to the continuing respect for palatine privilege induced by the dominant political culture in combination with three specific factors which will be explored in the next chapter: the birth of a new prince of Wales, the death of Cromwell himself and the return of the country to war.

Minshull (24, 30 Oct. 1532: STAC 2/29/145) and the writ for the examination of George Calveley (20 Nov. 1532: STAC 2/34/96). The shrievalty of Edward Fitton referred to began with appointment on 24 November 1531 and ended when George Poulett was appointed on 8 December 1532: 39 DKR, 56.

157 Pardons: 8 Feb. 1533; 11 Feb. 1534: LP vi. 196(19); vii. 262(7). Settlement: Bangor Mostyn Collection, 586–7 (21 Mar. 1533/4).

158 PRO, STAC 2/28/14, 24; see pp. 125–8 above.

10

The Late 1530s and After

Before 1536, it has been argued here, the palatinate was the major factor in local political life. It has further been argued that the legislative changes of 1536 were not triggered by local political developments. These changes could have influenced local political life, yet 1536 was not a decisive watershed in Cheshire politics. Much had been destroyed – the immediate nexus of William Brereton's power and, more broadly, some of the features of the county's palatine privileges. Between 1536 and 1560 the effects of this destruction worked themselves out. The strife engendered by the disappearance of William Brereton gradually subsided; Cheshire gentry politics remained largely autonomous; a new prince was born; and, as war came to dominate life as it had not done for a century, the Cheshire community's response strengthened its corporate identity and thereby the palatinate.

It has been argued that the destruction of William Brereton, as well as ushering in a new policy of constitutional reform in Wales and Cheshire, also saw the end of the domination of office in the county by one man.[1] This is to exaggerate Brereton's influence in the 1530s and to under-estimate the success of dominant county gentry in taking on his offices, although there seems to have been little system behind the redistribution of Brereton's grants. Urian Brereton received his brother's largest landed holding in Cheshire, four messuages and 200 acres in Chorlton, Hampton and Shocklach. He also obtained his brother's office of escheator of Chester. In conjunction with Ranulph Woodall, Urian also became serjeant of the peace in Bromfield and Yale a few months later.[2] Edmund Peckham, cofferer of the household, received Etchells, Alderley and Aldford, with the stewardship of Longdendale, on 9 June 1536.[3] Of Brereton's other offices, the controllership of Chester and Flint went to Ralph Worseley; and Hugh Starkey, gentleman usher of the chamber, became steward of Tattenhall and Newhall.[4] In Wales, George Cotton and Thomas Seymour received the stewardships of the Holt, Bromfield and Yale, along with Chirk and Chirkland and of Cynllaith and Owen, Percival Harte, one of the king's sewers, became sheriff of Flint, and

---

[1] Ives, 'Court and county palatine', 33–4.
[2] *LP* x. 1256(8) (8 June 1536); x. 1256(29) (3, 14 June 1536); xi. 1217(7) (3, 10 Nov. 1536).
[3] *LP* x. 1256(14); Bindoff, *House of Commons, 1509–58*, iii. 78–9. A list in Wriothesley's hand proposed Peckham; on 2 June Peckham had already leased a farm in Etchells: *LP* x. 870, 1041.
[4] *LP* x. 1256(9, 43) (12, 22 June 1536).

Hugh David, yeoman of the guard, took on the keepership of Merseley park in Bromfield and Yale.[5]

More significant, and most controversial, in the redistribution of William Brereton's offices were the grants relating to Delamere forest and the duchy of Lancaster lordship of Halton. Cromwell appears to have considered both Sir Piers Dutton and Sir John Done for the rangership of Delamere, but in the event, on 2 June, Sir Piers Dutton received a grant.[6] Delamere was a dangerous point of tension. Sir Piers Dutton's house, for which he had struggled for so long, lay within the bounds of the forest, and the hereditary foresters, the Done family, supporters of William Brereton, represented a threat to his authority in the area. A petition put in by John Done against Dutton, and probably to be dated to the latter part of 1536 when Dutton was sheriff and Ralph Manning his deputy, complained of Dutton's placing his servants on juries and taking money for the return of writs; and alleged that he was responsible for the killing of a deer in Delamere, under colour of the rangership, and for a riot against Sir John Done's man, a forester, thereby preventing the fetching in of a strayed hart.[7] One of Done's men may have been murdered at Dutton's instigation in July 1535.[8] Sir Piers also made allegations against Done.[9] Although in Halton Dutton was less successful, he had high hopes that this would not be a permanent set-back. Sir Edward Nevill, who married Elizabeth, Lady Savage, Brereton's widow,[10] wanted to sell the office during John Savage's minority, yet, Dutton alleged, Sir William Brereton was preventing Nevill from accepting the fee Dutton was willing to pay.[11]

Although Cheshire, like the rest of northern England, was troubled in the

5 *LP* xi. 943(1); x. 1256(32) (31 May, 17 June 1536); xi. 385(2) (2 Aug. 1536).
6 A list in Wriothesley's hand suggested Sir Piers Dutton for the stewardship of Halton and rangership of Delamere. Another note associated Delamere, Shotwick and the escheatorship with Henry Annesley, groom of the chamber. Shortly after 20 May 1536 Cromwell noted Done's name in connection with the forestership: *LP* x. 870, 871, 879(6), 929(iii). For the grant see *LP* x. 1256(17) (2, 10 June 1536).
7 It also complained that George Holford, Ralph Manning and William Glasier had got Piers Felday to accuse Piers Bruen, Done's servant, leading to Bruen's imprisonment in the Tower, and that Dutton now had a supersedeas to prevent him being sued: BL, MS Harley 283, fos 15–16 (*LP* viii. 22(2), no earlier than 10 July 1536).
8 This is reported as having occurred about the previous 23 July, in a document probably to be dated to 1535, since it described the murder of Randal Davenport as having happened 3 years previously: *LP* viii. 496.
9 Done responded by complaining of an inquisition held before Ralph Birkenhead, ranger of the forest and undersheriff of the county, who, he said, had great malice towards John Done his grandfather. Dutton also raised the issue of a mill at Utkinton, and Done's taking fish within the forest: PRO, SP 1/117, fos 105r–v (stamped foliation) (*LP* xii/1, 717).
10 Nevill's first wife, Eleanor, widow of Ralph, Lord Scrope of Upsall, died before 25 March 1531: *CP* xi. 572. Nevill was executed late in 1538: *DNB* (1894), xl. 250 (which does not mention his second wife.)
11 *LP* xii/2, 1215 (placed at 15 Dec. 1537 by the editors because of the alleged length of the remainder of John Savage's minority, about 7 years; but the last in the sequence of Dutton

latter part of 1536 and early 1537, it was not the Pilgrimage of Grace which disturbed the order of the shire. The troubles that afflicted Cheshire in 1536–7 were due to the feuds exacerbated by the fall of William Brereton, especially that between Brereton and Dutton.[12] Just as the legislation relating to Cheshire was contradictory and disruptive in its effects, so was the more immediate political intervention of Thomas Cromwell. The Pilgrims knew that the rulers of Cheshire could not agree, and that the county was therefore unlikely to join the rising.[13] Confusion in the household of the earl of Derby was not relevant to Cheshire.[14] Although some Cheshire gentlemen did play a role in suppressing the rebellion, in the train of the earl of Derby,[15] the rulers were far too busy with their local struggles, insulated behind the county's autonomy. The best-known example of this surrounds the dissolution, in October 1536, of the abbey of Norton, close to Sir Piers Dutton's newly won seat at Dutton, during which a disturbance allegedly occurred.[16] Dutton reported to Chancellor Audley that he had dispersed the rebels and taken the abbot and three of the canons to Halton Castle.[17] Dutton alleged that Sir William Brereton was reluctant to act against the abbot; Sir William may have encouraged the trouble to embarrass Sheriff Dutton at a time of political tension over the Pilgrimage.[18] After Brereton succeeded in June 1537 in discrediting Felday's confession (the basis of Dutton's charges in the coining case), Cromwell ordered the abbot and canons of Norton to be freed in August 1537.[19] More directly, the death of William Brereton reopened the question of the inquisition on his father, Sir Randal, who had died in 1530.[20]

One of the reasons why this struggle for local dominance was occasionally exaggeratedly portrayed as rampant crime was the county's sometimes problematic relationship with the Council in the Marches. The classic instance is

---

shrievalties began in November 1536, so the thanks expressed for the shrievalty by Dutton must place it in December 1536.)

[12] Other gentry were involved in serious disputes, for example Hugh Starkey, a powerful Chamber servant, accused of torture at Holt between 1537 and 1538: PRO, STAC 2/28/74.

[13] *LP* xi. 1253. See the contrary argument of Madeleine Hope Dodds and Ruth Dodds, *The Pilgrimage of Grace 1536–37 and the Exeter conspiracy, 1538*, London 1915, repr. London 1971, map I, who describe Cheshire as in 'open rebellion'.

[14] *LP* xi. 859; Elton, *Policy and police*, 328.

[15] Sir William Stanley served with 121 men, Edward Warren 59, Piers Legh 201, Thomas Venables 9 and Sir Edward Fitton 250: *LP* xi. 1251.

[16] This episode was used by G. R. Elton to show how far out of the control of central authority local events could get: *Policy and police*, 321–5. See also Chesters, 'Power politics in Cheshire', 25–6, and 'Power politics and roguery, part II', 45–7, 57.

[17] *LP* xi. 681.

[18] *LP* xi. 1212. Randal Brereton was involved in the attempt to save the convent: Ives, 'Court and county palatine', 27.

[19] Dutton had to hurry the coiner to the scaffold to silence him: *LP* xii/2, 58, 597 (*Memorials of the Duttons*, 126–30, 130–2).

[20] Ormerod, *Chester*, iii. 901; *LP* xi. 1310 (misdated to 1536); xii/2, 1123; xiii/1, 17.

a statement by Rowland Lee concerning the Mainwaring–Cholmondeley affray in 1537–8.[21] At the end of 1537 the dispute between Richard Cholmondeley of Cholmondeley and Sir Randal Mainwaring of Baddiley broke into open violence. Richard Cholmondeley had a long-standing grievance against the Mainwarings. He had taken a lease of the vicarage of Acton from the vicar there, Richard Ormyshaw, at Michaelmas 1531 and claimed that he was promised an extension at the end of the lease if he wished. On the expiry of the agreement, however, the property was let to Randal Mainwaring, and Cholmondeley complained to the chancellor. Ormyshaw also put in a bill of complaint, citing Cholmondeley's alleged failure to pay rent, repair buildings and keep 'hospytalyte ther as he ys bounde to do'. The matter was put in arbitration in December 1534 before Sir Henry Delves and Ralph Broke.[22] One of Mainwaring's household servants, also called Randal, had on 10 April 1537 been bound in £200, in his view unfairly, to keep the peace towards Richard. Tension was reaching the point where each party took to travelling armed, and in December 1537 they came to blows.[23] Knowing Randal was in London, Richard allegedly set Hugh Lowther to wait on Randal's route home. Having spotted him, Lowther summoned Cholmondeley to Chalton (Staffs.) where on 1 December 1537 they attacked Randal and his companions; Randal and Humphrey Baskervile his servant were left for dead. Cholmondeley replied with an accusation that it was he who had been subjected to the initial assault, on 30 November 1537.[24] On 15 December Sir Piers Dutton wrote to Cromwell reporting the riot.[25] Cholmondeley was a close Brereton connection, and Dutton was concerned at his behaviour and at the apparent support for Thomas Brereton shown by Cromwell in connection with Randal Brereton's inquisition *post mortem*. Dutton's letter quickly led to the intervention of the Council in the Marches, on Cromwell's instructions.[26] About 26 December Richard Cholmondeley was imprisoned at Shrewsbury;[27] refusing to put in bonds to keep the peace towards Randal Mainwaring, he was

---

[21] For example, VCH, *County of Chester*, ii. 31.

[22] PRO, C 1/754/46–7; C 1/865/29. Ormyshaw also came into conflict with Cholmondeley over 240 acres in Acton which Cholmondeley claimed had been let by the abbot of Combermere to Sir Roger Cholmondeley of London, serjeant-at-law. Ormyshaw had resisted removal of his cattle from the land, probably in 1535: C 1/755/27; C 1/771/11–14.

[23] PRO, STAC 2/8/272; STAC 2/29/182 (*Collections for a History of Staffordshire* n.s. x/1 [1907], 157–8, 188; [1912], 118–21).

[24] *Collections for a History of Staffordshire* n.s. x/1 (1907), 157–8.

[25] PRO, SP 1/112, p. 241 (*LP* xi. 1310) (misdated 1536).

[26] The letter from Lee to Cromwell of 29 March 1538 refers to an instruction sent with Justice Porte that the case be examined by the Council in the Marches, apparently before the committing of Cholmondeley to Wigmore prison: PRO, SP 1/130, pp. 192–202 (*LP* xiii/1, 624).

[27] *Collections for a History of Staffordshire* (1912), 120. Rowland Lee later said Cholmondeley had been in prison at Wigmore since Christmas, but this seems to ignore his stay at Shrewsbury: PRO, SP 1/130, pp. 192–202 (*LP* xiii/1, 624).

committed to 'straighter custody' in Wigmore Castle on 26 January.[28] The case occurred at an important time: as well as the possibility of Cromwell's support for the Breretons over the inquisition *post mortem*, there were other signs of a threat to Dutton. On 27 January Richard Hough reminded Cromwell of a promise of the ridership of Delamere forest: in the same letter he reported 'so it is sir Peires Dutton is nowe comen up to london'.[29]

Responses to the riot must be seen in the context of the activity of the Council in the Marches. The council was not used to forge closer links between Cheshire and the central government in the 1530s or as a directly controlled crime-fighting authority; it had considerable autonomy.[30] The correspondence between Thomas Cromwell and Rowland Lee, president of the Council in the Marches, extends from 3 July 1534 until 19 May 1540.[31] Unfortunately we have only one side to the correspondence, the letters sent by Lee, and no definite idea of the level of loss among these. What the correspondence does give us is a body of 174 letters from the major government servant in the region to the king's chief minister. It is a confident correspondence: Lee was not afraid to report what he considered necessary to his mission and, on occasion, to attack Cromwell's policy.

Lee moved about the marches as he saw fit, and the places he chose to visit indicate where his priorities lay and influenced the information he could give Cromwell. He spent little time in Cheshire. The 174 letters were dated at twenty identifiable places. Shrewsbury occurs most frequently, with thirty-seven letters. Next come Ludlow, with twenty-six, and Bewdley with fifteen. From nowhere else came more than eight letters, and only five originated from the city of Chester and just one from nearby Holt.[32] Considering the periods covered by two or more letters dated at one place, without any intervening letter from elsewhere, and assuming this represented an uninterrupted stay, the letters indicate that Lee spent the majority of his time in Wigmore, Ludlow, Shrewsbury and Hereford.[33] Stays totalling only thirty days can be allocated to Chester, in 1534 and 1538,[34] although this is the eighth highest total.

We do not know the impact of loss of letters on this pattern. The letters' contents indicate that Lee actually visited Chester at least twice more, in 1537 and 1539, but neither visit resulted in letters being sent thence.[35]

---

[28] PRO, SP 3/xv/15 (*LP* xii/1, 149); *Collections for a History of Staffordshire* (1912), 120.

[29] With Wriothesley's support: PRO, SP 1/128, p. 128 (*LP* xiii/1, 153.)

[30] Cf. Roberts, ' "Acts of union" and the Tudor settlement of Wales', 113.

[31] Calendared in *LP* vii–xv.

[32] *LP* vii. 1151; xiii/1, 1042, 1044, 1087, 1153. (Holt is at xiii/1, 958.)

[33] This too is an arbitrary method, but from it we may suggest that Lee's location is known for 1,051 out of 2,148 days for the period covered by the letters. Of these 1,051 days, 259 can be allocated to Wigmore, 225 to Ludlow, 147 to Shrewsbury and 107 to Hereford.

[34] Respectively, the letters quoted in n. 32 above from *LP* vii (1534); xiii/1 (1538).

[35] On 6 July 1537 Lee reported that he was going to Chester until mid-August; by 28 September he was back at Shrewsbury, whence he referred to a summer visit to Cheshire and

Cheshire seems to have been unremarkable in Lee's eyes and, on at least two of his visits, not to have deserved immediate reporting. The content of the letters again sees Cheshire playing a minor role. If the county is the source of just 2.87 per cent of the letters, its affairs are mentioned in few more. Of the 174 letters considered only thirty or thirty-one mention Cheshire affairs. Some are not concerned with anything other than interesting phenomena, such as the 1534 earthquake.[36] Seven letters contain patronage requests concerning the county,[37] and twenty-two contain political news. The influence of the Council in the Marches did not therefore mean subjection to Westminster since communication between the two relating to Cheshire was minimal. It has already been suggested that the relationship between the Chester exchequer and the marcher council was a complex one between two autonomous institutions. During the early years of Lee's presidency, the Council in the Marches did not represent a strong link between Cheshire and the centre: the vast majority of Lee's letters concerning Cheshire (seventeen) were written during the years 1537–9, after the legislation concerning the marches of Wales in 1534–6, and cannot be seen as contributing to it.

In this context, the exceptional nature of the Mainwaring–Cholmondeley dispute is evident from the way it was treated. Despite his imprisonment at Wigmore, by mid-February 1538 Richard Cholmondeley had not yet been indicted in Cheshire. This took place during the county court session of 26 February 1538, and there are clear signs that the indictment was tampered with to protect him, perhaps through the packing of the jury; although the bill was found, considerable portions of the indictment (including all specific references to Mainwaring, and to the movement of the rioters from Cholmondeley to Chalton) were deleted and a new version written out, leaving only the general allegation of riot.[38] Perhaps at Dutton's suggestion, backed by the obvious lack of action locally, on 17 February 1538 Chancellor Audley instructed the council in the marches to send Cholmondeley to London.[39] This triggered Rowland Lee's most intensive intervention in the palatinate during his spell as president. On 5 March 1538 he announced his intention to 'Remove after Easter to Chesshire . . . for the redresse of suche enormyties and mysdemeanors as haue bene there of late vsed'.[40] On 16 March Lee explained to Cromwell the underlying cause of the problem: 'the dissention

---

Flintshire: *LP* xii/2, 222, 770, 896. In 1539 a fever prevented him from spending a month in Chester from the Tuesday before Pentecost. On 24 May he was still at Wigmore, but by 19 July at Montgomery he reported lately having been at Chester: *LP* xiv/1, 715, 1020, 1289.

[36] *LP* vii. 1151.

[37] *LP* xii/2, 770; xiii/1, 1044, 1087, 1361; xiii/2, 1031; xiv/1, 830; xv. 128.

[38] PRO, CHES 24/89(2). The grand jury included several close neighbours of Cholmondeley in Broxton hundred, for example John Stringer of Crewe. The sheriff was Dutton's enemy, Sir Henry Delves.

[39] PRO, SP 1/101, pp. 112–13 (*LP* x. 310) (misdated 1536).

[40] PRO, SP 1/129, p. 160 (*LP* xiii/1, 426).

betwene Brearton and Dutton destroyeth all goode order'.[41] The fundamental point for Lee, however, was whether the Council in the Marches was going to be allowed to tackle the problem alone and without interference from London: Audley's instruction of 17 February suggested that this was unlikely. Although Lee was willing to comply with Audley's request that he demand sureties from Cholmondeley to appear in Star Chamber at Easter, he asked Cromwell to support him in having the case heard in Cheshire.[42] By 8 May Lee was at Holt; five days later Cromwell wrote to him saying that the case should not be heard before the Council in the Marches if the offence was committed outside their commission, as was the case. Lee again asked for the case to be kept before his court in a letter of 21 May from Chester itself.[43] It is significant that it is in this context that the letter emphasised disorder in the county. There was an element of special pleading here: Lee had to emphasise Cheshire's special problems and his own competence to solve them if he was to defend his jurisdiction, which he believed was the only sure way of suppressing disorder in the marches. There are signs that Lee's concern was partly due to the behaviour of Sir Piers Dutton in Cheshire at the time. Richard Cholmondeley was a Brereton connection: his sureties in 1538 included Sir Richard Brereton and Philip Egerton of Egerton.[44] Dutton's move to inform Cromwell of the riot was designed to remove it from local jurisdiction, his ride to London to extract it from Lee's too.[45] Lee's concern with the Duttons' behaviour was clear when he imprisoned the grand jury which had sat at the sessions in Chester in March 1538 for, as he told Cromwell, finding 'murders to be manslaughters and Ryottes to be mysbehavors'.[46] Among the indictments they had found, in Lee's view too leniently, for trespass, were two which related to large groups led by the Duttons.[47] In June of the same year, at a time when Lee was almost certainly in Cheshire himself, further indictments were found against Peter Leicester of Nether Tabley and Ranulph Dudley of Nether Peover, labourer, and a group of ten headed by Sir Piers Dutton himself.[48] By June, however, the Cholmondeley–

---

41 PRO, SP 1/130, pp. 63–4 (*LP* xiii/1, 519).

42 PRO, SP 1/130, pp. 192–202 (*LP* xiii/1, 624); SP 1/102, fo. 42 (*LP* x. 310) (Audley's command: misdated 1536).

43 PRO, SP 1/132, pp. 163–4 (*LP* xiii/1, 1042). It was committed in Staffordshire.

44 PRO, SP 1/130, pp. 192–202 (*LP* xiii/1, 624).

45 Lee's scepticism is very clear: PRO, SP 1/132, pp. 163–4 (*LP* xiii/1, 1042).

46 PRO, SP 1/134, p. 204 (*LP* xiii/1, 1411: 18 July). The sessional file for the session of 26 March 1538 (among CHES 24/89(1)) is damaged; it is impossible to recover the evidence for this episode provided by the grand jury panel.

47 Two indictments, one of 23 people, the other of 8, were headed by Thomas Dutton of Marsh, one of Lawrence Dutton's bastards; two others were headed by Lawrence Dutton of Manley. In all cases the Duttons' target was John Birkenhead: PRO, CHES 20/5, rot. 4; CHES 24/89(1), file for the session of 26 March 1538.

48 The latter indictment was linked with one of those found in March through the presence in both of the name of Ranulph Wirrall, son of Hugh Wirrall, of 'Leigh-iuxta-Weverham' (Little Leigh, in the parish of Great Budworth), yeoman: PRO, CHES 20/5, rot. 4v.

Mainwaring case had come before Star Chamber: Lee's alarmism had failed.[49] Lee continued to present violence as endemic in Cheshire if he had a reason to do so, but he could do the opposite if necessary.[50] His relative lack of activity in the shire suggests that disorder was not a serious concern and the underlying pattern of Cheshire politics had been little disrupted. The confusion over jurisdictions and the failure to achieve a resolution of the incident for many months indicate again the continuing insularity of the palatine political system and the degree to which those at the centre were happy for it to remain so. Such disputes produced a complex series of pressures, by no means all of which tended to undermine local autonomy.

It was only when the dispute impinged on the capital and involved murder that really decisive action was taken. In January 1539 John Mainwaring killed Roger Cholmondeley in St Paul's churchyard, and then fled to sanctuary at Westminster. Ralph Mainwaring was indicted but acquitted; but John was hanged in London, along with two accomplices, Robert Jones and Thomas Potter. Two others who were involved, William Edwards and Hugh Griffyth, were sent to Cholmondeley for execution.[51] This is usually taken as a good example of the erosion of sanctuary and possibly the cause of the abolition of sanctuary for major crimes in the next session of parliament[52] – but, given the previous history of the dispute, it paradoxically illustrates the continued impenetrability of Cheshire's jurisdictions, even after the reforms. The gaol delivery was conducted by Thomas Cromwell, Richard Rich, John Hales and William Forman, lord mayor of London, and so the refusal to look beyond the immediate murder in London and convict Ralph Mainwaring is particularly striking.[53] The quickening recovery in the power of the palatinate – and a major reason for it – are suggested by the fact that the guilty men were hanged in the infant Prince Edward's livery.

Another sign of the restored and even increased autonomy of the palatinate is to be found in the creation of the bishopric of Chester in 1541.[54] Although the precise form of the new diocese, pairing the archdeaconries of Chester and Richmond, was not originally intended, Chester's place as the seat of a new bishopric founded on the monastic heritage of St Werburgh's

---

[49] A *dedimus potestatem* was issued to Sir Edward Aston and others on 22 June: PRO, STAC 2/29/182 (*Collections for a History of Staffordshire* [1912], 121).

[50] The contrast in 1539 between PRO, SP 1/150, pp. 91–2, and SP 1/152, p. 143 (*LP* xiv/1, 715, 1289) should be noted.

[51] PRO, KB 9/541/85–7; KB 27/1112, Rex, r.9–9a; Halle, *Chronicle*, 827 (who has John Jones, John Potter and William 'Maneryng' being hanged); Holinshed, *Chronicles*, iii. 807; Wriothesley, *Chronicle*, 93. Stow (*Annales* [1615], 575) follows Halle in naming Mainwaring William and Jones and Potter both John.

[52] Elton, *Policy and police*, 289–90; Thornley, 'Destruction of sanctuary', 203–4; 32 Henry VIII, c.12 (*SR* iii. 756–8).

[53] PRO, KB 9/541/85–7; KB 27/1112, Rex, r.9–9a.

[54] Heath, 'Medieval archdeaconry and Tudor bishopric of Chester', 243–52. (Heath's overall conceptual framework is, however, one which treats the regime as intent on the 'curtailment of privilege'.)

had been assured from the start. Chester's archdeaconry had always fitted uneasily within the diocese of Coventry and Lichfield; memories of Chester's housing the *cathedra* in the late eleventh century remained strong, and the popular association of the bishopric with the town meant a continued tradition of referring to the bishop of Coventry and Lichfield as the 'bishop of Chester' through the late Middle Ages. Even Rowland Lee found that the archdeacon 'regards himself as an ordinary'.[55] Legislation has treated Chester archdeaconry as distinct, for example in the 1529 Mortuaries Act, which associated it with the Welsh dioceses.[56] Most important for our purposes is the fact that there had been a long tradition of associating the autonomy of the archdeaconry with the palatinate's rights, most notably when Bishop Booth and Bishop Boulers challenged the archdeacon's powers in 1449–55. If, before 1540, Cheshire had existed in an uneasy state of subjection to an ecclesiastical jurisdiction based outside its borders, from 1541 the palatinate's premier churchman was now unchallenged in his jurisdiction.

Not only did the palatinate's politics begin to regain something of their autonomy from outside interference, internally, the palatinate adjusted and grew stronger. The two judicial innovations of the 1530s and 1540s, the Chester sessions and the commission of the peace, indicate the continuing operation of palatine institutions and co-operation among the gentry. There were, admittedly, signs that the concern, expressed in the parliamentary petition of 1541,[57] that the county's judicial structures were crumbling, was justified. Although in the eight sessions of the county court held in 1539 at least forty-one different indictments were recorded, there do not seem to have been any indictments found in 1540 until the sessions beginning 18 October, the first of the new-style great sessions. The number of indictments found at the court of 2 October 1541 was also low, at fifteen, each of no more than three people.[58] Yet the disruption was short-lived. The average number of indictments before the county court dropped from between thirty-five and forty-five a year, as the sittings of the JPs began to offer an alternative destination for criminals who would previously have been indicted at the county court, but the figure stabilised at the still significant figure of about twenty-five *per annum*. Overall, the business of the county court remained fairly steady during the last years of Henry VIII,[59] fell slightly under Edward VI[60]

---

[55] *LP* ix. 712.

[56] 21 Henry VIII, c.6 (*SR* iii. 288–9); cf. p. 125 above.

[57] See pp. 131–2 above.

[58] CHES 20/5, rot. 11. There were also, of course, indictments (rot. 11v.) before JPs which resulted in action in the sessions.

[59] This is judged from the admittedly crude measure of the size of the plea roll: PRO, CHES 29/246 (autumn 1542, 13 rotulets); 247 (spring 1543, 20); 248 (autumn 1543, 20); 249 (spring 1544, 15); 250 (autumn 1544, 14); 251 (spring 1545, 13); 252 (autumn 1545, 18); 253 (spring 1546, 13); 254 (autumn 1546, 8).

[60] PRO, CHES 29/255 (Apr., May 1547, 17); 256 (Apr., Oct. 2 Edward VI, 16); 257 (Apr.,

and then recovered under Mary.[61] This recovery in the level of business in the court is reflected, for example, by the number of attorneys active there which rose from two in the 1540s, invariably Thomas Hurleston and Thomas Birkenhead, to four or even five in the later 1550s.[62] There were also signs of initial problems with the commission of the peace, as it did not become effective for many months after the passage of the legislation. The first known Cheshire commission of the peace dates from July 1539,[63] before the first Welsh commissions, dating from 1542. The first trace of activity before commissioners of the peace in Cheshire probably dates from the first weeks of 1539, in connection with a trespass in Disley on 19 August 1538.[64] Also ominously for the autonomy of the county community, the membership of the commission was dominated by the Council in the Marches: although the members of the commission were listed by status group, council members had precedence within each, and they represented more than a third of working members of the commission.[65] Yet the Cheshire gentry involved were a comprehensive cross-section of the community,[66] and by 1542 they would make up more than half the commission.[67] The last commission of Henry

---

Sept. 3 Edward VI, 15); 258 (Apr., Sept. 5 Edward VI, 27); 259 (Apr., Sept. 6 Edward VI, 30).

[61] PRO, CHES 29/260 (Oct. 1553, 24); 261 (May 1554, 22); 262 (Oct. 1554, 21); 263 (May 1555, 14); 264 (Sept. 1555, 27); 265 (May 1556, 18); 266 (Aug. 1556, 19); 267 (May 1557, 24); 268 (May 1558, 17); 269 (Oct. 1558, 18).

[62] PRO, CHES 29/246-7 (Hurleston and Birkenhead alone, 1542-3); 266 (Robert Brock, Richard Nuttall, John Banester, Thomas Birkenhead and Thomas Browne, Aug. 1556), 269 (Nuttall, Brock, Browne and both Thomas and Henry Birkenhead, Oct. 1558).

[63] PRO, C 66/687, m. 8d. (*LP* xiv/1, 1354(9) [3 July 1539; partially misprinted]).

[64] PRO, STAC 2/13/278-86 (*L&C Star Chamber*, 92-4). The indictments took place before JPs about three weeks before the presentation of the bill, which must have been shortly before the issue of a commission from the Court of Star Chamber on 14 February 1539.

[65] Marriott, 'Commission of the peace', 21-2.

[66] Sir Piers Dutton, Sir William Brereton of Brereton, Sir William Stanley, Sir William Venables (not in the *LP* entry for 1539, but in that for 1540), Sir Henry Delves, Sir Edward Fitton, Sir John Done, Sir Ranulph Mainwaring, Sir John Holford, Thomas Holcroft, John Holcroft, John Massey, Edmund Savage, Urian Brereton, William Moreton, Richard Hassall and John Birkenhead. The second commission, of 9 February 1540, changed the first only in the addition of Hugh Starkey of Oulton: *LP* xv. 282(34). From Easter 1542, the *nomina ministrorum* in the assize records include the names of working justices, omitting the dignitaries until 4 Edward VI: PRO, CHES 24/90 (Easter and Michaelmas, 33 Henry VIII). The Easter 1542 *nomina* records the addition of Lawrence Smith of the Hough, whose father had died in summer 1538, Edward Warren of Poynton and Robert Tatton of Wythenshawe, and the temporary omissions of Sir Edward Croft, Roger Wigston, John Vernon and Sir Thomas Holcroft, the latter perhaps due to his involvement in Scottish affairs.

[67] The commission added Thomas Venables, almost immediately after his father's death, Sir Thomas Fouleshurst, perhaps the most prominent man so far excluded, George Booth, just 25 years old in summer 1542 and to die a year later, John Carrington and Piers Legh, a relative newcomer to Cheshire: PRO, C 193/12/1, m. 38v (*LP* xvii. 1154(75)).

VIII's reign, that of 28 June 1543, continued the position much as before.[68] By 1543, therefore, the commission included all the heads of the most senior Cheshire gentry families. If we compare it with the list of men required to produce more than forty men for military service in 1544–5, we find that only Sir Piers Warburton, Sir Richard Brereton and Ralph Done had been omitted from the commission. It also included a body of lawyer-administrators of slightly lesser status, all men closely linked with the administration of the palatinate. Richard Hassall served as deputy justice of Cheshire in the early 1540s, an office in which he had been preceded by John Birkenhead, head of the family that dominated the office of clerk and prothonotary of Cheshire and Flint in the sixteenth century, and Robert Tatton was clerk of the Chester exchequer. The Cheshire commission rapidly became far more than just another manifestation of the Council in the Marches, providing an effective opportunity to express the coherence and identity of the elite of Cheshire gentry families. There are few signs of significant, still less of deliberate, exclusions; and the presence of some of the key judicial administrators of the palatinate ensured that ultimately the activity of the commission could be integrated with the older judicial structures of the palatinate.[69]

War and Cheshire, 1540–60

If a new stability and confidence in the palatinate community began to emerge after 1536, as seen in the commission of the peace, it drew on several factors. One of these was the birth of Edward, son of Jane Seymour and Henry VIII, news of which had reached the marches by 25 October.[70] Although Edward was never officially created prince of Wales and earl of Chester, his birth stimulated thoughts on his potential role in those territories, both literary and specifically political.[71] The birth of an heir to the throne helped to

---

68 Sir William Brereton had died in 1541, Sir William Venables had been succeeded by Thomas and Sir Piers Dutton served as sheriff in 1542–3 and was to die in August 1545. These were understandable changes. That left Sir William Stanley, Sir Henry Delves, Sir Edward Fitton, Sir Thomas Fouleshurst, Sir John Done, Sir Ranulph Mainwaring, Sir John Holford, Thomas Holcroft, Edward Warren, Richard Hassall, Peter Legh, John Massey, Lawrence Smith, George Booth, Edward Savage, Hugh Starkey, Urian Brereton, Robert Tatton, John Carrington, Jr, William Moreton and John Birkenhead. John Holcroft no longer appeared: PRO, C 67/1, m. 12 (*LP* xx/1, 622(7)). Sir Ranulph Mainwaring is mistranscribed 'Francis'.

69 In this sense the commission seems to have been more focused on the elite (of both gentry society and palatinate administration) than that of the West Riding of Yorkshire by the 1540s: Smith, *Land and politics*, 156.

70 *LP* xii/2, 985.

71 Leland, *Genethliacon illustrissimi Eaduerdi*; ' "A breviat of the effectes devised for Wales" '; and in general see pp. 57, 128–31 above. The possibility of a new marcher council, discussed by Roberts, was apparent almost immediately: Richard Hassall wrote to Cromwell on 28 October 1537 saying that he was solicitor when Mary came to the marches and, now

revive the palatinate community through one of its most important elements: the existence, if only potentially, of an earl of Chester. The influence of the prince's servants might be disruptive, as has been seen in the case of the participants in the Cholmondeley–Mainwaring feud hanged in his livery. It also gave the Cottons' arrival in Cheshire society added weight and legitimacy: as comptroller and cofferer of the prince, Sir Richard Cotton commanded tremendous authority in the county, both generally and in the specifics of county administration. So too did George Cotton: when John Mainwaring of Ightfield acted as deputy chamberlain in 1537 he was described as George's servant.[72] Even more unsettling problems were caused by Edward's birth, as Rowland Lee reported: 'A little the thieves begin to steal, trusting of white books [of pardon] by the birth of the prince.'[73] The influence of the new prince might therefore be disruptive, but this was disruption experienced by a dynamic society which might once again find its focus in an earl of its own. Also important was the fall of Cromwell in 1540: after his death no minister of the crown proposed a scheme of reform for Cheshire on the scale of that devised in 1533–6.

Most important in the long term, however, was war. The return of England to war in the 1540s helped to strengthen the pattern of Cheshire gentry politics. After a largely peaceful decade in the 1530s,[74] the situation in Ireland and the need to defend against invasion provided the first calls to arms. In October 1539 Sir William Brereton, whose presence in the county in and after 1536 had exacerbated conflict, was ordered back to Ireland where he had previously served from 1534.[75] Over the next few years Brereton played a

---

that the prince had been born, he hoped Cromwell would remember him when the king appointed officers in the marches: *LP* xii/2, 997.

[72] JRUL, Arley charters 17/2. Mainwaring acted for Cotton again in the following year, although he was no longer described as vice-chamberlain: ibid. 17/9, 15.

[73] *LP* xii/2, 985 (25 Oct. 1537). For the possibilities presented by a marriage of Edward to the heir to the Scottish kingdom see A. H. Williamson, 'Scotland, AntiChrist, and the invention of Britain', in John Dwyer, Roger A. Mason and Alexander Murdoch (eds), *New perspectives on the politics and culture of early modern Scotland*, Edinburgh 1982, 34–58; Roger A. Mason, 'The Reformation and Anglo-British imperialism', in Roger A. Mason (ed.), *Scots and Britons: Scottish political thought and union of 1603*, Cambridge 1994, 167–71; M. Merriman, 'James Henrisoun and "Great Britain": British union and the Scottish commonweal', in Roger A. Mason (ed.), *Scotland and England, 1286–1815*, Edinburgh 1987, 85–112; D. M. Head, 'Henry VIII's Scottish policy: a reassessment', *Scottish Historical Review* lxi (1982), 1–24.

[74] Although musters were occasionally necessary for the defence of the northern border, of course. See, for example, *Tudor royal proclamations*, 205 (no. 137; 26 Oct. 1532).

[75] On coastal defence see PRO, SP 1/143, pp. 185–95 (*LP* xiv/1, 398); SP 1/150, p. 157 (*LP* xiv/1, 801), forwarded to Cromwell by Lee on 22 Apr.; SP 1/150, pp. 182–3 (*LP* xiv/1, 830). On Brereton see SP 1/154, pp. 8–9 (*LP* xiv/2, 303) (2 Oct. 1539); Bangor, Mostyn Collection, 5410–11, settlement by Sir William Brereton on 25 Oct., 31 Oct. 1539. Brereton was in Ireland in 1540, in spite of his continuing to be vice-chamberlain of Chester: STAC 2/20/264.

major role in the military and diplomatic campaign there, ultimately as justice of Ireland; and he died there in 1541.[76]

The Brereton campaign in Ireland involved only a few hundred men, not all of them from Cheshire. The wars of the early 1540s spread the impact of mobilisation more widely within the county. Some Cheshire men served in France: on 20 June 1544 Thomas Croxton of Ravenscroft made his will after receiving the order to serve in France; and a muster book for the campaign includes Urian Brereton.[77] There was a tradition of service by Cheshire men across the Channel, in particular among the Holfords, one of the few local families with a continued commitment to the last stages of the Hundred Years War, and Sir George Holford and Thomas Bulkeley served in 1489.[78] But this was a limited commitment. The attractions of continental campaigning cannot have been increased by experiences of the French war in the 1520s. Hamlet, Edward and Robert Massey, and Ralph and Thomas Forest were alleged to have said at Calais during the 1522 campaign that 'ther was not oon good capteyn in all my lordes armye'. In their defence they produced several witnesses to corruption by captains and demonstrated that there was a widespread feeling among the troops that they were sent abroad 'to the entent they shuld be cast awey & distroyed'.[79] War in Scotland, however, involved far more Cheshire men and with greater enthusiasm and success. On 24 August 1542 the duke of Norfolk was commissioned to campaign against the Scots with, amongst others, the men of Cheshire, and although it was the Scottish counter-attack into the western marches which resulted in a crushing defeat for the Scots at Solway Moss, those with Norfolk could revel in the triumph.[80] Early in 1544, as part of the retaliation for the failure of the treaties of Greenwich, Cheshire men were again going north: on 8 March one James Clulaw's mare was commandeered by Sir Edward Fitton as he prepared to lead the men of the lordship of Leek in Staffordshire towards Scotland, and Edward Seymour and his colleagues reported to the king on 27 March 1544 that gentlemen of Cheshire were daily arriving for the campaign. By early May, 1,500 Cheshiremen under twenty-eight leaders

---

76 PRO, SP 60/9/25 (*LP* xv. 649) (7 May 1540). His grandson was given livery of his lands on 28 June 1542: *LP* xvii. 443(76). William's son John won distinction in the Irish wars: SP 60/10/68 (*LP* xvii. 664); SP 60/11/5 (*LP* xviii/1, 550).

77 PRO, SP 1/184, fos 85, 222, 224, 226, 228, 230 (*LP* xix/1, 743); *LP* xix/1, 273.

78 Driver, *Cheshire in the later Middle Ages*, 15–16; PRO, E 36/130, fos 19v–31v; Bennett, 'Henry VII and the northern rising of 1489', 54; CHES 1/2/74 (signed bill, Westminster, 26 February; Holford excused appearance in the Chester exchequer, on the grounds that he was appointed 'to doo us service in our Armee unto the parties of Bretain').

79 PRO, STAC 2/21/197.

80 *LP* xvii. 661, 686, 808; APC i. 24; Bangor, Mostyn Collection, 588 (warrant to Richard Hough to raise men, 25 Aug. 1542). On 19 September 1542 the commissioners at York deferred the arrival of Cheshire troops to 7 October. Cf. HMC, *Rutland*, i. 30. It was probably refusal to serve in this campaign that led to the eviction of Thomas Johnson from a messuage and mill in Wettenhall by Thomas Brereton: PRO, STAC 2/6/66 (*L&C Star Chamber*, 38–9). See also J. J. Scarisbrick, *Henry VIII*, London 1968, 435–6.

mustered in Newcastle. Among others, Sir William Brereton, Sir Edmund Savage, Sir John Done and Sir Lawrence Smith marched their troops from Chester, and Sir Hugh Cholmondeley came from Cholmondeley. With Cheshire's help, Leith and Edinburgh suffered the devastating wrath of the English.[81] The scale of the operation had obvious implications for the future service of Cheshiremen. At least one woman property-owner made arrangements for her tenants' service: on 14 October 1544 Eleanor Baskervile made Sir Randal Mainwaring her steward in Withington, Old Withington, Chelford and elsewhere with the express power to lead her tenants 'to serue the kynges hignes in his graces warres', and to evict those who did not follow him.[82] Early 1545 saw the English without allies and suffering defeat by the Scots at Ancrum on 27 February; Cheshire forces played a part in the preparations of the following summer and of 1546.[83] Henry's demise did nothing to reduce military efforts against Scotland, for this was one of Protector Somerset's obsessions.[84] Cheshiremen took part in and remembered with pride the victory gained at Pinkie in 1547.[85] Subsequently, a garrisoning policy was combined with further invasions in August 1548 and in January and July 1549.[86] At least two Cheshire captains were involved, Sir John Savage and Sir Thomas Venables.[87] Yet the disastrous failure of this and other of Somerset's policies led to their abandonment, and the duke of Northumberland led the country to peace with France in March 1550 and with Scotland a year later.[88]

Cheshire's involvement in war against the Scots continued under Mary, however. An uneasy peace between the Marian regime and the French was

[81] PRO, C 1/1111/61; SP 1/184, fo. 26 (LP xix/1, 251); HMC, *Salisbury*, i. 37 (item 156, which is LP xix/1, 471); HMC, *Report on the manuscripts of the most honourable the marquess of Bath preserved at Longleat, IV: Seymour Papers, 1532–1686*, London 1968, 58–60, 66–7, 69–72, 96, 101; F. H. Cheetham, 'Cheshire men in the Scottish expedition of 1544', THSLC n.s. xxxvii (1922 [1921]), 232; Scarisbrick, *Henry VIII*, 442–4.

[82] JRUL, Mainwaring charters 347.

[83] LP xx/1, 538; PRO, SP 49/8/73 (LP xx/2, 308); SP 49/8/85 (LP xx/2, 432); Scarisbrick, *Henry VIII*, 452–6, 469; LP xxi/2, 433.

[84] Guy, *Tudor England*, 201–3; M. L. Bush, *The government policy of Protector Somerset*, London 1975, 7–39.

[85] While the conveying of troops to Scotland was being arranged in August 1547, an assault took place near Macclesfield: PRO, STAC 2/25/302 (*Collections for a History of Staffordshire* [1912], 4–5, misdated to Henry VIII's reign). Morris believed the reference to three knights and 300 men from Cheshire fighting in Scotland (BL, MS Harleian 2145), refers to Pinkie: *Chester in the Plantagenet and Tudor reigns*, 69. See p. 233 below for the poem 'Musleboorrowe ffeild'. Again, Chester was a port of transit for Irish kerne: Morris, *Chester in the Plantagenet and Tudor reigns*, 69–70.

[86] CSPD, *1547–53*, pp. 28–30, item 82 (muster roll, Northwich hundred, 27 Feb. 1548).

[87] HMC, *Rutland*, i. 36–7.

[88] In spring 1549 120 Lancashire and Cheshire men deserted: HMC, *Rutland*, i. 35–6; Jordan, *Edward VI: the young king*, 297. See also Guy, *Tudor England*, 219. Sir Thomas Holcroft was involved in negotiations in Scotland in November 1549: HMC, *Rutland*, i. 33, 46–8; cf. Jordan, *Edward VI: the young king*, 280; Jordan, *Edward VI: the threshold of power*, 93, 112.

finally ended in 1557 after the raid on Scarborough by Thomas Stafford in April of that year. Awareness of the eventual inevitability of war may have lain behind the agreement by Hamo Billyncham of Macefen in December 1556 that he would give his service in war in the retinue of Hugh Cholmondeley.[89] In February 1557 Thomas Pillyn, as feodary of Cheshire, was warned to prepare farmers of crown lands and other royal dependants for a muster, a command which he passed on to, amongst others, the people of Bebington.[90] During July 1557 the Scots and their French allies began raiding across the northern border. King Philip's determination to avoid conflict, however, combined with Scots reluctance and the unwillingness of the French to send aid to ensure that no full-scale war resulted. Yet there was sufficient concern on the English side of the border for Berwick to be reinforced and for a force of light horse to be mobilised under the earls of Westmorland and Shrewsbury. Thanks to Shrewsbury's caution, the forces of the northern shires were never committed.[91] Even then, although the main focus of the English war effort was in the Low Countries and the country was exhausted by harvest failure and epidemic disease,[92] the demands on Cheshire for northern defence did not end. In 1558 200 Cheshire men were sent to the border under the command of Sir William Brereton, and on 7 September the Privy Council wrote to a group including Brereton and Sir Richard Cholmondeley thanking them for their efforts in an 'exploit' at Coldingham.[93]

Scotland was therefore once again a forum in which the gentry of Cheshire could display their martial prowess. The reigns of Henry VIII, Edward VI and Mary also saw the opening to Cheshiremen of a new avenue for activity and advancement – Ireland.[94] From the time when Sir William Brereton served as lord justice of Ireland in the 1530s, increasing numbers of Cheshire gentlemen and others went across the Irish Sea to fight, administer and ultimately settle. Throughout the 1540s and 1550s the Brereton family, including Andrew, Arthur, Edward and John, sons of Sir William, was prominent in Ireland. Andrew eventually married Catherine, daughter Sir Andrew

---

[89] CCRO, DCH X/12/12 (12 Dec. 1556).
[90] CCRO, DDX 43/50 (23 Feb. 1557).
[91] Loades, *Reign of Mary Tudor*, 304–11; Bernard, *Power of the early Tudor nobility*, 128–9; C. S. L. Davies, 'England and the French war, 1557–59', in Jennifer Loach and Robert Tittler (eds), *The mid-Tudor polity, 1540–1560*, London 1980, 166–8.
[92] Loades, *Reign of Mary Tudor*, 312–28, and *Mary Tudor*, 274–82, 291–305; Davies, 'England and the French war', 159–85.
[93] APC vi. 244, 396. On 22 August 1559 it was suggested that for border security 8,000 men should be sent to the warden of the western march from Yorkshire, Nottinghamshire and Cheshire: *Calendar of state papers, foreign series, of the reign of Elizabeth, 1558–1559*, ed. Joseph Stevenson, London 1863, 491.
[94] There had always been a very small-scale involvement by Cheshiremen in Ireland, of which the Irish expeditions of Richard II and the service of Sir John Stanley are the most prominent examples. Ireland had not, however, to this point offered the sort of opportunities for extensive service provided by campaigns against Scotland.

Fitzsimmons of Ireland.[95] Also in Ireland were George Delves, a prominent captain in the 1560s, and members of the Mainwaring family, such as Robert Mainwaring.[96]

The benefits of the conflict in Scotland were particularly evident, especially as crystallised in the mass knighting of Cheshire gentry in 1544.[97] On 11 May, before Leith, Thomas Holcroft, William Brereton, Hugh Cholmondeley, Edward Warren, Piers Legh, Hugh Calveley, Edmund Trafford, Richard Egerton, Lawrence Smith and John Legh of Booths were made knights by the earl of Hertford. Thomas Venables was made knight that day at Edinburgh. On the 13th, also at Leith, Roger Brereton, Urian Brereton and Philip Egerton joined them. Five days later at Butterden, William Davenport, Ralph Leicester, Edmund Savage and John Massey completed a tally of eighteen Cheshiremen knighted. Certain gentlemen were created esquires, including Richard Birkenhead, Roger Boydell, Thomas Cowper, Hugh Dutton, Ralph Leech, William Sneyd and Adam Troutbeck.[98] This was a large proportion of the major Cheshire gentlemen, and united with them were relative newcomers like Richard Birkenhead and William Sneyd, palatinate officials making good in Cheshire society. There were obvious material rewards from the campaigns. The Lancashire gentleman Richard Asheton of Middleton included the arms of the two important Scots he had captured at Flodden on his own coat of arms, and William Norris of Speke had loot taken from Edinburgh in 1544. The church of St Michael-in-Wyre in Amounderness still owns a bell made in 1458 for the donor, Catherine de Bernieules, which originated in the Boulonnais.[99] More importantly, however, campaigns against the Scots increased the self-identification and coherence of the Cheshire

95 *Calendar of state papers, Ireland, of the reigns of Henry VIII., Edward VI., Mary, and Elizabeth, 1509–1573*, ed. Hans Claude Hamilton, London 1860, 65, 69, 73, 79, 81, 87, 91, 98, 102–4, 118, etc; Ormerod, *Chester*, iii. 89. Sir Antony St Leger recommended Randal Brereton to Sir Michael Stanhope on 16 February 1550–1 at Kilmainham: HMC, *Salisbury*, i. 82. See the voluntary service of a Chester bowyer, reported in May 1548, and the 100 Cheshire archers raised in autumn 1553 under Robert St Leger and Andrew Brereton: APC ii. 198; iv. 355.

96 CSP, *Ireland, 1509–73*, 169, 205, 208, 210, 248, 257, 258, 339, 341, 403, 471 (Delves); 82, 134, 410 (Robert Mainwaring).

97 LP xix/1, 531. Sir William Brereton was successful in a patronage suit because of his service in Ireland: PRO, SP 60/9/49 (LP xvi. 22.)

98 William A. Shaw, *The knights of England*, London 1906, ii. 54–6; Holinshed, *Chronicles*, iii. 837; Driver, *Cheshire in the later Middle Ages*, 21–2. There were more knighthoods, including ones for George Audley, John Holcroft and Arthur Mainwaring in September–October 1547: Shaw, *Knights of England*, ii. 61, 63. On 10 March 1544, as *armiger*, Roger Brereton entered a bond to keep an arbitration award to be made after his return from Scotland; the title was later altered in the bond to *miles*: CCRO, U/2.

99 *Visitation of Lancashire and a part of Cheshire made in 1533*, 59; Herbert Winstanley, 'Speke hall', *THSLC* n.s. xxxv (1920 [1919]), 9–14; George Ormerod, 'A memoir of the Lancashire house of Le Noreis or Norres, and of its Speke branch in particular, &c., with notices of its connexion with military transactions at Flodden, Edinburgh and Musselburgh', *THSLC* ii (1850 [1849]), 138–82, esp. pp. 162–6, 167–8, 179, 181–2; F. H. Cheetham, 'The church of

community, and the advantages clearly outweighed the negative impact, although this was more apparent in the later years of the decade.[100]

War also produced social disruption. The local action on the Star Chamber case of *Thomas Pigot v. William Newton, James Smyth, clerk, and others*, for ouster from Butley manor and assault on the plaintiff's tenant, was lost in the confusion.[101] Sir William Brereton's departure for Ireland in 1539 led him to express a fear that the old Brereton enemy, Sir Piers Dutton, might use the opportunity it provided to 'vnfrendly vse & handle' his friends.[102] In one Star Chamber case, the absence of Sir William, the deputy chamberlain, was cited as a reason why the plaintiff could not get justice in the locality.[103] The passage of Irish kerne through Chester caused 'a great Fray' in 1549.[104] Competing demands for service, from Sir William Brereton and Sir John Holford, caused trouble for Thomas Croxton.[105] Yet there was little opposition to war from the Cheshire gentry community. On 18 June 1542 the Privy Council received letters from the commissioners for the loan stating that the response of the gentry had been good, although that of some merchants had been poor.[106] Technical reasons account for any lack of eagerness for active service: for example, in 1545, Sir Thomas Venables wished to be excused on the grounds that he was sheriff, and the commissioners charged with raising troops in Cheshire told the earl of Shrewsbury that difficulties in levying the 3,000 men demanded were due to the earl of Derby recruiting many of the county's men.[107]

St Michael-in-Wyre in Amounderness', *THSLC* n.s. xxx (1915 [1914]), 181–227, illustration facing p. 208.

[100] The costs of involvement, not only the direct expense and danger of service but also the loans and benevolences raised by the king, were heavy: Sir William Brereton owed the crown £350; his military service meant his wife, with Sir Robert Needham and Sir Alexander Ratcliffe, had to write to Cromwell asking for respite: PRO, SP 1/158, fos 66–7 (*LP* xv. 354). In the 1520s Sir John Warburton borrowed from Thomas Thornton of Chester 'towardes his charges in his Journey ageinst the Scottes at ther last invading this Royalme of England': C 1/1503/3. Absence on service abroad made one's position at home vulnerable: SP 1/153, p. 126 (*LP* xiv/2, 166). Oliver Arrowsmith was murdered while one of 'your graces retynue in the parties of Ireland' by John Davenport of Davenport: STAC 2/25/166. For the 1545 benevolence see *LP* xx/1, 52. For the community represented and strengthened in the great French campaigns of the fourteenth century, and the smaller group who pursued the war into the phase of defence and garrisons, and the costs they faced see Morgan, *War and society*, ch. iv, esp. pp. 154–61, and Nigel Saul, *Knights and esquires: the Gloucestershire gentry in the fourteenth century*, Oxford 1981, ch. ii.

[101] PRO, STAC 2/30/86; *LP* Add.i/2, 550.

[102] He wrote to Cromwell on 9 October 1539 asking that no sheriff partial to Dutton be appointed: PRO, SP 1/154, p. 10 (*LP* xiv/2, 304.)

[103] PRO, STAC 2/20/264.

[104] Smith, *Vale-royall*, 83; Webb, 'Vale-royall', 196 (annals printed under 1549); *Sheaf* 3rd ser. viii (1911), 88 (no. 1768).

[105] CCRO, DCH J/27.

[106] *LP* xvii. 412; APC i. 14.

[107] *LP* xx/1, 579, 574.

War provided a focus for the extension of the influence of new additions to the county elite, often brought into the county with the aid of dissolution spoils. This was particularly true of Thomas Holcroft, a Scottish specialist.[108] When Sir Piers Dutton died, it was the earl of Hertford, commander in Scotland, who recommended Holcroft for the ridership of Delamere forest.[109] The influence of such men was not always welcome: there was a fierce conflict between Lady Katherine Smith, widow of Chester merchant Sir Thomas Smith, whose son Lawrence was to be knighted at Leith, and John Massey of Puddington.[110] On the whole, however, war helped ensure that this limited influx of new men was soon integrated into Cheshire society.

It was military activity in Ireland and the wars with Scotland, especially as they affected Ireland, which brought Cheshire to the attention of the Privy Council during the 1540s. What is significant here is that the need for central co-ordination of the military efforts of Henry's kingdoms, seen through the council, did not undermine palatine autonomy, for interventions were limited and infrequent.[111] Attempts to foster an English party in Scotland meant that Chester shipping was needed to convey men like Lennox and the bishop of the Isles around the Irish Sea.[112] In the operations instigated by Somerset, Irish kerne were recruited to the English side, and their passage through Chester, already noted for its potentially disruptive effects in the locality, meant that the council's attention occasionally fell on the city.[113] Ireland was also a concern of the council, and Chester was a key port for passage to and from Ireland which meant it occasionally appeared in their considerations.[114] Apart from these reasons, Cheshire's name was mentioned at the council board infrequently: in the internal government and politics of the shire there was no interest; and few if any in the shire took the opportunity to go to the council to air their grievances.[115] If anything, the contrary

---

[108] *LP* xvii. 745; xix/1, 589.

[109] PRO, SP 1/206, fo. 22 (*LP* xx/2, 160) (18 Aug. 1545). There was also opposition to the intrusion of outsiders into the army raised by Sir William Brereton; for him, the expedition was to be a family and county affair: SP 1/154, pp. 11–12 (*LP* xiv/2, 303).

[110] PRO, SP 1/154, fo. 31 (*LP* xiv/2, 351) (18 Oct. 1539); STAC 2/18/219, 199, 126 (printed in *L&C Star Chamber*, 117–18). See *Lawrence Smyth v. Sir Henry Delves*, re. manors of Weston and Chorlton: STAC 2/19/97, 134 (*L&C Star Chamber*, 126). See also a dispute between Sir John Done and Thomas Holcroft that was arbitrated by the Privy Council on 22 Nov. 1540: *LP* xvi. 286.

[111] A Welsh comparison in provided by Melanie Katina Lloyd, 'The Privy Council, Star Chamber and Wales, 1540–1572', unpubl. PhD diss. Swansea 1987, esp. ch. iv. She expected Privy Council involvement in Welsh affairs and therefore expresses surprise when she did not find it.

[112] *APC* i. 240, 248, 253, 276, 379, 439–40, 480–1, 483–4. This role in Scottish policy is probably the reason for the otherwise atypical interest of the council in the mayoral election following the death of William Holcroft in 1546: *APC* i. 448.

[113] *APC* iii. 79, 80, 94 (kerne returning to Ireland in 1550, some from Calais).

[114] *APC* ii. 133, 202, 210, 271, 396; iv. 406; vi. 153, 242. See also orders to victual men *en route* for Ireland in 1558: *APC* vi. 288, 308.

[115] Possible exceptions here include John Warburton's suit for the farm of Acton Grange,

tendency was apparent. When Sir John Massey's over-vigilant attitude as searcher of Chester brought him to the attention of the council, it intervened to restrain him.[116]

The return to war was one factor which, with an end to meddling with Cheshire's liberties, ushered in a period of greater constitutional stability. The palatinate reasserted itself as the forum for local political life with a new confidence. The wars of the 1540s corrected the inglorious interlude in Cheshire's war record that had occurred between the mid fifteenth century and the 1530s. This had seen rather desperate defence of the county's honour of the kind expressed in *Flodden Field*, battling in the face of mocking such as that of John Skelton in *Why come ye nat to court?*, regarding the unhappy experience of September 1522:

> What here ye of Chesshyre?
> They have layde all in the myre.
> They grugyd and sayde
> Theyr wages were nat payde.
> Some sayde they were afrayde
> Of the Scottyshe hoost.
> For all theyr crack and bost
> Wylde fyre and thonder;
> For all this worldly wonder,
> A hundred myle asonder
> They were, whan they were next.
> This is a trew text![117]

The Cheshire community was therefore able to reshape its history, building on the plentiful materials to be found in previous great military feats under the Black Prince. Holinshed proudly recalled the Legh family's origins, holding Handley because of the capture of the 'earl of Tankerville' at Caen in 1346, 'by one surnamed Legh, ancestor to Sir Peter Legh now living'.[118] And

---

referred to Augmentations early in 1550, and Robert Drihurst's complaint against John Burgonyn, a Frenchman, referred to the Council in the Marches for resolution in the city of Chester in 1557: APC ii. 396; vi. 155. Also, Ralph Dutton entered a bond before the council in 1552 for good behaviour towards Richard Bostock and John Bromeley: APC iv. 172, 194, 195, 211.

[116] For Massey see APC i. 184 (7 June 1545); cf. i. 499 (29 July 1546). Religion appears little, although Bishop Cotes found himself summoned to the council for his sermons in 1547: APC ii. 483 (18 Apr. 1547); cf. ii. 379 (2 Feb. 1549/50; bishop and archdeacon). The dean of Chester was summoned for allegedly stripping lead from the cathedral buildings: iv. 163, 218, 230. For the absence of religious issues originating in Wales see Lloyd, 'Privy Council, Star Chamber and Wales', 51–2.

[117] *Bishop Percy's folio manuscript*, i. 320–1; Skelton, *Poems*, 285, lines 250–61. For Shrewsbury's complaints see LP iii. 2524. Cheshire's disgrace contrasted with the praise heaped on some of the Shropshire contingent for their efforts against the duke of Albany in November 1523: CCityRO, CR 63/2/843/1.

[118] Holinshed, *Chronicles*, ii. 635. The capture of the lord of Tancarville was achieved by Thomas Danyers, from whom Handley passed to the Leghs: Morgan, *War and society*, 142;

the community could now look back to Flodden and Bosworth and integrate them with current experience in a myth of the warrior palatinate, the prowess of which sprang from its special status. Holinshed erased, literally, embarrassing episodes in the county's recent past at Flodden.[119] The people of Cheshire were, according to William Smith, 'of stomack, bold, and hardy; of stature, tall and mighty; withall impatient of wrong, and ready to resist the Enemy or Stranger, that shall invade their Countrey: The very name whereof they cannot abide, and namely, of a Scot'.[120] Victory over the Scots was a chronological marker by which other events could be located in time: one witness who gave evidence in October 1530 in a dispute over property at Wistaston and Monks Coppenhall recalled the purchase of two oxen there 'afore the first Scotishefyld'.[121] Cheshire men proudly recalled the battle of Pinkie in the ballad 'Musleboorrowe ffeild':

> The Lord Huntley, we had him there,
> with him hee brought 10000: men
> yett, god be thanked, wee made them such a banquett
> that none of them returned againe[.][122]

The members of the county community were bound together in war far more effectively than they had been since the days of Edward III's *chevauchées* in France. A relatively peaceful county was now characterised by ordered stability. The effects of the Welsh legislation of 1543 seemed minimal when in 1553 the new prothonotary for Cheshire and Flintshire was appointed as before, ignoring the new judicial circuit of north-east Wales.[123] The MPs who represented Cheshire in the 1540s, who had all been knighted together, helped ensure Westminster legislation concerned itself with refining and improving details of Cheshire's judicial position, while Edward VI's accession saw the traditional grant of the mise in return for the county's privileges.[124]

The effects of war were not the only source of potential disruption in a

---

Richard Barber, *Edward, prince of Wales and Aquitaine: a biography of the Black Prince*, Woodbridge 1978, 55, 67.

119 References to the presence of Cheshiremen under Sir Edmund Howard, and to the accusation of cowardice made against them to the king, present in Halle (*Chronicle*, 557–8, 564), disappear in Holinshed (*Chronicles*, 592, 596–7). In Holinshed the king instead thanks all for their good service, wishing that they be sent letters in appreciation (p. 599); the transformation is complete when Stow provides a transcript of the letter to William Molineux: *Annales* (1615), 494–6.

120 Smith, 'Vale-royall', 19. See also Morgan, *War and society*, 3–4 (where the creation of the tradition is dated to 1540–1620).

121 PRO, STAC 2/6/253 (*L&C Star Chamber*, 57).

122 *Bishop Percy's folio manuscript*, i. 123–6 at lines 25–8.

123 *List of the records of the palatinates*, pp. iv–v.

124 Compare the list of MPs in Bindoff, *House of Commons, 1509–1558*, i. 43, with the list (at p. 229 above) of those knighted. For legislation see pp. 133–7 above.

community that was otherwise strengthening. Religious affairs too threatened division, although again this was accommodated by the community. There is evidence of religious heterodoxy in Cheshire.[125] The marriage of Sir Piers Dutton to Juliana, the widow of Henry Patmore and daughter of William Poyntz of North Ockendon, Essex, was an extraordinary alliance – Cheshire gentlemen did not, in general, marry the daughters of Essex men or the widows of London merchants during this period.[126] Their connection was possibly due to shared religious sympathies. Thomas Patmore was an evangelical and suffered for his faith. William Poyntz was linked to Thomas Poyntz who sheltered Tyndale in his later years.[127] As Susan Brigden has pointed out, the wives of such men tended to seek remarriage within the same religious environment, so Sir Piers Dutton's religion may have been more radical than we might have expected. His role when the priory of Norton was dissolved, standing by and even exploiting the fact that there was resistance to create difficulties for Sir William Brereton,[128] does not suggest sympathy for monasticism, especially given that Norton was the Dutton ancestral burial place.[129]

It is therefore questionable whether we should date the advent of the Reformation in Cheshire to the reign of Edward VI, as most historians have done. There are signs that Protestantism began to make its first impact in the 1540s or even before. Cheshire's contacts with the rest of England were by no means so negligible as to make conversion of Cheshire people while out of the county impossible. Christopher Haigh has noted the importance of contacts at the Inns of Court and at the University of Cambridge, and there was also scope for religious influences to operate at court and elsewhere. George Blage was in trouble for his evangelical views on the sacrament of the altar at court in July 1546; his family origins and continuing ties in Cheshire can be seen in the fact that his accusers were Sir Henry Calveley and Edward Littleton.[130] Other men came into the region as a result of the clerical

---

[125] This is contrary to much recent writing on the Reformation in the north-west, in particular Haigh, *Reformation and resistance*.

[126] Ormerod, *Chester*, i. 650–1; ii. 796. Henry's son is thought by Susan Brigden to have been the Thomas Patmore who was sentenced to perpetual imprisonment for heresy, but she seems confused and a chancery case demonstrates that there were more Patmore sons than she thought: *London and the Reformation*, Oxford 1989, paperback edn 1991, 206; PRO, C 1/558/60 (the plaintiff is Henry's son John).

[127] *LP* ix. 182 (Thomas to John Poyntz, Aug. 1535). The marriage had taken place before Wolsey's resignation from the chancellorship, and possibly therefore before the Patmore–Poyntz connection with heresy was very clear: PRO, C 1/558/60; or possibly even from 1515–18: C 1/381/1. They were apparently married by 1523–4: Ormerod, *Chester*, i. 651.

[128] Elton, *Policy and police*, 321–4; see also p. 216.

[129] Patrick Greene, *Norton priory: the archaeology of a medieval religious house*, Cambridge 1989, 9–15. It had recently seen the burial of Lawrence Dutton: *Lancashire and Cheshire wills . . . from the ecclesiastical court*, 22–9.

[130] Wriothesley, *Chronicle*, 169–70. One of those prosecuted under the Act of Six Articles

appointments of Henry's later years. One such was Henry Man, dean of Chester. In two chancery bills to Thomas Wriothesley, Edward Plankney of London complained that when Thomas Brereton was about to present in the exchequer 'certeyne grevose and weighty informacons of dyvers and sondry offences transgressions and commitments agenst the statute of vi articles by Henry Man', the dean, 'knowyng hymselfe gylty and culpable in soche thynges as the sayd Thomas wold have presentyd agenste hym' and realising that this 'shulde haue ben to the greate dishonestie of the said Deane', sent men to Plankney to promise him the clerkship of the chapter if he would get the allegation dropped.[131] Henry Man was a Carthusian who supported the Nun of Kent and then, when he made his will years later, left his books to Sheen, should it be refounded. The inference usually drawn from this evidence is that he was a hard-line conservative who never gave up hope of religious restoration – just the sort of man to run the Church in the conservative north-west.[132] Yet Man thought in the 1540s that he might have offended against the Act of Six Articles and he was promoted to the bishopric of Man in 1546 at the instance of the evangelical patron Sir Anthony Denny.[133]

With the accession of Mary, the tide turned against the Protestants, and staunch conservatives were appointed to Chester posts. The bishop, Dr Cotes, had been in trouble with the Privy Council early in Edward VI's reign for 'lewd behaviour' in preaching.[134] Yet Protestant activity continued in Cheshire, suggesting it had had time to establish roots. The most obvious example of this in Chester was paradoxically the burning of George Marsh. Born at Dean near Bolton, Marsh was ordained c. 1542. His Protestantism had been inspired in Cambridge, and he was a close associate of John Bradford, the most prominent Protestant evangelist of the north. Bradford was included in Edward VI's plan to have six chaplains touring the conservative regions, and Marsh and he preached to large crowds in the Manchester area according to the perhaps over-enthusiastic testimony of John Foxe.[135] In his death at least Marsh demonstrated that some sympathy for reform had come

---

was Richard Bostock, priest, of St Botolph's-without-Aldgate, whose surname suggests Cheshire origins: *The acts and monuments of John Foxe: a new and complete edition*, ed. Stephen Reed Cattley, London 1837–41, v. 447.

131 PRO, C 1/1149/43–4. Edward Plankney resigned the registrarship of Chester to George Wilmesley in 1544: Haigh, 'George Wilmesley', 8–9. His arrest was ordered early in the reign of Mary: APC iv. 314 (9 Aug. 1553).

132 Haigh, *Reformation and resistance*, 111.

133 LP xxi/1, 148 (20–2).

134 APC ii (1547–50), appendix, p. 483; Jordan, *Edward VI: the young king*, 224 (18 Apr. 1547).

135 Although he was never appointed: *Chronicle of Edward VI*, 101; Jordan, *Edward VI: the threshold of power*, 274. Bradford, a friend of Bucer, was converted by Latimer: Jordan, *Edward VI: the young king*, 341. Haigh, *Reformation and resistance*, 168–73, is sceptical of Bradford's influence: he identified only 40 Protestants, all in the Manchester area (especially in Prestwich and Bolton), and all but three closely associated to the Bradford and Marsh circle.

to Cheshire. Arrested for preaching near Bolton, he was brought to Chester and burned at Spital in Boughton in April 1555. This was the occasion for a rescue attempt, led by city sheriff John Cooper, in which by some accounts many Chester people participated. They were resisted by the vice-chamberlain and the other sheriff, Robert Amory. It seems unlikely that many were involved in the attempt, for Cooper had to flee across Holt bridge into Wales, where he remained an outlaw until the end of the reign.[136]

One anecdote which suggests that at least one woman in the city had become a Protestant relates to the visit of Dr Henry Cole to the city *en route* for Ireland in 1558. He had with him a commission to prosecute heresy in Ireland, but during his stay Lady Ann Smith, wife of Sir Lawrence and daughter of Thomas Fouleshurst, substituted for it a pack of cards, the knave of clubs uppermost. The trick was not discovered until Cole reached Ireland, and since he was unable to get a new commission before Mary's death, many Protestant lives were saved.[137]

Ann's husband, Sir Lawrence, had attacked one of the government's bills in the 1555 parliament.[138] The survey of the Cheshire gentry made in 1564 adds some suggestive detail. Lawrence Smith was one of eleven JPs who were believed to be favourable to Elizabethan religious policies.[139] Along with him in Nantwich hundred John Delves was listed as favourable, but Bucklow and Macclesfield hundreds could only muster one each, Sir Ralph Leicester of Toft and Sir Edward Fitton of Gawsworth. Sir John Savage of Clifton and Ralph Done of Utkinton from Eddisbury, Richard Hough of Leighton and William Glastor[Glasior?] of Wirral, and Sir Hugh Cholmondeley of Cholmondeley, George Calverley of Lea and Richard Hurleston of Pickton complete the list. In the county as a whole, the positively unfavourable numbered only nine.[140]

---

136 Fenwick, *History of Chester*, 171–2; Morris, *Chester in the Plantagenet and Tudor reigns*, 71. Smith, 'Vale-royall', 82, and Webb, 'Vale-royall', 197, both written under Protestatism, say that Marsh died 'for the Gospel'. Webb's version adds that he 'did constantly indure his Martyrdome with such patience, as was wonderfull'. Bradford was, however, the only martyr in a county that produced none of its own: D. M. Loades, *The Oxford martyrs*, 2nd edn, Bangor 1992, 12.

137 Fenwick, *History of Chester*, 171–2. Accounts differ as to the identity of the culprit. Morris made her Mrs Elizabeth Mottershead, the innkeeper at the Blue Posts Inn where Cole stayed: *Chester in the Plantagenet and Tudor reigns*, 72.

138 Jane, widow of Sir William Brereton (another possible Protestant), married Smith as his second wife in January 1560–1: Ormerod, *Chester*, iii. 503; Bindoff, *House of Commons, 1509–1558*, iii. 334–5.

139 'A collection of original letters from the bishops to the Privy Council, 1564', ed. Mary Bateson, in *Camden Miscellany*, IX (Camden n.s. liii, 1895), 75–6. Opinions might have altered over the preceding 10 years.

140 John Bruen of Stapleford, John Dutton of Dutton, Sir Henry Brereton of Handforth, Sir William Davenport of Bramhall, Robert Tatton of Wythenshawe, Sir Piers Legh of Lyme, John Warren of Poynton, Sir Thomas Venables of Kinderton and William Massey of Puddington (who was, however, noted to be 'a good Justice').

The lack of factionalism resulting from these religious differences and the continued coherence of the county community were indicated by the history of the commission of the peace under Edward and Mary. The commission of 26 May 1547[141] added John Bird, bishop of Chester since 1541. There were three omissions among the gentry, Sir Edward Fitton, who was to die in February 1548, Sir Thomas Fouleshurst and John Carrington. It has been suggested that the latter two omissions may have been for religious reasons,[142] but there is little to support this conjecture.[143] Fouleshurst was also omitted from the commission under Mary, and Carrington's son John made only an isolated appearance in May 1554: it is unlikely religion played a part in earlier exclusions.[144] There were several additions to the commission – Thomas Aston, Hugh Cholmondeley, Sir Philip Egerton, Sir Richard Egerton and Thomas Grosvenor of Eaton were included, as were William Brereton of Brereton and Rowland Stanley of Hooton, after the deaths of their fathers, who had already served. A number of Lancashire men were also added: Sir Edmund Trafford of Trafford, whose family had had strong Cheshire connections, Sir William Norris of Speke, who represented the earl of Oxford's interests around Chester, and Sir John Holcroft. The total membership of the commission was now forty-seven. The Cheshiremen added to the list came from the second most senior rank in the county gentry, of the status of the men assessed for service with twenty to forty men in 1544–5.[145] This did mean, however, that many of similar prominence were being excluded from the commission. The reason for the choice is unclear, but this extension almost certainly contributed to the pressure which led to the further expansion of the commission in the next few years.

The exception to this picture of a gradually growing bench composed of the Cheshire elite was of brief duration and proves the rule. One factor behind the commission's expansion was a search for support by Northumberland, and especially by his main agent in the marches, William Herbert, earl of Pembroke. In 1551 the *nomina ministrorum* for the first time includes the names of JPs who were dignitaries and non-working members. This is significant, since the list adds fourteen non-locals, only two with definite connections to the Council in the Marches, and all probably supporters of the earl of

---

141 *CPR, Edward VI*, i. 81.

142 Marriott, 'Commission of the peace', 38–9.

143 Diarmaid MacCulloch, *The later Reformation in England, 1547–1603*, Basingstoke–London 1990, 24–5, and *Suffolk*, 165–8, 231; E. J. Bourgeois II, 'A ruling élite: the government of Cambridgeshire, circa 1524–88', unpubl. PhD diss. Cambridge 1988, 191–3, 215.

144 Carrington died in 1553; although Fouleshurst, whose elder brother had been found an idiot early in the 1520s, was to live on until 1558, by 1547 he was probably in his late forties. If anything, the reformist sympathies of Fouleshurst's daughter should have indicated his suitability for office under a Protestant regime.

145 Hugh Cholmondeley and Richard Egerton were responsible for 40 men, Philip Egerton and Thomas Grosvenor for 30.

Pembroke.[146] The seventeen additions to the commission in 1551 are striking in that they took the commission from a strength of fifty-six to sixty-seven, leaving it twice the size it had been at the death of Henry VIII. John Pollard had joined the Council in the Marches in mid-1550 to escape the pressures of Westminster, and Richard, bishop of St Asaph, had succeeded Robert Warton alias Parfew in that see. Sir Richard Cotton, comptroller of the king's household, also had local interests but he is more significant as a key figure in the attempt to take over the commission using close associates of Dudley and his allies. The most important connection was that of the Herbert family, represented most directly by George and Walter Herbert, kinsmen of William Herbert himself;[147] and more broadly by gentlemen from Gloucestershire, Herefordshire and Worcestershire. Some clearly shared the radical religious outlook of the regime. Sir Anthony Kingston, famous for his violent suppression of the south-western rebels in 1549 and for his forthright opposition in the parliament of 1555, was joined by Sir John St Loe, who was involved in the Wyatt rebellion of 1554 and the Dudley conspiracy of 1556.[148] Sir James Croft was another of the new men whose active commitment to the Dudley regime is clear: a kinsman of Sir William Herbert who acted as his vice-president on the Council in the Marches, he was condemned to death for involvement in the Wyatt rebellion in 1554.[149] In the appointment of the Cheshire justices in 1551 the prime concern was to achieve the domination of the Herbert connection, not primarily to secure a majority for Protestantism.[150] The determination to control the palatinate is shown most clearly in the grant of the reversion of the chamberlainship to Sir Richard Cotton on the same day as Edward VI's attempt to direct the succession to Jane Grey.[151]

If there were tensions present here, and there almost certainly were, they were concealed until the accession of Mary. The partisan nature of some appointments to the bench under Edward is confirmed by the fact that Mary's first Cheshire commission omitted eleven of the new men of 1551.[152] Only

---

[146] PRO, CHES 24/92/7 (Apr. 4 Edward VI, 1550); CHES 24/92/9 (Apr. 5 Edward VI, 1551); Marriott, 'Commission of the peace', 49–51.

[147] Bindoff, *House of Commons, 1509–1558*, ii. 337–8, 340–1.

[148] Ibid. ii. 468–70; iii. 259–60.

[149] Ibid. i. 724–5. He was later pardoned. Religious commitment, as well as a landed position in Worcestershire, probably also lay behind the appointment of Robert Acton. Sir Walter Dennis and Sir Nicholas Arnold, brothers-in-law, were important figures in Gloucestershire and Monmouthshire; William Sheldon, of Beoley in Worcestershire, had had connections with the Seymours, but there are signs that he was moving into the circle of the Dudleys: ibid. i. 291–2, 330–1; ii. 36–7; iii. 306–7.

[150] Sir John Bridges and John Scudamore were both committed Catholics, but possessed considerable marcher influence: ibid. i. 533–4; iii. 284–5. In 1551–3 arrangements for lieutenancies apparently included Cheshire in Pembroke's commission for Wales as lord president: APC iii. 258–9; iv. 49–50, 276–8.

[151] CPR, 1553, 18.

[152] *Sheaf* 3rd ser. xvii (1922), 86–7.

five of the Edwardian justices from outside the county were reappointed. Yet this purge did not affect local membership: most of the Cheshire gentlemen removed had been reappointed by 1555. Six such Edwardian justices were initially omitted, to be reappointed shortly afterwards. These included Sir William Brereton, notable for his removal from the shrievalty on Mary's accession,[153] Sir Edward Fitton, Sir John Holcroft and Sir William Norris.[154] In September 1556 the commission was seventy-one strong, falling to sixty-four late in that year, and rising again to seventy-one in 1558.[155] After initial hesitancy over Brereton and Fitton there was therefore no sign of a lasting religious purge of local Cheshire JPs: the senior gentry of the county continued to act together in this important judicial and administrative role relatively cohesively, and the Marian regime appreciated this. There was no attempt to swamp the Cheshire commission with outsiders. Even Sir Lawrence Smith, a known opponent of the government's religious policies, remained a JP for all but the commissions of May 1556-7, returning in October 1557. If this was a punishment for his opposition in the parliament of 1555, the penalty was not severe. The divisions in local society along religious lines that were appearing in some southern counties under Mary had not yet emerged in Cheshire.[156] Mary's seizure of the English throne has left no evidence of division or opposition within Cheshire. While in some areas Lady Jane Grey garnered considerable initial support, in Cheshire there is little sign of any question but that the county would support Mary, responding to her prompt command; in the case of Sir Hugh Cholmondeley, Mary wrote from Kenninghall on 12 July 1553 commanding his allegiance.[157] Cheshire had had strong ties with Mary since her time in the marches. Even

---

153 Since Sir William Brereton died in 1559, we are denied any judgement which might reflect on his beliefs under Mary, but this removal was almost certainly a result of suspect religion.

154 The absence of representatives of the Booth of Dunham Massey and Starkey of Oulton families is not surprising: George Booth died in 1543, aged 27, leaving a young son William, and Hugh Starkey died in September 1555, to be succeeded by James who died about 13 months later. Nor is the omission of Thomas Aston, who died at the end of the reign of Edward VI, or Thomas Grosvenor of Eaton, who died 4 Edward VI and whose son Thomas did not reach his majority until the beginning of Elizabeth's reign. That leaves unaccounted for only the omissions of Robert Tatton and John Birkenhead, administrators who had served previously, and possibly the continued absence of Sir John Warburton.

155 *Nomina ministrorum*: 1&2 Philip and Mary: PRO, CHES 24/93/3-4 (1554-5); 2&3 Philip and Mary: CHES 24/93/5-6 (1555-6); 3&4 Philip and Mary: CHES 24/94/1-2 (1556-7); 4&5 Philip and Mary: CHES 24/93/3-4 (1557-8).

156 MacCulloch, *Later Reformation*, 24-5; Peter Clark, *English provincial society from the Reformation to the revolution: religion, politics and society in Kent 1500-1640*, Hassocks 1977, 98; R. Fritze, 'Faith and faction: religious changes, national politics and the development of local factionalism in Hampshire, 1485-1570', unpubl. PhD diss. Cambridge 1982, 28-9; Bourgeois, 'Ruling élite', 62, 223.

157 Morris, *Chester during the Plantagenet and Tudor reigns*, 70-1. The Privy Council commended the 'serviceable doings' of the mayor of Chester on 4 August 1553, and the marquess of Northampton's barber was arrested there in September: APC iv. 311, 348. Of

in 1547 one of the properties she was granted was Shotwick in the Wirral.[158] Several Cheshiremen were prominent in her household and subsequently in her regime, especially Richard Wilbraham, a favourite of Mary and a key financial official.[159]

Nor, in spite of a riot in Neston against an enclosure by the earl of Oxford which the rioters claimed had been found to be illegal, is there much sign of the 'generall plage of rebelling' which scarred other areas of England around the year 1549.[160] Instead there was relative cohesion: the palatinate had survived a time of uncertainty that was little of its own making because it demonstrated that it was still a useful asset to the crown, because none of the various regimes that held sway at Westminster had ever been convinced that it was an anachronistic institution that had to be swept away and because those who operated within it knew that fundamentally it worked and brought them great advantages. An old conception of the coherence and purpose of the territories of the English crown was dying in the early Tudor period. No longer did the claim to the French throne as part of a complex of territories

the 2,100 footmen appointed for the queen's escort in early 1554, 500 were to be provided by the earl of Derby and 500 by Sir Rees Mansell, Chester's chamberlain: iv. 392, 399.

[158] Loades, *Mary Tudor*, 137–8.

[159] He was, for example, receiver for the loan in 1557: *CSPD, 1547–80*, 95, 104. He had described himself as 'seruant & dayly attendant appon the Right honorable the lady Maryes grace' or 'vnto the right honorable the ladie Marie' when litigating in chancery during Edward VI's reign: PRO, C 1/1279/43; C 1/1276/49. Mary's abrupt seizure of the throne and determinedly Catholic and pro-Spanish policies did cause some tension aside from the removal of Sir Lawrence Smith from the bench and Sir William Brereton from the shrievalty. There was a considerable drop in numbers attesting Cheshire election indentures after her accession: at least 29 names were appended to the indenture in September 1553, but in October 1554 the number was only 6, in October 1555 just 8, and there were even fewer in January 1558: C 219/21/16; C 219/23/18; C 219/24/19;C 219/25/16 (the latter is seriously damaged). On the December 1544 indenture there are 70 names: C 219/18C/10. Cheshire also produced at least one man who, although a Catholic, was a notable opponent of the Spanish marriage: John Bradford of Nantwich in Cheshire, author of 'The copye of a letter . . . to the right honorable lordes the erles of Arundel, Darbie, Shrewsbury and Penbroke'. Involved in the Dudley conspiracy, he was executed for his part in Thomas Stafford's Scarborough raid in 1557. He was anti-Protestant, but also anti-Spaniard and had been insinuated as a spy into the household of the duke of Medina Celi between 1554 and 1556: D. M. Loades, 'The authorship and publication of "The copye of a letter sent by John Bradforth to the right honorable lordes the erles of Arundel, Darbie, Shrewsbury and Penbroke" ', *Transactions of the Cambridge Bibliographical Society* iii (1959–63), 155–60. For the hostility to the Spaniards of the earl of Derby, whose son killed two chief Spaniards on 8 August 1554, see Bernard, *Power of the early Tudor nobility*, 86ff. Even so, this evidence does not add up to serious religious or political opposition to the Marian regime in Cheshire.

[160] PRO, C 1/1275/49–51; HMC, *Rutland*, i. 41–2 (quotation); B. L. Beer, *Rebellion and riot: popular disorder in England during the reign of Edward VI*, Kent, Ohio 1982. Shrewsbury kept order in the north midlands in 1549: Bernard, *Power of the early Tudor nobility*, 61. The rioters' target was an outsider to Cheshire society: cf. the resistance to Oxford's claim to appoint the mayor of Chester's serjeant: STAC 2/27/116.

bound together through the royal kin hold much attraction for monarchs, governments or people. Cheshire had possessed a powerful stake in this conception of political identity and purpose, through its special relationship with the heir to the throne, the county's earl; but its loss was not fatal to the palatinate. If a new conception of England was beginning to be created, a country that was Protestant and anti-Catholic, especially anti-Spanish Catholic, and which was opposed in its civilisation to barbaric neighbours like the Scots and Irish and even more to the peoples of the new world, then it was possible for Cheshire to be integrated within it without losing its privileges.[161] One of the most important historiographers of the new English identity, Raphael Holinshed, had grown up in the 1530s as a favoured student of William Bridges in Macclesfield grammar school,[162] and he incorporated within his work many of the most important parts of the palatine tradition.[163] Like Wales, Cheshire could draw on its western British traditions to claim some connection with the Celtic Church, and hence assist in the vital search for Protestant religious legitimacy.[164] And as a community it was well placed in its traditions and contemporary experience to take its own special position at the battlefront between the civility of the English commonwealth and the barbarism of its neighbours. When Elizabeth ascended the throne, Cheshiremen could be confident that provincial privilege (in their own and in other similar territories) was to be an essential part of the political life of many subjects of the English crown for decades to come.

---

161 David Cressy, *Bonfires and bells: national memory and the Protestant calendar in Elizabethan and Stuart England*, London 1989; O. W. Furley, 'The pope-burning processions of the late seventeenth century', *History* xliv (1959), 16–23; William S. Maltby, *The black legend in England: the development of anti-Spanish sentiment, 1558–1660*, Durham, NC 1971; Nicholas P. Canny, 'The ideology of English colonization: from Ireland to America', *William and Mary Quarterly* 3rd ser. xxx (1973), 575–98, and *Kingdom and colony: Ireland and the Atlantic world, 1560–1800*, Baltimore 1988; Andrew Hadfield, 'Briton and Scythian: Tudor representations of Irish origins', *Irish Historical Studies* xxviii (1993), 391–408.

162 Holinshed received 6s. 8d. in Bridge's will (10 Mar. 1536): *Lancashire and Cheshire wills . . . from the ecclesiastical court*, 164–8 at p. 167. The Holinshead who matriculated from Christ's College, Cambridge, in May 1544 was possibly the same man: *DNB* ix. 1024.

163 Holinshed relied on Henry Bradshaw, the best previous compilation of Cheshire tradition, for example for Leon Gauer's foundation of Chester: *Chronicles*, i. 446. Holinshed elided the Anglo-Saxon earls of Mercia with earls of Chester (for instance Leofric, 'the noble earl of Chester, or Mercia': i. 740, 743, 750); told the story of Harold II's connection with Chester (i. 762; ii. 1); described the Cheshire barons (ii. 33); and mentioned the post-Conquest earls of Chester frequently (ii. 152, 182, 349–50: Ranulph III's achievements and taking of a tax). After he described the death of the last earl, he added, 'I have thought it not impertinent for the honour of so noble a lineage, to set downe the descent of the same earles' (ii. 381). It is striking that he makes no apparent mention of the Welsh reform legislation. It is also significant that one of Holinshed's most important co-workers, John Hooker, had ties to Cornwall and Devon: McKisack, *Medieval history in the Tudor age*, 128–31.

164 Roberts, 'Union with England and the identity of "Anglican" Wales'.

Conclusion

This book began by asserting the importance of the palatinate of Chester and its privileges in the fifteenth century. The surviving petitions of the county suggest that the people of the palatinate believed their county to be an entire political system of itself with its own parliament, council, courts and administration. The first part of the book then demonstrated that this autonomous system was still a reality in the early Tudor period. The culture of centre and locality justified and glorified the palatinate. Taxation, a crucial point in the nexus of crown–locality relations, was still agreed through a local parliament and paid in the traditional manner; and the council of the earl of Chester was potent enough to tap the demand for equitable justice, giving birth to the Chester exchequer.

It has not been the intention of this book, however, to argue that nothing changed during the early Tudor period in Cheshire. Such an argument would ignore the shifting patterns of litigation by Cheshire people, the legislative changes that affected the shire and the way that royal patronage influenced the character of the body of officers who administered the county. Part II thus concluded that Cheshire developed a different relationship with royal government. By 1560 Cheshire people were becoming more accustomed to litigation in chancery or Star Chamber, their officers were more frequently courtiers or members of the Council in the Marches of Wales and new laws meant writs ran in the king's name. JPs presided over quarter sessions in the county, and Cheshire MPs sat at Westminster. These changes were, however, limited and never intended to destroy the special status of the Chester palatinate. Neither political imperatives, nor administrative momentum, nor the imperial ideal present particularly in the work of Thomas Cromwell were to result in the incorporation of the palatinate. Cromwell's ideal was not a vision of uniformity but of supreme sovereignty projected into varied jurisdictions. Neither in its humanist elements nor in its British roots did it seriously depart from a vision of the king's territories as an association of varied particular and particularist elements.[1] Because of this, many of the changes were made for reasons that related only indirectly to Cheshire, and their

---

[1] I depart from the interpretation of John Morrill and Brendan Bradshaw: John Morrill, 'The British problem, c. 1534–1707', in Bradshaw and Morrill, *The British problem*, for example at p. 22. Bradshaw, 'Tudor Reformation and revolution', 42, urges a return to earlier work on the imperial idea, citing Frances Yates, *Astraea: the imperial theme in the sixteenth century*, London 1975, and J. N. Figgis, *The divine right of kings*, 2nd edn, Cambridge 1922. His unspoken and untested assumption is that imperial ideas assumed uniformity and centralisation.

impact was unpredictable and could be shaped by local people. The Chester palatinate as a cultural, social and political institution emerged in the 1560s altered but still formidable.

Part III showed that the palatinate remained an important context for the county's political life into the reign of Elizabeth. Cheshire did not become just another ordinary English county. Henry VII's policy in the shire, although more intensive in its enforcement of his lordship, was determined by the precedents and institutions of the palatinate. This finding forms an interesting parallel with one of the most important approaches to 'centralisation' from a continental European scholar of the last half century. Bernard Guenée argued that late medieval and early modern France saw not personal centralisation or geographical centralisation – the direct personal control of the king, or of institutions based in the capital – but the sponsorship of local institutions by the crown, often in the face of criticism from the officials of the central institutions.[2] This he called institutional centralisation, citing as evidence the formation of the *parlements* of Dijon and Aix. This was a stronger form of centralisation than that practised in Cheshire. In the French case, local representative institutions were allowed and indeed encouraged to wither, while the new *parlements* were deliberate royal creations, often with (at least superficially) stringent rules to ensure that local councillors did not dominate or control them. In Cheshire's case under Henry VII, it was on traditional institutions that the crown relied; if new institutions emerged, for example the exchequer, they did so largely on the initiative of local office-holders and litigants, and the crown played a minimal role in sponsoring them. Under Henry VIII, Wolsey's policy challenged some elements of palatine privilege more directly, but it was interference rather than systematic assault, still less systematic reconstruction. Cromwell's reforms, framed as they were on the level of general principles, altered more: there was serious disruption of the pattern of day-to-day politics and administration in the shire. After 1540, however, the palatinate community managed to find a new *modus vivendi* with the culture and institutions of politics in the shire and its relationship with the other territories of the English crown. The birth of a new prince at this crucial time and the participation of the county community in war strengthened its coherence and the stability of the palatinate.

The general theme of this book is therefore the longevity of the palatinate and its continuing importance into the early modern period. This has profound implications for the way we see the early Tudor state as a whole. The territories of the English king were far less unified and centralised than has been argued. As the early parts of this study showed, it was not just Cheshire which remained autonomous in many respects through the late Middle Ages and into the early Tudor period.[3] The historiography of

---

[2] Bernard Guenée, 'Espace et état dans la France du bas moyen âge', *Annales* xxiii (1968), 744–58.
[3] Griffiths, 'King's realm and dominions', began discussion for the later medieval period.

Durham's palatinate has developed in much the same manner as Cheshire's: the account of the decline of the Durham palatinate produced by Lapsley in 1900, from a microcosm of conquest England in 1100 to a phantom by the seventeenth century, has been progressively exaggerated as writers have emphasised an ever earlier debasement and collapse of its privileges.[4] More recently, a McFarlane-ite approach to the history of the north-east of England in the fifteenth century has stressed gentry solidarities and down-played palatine influence.[5] The same might be said of Ireland, Wales, the Isle of Man, the Channel Islands and, to a lesser extent, Cornwall.[6] Yet in fiscal and judicial matters, and in their political cultures, the local jurisdictions and polities of Durham and the rest were as strong if not stronger than those of the palatinate of Chester. Changes came to these territories in the Tudor period, as they did to Cheshire; but they came in varied form and their effects were equivocal. It is impossible to argue that any of them were rendered merely part of the unified fiscal, judicial, administrative, cultural and political system of England. Of all these areas, Cheshire had always had the least potent claims to difference and it was subjected to the most thorough challenge to its privileges. If Cheshire's palatinate survived, then it is not surprising that so too did Durham and the others. Indeed, it has been demon-strated that in many respects the early Tudor period saw the strengthening of

His 'The provinces and the dominions in the age of the Wars of the Roses', in Sharon D. Michalove and A. Compton Reeves (eds), *Estrangement, enterprise and education in fifteenth-century England*, Stroud 1998, 1–25, attempts a 'British' perspective to the Wars of the Roses.

4   Lapsley, *County palatine of Durham*; Constance M. Fraser, 'Prerogative and the bishops of Durham, 1267–1376', *EHR* lxxiv (1959), 467–76; Jean Scammell, 'The origin and limita-tions of the liberty of Durham', ibid. lxxxi (1966), 449–73; M. E. James, *Family, lineage and civil society: a study of society, politics and mentality in the Durham region, 1500–1640*, Oxford 1974; *Northern petitions, illustrative of life in Berwick, Cumbria and Durham in the fourteenth century*, ed. C. M. Fraser (Surtees Society cxciv, 1982 [1981]); Emsley and Fraser, *Courts of Durham*. For both Durham and Cheshire see James W. Alexander, 'The English palatinates and Edward I', *Journal of British Studies* xxii (1983), 1–22; W. J. Jones, 'Palatine performance in the seventeenth century', in Peter Clark, Alan G. R. Smith, and Nicholas Tyacke (eds), *The English commonwealth, 1547–1640: essays in politics and society presented to Joel Hurstfield*, Leicester 1979, 189–204.

5   Pollard, *North-eastern England*, and 'The crown and the palatinate of Durham, 1437–94', in A. J. Pollard (ed.), *The north of England in the age of Richard III*, Stroud 1996, 67–87.

6   The historiography of the Channel Islands and of the Isle of Man during this period is limited and Whiggish in tone: A. J. Eagleston, *The Channel Islands under Tudor government, 1485–1642: a study in administrative history*, Cambridge 1949; A. W. Moore, *A history of the Isle of Man*, London 1900, repr. Douglas, Isle of Man 1992; Kinvig, *Isle of Man*. An exception is John le Patourel, *The medieval administration of the Channel Islands, 1199–1399*, London 1937. For Cornwall see A. L. Rowse, *Tudor Cornwall: portrait of a society*, new edn, London 1969; Philip Payton, *The making of modern Cornwall: historical experience and the persistence of 'difference'*, Redruth [1992]; and the alternative approaches suggested in Thornton, 'Dynasty and territory' and J. P. D. Cooper, 'Propaganda, allegiance and sedition in the Tudor south-west c. 1497–1570', unpubl. DPhil. diss. Oxford 1999.

the judicial and fiscal privileges of some of these territories, such as the Channel Islands and Ireland. It is dangerous to talk of system in this series of developments, but it might be said that under the Tudors the non-English territories of the crown were systematised and the sovereignty of the king projected more effectively into them.[7] In the process, the ability of Ireland and the Channel Islands to exclude, for example, the immense power of the Westminster equity courts grew. The result after 1603 was not a tripartite system of relatively centralised and coherent monarchies, with the possible added complexity of the land of Wales, but an association of three composite monarchies, each with a complex hierarchy of autonomous elements associated with and within them.

There may be contemporary reasons for an increased questioning of conventional patterns of territorial relationships. Under either Whig or Marxist interpretations, local autonomy and privilege tends only to decline. Centralisation is a key concept, descriptive and at the same time a measurement of success or failure for society. Both Whig and Marxist interpretations are, however, teleologies. They reflect the perceived end of their teleology – the supposedly centralised state of the Victorian period and the first three-quarters of the twentieth century. In particular, the central fifty years of the present century saw a remarkably unanimous belief in the homogeneity of the British political system.[8] Reflected strongly in the historiography, this belief was also systematised and expressed in works of political science.

Indications of change had, however, appeared with the Carmarthen and Hamilton by-elections of 1966–7. They did not have an immediate impact in the academic literature, and even when political scientists responded they were not unanimous, but by the early 1980s an author like Jim Bulpitt could criticise previous approaches to the problem of what he called territorial politics.[9] Bulpitt broadly supported the internal colonialism thesis, applied to Britain by Michael Hechter.[10] Hechter argued that inequality and dependency led to central domination over the localities, and that the reinforcement of cultural difference permitted their exploitation. For Bulpitt, Hechter was strongest when criticising the centralisation–decentralisation dichotomy for its crude emphasis that growing central power and modernisation implied diffusion and homogenisation. Bulpitt emphasised the 'official mind' of those at the centre, which preferred informal domination and government in the central interest by local elites to direct central control.[11] It was only when

---

7   As implied by Morrill, 'British problem', 11.
8   An overview of politics and political science is provided by William H. Field, *Regional dynamics: the basis of electoral support in Britain*, London 1997.
9   Jim Bulpitt, *Territory and power in the United Kingdom: an interpretation*, Manchester 1983.
10 Ibid. 34–45; Michael Hechter, *Internal colonialism: the celtic fringe in British national development, 1536–1966*, London 1975. See criticisms of Hechter in Jenny Wormald, 'The creation of Britain: multiple kingdoms or core and colonies?', *TRHS* 6th ser. ii (1992), 183–94.
11 Bulpitt, *Territory and power*, 75–87.

growing instability in England and greater dangers posed by her European neighbours forced a change in this 'official mind' that there was a shift towards 'formal empire', the centralisation which had been seen as inevitable by many other writers.[12]

The response among historians to the break-down of the supposed homogeneity of the United Kingdom has been somewhat different. The 1960s brought increased historical attention to the localities, especially for the later Middle Ages through the influence of McFarlane and for the early modern period in the Leicester School of Hoskins and Everitt.[13] This was, however, an emphasis on the locality, especially on the county, and not the nation or region; and if this meant that the spotlight no longer fell uniquely on the centre, the shires that were studied were portrayed as the fairly homogenous building-blocks of a more decentralised but none the less fairly unified kingdom. Historians turned much more slowly to the study of the sort of nationalism and regionalism that political scientists had discovered after 1966. Although the scholarly historical study of Ireland, Scotland and Wales received a tremendous boost after 1945, it remained largely the preserve of historians resident in each country, who wrote history which dealt with their own 'nation' in relative isolation. The 'national', and indeed 'nationalist', historiography of these areas was paradoxically as convinced of the success and inevitability of English centralisation as any Oxford-based historian. From the anglophile W. Llewelyn Williams's *The making of modern Wales* (1919), written in the tradition of George Owen, to A. O. H. Jarman and his work on the origins of nationalism, Welsh historiography was an account of ever-closer rule from Westminster.[14] Disillusion with centralised planning and increased awareness of economic inequality reinforced nationalist historiographies which bore far more relation to the aspirations of local present-day political elites than to the realities of life in late medieval or early modern Wales or Ireland.[15] It was only in the 1970s, following the publication of the seminal manifesto by J. G. A. Pocock, 'British history: a plea for a new subject', that the integration of the history of these areas into what has been called a 'new British history' occurred.[16] A stream of new work reinter-

[12] Ibid. 87–98.

[13] See introduction, nn. 51–2.

[14] For example, J. C. Beckett, *The making of modern Ireland, 1603–1923*, London 1996; Rosalind Mitchison, *A history of Scotland*, London 1970; David Williams, *A history of modern Wales*, 2nd edn, London 1977; B. Lenman, 'The teaching of Scottish history in the Scottish universities', *Scottish Historical Review* lii (1973), 165–90; Philip Jenkins, *A history of modern Wales, 1536–1990*, London 1992, 407–29; R. F. Foster, 'History and the Irish question', *TRHS* 5th ser. xxxiii (1983), 169–92.

[15] Derek W. Urwin, 'Conclusions: perspectives on conditions of regional protest and accommodation', in S. Rokkan and Derek W. Urwin, *The politics of territorial identity: studies in European identity*, London 1982, 425–36 at pp. 429–30. In the latter case see Steven G. Ellis, 'Nationalist historiography and the English and Gaelic worlds in the late Middle Ages', *Irish Historical Studies* xxv (1986), 1–18.

[16] Published in the *Journal of Modern History* xlvii (1975), 601–28.

preted 'English' history in the light of the newly recognised importance of Scotland, Ireland and, to a lesser degree, Wales.[17] Much of this writing posed difficulties, however, because, although it raised the question of Britishness and demonstrated its problematic nature, it tended to consider this problem through the use of concepts based on the coherence of the 'nations' from which Britishness is described as being composed: 'Englishness', 'Scottishness', 'Irishness' and 'Welshness'.[18] These 'nations' are equally problematic, not least in the issues raised by the frontiers between them.[19]

It is to Ireland that we must look for a wider historiographical context for the present work, for it is with regard to Ireland that the most vigorous debate has occurred in recent years over the territorial and political relationships between these islands and their composite elements. The starting point of most recent writers on Tudor Ireland was a tradition of scholarship which often concentrated more heavily on the aggressively centralising tendencies of the English monarchy than even the English historiography did. Brendan Bradshaw had at the end of the 1970s argued that a constitutional revolution had occurred in sixteenth-century Ireland. Following in the path newly defined by Elton but with predecessors running back into Whig and Marxist accounts of Ireland, Bradshaw's opinion of the purpose of Cromwellian policy was clear. By the beginning of the sixteenth century, 'the continued ineffectualness of central government' meant that Ireland was 'well on the way

17 This included in particular R. R. Davies, *Domination and conquest: the experience of Ireland, Scotland and Wales, 1100–1300*, Cambridge 1990; Conrad Russell, 'The British problem and the English civil war', *History* lxxii (1987), 395–415, and *The fall of the British monarchies, 1637–1642*, Oxford 1992.

18 The last thirty years have brought few challenging new considerations of 'Englishness'. Robert Colls and Philip Dodd (eds), *Englishness: politics and culture, 1880–1920*, Beckenham 1986, and Gerald Newman, *The rise of English nationalism: a cultural history, 1740–1830*, 1987, revised edn, London 1997, are honourable, although late, exceptions. G. R. Elton's *The English*, Oxford 1992, is an example of continuing glorification of a difficult concept.

19 Few British works stand comparison with P. Sahlins, *Boundaries: the making of France and Spain in the Pyrenees*, Berkeley 1989, although useful work includes Davies, *Lordship and society*; Cynthia J. Neville, *Violence, custom and law: the Anglo-Scottish border lands in the later Middle Ages*, Edinburgh 1998; Anne A. Cardew, 'A study of society in the Anglo-Scottish borders, 1455–1502', unpubl. PhD diss. St Andrews 1974; Thomas I. Rae, *The administration of the Scottish frontier, 1513–1603*, Edinburgh 1966; J. A. Tuck, 'Northumbrian society in the fourteenth century', *NH* vi (1971), 22–39; Denys Hay, 'England, Scotland and Europe: the problem of the frontier', *TRHS* 5th ser. xxv (1975), 77–91; R. L. Storey, 'The wardens of the marches of England towards Scotland, 1377–1489', *EHR* lxxii (1957), 593–615; M. L. Bush, 'The problem of the far north: a study of the crisis of 1537 and its consequences', *NH* vi (1971), 40–63; Alexander Grant, 'Scotland's "celtic fringe" in the late Middle Ages: the Macdonald lords of the Isles and the kingdom of Scotland', in R. R. Davies (ed.), *The British Isles, 1100–1500: comparisons, contrasts and connections*, Edinburgh 1988, 118–41; Jane H. Ohlmeyer, *Civil war and restoration in the three Stuart kingdoms: the career of Randal MacDonnell, marquis of Antrim, 1609–1683*, Cambridge 1993. The interface between the English and the French, represented by the English possessions in France to the mid-fifteenth century, and later by Calais and the Channel Islands, has received relatively little attention.

towards fragmenting politically into a number of sovereign dynastic principalities'. In response, 'Cromwell's programme was designed to undermine the administrative and jurisdictional integrity of the government of the Irish Lordship, to shift its centre from Dublin to London, and to transform the Dublin administration from a central government into a regional council.'[20] Although, as he himself admitted, we have no statement from Cromwell of these alleged principles behind his policy, Bradshaw was confident that they could be divined from the ideas of Archbishop Alen and Chancellor Audley. Alen, in a commentary on the status of his see, described it as a handmaid of the English Church; Audley, in a letter to Cromwell, proposed a union of ecclesiastical jurisdictions under Canterbury.[21] Yet these are both statements regarding the position of the Irish Church, and in the latter case an abortive one at that. In England too the position of the Church and its jurisdiction was subject to a dramatic review as a consequence of the royal supremacy. In neither case, however, it is safe to extrapolate from the position of the Church to secular jurisdiction. Bradshaw could not therefore properly explain the continuation of the Irish parliament as an important part of the government of Ireland and the lack of a 'territorial union'. Instead there was a 'personal union, in the imperial crown, of two distinct constitutional and jurisdictional entities', and this was 'precisely what was expressed by [what Bradshaw perceived as] the Anglo-Irish separatist tradition of the fifteenth century'.[22]

Bradshaw's revolution was placed in a different light by Steven Ellis's reformulation of developments in fifteenth- and sixteenth-century Ireland. Ellis simultaneously emphasised the viability of the late medieval political settlement and the impact of the changes that superseded it. Ellis questioned the traditional emphasis on 'the borderlands . . . as untypical, disordered and long requiring special treatment until eventually incorporated into a consolidated realm when Henry VIII swept away "the few lingering exceptions to a uniform government from the centre" '.[23] In government, both in terms of institutions and political connection, in foreign policy, and in political protest and revolt, Ellis found provincial autonomy to be thriving in 1500. Indeed, Ellis usefully redefined Englishness to escape from a reliance on terri-

---

[20] Bradshaw, *Irish constitutional revolution*, 19, 161.

[21] Ibid. 162, citing *Calendar of Archbishop Alen's register*, ed. C. McNeill, Dublin 1950, 281, 288, and *State papers published under the authority of His Majesty's commission: King Henry the Eighth*, London 1830–52, i. 438.

[22] Bradshaw's theory demanded the 'discontinuance of a separate parliament for Ireland, and the attendance of members from the new Pale at the Westminster parliament'; he explained simply that 'the situation in Ireland was obviously not ripe for such an innovation in 1536': Bradshaw, *Irish constitutional revolution*, 161–3. See also his 'Tudor Reformation and revolution'.

[23] Ellis, 'Crown, community and government', 187 (quoting D. M. Palliser, *The age of Elizabeth: England under the later Tudors, 1547–1603*, London 1983, 9); 'England in the Tudor state', 210–12; and 'Tudor state formation'.

toriality: 'before *c*. 1550 the characteristics of its Englishness [i.e. of the English state] were more loosely defined and that Englishness and the English political community were not synonymous with England'. Law, government systems, customs and language were identifiably English but were neither confined to England nor universal there. Hence Englishness could articulate an apparently diverse grouping of territories. In some ways, this approach was reminiscent of the most orthodox of the Whig historians: Ellis described the awareness of the kings of England that an attack on franchises might alienate the nobles upon whom they depended. But his insight allowed a new perspective, for he also made a comparison with France, which had seen the evolution of a powerful nation state alongside the maintenance of considerable decentralisation. England in 1500, Ellis said, was close to achieving the same development. It did not, however, come to fruition, and in explaining this Ellis reverted to more conventional models. A combination of the 'crown's changing perception of the Irish problem' and 'more general changes in the character of royal government, *c*. 1530–75' destroyed the late medieval political system and produced a 'split into separate political entities on different lines'. Thus the constitutional revolution of the sixteenth century gained considerably in its significance, no longer simply far-reaching but unexpected.[24]

Central to Ellis's interpretation – indeed central to all explanations of this period of Irish history – was the relationship of the Kildare rebellion to the Irish policy of the regime at Westminster and its agents in Dublin. If that rebellion was a consequence of the introduction of a policy of administrative and jurisdictional subjugation, as Bradshaw and others argued, then it was a reactionary step protesting against Tudor centralisation. If, on the other hand, what new policy there was before the rebellion, although aimed at reviving the English position in Ireland, was intended to work not against but through existing noble networks of power, then the rebels' actions might become a cause of and not a response to the changes that ensued. In Ciaran Brady's recent formulation, the rebellion 'disturbed political relationships that had been in place for more than half a century, introduced new volatile factors into Irish politics and forced the English governors to assume a new pre-eminence in Irish affairs far beyond that anticipated in the original reform schemes of the early 1530s, simply in order to survive'.[25] This attempt failed, being perceived by its enemies as corruption and venality on a massive scale.[26] The result was the introduction of a new strand of reform, with the

[24] Idem, 'Crown, community and government', 188–91, 192, 193, 195, 201–2.
[25] Brady, *Chief governors*, p. xiv, prologue; 'Comparable histories: Tudor reform in Wales and Ireland', in Ellis and Barber, *Conquest and union*, 64–86; 'England's defence and Ireland's reform: the dilemmas of the Irish viceroys, 1541–1641', in Bradshaw and Morrill, *The British problem*, 89–117.
[26] Brady, *Chief governors*, p. xiii and ch. 1. This corruption was 'highly functional, and . . . supported his far larger attempt to shape a coalition of support for his government throughout the country'.

same objective of constitutional reconstruction but with a radically more aggressive means of achieving it. Brady refers to a 'dire Heisenbergian principle', by which reform itself redefined the nature – and in the end the difficulty – of the problems it was designed to resolve.[27] By the 1580s the savage repression perpetrated by Arthur Lord Grey de Wilton and the failure of the reforms attempted by Sir John Perrot pointed the way towards a fatal conclusion: 'English government could be maintained in Ireland not by peaceful, diplomatic persuasion, but only by a massive reassertion of English military might.'[28]

This has taken the historiography of Tudor Ireland into a phase in which the shift towards repressive centralisation is seen as the result of 'exhaustion, disillusion and neglect', rather than any deliberate ideological or political imperative.[29] Even so, the lesson is still that pressures during the sixteenth century tended to move events towards a reduction of local liberties and the aggressive assertion of central rule, if more by accident rather than design. Such an approach begs many questions for the experience of privileged communities elsewhere amongst the dominions of the English crown. Where the conditions that produced this drift in Ireland were lacking, what were the implications of Tudor policy for the survival of provincial privileges? If change was intended to be achieved through existing political structures, not against them, then what were the consequences for those areas where the strategy worked and local political structures were indeed the conduit for the reinforcement of the king's sovereignty and ultimate political control?[30] And what of the pressures for reform in the first instance? Brady's formulation of these pressures is limited and is one of the areas of his work in which he chooses to defer to Bradshaw. Yet if the design was as minimal in Ireland as it appears to have been, how should we understand the parallel pressures elsewhere? Ellis's formulation, positive though it is about the possibilities for an association of autonomous territorial elements in 1500, is linked to an analysis of the pressures for change which is little short of apocalyptic – and with which Brady would disagree. If we marry Ellis's understanding of the viability of autonomy in 1500 with Brady's conception of the accidental nature of the reform campaign, we have the possibility that the English king in 1603 might have ruled a highly decentralised yet still coherent composite monarchy. If we recognise that the accident which brought repressive centralisation to Ireland was an accident particular to that territory, it might just be possible that he in fact did.

[27] Ibid. p. xiv.
[28] Ibid. epilogue, esp. pp. 296–300.
[29] Ibid. 300. See also the emphasis on defence in Hiram Morgan, 'British policies before the British state', in Bradshaw and Morrill, *The British problem*, 66–88.
[30] Note the disagreement between P. R. Roberts, 'The English crown, the principality of Wales and the Council in the Marches, 1534–1641', in Bradshaw and Morrill, *The British problem*, 122, and Glanmor Williams, *Wales and the Act of Union*, Bangor 1992, 25.

It is only in this light that we can understand how the territories of the English crown at the start of the English Civil War were so diverse in their interconnection that no account of the outbreak of war can be complete without a reference to the problem of multiple kingdoms and composite monarchies.[31] Only this perspective can explain how the creation of English North America enshrined principles of local autonomy on a scale unequalled in the empires of other European powers.[32] It also explains why the first British empire was never a systematically-unified entity, and why when greater unity was attempted in the late eighteenth century the result was revolution.[33]

A major reason for the problematic nature of the historiography of centralisation in the English territories is also the key to its solution. There is no doubt that a very significant section of the territory of England was precociously highly centralised. In James Campbell's phrase, the Old English monarchy was 'a formidably organised state', with long traditions of effective rule under a single king and habits of unity, regularity and common experience – but only in those areas south-east of a line connecting the Severn with the Wash. Beyond that line, the areas under English control were part of an essentially voluntary coalition occasionally encouraged by violence.[34] England was unified as early as the tenth century if we accept a definition of England which depends upon indications of unification and centralisation: but England was more, in terms of territory, communities and political identities, than that.[35]

It is now almost universally accepted that the 'British history' called for by John Pocock over twenty years ago is necessary for an understanding of

---

[31] Especially clear in her insistence that closer union between England and Scotland in 1707 occurred '*faute de mieux*' is Wormald, 'Creation of Britain', 193–4.

[32] On the problems of American privileges and the debates surrounding the multiple kingdoms of sixteenth- and seventeenth-century Britain see Harvey Wheeler, 'Calvin's case (1608) and the McIlwain–Schuyler debate', *American Historical Review* lxi (1956), 587–97.

[33] J. H. Elliott, 'A Europe of composite monarchies', *Past and Present* cxxxvii (Nov. 1992), 48–71. For France and Brittany see Jones, ' "Mon Pais et ma nation" ', 144–68, and ' "Bons Bretons et bons Francoys": the language and meaning of treason in later medieval France', *TRHS* 5th ser. xxxii (1982), 91–112; P. S. Lewis, 'War propaganda and historiography in fifteenth-century France and England', *TRHS* 5th ser. xv (1965), 1–21; Joseph R. Strayer, 'France: the holy land, the chosen people and the most Christian king', in Theodore K. Rabb and Jerrold E. Seigel (eds), *Action and conviction in early modern Europe*, Princeton 1969, 3–16; Bernard Guenée, *States and rulers in later medieval Europe*, Oxford 1985, 49–65, 216–20.

[34] Compare James Campbell, *Essays in Anglo-Saxon history*, London 1986, pp. x–xi; *Stubbs and the English state* (The Stenton Lecture), Reading 1987; and 'The late Anglo-Saxon state: a maximum view', *Proceedings of the British Academy* lxxxvii (1995), 39–66, with Pauline Stafford, *Unification and conquest: a political and social history of England in the tenth and eleventh centuries*, London 1989, with her emphasis (esp. pp. 125–8) on the lack of inevitability in the creation of the England of the twelfth century.

[35] Ellis, 'Crown, community and government', and 'England in the Tudor state'.

society, economy and politics in all parts of these islands.[36] The work which builds on these foundations tends, however, to display the same certainties of unity within each of the three kingdoms of England, Scotland and Ireland which it criticised in the old historiographical elision of England with Great Britain or the British Isles. Some versions of the 'new British history' may escape the crime of which Conrad Russell has been accused, of writing new English history with additional players in the opera,[37] but they still assume the work to take the form of a trio.[38]

At the heart of the problem lies the political culture which explained the relationships between political communities, and which supported the existence of autonomous jurisdiction. Rees Davies has recently emphasised the importance of regnal solidarities in ensuring the crystallisation of national communities: 'an institutional corset for the well-developed sense of common ethnicity'.[39] Yet ethnicity and the national community were neither co-extensive nor the overwhelmingly dominant adhesives for political community. Even if regnal solidarity were such a catalyst of community identity, there is a danger of assuming that this implies unyielding unity. Even on the most optimistic definition of royal kin structures in the British Isles as patrilineal, none of the monarchies of the British Isles lost at least the basic complexity inherent in the existence of a king's wife and an eldest son and heir: regnal solidarity in its territorial aspects was inevitably multifaceted.[40] The institutional corset was therefore a complex garment, worn over a huge variety of important underclothes, and from which some of these undergarments protruded. What Cheshire had in common with many of the communities referred to in this book was a position not just beyond the core territory of England, but at the interface – in many ways the centre – of the influences of the various core territories which made up the British Isles in the late medieval and early modern period. It bordered Wales and the palatine county of Lancaster, formed a recruiting ground against the Scots and was the port of departure to and arrival from Ireland and the Isle of Man. In this lay its importance for the contemporary mind, and therefore for the historian.

This means we must consider more than the pure legal theory which

---

36 This is despite the fact that the first major texts on this theme have been published relatively recently: Ronald G. Asch (ed.), *Three nations: a common history?: England, Scotland, Ireland and British history c. 1600–1920*, Bochum 1992; Ellis and Barber, *Conquest and union*; Grant and Stringer, *Uniting the kingdom?*; Bradshaw and Morrill, *The British problem*.

37 Morrill, 'British problem', 28–32, and *The nature of the English Civil War*, London 1993, 259–62; K. M. Brown, 'British history: a sceptical comment', in Asch, *Three nations*, 117–27.

38 Keith Robbins, for example, although he adds important *caveats* to his assembly of 'ingredients' (England, Scotland and Wales), allows these little role in his account of early modern and later developments: *Great Britain: identities, institutions and the idea of Britishness*, London–New York 1998, ch. i and passim.

39 R. R. Davies, 'The peoples of Britain and Ireland, 1100–1400, II: Names, boundaries and regnal solidarities', *TRHS* 6th ser. v (1995), 19.

40 Pauline Stafford, *Queens, concubines and dowagers: the king's wife in the early Middle Ages*, London 1983; Griffiths, 'King's realm and dominions'.

expressed these regnal solidarities, although this was important. In the eyes of the lawyers, there were clear differences between the territories of the English crown: it was asserted that while Wales, Gascony and Calais had been added to the realm by conquest, Chester and Durham proceeded out of it by grants.[41] Even so, the impression gained from the year books is of uncertainty and open debate on Cheshire's status. In Pilkington's case, in the exchequer chamber in 1433, John Fortescue argued that Ireland was 'seuere del roialme dengleterre', giving as his grounds for this the fact that a fifteenth and tenth voted in England would not bind Ireland. Fortescue was in the minority on this occasion; another serjeant argued that the position of Cheshire and Durham was not separation despite their similar taxation privileges.[42] Yet Fortescue's brother Henry had been chief justice of the King's Bench in Ireland in 1426–9,[43] so he had informed knowledge of the position there at least. And neither he nor John Needham, supporter of the 1450 petition for Cheshire privileges, can be accused of ignorance of the law: Fortescue's works are famous and Needham was a justice of both Common Pleas and King's Bench.[44] The distinction of Cheshire from Wales had been recognised by Fortescue himself late in the reign of Henry VI, yet at the same time he and others produced opinions that protected the palatinate's privileges, for example against the vouching of persons in Cheshire and recovery *in banco* of land there.[45] Both conquest and grant were complex grounds for privileges, and, although they might both have been vulnerable to criticism, far more powerful were their attractions to the contemporary mind.[46] Academic texts and the year books may provide one context for the changing position of the territories of the English crown, but are misleading on their own. In the broader political imagination being 'Cheshire' was easy to understand. It implied being English, but this state of 'Englishness' was far more complicated.[47] In the Middle Ages and well into the early modern period, the myths upon which it was based, centring on Brut and Arthur, lacked a coherent political core. They sprang, after all, from Geoffrey of Monmouth's *History*, which was created for the multi-national assemblage of the Angevin

[41] Chrimes, *English constitutional ideas*.
[42] *Select cases in the exchequer chamber*, 81–4. See Lydon, *Lordship of Ireland*, 263–5, and *Ireland in the later Middle Ages*, 144–5; Cosgrove, 'Parliament and the Anglo-Irish community', 28–30.
[43] Ibid. 30.
[44] Clayton, *Administration*, 157.
[45] Lapsley, *County palatine of Durham*, 234, 243, 258.
[46] See Hans S. Pawlisch, *Sir John Davies and the conquest of Ireland: a study in legal imperialism*, Cambridge 1985, esp. pp. 162–9, and criticism in Paul Christianson, 'Political thought in early Stuart England', *HJ* xxx (1987), 955–70 (Davies acting as a common lawyer, pillaging from canon lawyers).
[47] See the complexities into which English representatives were forced to enter in order to defeat French criticism of English claims to nationhood at the Council of Constance, including the *nationes particulares* within the English nation: A. O. H. Jarman, 'Wales and the Council of Constance', *Bulletin of the Board for Celtic Studies* xiv (1950–2), 220–2.

empire.[48] They could accommodate – indeed they positively encouraged – local identities in all their complexity, both Welsh and English, both Celtic and Saxon, both English and French, and also identities within each of these.[49] Richard Helgerson has influentially argued that the late Tudor period saw the imagination, or perhaps the reimagination, of England, its conscious reinvention in the work of lawyers like Coke, antiquarians like Camden, poets like Drayton and Spenser and historians like Holinshed. This approach offers many advantages; unfortunately, as put into practice by Helgerson, it tends to reproduce the same emphases as the established historiography of the national community, an historiography founded upon a study of political and social transaction – and the very historiography which it seeks to complement or even replace. This is largely because it is dependent on the work of historians, especially Elton, who emphasise the unity of the English political community in the sixteenth century.[50] If for these writers there was division, it was division that reflected this national unity: some other interest – 'the nobility, the law, the land, the economy, the common people, the church' – competed with the crown in the writing Helgerson discussed.[51]

[48] R. Howard Bloch, *Etymologies and genealogies: a literary anthropology of the French Middle Ages*, Chicago 1983; Christopher Brooke, 'Geoffrey of Monmouth as a historian', in Christopher Brooke and others (eds), *Church and government in the Middle Ages: essays presented to C. R. Cheney on his 70th birthday*, Cambridge 1976, 77–91, esp. p. 88 (Brooke's emphasis on Geoffrey as a parodist does not undermine his subsidiary point that the beneficiary was the Angevin dynasty); R. William Leckie, Jr, *The passage of dominion: Geoffrey of Monmouth and the periodisation of insular history in the twelfth century*, Toronto 1991. See also John Gillingham, 'The context and purposes of Geoffrey of Monmouth's *History of the kings of Britain*', *Anglo-Norman Studies XIII: Proceedings of the Battle Conference 1990*, Woodbridge 1991, 99–118, whose emphasis on the immediate context and on Geoffrey's defence of the Welsh character leads him to under-estimate the importance of the broader political context. For the later Middle Ages see Anne F. Sutton and Livia Visser-Fuchs, *Richard III's books: ideal and reality in the life and library of a medieval prince*, Stroud 1990, ch. viii.
[49] Davies, 'Names, boundaries and regnal solidarities', 1–20. See also Anglo, 'British history in early Tudor propaganda'; Allan, 'Yorkist propaganda'; G. R. Elton, 'English national selfconsciousness and the parliament in the sixteenth century', in *Nationalismus in Vorindustrieller Zeit: Herausgegeben von Otto Dann*, Munchen 1986, 73–82; Laura Keeler, 'The *Historia regum Britanniae* and four medieval chroniclers', *Speculum* xxi (1946), 24–37; Denys Hay, 'The use of the term "Great Britain" in the Middle Ages', *Proceedings of the Society of Antiquaries of Scotland* lxxxix (1958 [1955–6]), 55–66; Roger Sherman Loomis, 'Edward I, Arthurian enthusiast', *Speculum* xxviii (1953), 114–27; Koebner, ' "The imperial crown of this realm" ', 29–52; A. E. Parsons, 'The Trojan legend in England: some instances of its application to the politics of the times', *The Modern Language Review* xxiv (1929), 253–64; W. A. Nitze, 'The exhumation of King Arthur at Glastonbury', *Speculum* ix (1934), 355–61; James Douglas Merriman, *The flower of kings: a study of the Arthurian legend in Britain between 1485 and 1835*, Manhattan, Wichita 1973; J. G. A. Pocock, 'England', in Orest Ranum (ed.), *National consciousness, history, and political culture in early-modern Europe*, Baltimore–London 1975, 98–117; Walter Ullmann, ' "This realm of England is an empire" ', *Journal of Ecclesiastical History* xxx (1979), 175–203.
[50] Richard Helgerson, *Forms of nationhood: the Elizabethan writing of England*, Chicago–London 1992, 4, 9, cites Elton and Corrigan and Sayer.
[51] Ibid. 10.

If a conscious process of 'reimagining' or even inventing England was taking place, it was not an England of unity and uniformity.[52] Spenser's *Faerie Queen* dramatised the territorial politics of the north-west and of north Wales, setting Arthur's education beside the river Dee, symbolic of Cheshire's position at this crucial frontier.[53] Drayton's *Poly-olbion* celebrated the diversity of the counties of England. More than that, the work preserved the stories of their history which had provided a foundation for their political particularism and privileges. In the case of Cheshire, the palatinate was mentioned early in the account of the county: 'And of countries, place of palatine doth hold, and thereto hath her high regalities enroll'd'.[54] Antiquarian chorography, exemplified by Camden's *Britannia*, also fails to show the 'writing' or 'imagination' of England as a unified, centralised system: the chapters on Cheshire and similar examples abound with discussion of provincial privilege and its antiquarian foundations. Hostile as he is to Chester's 'British' history, he strongly affirms Cheshire palatinate status, concluding with the observation that the county 'retains that Prerogative to this day'.[55] The legal writing of the same period, for Helgerson the nearest approach to a codification of English law, crystallised and therefore helped to preserve the provincial privilege which he claims was being eradicated.[56] Coke's *Fourth part of the institutes of the laws of England*, which describes the courts of the country, set out in precise detail not just the 'national' courts of Westminster, but also the most minor and most dubious of the provincial jurisdictions. Of course Coke was able to dismiss the alleged franchisal courts of Wight or Hexhamshire.[57] Yet he ensured that Chester's privileges were carefully enumerated. This meant recording some of the legal judgements of Hilary 29 Elizabeth and Hilary 11 James I in which Chester's position with regard to writs of error was clarified and to an extent limited. Still, the chapter opened

---

52 Ibid. 136, accepts that provincial particularism, including the palatine jurisdiction of Chester as well as the past privileges of Pembroke and the independent histories of Wales, Kent and Cornwall, played a role in defining locality. His comment at p. 138, however, illustrates the weakness of this perception: 'the nation, unlike the dynasty, is in turn strengthened by its very receptiveness to such individual and communal autonomy'.

53 Spenser, *Faerie Queen* I. ix. 2; Andrew Hadfield, 'From English to British literature: John Lyly's *Euphues* and Edmund Spenser's *The Faerie Queene*', in Brendan Bradshaw and Peter Roberts (eds), *British consciousness and identity: the making of Britain, 1534–1707*, Cambridge 1998, 152. Hadfield notes that the name of Britomart's father, Ryence, derives from the king of north Wales in Malory.

54 *The works of Michael Drayton, esq.*, London 1748, 290. Helgerson misleads in his account of the opening of the work – it commences with the 'French islands' of Jersey and Guernsey, not with Cornwall: *Forms of nationhood*, 139.

55 Camden, *Britannia*, 1586 edn, pp. 342–6; cf. the English version as republished in 1695: *Camden's Britannia, 1695: a facsimile of the 1695 edition published by Edward Gibson*, intro. by Stuart Piggott, Newton Abbot 1971, cols 554–66; quotation at col. 566.

56 Helgerson, *Forms of nationhood*, ch. ii.

57 Edward Coke, *The fourth part of the institutes of the laws of England*, London 1648, 222, 287.

with uncompromising support for the palatinate: 'the most ancient and most honourable County Palatine remaining in England at this day'. Coke also repeated the account of the creation of the palatinate by William the Conqueror. There was even a description of the Cheshire barons, the 'first visible mark of a County Palatine'.[58] Coke provided the same service for Durham; and his discussion of the Council in the Marches of Wales was enlivened by an account of Rhodri the Great and his sons.[59] In Tudor historical writing, too, diversity was enshrined, so the England 'written' in such work as Holinshed's *Chronicles* was one of composite monarchies and multiple kingdoms. In its very authorship it encapsulated the nature of the territories of the English crown: Holinshed the Cheshireman, Hooker from the south-west, Stanihurst from Ireland.[60] The reality of Cheshire's imagined and transacted identity can be extrapolated to other regions under the rule of the English king, revealing an easy tension between centralised monarchy and territorial autonomy that characterised the Tudor state and exists even today.

[58] Ibid. 211–15.
[59] Ibid. 216, 243.
[60] Annabel Patterson, *Reading Holinshed's chronicles*, Chicago–London 1994, criticised F. J. Levy's belief in the shapelessness of the chronicles (*Tudor historical thought*, 168, 183–4), and D. R. Woolf's that the history was providentialist and therefore served to legitimate the ruling dynasty (*The idea of history in early Stuart England*, Toronto 1990). For her, the work was deliberately multi-vocal (pp. 4–7 and passim), although she does not see territorial autonomy as one of the 'diversities' celebrated in the work.

Bibliography

Unpublished primary sources

Bangor, University of Wales
Mostyn Collection, 7773–4

Cambridge, Corpus Christi College
MS 369

Chester, Cheshire County Record Office
DAR   Arderne of Alvanley and Harden
DBA   Barnston of Churton
DBC   Birch, Cullimore & Co., Chester
DBD   Brown, Dobie & Rogers, Chester
DBN   Brooke of Norton
DBW   Baker-Wilbraham of Odd Rode
DCB   Charlton & Co., Chester
DCC   Cowper MSS
DCH   Chomondeley of Cholmondeley
DCR   Crewe of Crewe
DDA   Davenport of Bramhall
DDS   Downes of Shrigley
DDX   Miscellaneous collections
DET   Egerton of Tatton
DLE   Leche of Carden
DLT   Leicester-Warren of Tabley
DMD   Moore Dutton of Tushingham
DNE   Needham (Kilmorey)
DOA   Orrell of Ashley
DOL   Oldfield of Leftwich
DSC   Sedgeley, Caldecott & Co., Knutsford
DSS   Shakerley of Hulme and Somerford
DTO   Toler
DVA   Venables of Agden
DVE   Vernon and Warren
DWN   Wilbraham of Nantwich
DWS   Wilson of Sandbach
QCX 1/2–5   Quarter Sessions, Clerk of the Peace: papers relating to abolition
                of Chester palatinate

Chester, Chester City Record Office
AB   Assembly minute books
AF   Assembly files

CR 63/1–2   Earwaker collection
SB   Sheriffs' books
SF   Sheriffs' files
SPR   Passage court rolls
SR   Pentice court rolls
MB   Mayors' books
ML   Mayors' letters
MR   Portmote court rolls
TAR   Treasurers' account rolls
COWPER   William Cowper, *Collectanea Devana*

Chester, Chester Diocesan Record Office
EDA 12/1   Court of High Commission, 1543: Crown Commissioners
          appointed to enforce prescribed forms of worship
P   Ecclesiastical parishes

Chester, Eaton Hall, Eaton (consulted at Chester City Record Office)
Eaton charters

Douglas, Isle of Man, Manx National Trust Museum and Library
Libi Placitorum, 1543–69

Hereford, Hereford Record Office
BG 11/29

Lancaster, Lancashire Record Office
DDTr marriages

London, British Library
Additional charters 21,480, 26,786, 43,368
MSS Additional 7099, 34,815
MSS Cotton Vitellius, 1, A xvi, C.1
MSS Harleian 283, 368, 1967, 1997, 1988, 2009, 2022, 2046, 2079, 2091, 2119,
    2125, 2151, 2155, 2177
MSS Lansdowne 163, 644
MS Stowe 141

London, Gray's Inn
MS 9

London, Public Record Office

Chancery
C 1   Early Chancery proceedings
C 2   Court of Chancery, preachings, series I, Elizabeth I to Charles I
C 82   Warrants for the great seal, series II
C 244   Chancery files, Tower and Rolls Chapel series, *corpus cum causa*

Court of Requests

REQ 1	Books
REQ 2	Proceedings

Duchy of Lancaster

DL 5	Court of duchy chamber, entry books of decrees and orders
DL 42	Cartularies, enrolments, surveys and other miscellaneous books

Exchequer

E 28	Council and privy seal records
E 36	Treasury of the receipt
E 101	King's remembrancer, accounts various
E 163	Exchequer king's remembrancer, miscellanea of the exchequer
E 179	Lay subsidy rolls, etc.
E 198	Documents relating to serjeanties, knights' fees, etc.
E 321	Court of Augmentations and Court of General Surveyors, legal proceedings

Palatinate of Chester

CHES 1	Chester warrants, etc.
CHES 2	Chester administrative enrolments
CHES 3	Chester inquisitions post mortem
CHES 5	Chester appearance rolls
CHES 7	Chester returns to writs of *certiorari*
CHES 14	Chester entry books of decrees and orders, etc.
CHES 15	Chester exchequer pleadings
CHES 20	Chester calendar rolls
CHES 24	Chester gaol files, writs, etc.
CHES 25	Chester indictment rolls and files
CHES 29	Chester plea rolls
CHES 31	Chester fines and recoveries
CHES 37	Chester warrants of attorney rolls
CHES 38–15	Chester miscellanea: summons of the exchequer

Prerogative Court of Canterbury

PROB 11	Will registers

Special Collections

SC 6	Ministers' and receivers' accounts

Star Chamber

STAC 1	Star Chamber proceedings Henry VII
STAC 2	Star Chamber proceedings Henry VIII
STAC 3	Star Chamber proceedings Edward VI
STAC 4	Star Chamber proceedings Philip & Mary

State Paper Office

SP 1   Letters and papers Henry VIII, general series
SP 2   Letters and papers Henry VIII, folios
SP 6

Manchester, John Rylands University Library
Arley charters
Bromley-Davenport muniments
Brooke of Mere MSS
Cornwall-Legh MSS
Dunham Massey muniments
Egerton of Tatton muniments
English MSS
Jodrell MSS
Legh of Lyme muniments
Mainwaring charters
Mainwaring MSS
Mascie of Tatton MSS
Roundell MSS
Rylands charters
Rylands MSS
Tatton of Wythenshawe MSS

Oxford, Bodleian Library
MS Lat. misc. c.66 (Capesthorne manuscript)
MS Don. C. 42 (William Latymer, 'Chronickille of Anne Bulleyne')

Published primary sources

Abstracts of inquisitions post mortem, made by Christopher Towneley and Roger Dodsworth, extracted from manuscripts at Towneley, ed. William Langton, ii (Chetham Society xcix, 1876)

Actes des états de l'île de Jersey, 1524–1800, I: 1524–1596 (12e publication de la société jersiaise, 1897)

Acts and monuments of John Foxe: a new and complete edition, ed. Stephen Reed Cattley, London 1837–41

Acts of the privy council of England, n.s., ed. John Roche Dasent and others, London 1890–

Amyot, T., 'A memorial from George Constantine', *Archaeologia* xxiii (1831), 50–78

Ancient Engleish metrical romances, ed. Joseph Ritson, London 1882

Annales cestriensis, ed. R. C. Christie (RSLC xiv, 1887)

Annual reports of the deputy keeper of the public records, London 1840–

Archbold, W. A. J., 'Sir William Stanley and Perkin Warbeck', *EHR* xiv (1899), 529–34

Babees book, ed. Frederick J. Furnivall (EETS xxxii, 1868)

Bacon's history of the reign of Henry VII, with notes by J. R. Lumby, Cambridge 1876

Bale, John, *Illustrium maioris Britanniae scriptorum*, Ipswich 1548

—— *Scriptorum illustrium maioris Brytanniae*, Basel [1557]

—— *Index Britanniae scriptorum*, ed. R. L. Poole and M. Bateson, Oxford 1902

Bayne, C. G. and William Huse Dunham, *Select cases in the council of Henry VII* (Selden Society lxxv, 1958 [1956])

Beamont, William, *Arley charters: a calendar of ancient family charters preserved at Arley Hall, Cheshire*, London 1866

Bentley, Samuel, *Excerpta historica, or, illustrations of English history*, London 1831

Bishop Percy's folio manuscript, ed. J. W. Hales and F. J. Furnivall, London 1868

Bodleian Library MS Fairfax 16, intro. John Norton-Smith, London 1979

Bradshaw, Henry, *The life of Saint Werburge of Chester*, ed. Carl Horstmann (EETS o.s. lxxxviii, 1887)

[Bradshaw, Henry], *The lyfe of Saynt Radegunde*, ed. F. Brittain, Cambridge 1926

Brereton, Owen Salusbury, 'Exhibition of coloured drawing of a window in Brereton church', *Archaeologia* ix (1799), 368–9

' "A breviat of the effectes devised for Wales", c. 1540–41', ed. P. R. Roberts, in *Camden Miscellany, XXVI* (Camden 4th ser. xiv, 1975), 31–47

Bridge, Joseph C., *Cheshire proverbs and other sayings and rhymes connected with the city and county of Chester*, Chester 1917

British Library Harleian manuscript 433, ed. Rosemary Horrox and P. W. Hammond, Upminster 1979–83

Calendar of ancient correspondence concerning Wales, ed. J. G. Edwards, Cardiff 1935

Calendar of Archbishop Alen's register, ed. C. McNeill, Dublin 1950

Calendar of the Caernarvonshire quarter sessions records, I: 1541–1558, ed. W. Ogwen Williams, Caernarvon 1956

Calendar of charter rolls, London 1903–16

Calendar of close rolls, London 1902–

Calendar of entries in the papal registers relating to Great Britain and Ireland: papal letters: XIII: 1471–1484, ed. J. A. Twemlow, London 1955

Calendar of entries in the papal registers relating to Great Britain and Ireland: papal letters: XIV: 1484–1492, ed. J. A. Twemlow, London 1960

Calendar of entries in the papal registers relating to Great Britain and Ireland: papal letters: XV: Innocent VIII: Lateran registers 1484–1492, ed. M. J. Haren, Dublin 1978

Calendar of entries in the papal registers relating to Great Britain and Ireland: papal letters: XVI: Alexander VI: Lateran registers, part 1, 1492–1503, ed. M. J. Haren, Dublin 1986

Calendar of entries in the papal registers relating to Great Britain and Ireland: papal letters: XVIII: Pius III and Julius II: Vatican registers 1503–1513, Lateran registers 1503–1508, ed. M. J. Haren, Dublin 1989

Calendar of fine rolls, London 1911–

Calendar of letters, despatches, and state papers, relating to the negotiations between England and Spain, preserved in the archives at Simancas and elsewhere, ed. G. A. Bergenroth and others, London 1862–1969

Calendar of patent rolls, London 1901–

Calendars of the proceedings in chancery in the reign of Queen Elizabeth; to which are prefixed examples of earlier proceedings in that court, namely from the reign of

Richard the Second to that of Queen Elizabeth, inclusive: from the originals in the Tower, London 1827–32

Calendar of Salusbury correspondence, 1555–c. 1700, ed. W. J. Smith, Cardiff 1954

Calendar of state papers, domestic series, London 1856–

Calendar of state papers, foreign series, of the reign of Elizabeth, 1558–1559, ed. Joseph Stevenson, London 1863

Calendar of state papers, Ireland, of the reigns of Henry VIII., Edward VI., Mary, and Elizabeth, 1509–1573, ed. Hans Claude Hamilton, London 1860

Calendar of Wynn (of Gwydir) papers, 1515–1690, in the National Library of Wales and elsewhere, Aberystwyth–Cardiff–London 1926

Camden, William, *Britannia*, London 1586

Camden's Britannia, 1695: a facsimile of the 1695 edition published by Edward Gibson, intro. Stuart Piggott, Newton Abbot 1971

St Caradoc of Llancarfan, *The historie of Cambria, now called Wales*, edn 'corrected, augmented and continued' by David Powell, London 1584

Cavendish, George, *The life and death of Cardinal Wolsey*, ed. Richard S. Sylvester (EETS ccxliii, 1959)

Chester mystery cycle, I: Text; II: Commentary and glossary, ed. R. M. Lumiansky and David Mills (EETS s.s. iii, ix, 1974, 1986)

Chester's triumph in honor of her prince as it was performed upon St George's day 1610, ed. T[homas] C[orser] (Chetham Society iii, 1844)

Chronicle and political papers of King Edward VI, ed. W. K. Jordan, London 1966

Chronicles of London, ed. C. L. Kingsford, Oxford 1905

Coke, Edward, *The fourth part of the institutes of the laws of England*, London 1648

'A collection of original letters from the bishops to the Privy Council, 1564', ed. Mary Bateson, in *Camden Miscellany, IX* (Camden n.s. liii, 1895)

Commons debates 1621, ed. Wallace Notestein, Frances Helen Relf and Hartley Simpson, New Haven–London 1935

Commons debates 1628, III: 21 April–27 May 1628, ed. Robert C. Johnson, Mary Frear Keeler, Maija Jansson Cole and William B. Bidwell, New Haven–London 1977

County community under Henry VIII: the military survey, 1522, and lay subsidy, 1524–5, for Rutland, ed. J. C. K. Cornwall (Rutland Record Series i, 1980)

D'Ewes, Sir Simonds, *A compleat journal of the votes, speeches and debates, both of the House of Lords and House of Commons throughout the whole reign of Queen Elizabeth, of glorious memory*, London 1693

Dictionary of national biography, ed. Leslie Stephen and Sidney Lee, Oxford 1917–

Dodridge, John, *The history of the ancient and moderne estate of the principality of Wales, dutchy of Cornewall, and earldome of Chester*, London 1630, facsimile edn, Amsterdam–New York 1973

Drayton, Michael, *Poly-olbion*, London 1612

Dugdale, William, *The baronage of England*, London 1675

The ecologues of Alexander Barclay, from the original edition by John Caward, ed. Beatrice White (EETS o.s. clxxv, 1928[1927])

Elias Ashmole (1617–1692): his autobiographical and historical notes, his correspondence, and other contemporary sources relating to his life and work, ed. C. H. Josten, Oxford 1966

Elyot, Thomas, *Bibliotheca Eliotae: Eliotis librarie*, London 1542

—— *Dictionary* (English Linguistics 1500–1800, A Collection of Facsimile Reprints, ed. R. C. Alston, no. 221, 1970)

—— *The boke named the gouernour deuised by Sir Thomas Elyot, knight*, ed. Henry H. S. Croft, London 1880

English historical documents, 1327–1485, ed. A. R. Myers, London 1969

Extracts from the manuscript liber Luciani de laude Cestriae, ed. M. V. Taylor (RSLC lxiv, 1912)

Fabyan, Robert, *The new chronicles of England and France*, London 1811

Fordun, Johannis de, *Chronica gentis Scotorum*, ed. William F. Skene, Edinburgh 1871

Fouke Fitz Warin: roman du XIVe siècle, ed. Louis Brandin, Paris 1930

Great chronicle of London, ed. A. H. Thomas and I. D. Thornley, London 1938

Halle, Edward, *Chronicle, containing the history of England, during the reign of Henry IV and succeeding monarchs to the end of the reign of Henry VII*, ed. H. Ellis, London 1809

Harrod, Henry Davies, *The muniments of Shavington*, Shrewsbury 1891

—— 'A defence of the liberties of Chester, 1450', *Archaeologia* 2nd ser. vii (1900), 71–80

Hinde, William, *A faithfull remonstrance of the holy life and happy death of John Bruen of Bruen-Stapleford in the county of Chester, esquire*, London 1641

Historiae Dunelmensis scriptores tres, Gaufridus de Coldingham, Robertus de Graystanes, et Willielmus de Chambre, ed. James Raine (Surtees Society ix, 1839)

HMC, *Annual reports*, London 1870–

HMC, *Calendar of the manuscripts of the most hon. the marquis of Salisbury KG, etc., preserved at Hatfield House, Hertfordshire*, London 1883–1976

HMC, *Calendar of the manuscripts of the marquis of Bath preserved at Longleat, Wiltshire*, ii, Dublin 1907; iv, London 1968

HMC, *Report on the manuscripts of Lord De L'Isle and Dudley preserved at Penshurst Place*, London 1925–66

HMC, *Report on the manuscripts of the late Reginald Rawdon Hastings, esq., of the Manor House, Ashby de la Zouch*, London 1928–

HMC, *Various collections*, ii, London 1903

HMC, *12th report, appendix, part IV: the manuscripts of his grace the duke of Rutland, GCB, preserved at Belvoir Castle*, London 1888–9

Holinshed, Raphael, *Chronicles of England, Scotland and Ireland*, London 1807

Irvine, William Fergusson, 'A list of the freeholders in Cheshire in the year 1578', in *Miscellanies relating to Lancashire and Cheshire*, iv (RSLC xliii, 1902), 1–24

Itinerary of John Leland in or about the years 1536–1539, ed. Lucy Toulmin Smith, London 1964

Itinerary of John Leland the antiquary, 3rd edn, ed. Thomas Hearne, Oxford 1769

James, Montague Rhodes, *A descriptive catalogue of the manuscripts in the library of Corpus Christi College*, Cambridge 1909–13

—— *Catalogue of MSS of Corpus Christi College Cambridge (nos 251–538)*, Cambridge 1911–12

Jefferson, G., *The lex scripta of the Isle of Man*, Douglas 1819

Journals of the House of Commons, London 1803

Journals of the House of Lords, London 1771–

Lancashire and Cheshire cases in the court of Star Chamber, ed. R. Stewart Brown (RSLC lxxi, 1916–17)

Lancashire and Cheshire wills and inventories at Chester, with an appendix of abstracts of wills now lost or destroyed, ed. J. P. Earwaker (Chetham Society n.s. iii, 1884)

Lancashire and Cheshire wills and inventories from the ecclesiastical court, Chester, ed. G. J. Piccope (Chetham Society xxxiii, li, liv, 1857, 1860, 1861)

Latymer, William, 'Chronickille of Anne Bulleyne', ed. Maria Dowling, in *Camden Miscellany, XXX* (Camden 4th ser. xxix, 1990), 23–65

Leigh, Egerton, *Ballads and legends of Cheshire*, London 1867

Leland, John, *Genethliacon illustrissimi Eaduerdi principis Cambriae, ducis Coriniae, & comitis Palatini*, London 1543, repr. in *The itinerary of John Leland the antiquary* (Hearne edn), v

—— *De rebus Britannicis collectanea*, ed. Thomas Hearne, Oxford 1774

Letters and accounts of William Brereton of Malpas, ed. E. W. Ives (RSLC cxvi, 1976)

Letters and papers, foreign and domestic, of the reign of Henry VIII, 1509–47, ed. J. S. Brewer, J. Gairdner and R. H. Brodie, London 1862–1910; *Addenda*, i, London, 1929–32

'Letters of the Cliffords, Lords Clifford and earls of Cumberland, c. 1500–c. 1565', ed. R. W. Hoyle, in *Camden Miscellany, XXXI* (Camden 4th ser. xliv, 1992), 1–189

List of early chancery proceedings preserved in the Public Record Office (PRO, Lists and Indexes xii, xvi, xx, xxix, xxxviii, xlviii, l, li, lii, liv, lv, 1901–36)

List of ministers' accounts: Edw. VI – 18th C. and analogous documents (PRO, Lists and Indexes, supplementary series ii, repr. New York 1967)

List of proceedings in the court of Requests, i (List and Index Society xxi, 1906)

List of proceedings in the court of Star Chamber, I: 1485–1558 (PRO, Lists and Indexes xiii, 1901)

List of the records of the palatinates of Chester, Durham and Lancaster (PRO, Lists and Indexes xl, 1914)

Madox, T., *Baronia anglica: an history of land-honors and baronies, and of tenure in capite*, London 1741

Mainwaring, Thomas, *A defence of Amicia, daughter of Hugh Cyveliok, earl of Chester*, London 1673

Manwood, John, *A treatise and discourse of the lawes of the forrest*, London 1598

Marcher lordships of South Wales, 1415–1536: select documents, ed. T. B. Pugh (Board of Celtic Studies, University of Wales, History and Law Series xx, 1963)

Metrical visions by George Cavendish, ed. A. S. G. Edwards (Renaissance English Text Society 5th ser. ix, 1980)

Miracles of King Henry VI: being an account and translation of twenty-three miracles taken from the manuscript in the British Museum (Royal 13 c.viii), intro. Ronald Knox and Shane Leslie, Cambridge 1923

Mum and the sothsegger, ed. M. Day and R. Steele (EETS o.s. cxcix, 1936 [1934])

Nixon's Cheshire prophecies, ed. W. E. A. Axon, Manchester–London 1873

Nixon's Cheshire prophecy at large, 5th edn, London 1716

Northern petitions, illustrative of life in Berwick, Cumbria and Durham in the fourteenth century, ed. C. M. Fraser (Surtees Society cxciv, 1982 [1981])

Palatine anthology: a collection of poems and ancient ballads relating to Lancashire and Cheshire, ed. J. O. Halliwell-Phillips, London 1850

Parliamentary writs and writs of military summons, together with the writs and muni-

ments relating to the suit and service due and performed to the king's high court of parliament and the councils of the realm, or affording evidence of attendance given at parliaments and councils, ed. Francis Palgrave, London 1827–34

Paston letters and papers of the fifteenth century, ed. N. Davis, Oxford 1971–6

Pegge, Samuel, 'Some observations on the paintings in the window of Brereton church', *Archaeologia* x (1792), 50–3

Plumpton correspondence, ed. Thomas Stapleton (Camden o.s. iv, 1839)

Plumpton letters and papers, ed. Joan Kirby (Camden 5th ser. viii, 1996)

Polychronicon Ranulphi Higden monachi cestriensis, ed. C. Babington and Joseph Rawson Lumby (Rolls Series xli, 1865–86)

'Proceedings in the court of Star Chamber, *temp*. Henry VIII. and Edward VI.', ed. W. K. Boyd, *Collections for a History of Staffordshire* (1910), 1–58

Proceedings in the parliaments of Elizabeth I, ed. T. E. Hartley, Leicester–London– New York 1981–95

Proceedings in parliament 1625, ed. Maija Jansson and William B. Bidwell, New Haven–London 1987

Pylkington, Robert, 'Narrative', in HMC, *Various collections*, ii

Records of early English drama: Chester, ed. Lawrence M. Clopper, Manchester 1979

Records of the guild of the Holy Trinity, St Mary, St John the Baptist and St Katherine of Coventry, ii, ed. Geoffrey Templeman (Dugdale Society xix, 1944)

Register of the guild of the Holy Trinity, St Mary, St John the Baptist and St Katherine of Coventry, ed. Mary Dormer Harris (Dugdale Society xiii, 1935)

Register of John Morton, archbishop of Canterbury, 1486–1500, ed. Christopher Harper-Bill (Canterbury and York Society lxxv, pt cxlviii, 1987)

'Rights and jurisdiction of the county palatine of Chester, the earls palatine, the chamberlain, and other officers', ed. J. B. Yates, in *Chetham Miscellanies, II* (Chetham Society xxxvii, 1856)

Rolls of the freemen of the city of Chester, I: 1392–1700, ed. J. H. E. Bennett (RSLC li, 1906)

Rotuli parliamentorum, ed. J. Strachey and others, London 1767–77

St German, Christopher, *Doctor and student*, ed. T. F. T. Plucknett and J. L. Barton (Selden Society xci, 1974)

Seacombe, John, *Memoirs, containing a genealogical and historical account of the ancient and honourable house of Stanley*, Liverpool 1737

Selden, John, *Titles of honor*, London 1614

Select cases in the exchequer chamber before all the justices of England, 1377–1461, ed. M. Hemmant (Selden Society li, 1933)

'Short and a brief memory . . . of the first progress of our sovereign lord Henry the seventh . . . etc.', in Leland, *De rebus Britannicis collectanea*, iv. 185–92

Skelton, John, *The complete English poems*, ed. John Scattergood, Harmondsworth 1983

Smith, William, *The particular description of England. 1588*, ed. with intro. by Henry B. Wheatley and Edmund W. Ashbee, London 1879

'Staffordshire suits in the court of Star Chamber, *temp*. Henry VII. and Henry VIII., abstracted from the original documents in the Public Record Office', ed. W. K. Boyd, *Collections for a History of Staffordshire*, x/1 (1907), 71–188

'Star Chamber proceedings. Henry VIII. and Edward VI.', *Collections for a History of Staffordshire* (1912), 1–207

State papers published under the authority of His Majesty's commission: King Henry the Eighth, London 1830–52

Statutes of the realm, London 1810–28

Stow, John, *The annales of England*, London 1601, 1615

Tudor royal proclamations, I: The early Tudors (1485–1553), ed. Paul L. Hughes and James F. Larkin, New Haven–London 1964

Twyne, John, *De rebus albionicis*, London 1590

The vale-royall of England, or the county palatine of Chester illustrated, publ. Daniel King, London 1656

Valor ecclesiasticus, ed. J. Caley and J. Hunter, London 1810–34

Venerabilis Baedae historiam ecclesiasticam gentis Anglorum, ed. Charles Plummer, Oxford 1896

Vergil, Polydore, *Historia anglica*, Basiliae 1555, repr. Menston 1972

——— *The anglica historia of Polydore Vergil AD 1485–1537*, ed. and trans. Denys Hay (Camden 3rd ser. lxxiv, 1950)

Visitation of Cheshire in the year 1580, made by Robert Glover, Somerset herald, for William Flower, Norroy King of Arms, ed. John Paul Rylands (Harleian Society xviii, 1882)

Visitation of Lancashire and a part of Cheshire made in the twenty-fourth year of the reign of King Henry the eighth, AD 1533, by special commission of Thomas Benalt, Clarencieux, ed. William Langton (Chetham Society xcviii, 1876)

Wharton, Thomas, *Anglia sacra*, London 1691

Works of Michael Drayton, esq., London 1748

Wriothesley, Charles, *A chronicle of England during the reigns of the Tudors, from AD 1485 to 1559*, ed. William Douglas Hamilton, i (Camden n.s. xi, 1875)

Wyatt, George, *Extracts from the life of the virtuous Christian and renowned Queen Anne Boleigne by George Wyatt*, in *The life of Cardinal Wolsey by George Cavendish*, ed. S. W. Singer, 2nd edn, London 1827

Secondary sources

Acheson, Eric, *A gentry community: Leicestershire in the fifteenth century, c. 1422–c. 1485*, Cambridge 1992

Adams, George Burton, *The history of England from the Norman Conquest to the death of John (1066–1216)*, London 1905

Alexander, James W., 'New evidence on the palatinate of Chester', *EHR* lxxxv (1970), 715–29

——— 'The alleged palatinates of Norman England', *Speculum* lvi (1981), 17–27

——— 'The English palatinates and Edward I', *Journal of British Studies* xxii (1983), 1–22

——— *Ranulf of Chester: a relic of the conquest*, Athens, Ga. 1983

Allan, Alison, 'Yorkist propaganda: pedigree, prophecy and the "British history" in the reign of Edward IV', in Ross, *Patronage, pedigree and power*, 171–92

Allmand, C. T., *Lancastrian Normandy, 1415–1450: the history of a medieval occupation*, Oxford 1983

Alsop, J. D., 'The theory and practice of Tudor taxation', *EHR* lxxxxvii (1982), 1–30

Anderson, Benedict R. O'G., *Imagined communities: reflections on the origin and spread of nationalism*, London 1983, rev. edn, London 1991

Anderson, Perry, *Lineages of the absolutist state*, London 1974

Anglo, Sydney, 'The British history in early Tudor propaganda', *BJRL* xliv (1961–2), 17–48

Arnold, Carol, 'The commission of the peace for the West Riding of Yorkshire, 1437–1509', in A. J. Pollard (ed.), *Property and politics: essays in later medieval English history*, Gloucester–New York 1984, 116–38

Arnold, Morris S., Thomas A. Green, Sally A. Scully and Stephen D. White (eds), *Of the laws and customs of England: essays in honor of Samuel E. Thorne*, Chapel Hill, NC 1981

Arthurson, Ian, 'A question of loyalty', *The Ricardian* vii, no. 97 (June 1987), 401–13

———— *The Perkin Warbeck conspiracy, 1491–1499*, Gloucester 1994

Asch, Ronald G. (ed.), *Three nations: a common history?: England, Scotland, Ireland and British history c. 1600–1920*, Bochum 1992

Ashton, J. W., ' "Rymes of . . . Randolf, erl of Chestre" ', *English Literary History* v (1938), 195–206

Avery, Margaret E., 'The history of the equitable jurisdiction of chancery before 1460', *BIHR* xlii (1969), 129–44

Barber, Richard, *Edward, prince of Wales and Aquitaine: a biography of the Black Prince*, Woodbridge 1978

Barnes, Thomas G., *Somerset, 1625–1640: a county's government during the 'personal rule'*, Cambridge, Mass. 1961

Barraclough, Geoffrey, 'The earldom and county palatine of Chester', *THSLC* ciii (1952 [1951]), 23–57

———— 'The annals of Dieulacres abbey', *Sheaf* 3rd ser. lii (1960 [Jan.–Dec. 1957]), 17–27

Beck, Joan, *Tudor Cheshire*, Chester 1969

Beckett, J. C., *The making of modern Ireland, 1603–1923*, London 1996

Beer, B. L., *Rebellion and riot: popular disorder in England during the reign of Edward VI*, Kent, Ohio 1982

Bellamy, John G., *Criminal law and society in late medieval and Tudor England*, Gloucester–New York 1984

———— *Bastard feudalism and the law*, London 1989

Benedict, P., *Rouen during the wars of religion*, Cambridge 1987

Bennett, H. S., *The Pastons and their England: studies in an age of transition*, Cambridge 1951

Bennett, Michael, 'A county community: social cohesion amongst the Cheshire gentry, 1400–25', *NH* viii (1973), 24–44

———— '*Sir Gawain and the Green Knight* and the literary achievement of the north-west midlands: the historical background', *Journal of Medieval History* v (1979), 63–88

———— 'Sources and problems in the study of social mobility: Cheshire in the later Middle Ages', *THSLC* cxxviii (1979), 59–95

———— ' "Good lords" and "king-makers": the Stanleys of Lathom in English politics, 1385–1485', *History Today* xxxi (July 1981), 12–17

———— *Community, class and careerism: Cheshire and Lancashire society in the age of Sir Gawain and the Green Knight*, Cambridge 1983

—————— *Lambert Simnel and the battle of Stoke*, Gloucester–New York 1987

—————— 'Careerism in late medieval England', in Rosenthal and Richmond, *People, politics and community*, 19–39

—————— 'Henry VII and the northern rising of 1489', *EHR* cv (1990), 34–59

Bernard, G. W., 'The fortunes of the Greys, earls of Kent, in the early sixteenth century', *HJ* xxv (1982), 671–85

—————— *The power of the early Tudor nobility: a study of the fourth and fifth earls of Shrewsbury*, Brighton 1985

—————— 'The fall of Anne Boleyn', *EHR* cvi (1991), 584–610

—————— (ed.), *The Tudor nobility*, Manchester 1992

Berry, Elizabeth, 'The vale royal of England', *Cheshire Round* i/9 (summer 1968), 304–10; i/10 (summer 1969), 338–43

Bindoff, S. T., *The House of Commons, 1509–1558*, London 1982

Bird, W. H. B., 'Taxation and representation in the county palatine of Chester', *EHR* xxx (1915), 303

Bloch, R. Howard, *Etymologies and genealogies: a literary anthropology of the French Middle Ages*, Chicago 1983

Booth, P. H. W., 'Taxation and public order: Cheshire in 1353', *NH* xii (1976), 16–31

—————— *The financial administration of the lordship and county of Chester, 1272–1377* (Chetham Society 3rd ser. xxviii, 1981)

Bossy, John, 'Blood and baptism: kinship, community and Christianity in western Europe from the fourteenth to the sixteenth centuries', in Derek Baker (ed.), *Sanctity and secularity: the Church and the world* (Studies in Church History x, 1973), 129–35

Braddick, Michael, 'State formation and social change in early modern England: a problem stated and approaches suggested', *Social History* xvi (1991), 1–17

—————— *Parliamentary taxation in seventeenth-century England: local administration and responses*, London 1994

Bradshaw, Brendan, *The Irish constitutional revolution of the sixteenth century*, Cambridge 1979

—————— 'The Tudor reformation and revolution in Wales and Ireland: the origins of the British problem', in Bradshaw and Morrill, *The British problem*, 39–65.

—————— and John Morrill (eds), *The British problem, c. 1534–1707: state formation in the Atlantic archipelago*, Basingstoke–London 1996

Brady, Ciaran, *The chief governors: the rise and fall of reform government in Tudor Ireland, 1536–1588*, Cambridge 1994

—————— 'Comparable histories: Tudor reform in Wales and Ireland', in Ellis and Barber, *Conquest and union*, 64–86

—————— 'England's defence and Ireland's reform: the dilemmas of the Irish viceroys, 1541–1641', in Bradshaw and Morrill, *The British problem*, 89–117

Brigden, Susan, *London and the Reformation*, Oxford 1989, paperback edn 1991

Bright, J. Franck, *A history of England*, 5th edn, London 1897

British Museum, *A guide to the medieval antiquities and objects of later date in the department of British and medieval antiquities*, London 1924

Brittain, F., *Saint Radegunde, patroness of Jesus College, Cambridge*, Cambridge 1925

Bromley, J., 'The heraldry of Ormskirk church', *THSLC* xxii (1907 [1906]), 64–90

Brooke, Christopher, 'Geoffrey of Monmouth as a historian', in Christopher Brooke and others (eds), *Church and government in the Middle Ages: essays presented to C. R. Cheney on his 70th birthday*, Cambridge 1976, 77–91

Brooke, R., 'On Handford Hall, in Cheshire . . .', *THSLC* ii (1849–50), 41–54

Brown, K. M., 'British history: a sceptical comment', in Asche, *Three nations*, 117–27

Brown, R. Stewart, 'The royal manor and park of Shotwick', *THSLC* lxiv (1913 [1912]), 82–142

—— 'The advowries of Cheshire', *EHR* xxix (1914), 41–55

—— 'The "domesday" roll of Chester', *EHR* xxxvii (1922), 481–500

—— 'Thwert-ut-nay and the custom of "thwertnic" in Cheshire', *EHR* xl (1925), 13–21

—— 'The Cheshire writs of *quo warranto* in 1499', *EHR* xxxxix (1934), 676–84

—— 'The exchequer of Chester', *EHR* lvii (1942), 289–97

Browne, A. L., 'Sir John Throckmorton of Feckenham, chief justice of Chester', *Journal of the Chester and North Wales Architectural, Archaeological and Historic Society* n.s. xxxi (1935), 55–71

Bryan, Donough, *Gerald Fitzgerald: the great earl of Kildare*, Dublin 1933

Buhler, Curt F., 'A note on the "balade to Saynt Werburge" ', *Modern Language Notes* lxviii (1953), 538–9

Bullock-Davies, Constance, *Menestrellorum multitudo: minstrels at a royal feast*, Cardiff 1978

Bulpitt, Jim, *Territory and power in the United Kingdom: an interpretation*, Manchester 1983

Burne, R. V. H., *Chester Cathedral from its founding by Henry VIII to the accession of Queen Victoria*, London 1958

—— *The monks of Chester: the history of St Werburgh's abbey*, London 1962

Busch, W., *England under the Tudors*, I: *King Henry VII (1485–1509)*, London 1895

Bush, M. L., 'The problem of the far north: a study of the crisis of 1537 and its consequences', *NH* vi (1971), 40–63

—— *The government policy of Protector Somerset*, London 1975

Cam, Helen M., 'The evolution of the medieval English franchise', in her *Law-finders and law-makers in medieval England: collected studies in legal and constitutional history*, London 1962, 22–43

—— 'The decline and fall of English feudalism', in her *Liberties and communities in medieval England: collected studies in local administration and topography*, London 1963, 205–22

Cameron, A., 'The giving of livery and retaining in Henry VII's reign', *Renaissance and Modern Studies* xviii (1974), 17–35

Campbell, James, *Essays in Anglo-Saxon history*, London 1986

—— *Stubbs and the English state* (The Stenton Lecture), Reading 1987

—— 'The late Anglo-Saxon state: a maximum view', *Proceedings of the British Academy* lxxxvii (1995), 39–66

Cannadine, David, 'British history as a "new subject": politics, perspectives and prospects', in Grant and Stringer, *Uniting the kingdom?*, 12–28

Canny, Nicholas P., 'The ideology of English colonization: from Ireland to America', *William and Mary Quarterly* 3rd ser. xxx (1973), 575–98

────── *Kingdom and colony: Ireland and the Atlantic world, 1560–1800*, Baltimore 1988

Carlson, David, 'King Arthur and court poems for the birth of Arthur Tudor in 1486', *Humanistica Lovaniensia* xxxvi (1987), 147–83

Carpenter, Christine, *Locality and polity: a study of Warwickshire landed society, 1401–1499*, Cambridge 1992

────── 'Gentry and community in medieval England', *Journal of British Studies* xxxiii (1995), 340–80

Chambers, E. K., *The medieval stage*, Oxford 1903

Cheetham, F. H., 'The church of St Michael-in-Wyre in Amounderness', *THSLC* n.s. xxx (1915 [1914]), 181–227

────── 'Cheshire men in the Scottish expedition of 1544', *THSLC* n.s. xxxvii (1922 [1921]), 232

Chesters, Geoffrey, 'Power politics in Cheshire', *Cheshire Round* i/1 (Dec. 1961), 25–6

────── 'Power politics and roguery in Tudor Cheshire', *Cheshire Round* i/2 (Oct. 1962), 45–7, 57

Chrimes, S. B., *English constitutional ideas in the fifteenth century*, Cambridge 1936, New York 1965

────── *Henry VII*, 2nd edn, London 1977

Christianson, Paul, 'Political thought in early Stuart England', *HJ* xxx (1987), 955–70

Clark, C., 'Women's names in post-Conquest England: observations and speculations', *Speculum* lxxx (1978), 223–51

Clark, Peter, *English provincial society from the Reformation to the revolution: religion, politics and society in Kent, 1500–1640*, Hassocks 1977

Clarke, M. V., *Medieval representation and consent: a study of early parliaments in England and Ireland, with special reference to the modus tenendi parliamentum*, New York 1964

────── and V. H. Galbraith, 'The deposition of Richard II', *BJRL* xiv (1930), 125–81

Clayton, D. J., 'The "Cheshire parliament" in the fifteenth century', *Cheshire History* vi (Sept. 1980), 13–27

────── 'Peace bonds and the maintenance of law and order in late medieval England: the example of Cheshire', *BIHR* lviii (1985), 133–48

────── *The administration of the county palatine of Chester, 1442–85* (Chetham Society 3rd ser. xxxv, 1990)

Cliffe, J. T., *The Yorkshire gentry from the Reformation to the Civil War*, London 1969

Clopper, Lawrence M., 'The history and development of the Chester cycle', *Modern Philology* lxxv (1977–8), 219–46

C[okayne], G. E., *The complete peerage*, rev. Vicary Gibbs and others, London 1910–59

Collinson, Patrick, *The religion of Protestants: the Church in English society, 1559–1625*, Oxford 1982

Colls, Robert and Philip Dodd (eds), *Englishness: politics and culture, 1880–1920*, Beckenham 1986

Condon, Margaret M., 'Ruling elites in the reign of Henry VII', in Ross, *Patronage, pedigree and power*, 109–42

———— 'An anachronism with intent?: Henry VII's council ordinance of 1491/2', in Ralph A. Griffiths and James Sherborne (eds), *Kings and nobles in the later Middle Ages*, Gloucester 1986, 228–53

Conway, Agnes, *Henry VII's relations with Scotland and Ireland, 1485–1498*, Cambridge 1932

Cooke, John H., *Bibliotheca cestriensis*, Warrington–Northwich–Winsford 1904

Cornwall, J. C. K., *Wealth and society in early sixteenth-century England*, London 1988

Corrigan, Philip and Derek Sayer, *The great arch: English state formation as cultural revolution*, Oxford 1985

Cosgrove, Art, 'Parliament and the Anglo-Irish community: the declaration of 1460', in Cosgrove and McGuire, *Parliament and community*, 25–41

———— (ed.), *Medieval Ireland, 1169–1534*, Oxford 1987

———— and J. I. McGuire (eds), *Parliament and community*, Belfast 1983

Coward, B., 'The lieutenancy of Lancashire and Cheshire in the sixteenth and early seventeenth centuries', *THSLC* cxix (1969 [1968]), 39–64

———— *The Stanleys, Lords Stanley and earls of Derby, 1395–1672: the origins, wealth and power of a landowning family* (Chetham Society 3rd ser. xxx, 1983)

Crane, Thomas, 'Remarks . . . on the Brereton window', *Archaeologia* xiii (1800), 406

Creasy, Edward, *The rise and progress of the English constitution*, 10th edn, London 1868

Cressy, David, *Bonfires and bells: national memory and the Protestant calendar in Elizabethan and Stuart England*, London 1989

Cross, Claire, David Loades and J. J. Scarisbrick (eds), *Law and government under the Tudors: essays presented to Sir Geoffrey Elton Regius Professor of Modern History in the University of Cambridge on the occasion of his retirement*, Cambridge 1988

Crouch, David, 'The administration of the Norman earldom', in Thacker, *The earldom of Chester*, 69–95

Cruikshank, C. G., 'Parliamentary representation of Tournai', *EHR* lxxxiii (1968), 775–6

Crump, C. G., 'A note on the criticism of records', *BJRL* viii (1924), 140–9

Cunningham, Sean, 'Henry VII and rebellion in north-eastern England, 1485–92: bonds of allegiance and the establishment of royal authority', *NH* xxxii (1996), 42–74

———— 'Henry VII, Sir Thomas Butler and the Stanley family: political control and the assertion of crown authority in north-western England, 1471–1521', in Tim Thornton (ed.), *Social Attitudes and Political Structures in the Fifteenth Century*, Stroud 2001, forthcoming

Curry, Anne E., 'Cheshire and the royal demesne, 1399–1422', *THSLC* cxxviii (1979 [1978]), 113–38

Daly, Kathleen, 'Some seigneurial archives and chronicles in fifteenth-century France', *Peritia* ii (1983), 59–73

———— 'Mixing business with pleasure: some French royal notaries and secretaries and their histories of France, c. 1459–1509', in Christopher Allmand (ed.), *Power, culture and religion in France, c. 1350–c. 1550*, Woodbridge 1989, 99–115

Davies, C. S. L., *Peace, print and Protestantism, 1450–1558*, London 1976

————— 'England and the French war, 1557–59', in Jennifer Loach and Robert Tittler (eds), *The mid-Tudor polity, 1540–1560*, London 1980, 159–85

————— 'Popular religion and the Pilgrimage of Grace', in A. Fletcher and J. Stevenson (eds), *Order and disorder in early modern England*, Cambridge 1985, 58–91

————— 'Tournai and the English crown, 1513–1519', *HJ* xli (1998), 1–26

Davies, R. R., 'Richard II and the principality of Chester', in F. R. H. du Boulay and Caroline M. Barron (eds), *The reign of Richard II: essays in honour of May McKisack*, London 1971, 256–79

————— *Lordship and society in the march of Wales, 1282–1400*, Oxford 1978

————— *Conquest, coexistence and change: Wales, 1063–1415*, Oxford–Cardiff 1987

————— *Domination and conquest: the experience of Ireland, Scotland and Wales, 1100–1300*, Cambridge 1990

————— 'The peoples of Britain and Ireland, 1100–1400, I: identities', *TRHS* 6th ser. iv (1994), 1–20; 'II: names, boundaries and regnal solidarities', v (1995), 1–20; 'III: laws and customs', vi (1996), 1–23; 'IV: language and historical mythology', vii (1997), 1–24

————— (ed.), *The British Isles, 1100–1500: comparisons, contrasts and connections*, Edinburgh 1988

Denton, William, *England in the fifteenth century*, ed. Charles A. Denton, London 1888

Dietz, Frederick C., *English government finance, 1485–1558*, 2nd edn, London 1964

————— *English public finance, 1558–1641*, 2nd edn, London 1964

Ditmas, Edith M. R., 'The curtana or sword of mercy', *Journal of the British Archaeological Association* 3rd ser. xxix (1966), 122–33

Dockray, K. R., 'Why did fifteenth-century English gentry marry?', in Jones, *Gentry and lesser nobility*, 61–80

Dodd, A. H., 'Wales's parliamentary apprenticeship (1536–1625)', *Transactions of the Honourable Society of the Cymmrodorion* (1944 [1942]), 8–72

Dodds, Madeleine Hope and Ruth Dodds, *The Pilgrimage of Grace 1536–7 and the Exeter conspiracy, 1538*, London 1915, repr. London 1971

Donovan, Mortimer J., 'Breton lays', in J. Burke Severs (ed.), *A manual of writings in middle English, 1050–1500*, New Haven 1967

Dorling, E. E., 'The heraldry of the font at Holt', *THSLC* xxiv (1909 for 1908), 97–104

Drexler, Marjorie, 'Fluid prejudice: Scottish origin myths in the later Middle Ages', in Rosenthal and Richmond, *People, politics and community*, 60–76

Driver, J. T., *Cheshire in the later Middle Ages, 1399–1540*, Chester 1971

Dunn, Diana E. S. (ed.), *Courts, counties and the capital in the later Middle Ages*, Stroud 1996

Dutton family, *Memorials of the Duttons of Dutton in Cheshire, with notes respecting the Sherborne branch of the family*, London–Chester 1901

Dwarris, Fortunatus, 'Observations on the history of one of the old Cheshire families', *Archaeologia* xxxiii (1849), 55–83

Eagleston, A. J., *The Channel Islands under Tudor government, 1485–1642: a study in administrative history*, Cambridge 1949

Earwaker, J. P., *East Cheshire: past and present: or a history of the hundred of Maccles-field*, London 1877–80

Edwards, J. G., 'Ranulph, monk of Chester', *EHR* xxxxvii (1932), 94

Edwards, Rhoda, *The itinerary of King Richard III, 1483–1485*, London 1983

Elliott, J. H., 'A Europe of composite monarchies', *Past and Present* cxxxvii (Nov. 1992), 48–71

Ellis, Steven G., 'Henry VII and Ireland, 1491–1496', in J. F. Lydon (ed.), *England and Ireland in the later Middle Ages*, Dublin 1981, 237–54

———— 'England in the Tudor state', *HJ* xxvi (1983), 201–12

———— 'Parliament and community in Yorkist and Tudor Ireland', in Cosgrove and McGuire, *Parliament and community*, 43–68

———— *Reform and revival: English government in Ireland, 1470–1534*, London 1984

———— *Tudor Ireland: crown, community and the conflict of cultures, 1470–1603*, London 1985

———— 'Crown, community and government in the English territories, 1450–1575', *History* lxxi (1986), 187–204

———— 'Nationalist historiography and the English and Gaelic worlds in the late Middle Ages', *Irish Historical Studies* xxv (1986), 1–18

———— 'A border baron and the Tudor state: the rise and fall of Lord Dacre of the north', *HJ* xxxv (1992), 253–77

———— 'Tudor state formation and the shaping of the British Isles', in Ellis and Barber, *Conquest and union*, 40–63.

———— and S. Barber (eds), *Conquest and union: fashioning a British state, 1485–1720*, London 1995

Elton, G. R., *England under the Tudors*, London 1955, repr. London 1967

———— *Policy and police: the enforcement of the Reformation in the age of Thomas Cromwell*, Cambridge 1972

———— 'Taxation for war and peace in early Tudor England', in J. M. Winter (ed.), *War and economic development: essays in memory of David Joslin*, Cambridge 1975, 33–48

———— 'Tudor government: the points of contact, I: parliament', *TRHS* 5th ser. xxiv (1974), 183–200; 'II: council', xxv (1975), 195–211; 'III: court', xxvi (1976), 211–28

———— *Reform and reformation: England 1509–1558*, London 1977

———— 'The English parliament in the sixteenth century: estates and statutes', in Cosgrave and McGuire, *Parliament and community*, 69–95

———— 'Wales in parliament, 1542–1581', in R. R. Davies and others (eds), *Welsh society and nationhood*, Cardiff 1984, 108–21 (repr. in *Studies in Tudor and Stuart politics and government*, Cambridge 1974–92, iv. 91–108)

———— 'English national selfconsciousness and the parliament in the sixteenth century', in *Nationalismus in Vorindustrieller Zeit: Herausgegeben von Otto Dann*, Munchen 1986, 73–82

———— *The parliament of England, 1559–1581*, Cambridge 1986

———— *The English*, Oxford 1992

Emden, A. B., *A biographical register of the University of Oxford to AD 1500*, Oxford 1957–9

———— *A biographical register of the University of Oxford, AD 1501–1540*, Oxford 1974

Emsley, Kenneth and C. M. Fraser, *The courts of the county palatine of Durham from the earliest times to 1971*, Durham 1984

Everitt, Alan, *The community of Kent and the great rebellion, 1640–60*, Leicester 1966

Fenwick, George Lee, *A history of the ancient city of Chester from the earliest times*, Chester 1896

Ferguson, Arthur B., *Clio unbound: perception of the social or cultural past in renaissance England*, Durham, NC 1979

Field, William H., *Regional dynamics: the basis of electoral support in Britain*, London 1997

Figgis, J. N., *The divine right of kings*, 2nd edn, Cambridge 1922

Finley, M. I., 'Myth, memory and history', *History and Theory* iv (1965), 281–302

Flower, Robin, 'Laurence Nowell and the discovery of England in Tudor times', *Proceedings of the British Academy* xxi (1935), 47–73

Foss, Edward, *The judges of England, with sketches of their lives, and miscellaneous notices connected with the courts at Westminster, from the time of the Conquest*, London 1848–64

Foster, Andrew W., 'The struggle for parliamentary representation for Durham, c. 1600–41', in Marcombe, *Last principality*, 176–201

Foster, R. F., 'History and the Irish question', *TRHS* 5th ser. xxxiii (1983), 169–92

Fox, Alistair, 'Prophecies and politics in the reign of Henry VIII', in Alistair Fox and J. A. Guy, *Reassessing the Henrician age: humanism, politics and reform, 1500–1550*, Oxford 1986, 77–94

Frame, Robin, 'Aristocracies and the political configuration of the British Isles', in Davies, *The British Isles*, 142–59

Fraser, Constance M., 'Prerogative and bishops of Durham, 1267–1376', *EHR* lxxiv (1959), 467–76

Freeman, Edward A., *The growth of the English constitution from the earliest times*, 3rd edn, London 1898

Friedmann, Paul, *Anne Boleyn: a chapter of English history, 1527–1536*, London 1884

Fryde, E. B., D. E. Greenway, S. Porter and I. Roy (eds), *Handbook of British chronology*, 3rd edn, London 1986

Fuller, Thomas, *The history of the worthies of England*, new edn with notes by John Nichols, London 1811

Furley, O. W., 'The pope-burning processions of the late seventeenth century', *History* xliv (1959), 16–23

Gairdner, James, *History of the life and reign of Richard the Third*, new and rev. edn, Cambridge 1898

Galliou, Patrick and Michael Jones, *The Bretons*, Oxford 1991

Garrett-Goodyear, Harold, 'The Tudor revival of *quo warranto* and local contributions to state building', in Arnold, Green, Scully and White, *On the laws and customs of England*, 231–95

Gillespie, J. L., 'Richard II's Cheshire archers', *THSLC* cxxv (1975), 1–39

———— 'Richard II's archers of the crown', *Journal of British Studies* xviii (1979), 14–29

———— 'Cheshiremen at Blore Heath: a swan dive', in Rosenthal and Richmond, *People, politics and community*, 77–89

Gillingham, John, 'The context and purposes of Geoffrey of Monmouth's *History of the kings of Britain*', *Anglo-Norman Studies XIII: Proceedings of the Battle Conference 1990*, Woodbridge 1991, 99–118

Gneist, Rudolph, *The history of the English constitution*, trans. Philip A. Ashworth, 2nd edn, London 1889

Godfrey, John Thomas, *The history of the parish and priory of Lenton in the county of Nottingham*, London 1884

Goodman, Anthony, *The loyal conspiracy: the lords appellant under Richard II*, London 1971

———— *The Wars of the Roses: military activity and English society, 1452–97*, London 1981

Goring, J. J., 'The general proscription of 1522', *EHR* lxxxvi (1971), 681–705

Gransden, Antonia, 'Antiquarian studies in fifteenth-century England', *The Antiquaries' Journal* lx (1980), 75–97

Grant, Alexander, 'Scotland's "celtic fringe" in the late Middle Ages: the Macdonald lords of the Isles and the kingdom of Scotland', in Davies, *The British Isles*, 118–41

———— and Keith J. Stringer (eds), *Uniting the kingdom?: the enigma of British history*, London 1995

Gras, Norman Scott Brien, *The early English customs system: a documentary study of the institutional and economic history of the customs from the thirteenth to the sixteenth century*, Cambridge 1918

Gray, Arthur, *The priory of Saint Radegunde, Cambridge* (Cambridge Antiquarian Society octavo publications xxxi, 1898)

Gray, H. L., 'The first benevolence', in Arthur H. Cole, A. L. Dunham and N. S. B. Gras (eds), *Facts and factors in economic history: articles by former students of Edwin Francis Gay*, Cambridge, Mass. 1932, 90–113

———— 'Incomes from land in England in 1436', *EHR* xxxxix (1934), 607–39

Grazebrook, H. S., 'The barons of Dudley', *Collections for a History of Staffordshire*, ix/2 (1888)

Green, John Richard, *A short history of the English people*, London 1878

Greene, Patrick, *Norton priory: the archaeology of a medieval religious house*, Cambridge 1989

Gregson, Matthew, *Second part of a portfolio of fragments, relative to the history and antiquities of the county palatine and duchy of Lancaster*, Liverpool 1817

Griffiths, Ralph A., *The principality of Wales in the later Middle Ages: the structure and personnel of government*, I: *South Wales, 1277–1536*, Cardiff 1972

———— 'Wales and the marches in the fifteenth century', in S. B. Chrimes, C. D. Ross and R. A. Griffiths (eds), *Fifteenth century England, 1399–1509*, Manchester 1972, 145–72

———— 'Patronage, politics and the principality of Wales, 1413–1461', in Hearder and Loyn, *British government and administration*, 69–86

———— 'Richard of York and the royal household in Wales, 1449–1450', *WHR* viii (1976), 14–25

———— 'Public and private bureaucracies in England and Wales in the fifteenth century', *TRHS* 5th ser. xxx (1980), 137–59

———— *The reign of Henry VI: the exercise of royal authority, 1422–1461*, London 1981

———— 'The English realm and dominions and the king's subjects in the later

Middle Ages', in J. G. Rowe (ed.), *Aspects of late medieval government and society*, Toronto 1986, 83–105

——— *King and country: England and Wales in the fifteenth century*, London–Rio-Grande 1991, 137–59.

——— 'The provinces and the dominions in the age of the Wars of the Roses', in Sharon D. Michalove and A. Compton Reeves (eds), *Estrangement, enterprise and education in fifteenth-century England*, Stroud 1998, 1–25

——— and Roger S. Thomas, *The making of the Tudor dynasty*, Gloucester 1985

——— (ed.), *Patronage, the crown and the provinces in later medieval England*, Gloucester–Atlantic Highlands, NJ 1987

Guenée, Bernard, 'Espace et état dans la France du bas moyen âge', *Annales* xxiii (1968), 744–58

——— *States and rulers in later medieval Europe*, Oxford 1985

Gunn, S. J., 'The regime of Charles, duke of Suffolk, in north Wales and the reform of Welsh government, 1509–25', *WHR* xii (1985), 461–94

——— 'The Act of Resumption of 1515', in Daniel Williams (ed.), *Early Tudor England: proceedings of the 1987 Harlaxton symposium*, Woodbridge 1989, 87–106

——— 'Peers, commons and gentry in the Lincolnshire revolt of 1536', *Past and Present* cxxiii (May 1989), 52–79

——— 'Chivalry and the politics of the early Tudor court', in Sydney Anglo (ed.), *Chivalry in the renaissance*, Woodbridge 1990, 107–28

——— 'Henry Bourchier, earl of Essex (1472–1540)', in Bernard, *Tudor nobility*, 134–79

——— 'The courtiers of Henry VII', *EHR* cviii (1993), 23–49

——— 'State development in England and the Burgundian dominions, *c.* 1460–*c.* 1560', in *L'Angleterre et les pays bourguignons: relations et comparaisons (XVe–XVIe s.)*, Neuchatel 1995, 133–49

——— and P. G. Lindley (eds), *Cardinal Wolsey: Church, State and art*, Cambridge 1991

Guth, DeLloyd J., 'Richard III, Henry VII and the city: London politics and the "dun cowe" ', in Ralph A. Griffiths and James Sherborne (eds), *Kings and nobles in the later Middle Ages*, Gloucester–New York 1986, 185–204

Guy, J. A., 'A conciliar court of audit at work in the last months of the reign of Henry VII', *BIHR* xlix (1976), 289–95

——— *The cardinal's court: the impact of Thomas Wolsey in Star Chamber*, Hassocks 1977

——— 'Thomas More as successor to Wolsey', *Thought: A Review of Culture and Ideas* lii (1977), 275–92

——— 'The development of equitable jurisdictions, 1450–1550', in E. W. Ives and A. H. Manchester (eds), *Law, litigants and the legal profession: papers presented to the fourth British legal history conference*, London 1983, 80–6

——— *The court of Star Chamber and its records to the reign of Elizabeth I* (PRO Handbooks xxi, 1985)

——— *Tudor England*, Oxford 1988

——— 'Wolsey and the parliament of 1523', in Cross, Loades and Scarisbrick, *Law and government*, 1–18

——— 'Wolsey and the Tudor polity', in Gunn and Lindley, *Cardinal Wolsey*, 54–75

Gwyn, Peter, *The king's cardinal: the rise and fall of Thomas Wolsey*, London 1990

Hadfield, Andrew, 'Briton and Scythian: Tudor representations of Irish origins', *Irish Historical Studies* xxviii (1993), 391–408

———— *Literature, politics and national identity: Reformation to Renaissance*, Cambridge 1994

———— 'From English to British literature: John Lyly's *Euphues* and Edmund Spenser's *The Faerie Queene*', in Brendan Bradshaw and Peter Roberts (eds), *British consciousness and identity: the making of Britain, 1534–1707*, Cambridge 1998, 140–58

Haigh, C. A., 'A mid-Tudor ecclesiastical official: the curious career of George Wilmesley', *THSLC* cxxii (1971 [1970]), 1–24

———— *Reformation and resistance in Tudor Lancashire*, Cambridge 1975

Hallam, Henry, *The constitutional history of England from the accession of Henry VII. to the death of George II.*, 4th edn, London 1842

Haller, William, *Foxe's Book of Martyrs and the elect nation*, London 1963

Hampton, W. E., 'The White Rose under the first Tudors, I', *The Ricardian* vii (97) (June 1987), 414–20

Hanham, Alison, *Richard III and his early historians*, Oxford 1975

Hanmer, in the county of Flint: some account of the parish church, and its destruction by fire, repr. from *Eddowes's Shrewsbury Journal*, Shrewsbury 1889

Hardacre, P. H., 'The earl marshal, the heralds, and the House of Commons, 1604–1641', *International Review of Social History* ii (1957), 106–25

Harding, Alan (ed.), *Law-making and law-makers in British history: papers presented to the Edinburgh legal history conference*, London 1980

Harris, B. E., 'Ranulph III, earl of Chester', *Journal of the Chester Archaeological Society* lviii (1975), 99–114

———— 'A Cheshire parliament', *Sheaf* 5th ser. i (1976–7), 1–2

———— 'Cover illustration: the Cheshire "parliament"', *Cheshire History* ii (1978), 57–8

———— and D. J. Clayton, 'Criminal procedure in Cheshire in the mid-fifteenth century', *THSLC* cxxviii (1979 [1978]), 161–72

Harrison, C. J., 'The petition of Edmund Dudley', *EHR* lxxxvii (1972), 82–99

Harriss, G. L., 'Aids, loans and benevolences', *HJ* vi (1963), 1–19

———— *King, parliament and public finance to 1369*, Oxford 1975

———— 'Theory and practice in royal taxation: some observations', *EHR* lxxxvii (1982), 811–19

Hasler, P. W., *The House of Commons, 1558–1603*, London 1981

Hastings, Margaret, *The court of common pleas in fifteenth century England: a study in legal administration and procedure*, Ithaca, NY 1947

Hawkyard, A. D. K., 'The enfranchisement of constituencies, 1509–1558', *Parliamentary History* x/1 (1991), 1–26

Hay, Denys, 'The use of the term "Great Britain" in the Middle Ages', *Proceedings of the Society of Antiquaries of Scotland* lxxxix (1958 [1955–6]), 55–66

———— 'England, Scotland and Europe: the problem of the frontier', *TRHS* 5th ser. xxv (1975), 77–91

Head, D. M. 'Henry VIII's Scottish policy: a reassessment', *Scottish Historical Review* lxi (1982), 1–24

Hearder, H. and H. R. Loyn (eds), *British government and administration: studies presented to S. B. Chrimes*, Cardiff 1974

Heath, Peter, 'The medieval archdeaconry and Tudor bishopric of Chester', *Journal of Ecclesiastical History* xx (1969), 243–52

────── 'The treason of Geoffrey Blythe, bishop of Coventry and Lichfield, 1503–1531', *BIHR* xlii (1969), 101–9

Hechter, Michael, *Internal colonialism: the celtic fringe in British national development, 1536–1966*, London 1975

Helgerson, Richard, *Forms of nationhood: the Elizabethan writing of England*, Chicago–London 1992

Henneman, John B., Jr, 'The Black Death and royal taxation in France, 1347–1351', *Speculum* xliii (1968), 405–28

────── *Royal taxation in fourteenth-century France: the captivity and ransom of John II, 1356–1370* (Memoirs of the American Philosophical Society cxvi, 1976)

Herbert, Ailsa, 'Herefordshire, 1413–61: some aspects of society and public order', in Griffiths, *Patronage, the crown and the provinces*, 103–22

Hewitt, H. J., *Medieval Cheshire: an economic and social history of Cheshire in the reign of the three Edwards* (Chetham Society n.s. lxxxviii, 1929)

────── *The Black Prince's expedition of 1355–1357*, Manchester 1958

────── *The organisation of war under Edward III*, Manchester 1966

────── *Cheshire under the three Edwards*, Chester 1967

Hicks, M. A., 'The changing role of the Wydevilles in Yorkist politics to 1483', in Ross, *Patronage, pedigree and power*, 60–86

────── 'Attainder, resumption and coercion, 1461–1529', *Parliamentary History* iii (1984), 15–31

────── 'The Yorkshire rebellion of 1489 reconsidered', *NH* xxii (1986), 39–62

────── 'The 1468 Statute of Livery', *Historical Research* lxiv (1991), 15–28

Hogrefe, Pearl, *The life and times of Sir Thomas Elyot Englishman*, Ames, Iowa 1967

Holdsworth, William, *A history of English law*, 7th edn, ed. A. L. Goodhart and H. G. Hanbury, London 1956

Holmes, Clive, 'The county community in Stuart historiography', *Journal of British Studies* xix (1980), 54–73

Holt, J. C., *Robin Hood*, London 1982

Horrox, Rosemary, 'Urban patronage and patrons in the fifteenth century', in Griffiths, *Patronage, the crown and the provinces*, 145–66

────── *Richard III: a study in service*, Cambridge 1991

Hosker, P., 'The Stanleys of Lathom and ecclesiastical patronage in the north-west of England during the fifteenth century', *NH* xviii (1982), 212–29

Hughes, Ann L., 'Warwickshire on the eve of the civil war: a "county community"?', *Midland History* vii (1982), 42–72

Hunnisett, R. F., *The medieval coroner*, Cambridge 1961

────── 'The reliability of inquisitions as historical evidence', in D. Bullough and R. L. Storey (eds), *The study of medieval records*, Oxford 1971, 206–35

Hurnard, Naomi D., 'The Anglo-Norman franchises', *EHR* lxiv (1949), 289–327

Husain, B. M. C., *Cheshire under the Norman earls 1066–1237*, Chester 1973

Hutchinson, W., *The history of the county palatine of Durham*, Durham 1823

Ingram, Martin, *Church courts, sex and marriage, 1570–1640*, Cambridge 1987, paperback edn 1990

Ives, E. W., 'Patronage at the court of Henry VIII: the case of Sir Ralph Egerton of Ridley', *BJRL* lii (1969–70), 346–74

———— 'Court and county palatine in the reign of Henry VIII: the career of William Brereton of Malpas', *THSLC* cxxiii (1971), 1–38

———— 'Faction at the court of Henry VIII: the fall of Anne Boleyn', *History* lvii (1972), 169–88

———— 'Crime, sanctuary and royal authority under Henry VIII: the exemplary sufferings of the Savage family', in Arnold, Green, Scully and White, *Of the laws and customs of England*, 296–320

———— *Anne Boleyn*, Oxford 1986

———— 'The fall of Wolsey', in Gunn and Lindley, *Cardinal Wolsey*, 286–315

———— 'Stress, faction and ideology in early Tudor England', *HJ* xxxiv (1991), 193–202

Jack, Sybil, 'Monastic lands in Leicestershire and their administration on the eve of the dissolution', *Transactions of the Leicestershire Archaeological and Historical Society* xli (1965–6), 9–40

James, M. E., *Family, lineage and civil society: a study of society, politics and mentality in the Durham region, 1500–1640*, Oxford 1974

———— *Society, politics and culture: studies in early modern England*, Cambridge 1986

Jansen, Sharon L., *Political protest and prophecy under Henry VIII*, Woodbridge 1991

———— *The Welles anthology: MS Rawlinson C.813. A critical edition*, Binghamton, NY 1991

Jarman, A. O. H., 'Wales and the Council of Constance', *Bulletin of the Board for Celtic Studies* xiv (1950–2), 220–2

Jenkins, Philip, *A history of modern Wales, 1536–1990*, London 1992

Jenkinson, Hilary, 'Plea rolls of the medieval county courts', *HJ* i (1923), 103–7

Jewell, Helen M., *English local administration in the Middle Ages*, Newton Abbot–New York 1972

Jones, Alexander, *The Cymry of '76 or Welshmen and their descendants of the American revolution*, New York 1855

Jones, D. Cyril, 'The Bulkeleys of Beaumaris, 1440–1547', *Transactions of the Anglesey Antiquarian Society and Field Club* (1961), 1–20

Jones, Douglas, *The Church in Chester, 1300–1540* (Chetham Society 3rd ser. vii, 1957)

Jones, J. Gwynfor, 'Government and the Welsh community: the north-east borderland in the fifteenth century', in Hearder and Loyn, *British government and administration*, 55–68

———— *Wales and the Tudor state: government, religious change and the social order, 1534–1603*, Cardiff 1989

Jones, Michael, ' "Mon Pais et ma nation": Breton identity in the fourteenth century', in C. T. Allmand (ed.), *War, literature and politics in the late Middle Ages*, Liverpool 1976, 144–68

———— ' "Bons Bretons et bons Francoys": the language and meaning of treason in later medieval France', *TRHS* 5th ser. xxxii (1982), 91–112

———— (ed.), *Gentry and lesser nobility in later medieval Europe*, Gloucester 1986

Jones, Michael K., 'Richard III and the Stanleys', in Rosemary Horrox (ed.), *Richard III and the north*, Hull 1986, 27–50

———— 'Sir William Stanley of Holt: politics and family allegiance in the late fifteenth century', *WHR* xiv (1988), 1–22

———— and Malcolm G. Underwood, *The king's mother: Lady Margaret Beaufort, countess of Richmond and Derby*, Cambridge, 1992

Jones, W. J., 'The exchequer of Chester in the last years of Elizabeth I', in Slavin, *Tudor men and institutions*, 123–70

———— 'Palatine performance in the seventeenth century', in Peter Clark, Alan G. R. Smith and Nicholas Tyacke (eds), *The English commonwealth, 1547–1640: essays in politics and society presented to Joel Hurstfield*, Leicester 1979, 189–204

Jordan, W. K., *The charities of London, 1480–1660: the aspirations and the achievements of the urban society*, London 1960

———— *Edward VI: the young king: the protectorship of the duke of Somerset*, London 1968

———— *Edward VI: the threshold of power: the dominance of the duke of Northumberland*, London 1970

Keating, Michael, *State and regional nationalism: territorial politics and the European state*, Brighton 1988

Keeler, Laura, 'The *Historia regum Britanniae* and four medieval chroniclers', *Speculum* xxi (1946), 24–37

Keen, Maurice, 'Chivalry, heralds and history', in R. H. C. Davies and J. M. Wallace-Hadrill (eds), *The writing of history in the Middle Ages: essays presented to Richard William Southern*, Oxford 1981, 393–414

———— *English society in the later Middle Ages, 1348–1500*, London 1990

Kendrick, T. D., *British antiquity*, London 1950

Ker, N. R., *Medieval manuscripts in British libraries*, London 1969–

Kerhervé, J., 'Aux Origines d'un sentiment national: les chroniquers Bretons de la fin du moyen âge, *Bulletin de la société archaeologique du Finistère* cviii (1980), 165–206

Kerly, D. M., *An historical sketch of the equitable jurisdiction of the court of chancery*, Cambridge 1890

Kingsford, C. L., *Prejudice and promise in XVth century England: the Ford lectures, 1923–24*, Oxford 1925

Kinvig, R. H., *The Isle of Man: a social, cultural and political history*, Liverpool 1975

Kitching, Christopher, 'The Durham palatinate and the courts of Westminster under the Tudors', in Marcombe, *Last principality*, 49–70

Koebner, Richard, ' "The imperial crown of this realm": Henry VIII, Constantine the Great and Polydore Vergil', *BIHR* xxvi (1953), 29–52

Lander, J. R., 'Bonds, coercion and fear: Henry VII and the peerage', in J. G. Rowe and W. H. Stockdale (eds), *Florilegium historiale: essays presented to Wallace K. Ferguson*, Toronto 1971, 327–67 (repr. in his *Crown and nobility*, 267–300)

———— 'Council, administration and councillors, 1461–85', in *Crown and nobility*, 309–20

———— *Crown and nobility, 1450–1509*, London 1976

———— *Conflict and stability in fifteenth-century England*, 3rd edn, London 1977

———— *English justices of the peace, 1461–1509*, Gloucester–Wolfeboro, NH 1989

Lapsley, Gaillard Thomas, *The county palatine of Durham: a study in constitutional history*, London 1900

Lawton, David A., 'Scottish Field: alliterative verse and Stanley encomium in the Percy folio', *Leeds Studies in English* n.s. x (1978), 42–57

Leckie, R. William, Jr, *The passage of dominion: Geoffrey of Monmouth and the periodisation of insular history in the twelfth century*, Toronto 1991

Legge, M. D., *Anglo-Norman literature and its background*, Oxford 1963

Lehmberg, S. E., *The Reformation Parliament, 1529–36*, Cambridge 1970

────── 'Sir Thomas Audley: a soul as black as marble?', in Slavin, *Tudor men and institutions*, 3–31

────── *The later parliaments of Henry VIII, 1536–1547*, Cambridge 1977

Lenman, B., 'The teaching of Scottish history in the Scottish universities', *Scottish Historical Review* lii (1973), 165–90

Levy, F. J., *Tudor historical thought*, San Marino, California 1967

Lewis, H. Elvet, 'Welsh Catholic poetry of the fifteenth century', *Transactions of the Honorable Society of the Cymmrodorion* (1913 [1911–12]), 23–41

Lewis, P. S., 'War propaganda and historiography in fifteenth-century France and England', *TRHS* 5th ser. xv (1965), 1–21

Loach, Jennifer, *Parliament and the crown in the reign of Mary Tudor*, Oxford 1986

────── 'Parliament: a "new air"?', in Christopher Coleman and David Starkey (eds), *Revolution reassessed: revisions in the history of Tudor government and administration*, Oxford 1986, 117–34

Loades, D. M., 'The authorship and publication of "The copye of a letter sent by John Bradforth to the right honorable lordes the erles of Arundel, Darbie, Shrewsbury and Penbroke" ', *Transactions of the Cambridge Bibliographical Society* iii (1959–63), 155–60

────── *The Oxford martyrs*, 1970, 2nd edn, Bangor 1992

────── 'The dissolution of the diocese of Durham, 1553–4', in Marcombe, *Last principality*, 101–16

────── *The reign of Mary Tudor*, 2nd edn, London 1991

────── *Mary Tudor: a life*, paperback edn, Oxford 1992

────── *Power in Tudor England*, Basingstoke–London 1997

Longstaffe, W. Hylton Dyer, 'The banner and cross of Saint Cuthbert', *Archæologia Æliana* 2nd ser. ii (1858), 51–65

────── 'Cardinal Wolsey's instructions to his officers at Durham', *Archæologia Æliana* 2nd ser. ii (1858), 39–40

Loomis, Roger Sherman, 'Edward I, Arthurian enthusiast', *Speculum* xxviii (1953), 114–27

Lowe, D. E., 'The council of the prince of Wales and the decline of the Herbert family during the second reign of Edward IV (1471–1483)', *Bulletin of the Board of Celtic Studies* xxvii/2 (1977), 278–97

Lowry, M. J. C., 'Caxton, St Winifred and the Lady Margaret Beaufort', *The Library* 6th ser. v (1983), 101–17

Luttrell, C. A., 'Three north-west midland manuscripts', *Neophilologus* xlii (1958), 38–50

Lydon, J. F., *The lordship of Ireland in the Middle Ages*, Dublin 1972

────── *Ireland in the later Middle Ages*, Dublin 1973

Lysons, Daniel and Samuel Lysons, *Magna Britannia*, London 1810, ii/2

Mabrey, Ann, 'Two taxations in Wirral', *Cheshire History* vi (1980), 28–46

MacCulloch, Diarmaid, *Suffolk and the Tudors: politics and religion in an English county, 1500–1600*, Oxford 1986

────── *The later Reformation in England, 1547–1603*, Basingstoke–London 1990

McFarlane, K. B., 'Parliament and "bastard feudalism" ', *TRHS* 4th ser. xxiv (1944), 53–79 (repr. in McFarlane, *England in the fifteenth century*, 1–21)

—— 'Bastard feudalism', *BIHR* xx (1945), 161–80 (repr. in McFarlane, *England in the fifteenth century*, 23–43)

—— 'The Wars of the Roses', *Proceedings of the British Academy* i (1964), 87–119 (repr. in McFarlane, *England in the fifteenth century*, 231–61)

—— *The nobility of later medieval England*, Oxford 1973

—— *England in the fifteenth century*, intro. G. L. Harriss, London 1981

—— *Letters to friends, 1940–1966*, ed. G. L. Hariss with a memoir by Karl Leyser, Oxford 1997

McKisack, May, *Medieval history in the Tudor age*, Oxford 1971

McNiven, Peter, 'The Cheshire rising of 1400', *BJRL* lii (1970), 375–96

—— 'The men of Cheshire and the rebellion of 1403', *THSLC* cxxix (1980), 1–29

Maddern, Philippa C., *Violence and social order: East Anglia, 1422–1442*, Oxford 1992

Maddicott, J. R., 'The county community and the making of public opinion in fourteenth-century England', *TRHS* 5th ser. xxviii (1978), 27–43

Maitland, F. W., *The constitutional history of England*, Cambridge 1908

—— *Equity: a course of lectures*, ed. A. H. Chaytor and W. J. Whittaker, rev. John Brunyate, Cambridge 1936

Maltby, William S., *The black legend in England: the development of anti-Spanish sentiment, 1558–1660*, Durham, NC 1971

Mann, Michael, *The sources of social power*, I: *A history of power from the beginning to AD 1760*, Cambridge 1986

A manual of the writings in Middle English 1050–1500, ed. J. Burke Severs and Albert E. Hartung, New Haven, Conn. 1967–

Marchant, Ronald A., *The church under the law: justice, administration and discipline in the diocese of York, 1560–1640*, Cambridge 1969

Marcombe, David, 'A rude and heady people: the local community and the rebellion of the northern earls', in Marcombe, *Last principality*, 117–51

—— (ed.), *The last principality: politics, religion and society in the bishopric of Durham, 1494–1660*, Nottingham 1987

Marsh, Deborah, ' "I see by sizt of evidence": information gathering in late medieval Cheshire', in Dunn, *Courts, counties and the capital*, 71–92

Mason, Emma, 'Legends of the Beauchamps' ancestors: the use of baronial propaganda in medieval England', *Journal of Medieval History* x (1984), 25–40

Mason, Roger A., 'The Reformation and Anglo-British imperialism', in Roger A. Mason (ed.), *Scots and Britons: Scottish political thought and union of 1603*, Cambridge 1994, 161–86

Mayer, T. F., 'Tournai and tyranny: imperial kingship and critical humanism', *HJ* xxxiv (1991), 257–77

—— 'On the road to 1534: the occupation of Tournai and Henry VIII's theory of sovereignty', in Dale Hoak (ed.), *Tudor political culture*, Cambridge 1995, 11–30

Medley, Dudley Julius, *A student's manual of English constitutional history*, 6th edn, Oxford 1925

Merriman, James Douglas, *The flower of kings: a study of the Arthurian legend in Britain between 1485 and 1835*, Manhattan, Wichita 1973

Merriman, M., 'James Henrisoun and "Great Britain": British union and the Scottish commonweal', in Roger A. Mason (ed.), *Scotland and England, 1286–1815*, Edinburgh 1987, 85–112

Metzger, Franz, 'The last phase of the medieval chancery', in Harding, *Law-making and law-makers*, 79–89

Miller, Helen, *Henry VIII and the English nobility*, Oxford 1986

Mills, David, 'The Chester mystery plays: truth and tradition', in Dunn, *Courts, counties and the capital*, 1–26

Mitchell, Sydney Knox, *Taxation in medieval England*, ed. Sidney Painter, New Haven, Conn. 1951

Mitchison, Rosalind, *A history of Scotland*, London 1970

Moore, A. W., *A history of the Isle of Man*, London 1900, repr. Douglas, Isle of Man 1992

Moreton, C. E., *The Townshends and their world: gentry, law, and land in Norfolk, c. 1450–1551*, Oxford 1992

Morgan, D. A. L., 'The king's affinity in the polity of Yorkist England', *TRHS* 5th ser. xxiii (1973), 1–25

———— 'The individual style of the English gentleman', in Jones, *Gentry and lesser nobility*, 15–35

Morgan, Hiram, 'British policies before the British state', in Bradshaw and Morrill, *The British problem*, 66–88

Morgan, Philip, *War and society in medieval Cheshire, 1277–1403* (Chetham Society 3rd ser. xxiv, 1987)

Morgan, Prys, 'Elis Gruffudd of Gronant – Tudor chronicler extraordinary', *Flintshire Historical Society Publications* xxv (1971–2), 9–20

Morrill, J. S., *Cheshire, 1630–1660: county government and society during the English revolution*, London 1974

———— *The Cheshire grand jury, 1625–1659*, Leicester 1976

———— *The nature of the English civil war*, London 1993

———— 'The fashioning of Britain', in Ellis and Barber, *Conquest and union*, 8–39

———— 'The British problem, c. 1534–1707', in Bradshaw and Morrill, *The British problem*, 1–38

Morris, Rupert H., *Chester in the Plantagenet and Tudor reigns*, Chester [1894]

Mortimer, W. W., 'The Norman earls of Chester', *THSLC* 1st ser. iv (1851–2), 85–97

Morton, A. L., *A people's history of England*, London 1938

Murray, K. M. E., *The constitutional history of the Cinque Ports*, Manchester 1935

Myers, A. R., 'Tudor Chester', *Journal of the Chester Archaeological Society* lxiii (1980), 43–57

Neale, J. E., 'November 17th', in his *Essays in Elizabethan history*, London 1958, 9–20

le Neve, John (comp. B. Jones), *Fasti ecclesiae Anglicanae, 1300–1541*, X: *Coventry and Lichfield diocese*, London 1964

Neville, Cynthia J., *Violence, custom and law: the Anglo-Scottish border lands in the later Middle Ages*, Edinburgh 1998

Newman, Gerald, *The rise of English nationalism: a cultural history, 1740–1830*, 1987, rev. edn, London 1997

Nicholson, Graham, 'The Act of Appeals and the English Reformation', in Cross, Loades and Scarisbrick, *Law and government*, 19–30

Nitze, W. A., 'The exhumation of King Arthur at Glastonbury', *Speculum* ix (1934), 355–61

Noyes, T. Herbert, Jr, 'Notices of the family of Newton', *Sussex Archaeological Collections* ix (1857), 312–42

Ohlmeyer, Jane H., *Civil war and restoration in the three Stuart kingdoms: the career of Randal MacDonnell, marquis of Antrim, 1609–1683*, Cambridge 1993

Ormerod, George, 'A memoir of the Lancashire house of Le Noreis or Norres, and of its Speke branch in particular, &c., with notices of its connexion with military transactions at Flodden, Edinburgh and Musselburgh', *THSLC* ii 1850 [1849], 138–82

——— *The history of the county palatine and city of Chester*, 2nd edn rev. and enlarged by Thomas Helsby, London 1882

Ormrod, W. M., 'An experiment in taxation: the English parish subsidy of 1371', *Speculum* lxviii (1988), 58–82

——— 'The origins of the *sub pena* writ', *Historical Research* lxi (1988), 11–20

Owen, Mr, ' "Saynt Maholde and Saynt Michell" ', *Proceedings of the Isle of Man Natural History and Antiquarian Society* n.s. ii (1923–6), 257–61

Painter, Sidney, *Studies in the history of the English feudal baronage*, Baltimore 1943

Palliser, D. M., *The age of Elizabeth: England under the later Tudors, 1547–1603*, 1983, new edn, London 1992

Palmer, Robert C., 'County year book reports: the professional lawyer in the medieval county court', *EHR* lxxxxi (1976), 776–801

Parmiter, Geoffrey de C., *The king's great matter: a study of anglo-papal relations, 1527–34*, London 1967

Parsons, A. E., 'The Trojan legend in England: some instances of its application to the politics of the times', *The Modern Language Review* xxiv (1929), 253–64

le Patourel, John, *The medieval administration of the Channel Islands, 1199–1399*, London 1937

——— 'The Plantagenet dominions', *History* i (1965), 289–308

——— *The Norman empire*, Oxford 1976

——— 'Is northern history a subject?', *NH* xii (1976), 1–15

Patterson, Annabel, *Reading Holinshed's chronicles*, Chicago–London 1994

Pawlisch, Hans S., *Sir John Davies and the conquest of Ireland: a study in legal imperialism*, Cambridge 1985

Payling, Simon, *Political society in Lancastrian England: the greater gentry of Nottinghamshire*, Oxford 1991

Payton, Philip, *The making of modern Cornwall: historical experience and the persistence of 'difference'*, Redruth [1992]

Petit-Dutaillis, Charles and George Lefebvre, *Studies and notes supplementary to Stubbs' Constitutional history*, Manchester 1930

Pevsner, Nikolaus and Edward Hubbard, *Cheshire*, Harmondsworth 1971

Pierce, Hazel, 'The king's cousin: the life, career and Welsh connection of Sir Richard Pole, 1458–1504', *WHR* xix (1998), 187–225

Piggott, Stuart, 'William Camden and his Britannia', *Proceedings of the British Academy* xxxvii (1951), 199–217

Plott, Robert, *The natural history of Stafford-shire*, Oxford 1686

Pocock, J. G. A., 'Time, institutions and action: an essay on traditions and their understanding', in P. King and B. C. Parekh (eds), *Politics and experience*, Cambridge 1968, 209–37

———— 'British history: a plea for a new subject', *Journal of Modern History* xlvii (1975), 601–28

———— 'England', in Orest Ranum (ed.), *National consciousness, history, and political culture in early-modern Europe*, Baltimore–London 1975, 98–117

———— *The ancient constitution and the feudal law: a study of English historical thought in the seventeenth century: a reissue with a retrospect*, Cambridge 1987

Pollard, A. F., *Wolsey*, illustrated edn, London 1953

Pollard, A. J., *North-eastern England during the Wars of the Roses: lay society, war, and politics, 1450–1500*, Oxford 1990

———— 'The crown and the palatinate of Durham, 1437–94', in A. J. Pollard (ed.), *The north of England in the age of Richard III*, Stroud 1996, 67–87

Post, J. B., 'Equitable resorts before 1450', in E. W. Ives and A. H. Manchester (eds), *Law, litigants and the legal profession: papers presented to the fourth British legal history conference*, London 1983, 68–79

Postles, D. A., 'The baptismal name in thirteenth-century England: processes and naming patterns', *Medieval Prosopography* xiii/2 (1992), 1–52

Pronay, Nicholas, 'The chancellor, the chancery, and the council at the end of the fifteenth century', in Hearder and Loyn, *British government and administration*, 87–103

Pugh, T. B., *The marcher lordships of South Wales, 1415–1536*, Cardiff 1963

———— 'Henry VII and the English nobility', in Bernard, *Tudor nobility*, 49–101

———— and C. D. Ross, 'The English baronage and the income tax of 1436', *BIHR* xxvi (1953), 1–28

Quintrell, B. W., 'Government in perspective: Lancashire and the privy council, 1570–1640', *THSLC* cxxxi (1982[1981]), 35–62

Radding, Charles M., 'The estates of Normandy and the revolts in the towns at the beginning of the reign of Charles VI', *Speculum* xlvii (1972), 79–90

Rae, Thomas I., *The administration of the Scottish frontier, 1513–1603*, Edinburgh 1966

Ramsey, James H., *Lancaster and York: a century of English history (AD 1399–1485)*, Oxford 1892

Rastall, G. R., 'The minstrel court in medieval England', *Proceedings of the Leeds Philosophical and Literary Society (Literary and Historical Section)* xviii (Apr. 1982–Dec. 1982), pt 1, 96–105

Rawcliffe, Carole, 'Baronial councils in the later Middle Ages', in Ross, *Patronage, pedigree and power*, 87–108

———— 'The great lord as peacekeeper: arbitration by English noblemen and their councils in the later Middle Ages', in J. A. Guy and H. G. Beale (eds), *Law and change in English history*, London 1984

Redworth, Glyn, *In defence of the Church Catholic: the life of Stephen Gardiner*, Oxford 1990

Reid, R. R., *The king's Council in the North*, London 1921

Renaud, Frank, *Contributions towards a history of the parish of Prestbury in Cheshire* (Chetham Society xcvii, 1876)

———— 'Memorial brasses of Sir Edward Fitton and Dean Robert Sutton in St Patrick's, Dublin', *Transactions of the Lancashire and Cheshire Antiquarian Society* xi (1893), 34–51

Reynolds, Susan, 'Medieval *origines gentium* and the community of the realm', *History* lxviii (1983), 375–90

Richards, Raymond, *Old Cheshire churches: a survey of their history, fabric and furniture with records of the older monuments*, rev., enlarged edn, Didsbury 1973

Richmond, Colin, 'The Pastons revisited: marriage and the family in fifteenth-century England', *BIHR* lviii (1985), 25–36

────── 'The Sulyard papers: the rewards of a small family archive', in Daniel Williams (ed.), *England in the fifteenth century: proceedings of the 1986 Harlaxton symposium*, Woodbridge 1987, 199–228

────── *The Paston family in the fifteenth century: the first phase*, Cambridge 1990

Robbins, Keith, *Great Britain: identities, institutions and the idea of Britishness*, London–New York 1998

Robbins, Rossell Hope, 'A Gawain epigone', *Modern Language Notes* lviii (1943), 361–6

────── 'The poems of Humfrey Newton esquire 1466–1536', *Publications of the Modern Language Association of America* lxv (1960), 249–81

Roberts, P. R., 'The union with England and the identity of "Anglican" Wales', *TRHS* 5th ser. xxii (1972), 49–70

────── 'Wales and England after the Tudor "union": crown, principality and parliament, 1543–1624', in Cross, Loades and Scarisbrick, *Law and government*, 111–38

────── 'The English crown, the principality of Wales and the Council in the Marches, 1534–1641', in Bradshaw and Morrill, *The British problem*, 118–47

Robertson, Mary L., ' "The art of the possible": Thomas Cromwell's management of west country government', *HJ* xxxii (1989), 793–816

Robinson, W. R. B., 'The marcher lords of Wales 1525–31', *Bulletin of the Board for Celtic Studies* xxvi (1974–6), 342–52

────── 'The Tudor revolution in Welsh government, 1536–1543: its effects on gentry participation', *EHR* ciii (1988), 1–20

────── 'Henry VIII's household in the fifteen-twenties: the Welsh connection', *Historical Research* lxviii (1995), 173–90

Rosenthal, Joel and Colin Richmond (eds), *People, politics and community in the later Middle Ages*, Gloucester–New York 1987

Ross, C. D., *Edward IV*, London 1974

────── *Richard III*, London 1981

────── 'Rumour, propaganda and popular opinion during the Wars of the Roses', in Griffiths, *Patronage, the crown and the provinces*, 15–32

────── (ed.), *Patronage, pedigree, and power in later medieval England*, Gloucester–Totowa, NJ 1979

Round, J. H., *Peerage and pedigree: studies in peerage law and family history*, London 1910

Rowe, B. J. H., 'Discipline in the Norman garrisons under Bedford, 1422–1435', *EHR* xlvi (1931), 194–208

────── 'The estates of Normandy under the duke of Bedford, 1422–1435', *EHR* xlvi (1931), 551–78

Rowse, A. L., *Tudor Cornwall: portrait of a society*, new edn, London 1969

Russell, Conrad, 'The British problem and the English civil war', *History* lxxii (1987), 395–415

────── *The fall of the British monarchies, 1637–1642*, Oxford 1992

Sahlins, P., *Boundaries: the making of France and Spain in the Pyrenees*, Berkeley 1989

Saul, Nigel, *Knights and esquires: the Gloucestershire gentry in the fourteenth century*, Oxford 1981

———— 'Conflict and consensus in English local society', in John Taylor and Wendy Childs (eds), *Politics and crisis in fourteenth century England*, Gloucester–New Hampshire 1990, 38–58

Scammell, Jean, 'The origin and limitations of the liberty of Durham', *EHR* lxxxi (1966), 449–73

Scarisbrick, J. J., *Henry VIII*, London 1968

Scattergood, V. J., *Politics and poetry in the fifteenth century*, London 1971

Schofield, R. S., 'Taxation and the political limits of the Tudor state', in Cross, Loades and Scarisbrick, *Law and government*, 227–55

Sharpe, J. A., *Crime in early modern England, 1550–1750*, London 1984

Sharpe, Kevin, 'The earl of Arundel, his circle and the opposition to the duke of Buckingham, 1618–1628', in Kevin Sharpe (ed.), *Faction and parliament: essays on early Stuart history*, paperback edn, London 1985, 209–44

Shaw, R. Cunliffe, *The royal forest of Lancaster*, Preston 1956

Shaw, Stebbing, *The history and antiquities of Staffordshire*, London 1798

Shaw, William A., *The knights of England*, London 1906

Skeel, Caroline A. J., *The Council in the Marches of Wales: a study in local government during the sixteenth and seventeenth centuries*, Cambridge 1904

Slavin, Arthur J. (ed.), *Tudor men and institutions: studies in English law and government*, Baton Rouge 1972

Smith, A. Hassell, *County and court: government and politics in Norfolk, 1558–1603*, Oxford 1974

Smith, Anthony D., *The ethnic origin of nations*, Oxford 1986

Smith, J. Beverley, 'Crown and community in the principality of north Wales in the reign of Henry Tudor', *WHR* iii (1966–7), 145–71

———— 'The legal position of Wales in the Middle Ages', in Harding, *Law-making and law-makers*, 21–53

Smith, L. B., 'The Arundel charters in the lordship of Chirk in the fourteenth century', *Bulletin of the Board for Celtic Studies* xxiii (1969), 153–66

Smith, R. B., *Land and politics in the England of Henry VIII: the West Riding of Yorkshire, 1530–46*, Oxford 1970

Smith-Bannister, Scott, *Names and naming patterns in England, 1538–1700*, Oxford–New York 1997

Somerville, R., 'Henry VII's "Council Learned in the Law" ', *EHR* liv (1939), 427–42

———— *History of the duchy of Lancaster*, London 1953

———— 'The palatine courts in Lancashire', in Harding, *Law-making and law-makers*, 54–63

Southworth, J., *The English medieval minstrel*, Woodbridge 1989

Stafford, Pauline, *Queens, concubines and dowagers: the king's wife in the early Middle Ages*, London 1983

———— *Unification and conquest: a political and social history of England in the tenth and eleventh centuries*, London 1989

Starkey, David, 'Representation through intimacy: a study in the symbolism of monarchy and court office in early modern England', in I. Lewis (ed.), *Symbols and sentiments: cross cultural studies in symbolism*, London 1977, 187–224

———— 'The age of the household: politics, society and the arts, *c.* 1350–*c.* 1550', in Stephen Medcalf (ed.), *The later Middle Ages*, London 1981, 225–90

———— *The reign of Henry VIII: personalities and politics*, London 1985

———— 'Intimacy and innovation: the rise of the privy chamber, 1485–1547', in Starkey and others, *English court*, 71–118

———— and others (eds), *The English court from the Wars of the Roses to the Civil War*, London–New York 1987

Steel, Anthony, *Richard II*, Cambridge 1941

———— *The receipt of the exchequer, 1377–1485*, Cambridge 1954

Steiner, B. C., 'Maryland's first courts', *Annual Report of the American Historical Association*, i, Washington 1902 [1901]

Stenton, Frank, *The first century of English feudalism, 1066–1166*, 2nd edn, Oxford 1961

Stephen, Leslie and S. Lee (eds), *Dictionary of national biography*, repr. London 1949–50

Storey, R. L., 'The wardens of the marches of England towards Scotland, 1377–1489', *EHR* lxxii (1957), 593–615

———— *Thomas Langley and the bishopric of Durham, 1406–1437*, London 1961

———— *The reign of Henry VII*, London 1968

———— 'Gentleman-bureaucrats', in Cecil H. Clough (ed.), *Profession, vocation and culture in later medieval England*, Liverpool 1982, 90–129

Strayer, Joseph R., 'France: the holy land, the chosen people and the most Christian king', in Theodore K. Rabb and Jerrold E. Seigel (eds), *Action and conviction in early modern Europe*, Princeton 1969, 3–16

———— and George Rudisill, Jr, 'Taxation and community in Wales and Ireland, 1272–1327', *Speculum* xxix (1954), 410–16

Strong, Roy C., 'The popular celebration of the accession day of Queen Elizabeth I', *Journal of the Warburg and Courtauld Institutes* xxi (1958), 86–103

Stubbs, William, *The constitutional history of England in its origin and development*, Oxford 1880, 5th edn, London 1891

Studd, J. R., 'The Lord Edward's lordship of Chester, 1254–72', *THSLC* cxxviii (1979 [1978]), 1–25

Sutton, Anne F. and Livia Visser-Fuchs, *Richard III's books: ideal and reality in the life and library of a medieval prince*, Stroud 1990

Sylvester, Dorothy, 'The open fields of Cheshire', *THSLC* cviii (1956), 1–33

———— 'The manor and the Cheshire landscape', *Transactions of the Lancashire and Cheshire Antiquarian Society* lxx (1960), 1–15

Tait, James, *Medieval Manchester and the beginnings of Lancashire*, Manchester 1904

———— 'Knight-service in Cheshire', *EHR* lvii (1942), 437–59

Tanner, Thomas, *Bibliotheca Britannico-Hibernica*, London 1748

Taylor, Henry, *Historic notices, with topographical and other gleanings, descriptive of the borough and county-town of Flint*, London 1883

Taylor, John, *The universal chronicle of Ranulph Higden*, Oxford 1966

———— *English historical literature in the fourteenth century*, Oxford 1987

Taylor, Rupert, *The political prophecy in England*, repr. New York 1911

Temperley, Gladys, *Henry VII*, London 1917

Thacker, A. T., 'The earls and their earldom', in Thacker, *The earldom of Chester*, 7–12

———— 'The cult of King Harold at Chester', in Tom Scott and Pat Starkey (eds), *The Middle Ages in the north-west*, Oxford 1995, 155–76

———— (ed.), *The earldom of Chester and its charters: a tribute to Geoffrey Barraclough*, *Journal of the Chester Archaeological Society* lxxi (1991)

Thomson, Gladys Scott, *Lords lieutenant in the sixteenth century: a study in Tudor local administration*, London 1923

Thornley, I. D., 'The destruction of sanctuary', in R. W. Seton-Watson (ed.), *Tudor studies: presented to the Board of Studies in History in the University of London to Albert Frederick Pollard, being the work of twelve of his colleagues and pupils*, London 1924, 182–207

Thornton, Tim, 'The integration of Cheshire into the Tudor nation state in the early sixteenth century', *NH* xxix (1993), 40–63

———— 'A defence of the liberties of Chester, 1451–2', *Historical Research* lxviii (1995), 338–54

———— 'Local equity jurisdictions in the territories of the English crown: the palatinate of Chester, 1450–1540', in Dunn, *Courts, counties and the capital*, 27–52

———— 'Reshaping the local future: the development and uses of provincial political prophecy, 1300–1900', in Bertrand Taithe and Tim Thornton (eds), *Prophecy: the power of inspired language in history, 1300–2000*, Stroud 1997, 51–67

———— 'Dynasty and territory in the early modern period: The princes of Wales and their western British inheritance', *WHR* xx (2000), 1–33

Trevelyan, George Macaulay, *England in the age of Wycliffe*, London 1899, 4th edn, London 1909

———— *History of England*, London 1926, 3rd edn with corrections, London 1952

Tuck, J. A., 'Northumbrian society in the fourteenth century', *NH* vi (1971), 22–39

———— *Richard II and the English nobility*, London 1973

Ullmann, Walter, ' "This realm of England is an empire" ', *Journal of Ecclesiastical History* xxx (1979), 175–203

Urwin, Derek W., 'The price of a kingdom: territory, identity and the centre-periphery dimension in western Europe', in Yves Meny and Vincent Wright (eds), *Centre-periphery relations in western Europe*, London 1985, 151–70

———— 'Conclusions: perspectives on conditions of regional protest and accommodation', in S. Rokkan and Derek W. Urwin, *The politics of territorial identity: studies in European identity*, London 1982, 425–36

VCH, *Cambridge and the Isle of Ely*,

VCH, *County of Cheshire*, ed. B. E. Harris, Oxford 1979–

VCH, *Leicestershire*, ed. William Page and W. G. Hoskins, Oxford 1907–

VCH, *Nottinghamshire*, ed. William Page, Oxford 1906–

VCH, *Staffordshire*, ed. William Page, M. W. Greenslade and others, Oxford 1908–

VCH, *Warwickshire*, ed. H. Arthur Doubleday and William Page, Oxford 1904–

Virgoe, Roger, 'The parliamentary subsidy of 1450', *BIHR* lv (1982), 125–37

———— 'The benevolence of 1481', *EHR* civ (1989), 25–45

———— 'Aspects of the county community in the fifteenth century', in M. A. Hicks (ed.), *Profit, piety and the professions in late medieval England*, Gloucester–Wolfeboro, NH 1990, 1–13

Walker, Greg, *John Skelton and the politics of the 1520s*, Cambridge 1988

Wall, Alison, 'Patterns of politics in England, 1558–1625', *HJ* xxxi (1988), 947–63

Warnicke, Retha M., *William Lambarde: Elizabethan antiquary, 1536–1601*, London–Chichester 1973

—— 'Sexual heresy at the court of Henry VIII', *HJ* xxx (1987), 247–68

Warton, Thomas, *History of English poetry from the twelfth to the close of the sixteenth century*, ed. W. C. Hazlitt, London 1871

Watts, J. L., 'The counsels of King Henry VI, *c.* 1435–1445', *EHR* cvi (1991), 279–98

Webb, Sidney and Beatrice Webb, *English local government from the revolution to the Municipal Corporations Act: the manor and the borough*, London 1908

Wedgewood, Josiah C., *History of parliament: biographies of members of the Commons House, 1439–1509*, London 1936

Wheeler, Harvey, 'Calvin's case (1608) and the McIlwain–Schuyler debate', *American Historical Review* lxi (1956), 587–97

Wilkie, William E., *The cardinal protectors of England: Rome and the Tudors before the Reformation*, Cambridge 1974

Williams, C. H., 'The rebellion of Humphrey Stafford in 1486', *EHR* xliii (1928), 181–9

Williams, David, *A history of modern Wales*, 2nd edn, London 1977

Williams, Glanmor, 'Prophecy, poetry, and politics in medieval and Tudor Wales', in Hearder and Loyn, *British government and administration*, 104–16

—— *Recovery, reorientation and reformation: Wales, c. 1415–1642*, Oxford 1987

—— *Wales and the Act of Union*, Bangor 1992

Williams, Penry, *The Council in the Marches of Wales under Elizabeth I*, Cardiff 1958

—— *The Tudor regime*, Oxford 1979

Williams, W. R., *The history of the great sessions in Wales, 1542–1830*, Brecknock 1899

Williamson, A. H., 'Scotland, AntiChrist, and the invention of Britain', in John Dwyer, Roger A. Mason and Alexander Murdoch (eds), *New perspectives on the politics and culture of early modern Scotland*, Edinburgh 1982, 34–58

Willis, Browne, *A survey of the cathedrals*, London 1727

Wilson, R. M., *The lost literature of medieval England*, 2nd rev. edn, London 1970

Winstanley, Herbert, 'Speke Hall', *THSLC* n.s. xxxv (1920 [1919]), 1–20

Wolffe, B. P., *The crown lands, 1461–1536: an aspect of Yorkist and early Tudor government*, London–New York 1970

—— *The royal demesne in English history: the crown estate in the governance of the realm from the Conquest to 1509*, London 1971

—— *Henry VI*, London 1981

Wood, Anthony A., *Athenae Oxoniensis*, ed. P. L. Bliss, London 1813

Woodward, D. M., 'The Chester leather industry, 1558–1625', *THSLC* cxix (1968 [1967]), 65–111

Woolf, D. R., 'The "common voice": history, folklore and oral tradition in early modern England', *Past and Present* cxx (Aug. 1988), 26–52

—— *The idea of history in early Stuart England*, Toronto 1990

Wormald, Jenny, 'The creation of Britain: multiple kingdoms or core and colonies?', *TRHS* 6th ser. ii (1992), 175–94

Wright, Susan M., *The Derbyshire gentry in the fifteenth century* (Derbyshire Record Society viii, 1983)

Yates, Frances, *Astraea: the imperial theme in the sixteenth century*, London 1975

Youings, Joyce, *The dissolution of the monasteries*, London 1971

Unpublished theses

Bourgeois, II, E. J., 'A ruling elite: the government of Cambridgeshire, circa 1524–88', unpubl. PhD diss. Cambridge 1988

Cardew, Anne A., 'A study of society in the Anglo-Scottish borders, 1455–1502', unpubl. PhD diss. St Andrews 1974

Clayton, D. J., 'The involvement of the gentry in the political, administrative and judicial affairs of the county palatine of Chester, 1442–85', unpubl. PhD diss. Liverpool 1980

Cooper, John P. P., 'Propaganda, allegiance and sedition in the Tudor south-west, c. 1497–1570', unpubl. DPhil. diss. Oxford 1999

Cunningham, Sean, 'The Stanley earls of Derby in the early Tudor period, 1485–c. 1536', unpubl. MA diss. Lancaster 1990

—— 'The establishment of the Tudor regime: Henry VII, rebellion and the financial control of the aristocracy, 1485–1509', unpubl. PhD diss. Lancaster 1995

Curry, Anne E., 'The demesne of the county palatine of Chester in the early fifteenth century', unpubl. MA diss. Manchester 1977

Dickinson, J. R., 'Aspects of the Isle of Man in the seventeenth century', unpubl. PhD diss. Liverpool 1991

Ferguson, Catherine M. F., 'Law and order on the Scottish borders, 1603–1707', unpubl. PhD diss. St Andrews 1980

Fritze, R., 'Faith and faction: religious changes, national politics and the development of local factionalism in Hampshire, 1485–1570', unpubl. PhD diss. Cambridge 1982

Griffiths, R. A., 'Royal government in the southern counties of the principality of Wales, 1422–85', unpubl. PhD diss. Bristol 1962

Johnson, A. M., 'Some aspects of the political, constitutional, social, and economic history of the city of Chester, 1550–1662', unpubl. DPhil. diss. Oxford 1970

Lloyd, Melanie Katina, 'The Privy Council, Star Chamber and Wales, 1540–1572', unpubl. PhD diss. Swansea 1987

Marriott, Patricia J., 'The commission of the peace in Cheshire, 1536–1603', unpubl. MA diss. Manchester 1974

Marsh, Deborah, 'Humphrey Newton of Newton and Pownall (1466–1536): a gentleman of Cheshire and his commonplace book', unpubl. PhD diss. Keele 1995

Morgan, P. T. J., 'The government of Calais, 1485–1558', unpubl. DPhil. diss. Oxford 1966

Roberts, P. R., 'The "acts of union" and the Tudor settlement of Wales', unpubl. PhD diss. Cambridge 1966

Schofield, R. S., 'Parliamentary lay taxation, 1485–1547', unpubl. PhD diss. Cambridge 1963

Thornton, Tim, 'Political society in early Tudor Cheshire, 1480–1560', unpubl. DPhil. diss. Oxford 1993

Williams, Joanna M., 'The Stanley family of Lathom and Knowsley, c. 1450–1504: a political study', unpubl. MA diss. Manchester 1979

Worthington, Paul, 'Royal government in the counties palatine of Lancashire and Cheshire, 1460–1509', unpubl. PhD diss. Swansea 1990

Index

All places referred to are county towns or in Cheshire unless otherwise stated.

games, illegal, 128
Gamull, Ralph, 120
Gardiner, Stephen, bishop of Winchester, 84
Gascony, 253
Gawain and the Green Knight, 41
Gawsworth, 98
Gee, Henry, 126, 127
genealogy, 58, 61
General Proscription (1522), 74
General Surveyors, court of, 113–14
Genethliacon, see John Leland
gentry, 10–12, 13, 23–35, 46, 49, 58, 73, 93, 112, 120–1, 124–5, 129, 131, 138, 165–6, 169, 170, 177–8, 182, 183, 184, 187, 188, 189, 190, 193, 205, 211, 213, 214, 244; and administration, 25–9, 151, 153, 156, 157, 222–4, 239; and community, 31–3, 61, 224–31; wealth of, 24–5
Geoffrey of Monmouth, 253
Gerard, Thomas, 183
Gerrard, Piers, 93, 185
Gerrard, William, 117, 141
Geryn, John, 88
Gifford, Richard, 197
Gigli, Giovanni, 181
gilds, 47
Glamorgan, 129, 130, 146, 151
Glaseor, William, 52–3, 96, 116, 126, 152, 215, 236
Glegge, Henry, 158, 169
Glegge, Thomas, of Gayton, 183
Gloucestershire, 33–4, 129, 139, 144, 238
Godbehere, Gilbert, 36, 206
godparents, 49
Goldsmith, Ralph, 206
Goodman, Robert, 120
Goodman, William, 127
Gordon, George, fourth earl of Huntley (d. 1562), 233
Gower, 66
Gramsci, Antonio, 7
grand jury, 26–8
Grappenhall, 22, 153
Graveley (Cambridgeshire), 36
'Great John' (Prussian merchant), 106
great sessions, courts of, 130, 131, 132, 222–3
Great Yarmouth (Norfolk), 175
Green, Thomas, 116
Greenwich, treaty of (1543), 226
Grene, Richard, of Congleton, 24
Gresley, Sir John, 104, 105

Grey family, earls of Kent, 21
Grey, Edmund, fourth Lord Grey of Ruthin, first earl of Kent (d. 1489), 120
Grey, Edward, Lord Grey of Powis (d. 1551), 135
Grey, George, second earl of Kent (d. 1503), 86
Grey, Jane, queen of England, 238, 239
Grey de Wilton, Lord Arthur, 250
Griffin, John, of Nantwich, 168
Griffyth, Hugh, 221
Grimesditch, Ralph, 75
Grosvenor, Ranlyn, 120
Grosvenor, Richard, of Eaton (d. 34 Henry VIII), 146, 212
Grosvenor, Robert, of Holme, 181
Grosvenor, Thomas, of Eaton (d. 4 Edward VI), 237, 239
Grosvenor, Thomas, of Eaton (d. 21 Elizabeth), 239
Groves, William, 203
Grymesdiche, Hugh, 169
Guenée, Bernard, 243
Guernsey, 65, 66, 113, 114, 255
Guildford, Sir Henry, 124
Guildford, Sir Richard, 175
Guildford (Surrey), 87, 123
Guy of Warwick, alias Wigod of Wallingford, 44, 45

Haigh, Christopher, 234
Hailes abbey (Gloucestershire), 36
Hale, John, of Chester, 208
Hale, Robert, 207–8
Hales, John, 221
Hallam, Henry, 7
Halle, Edward, 172, 173–4, 176
Halton: castle, 97, 216; barony of, 50; honour of, 196, 215
Hamilton by-election (1967), 245
Hammond, John, 24
'Hamo', as a Christian name, 54
Hampshire, 124, 154
Hampton, 197, 214
Handford family, 170
Handley, 232
Hanky, John, of Churton, 169
Hannell, Joyes, wife of Thomas Hannell, 91
Hannell, Thomas, 91
haquebuts, 140
harbours, 139
Harcorte, John, 22
Harden, 107

'Neomagus' (alleged original name for Chester), 56
Neston, 240
Nevill family, 174
Nevill, Sir Edward, 215
Nevill, Eleanor, wife of Sir Edward Nevill, 215
Neville, Henry, fifth earl of Westmorland (d. 1563), 228
Newcastle (Northumberland), 87, 227
Newcastle-under-Lyme (Staffordshire), 47, 121, 123
Newhall, 21, 214
Newhall Tower, 21
'New Monarchy', 5
Newton, Humphrey of Pownall, 41, 42, 46, 60
Newton, Peter, 86, 183
Newton, Richard, 41
Newton, William, 230
Newton, 107
Newton-by-Middlewich, 168
New World, see America,
Nixon, William or Robert, prophet, 60
nobility, 6–7, 10–11, 13, 17–23, 46, 73, 82, 123, 165, 183
Norfolk, 8, 24, 34, 121
Norfolk, dukes of, see Howard
Norman Conquest, 3, 58
Norman, Richard, prior of Birkenhead, 120
Normandy, 71–2
Normandy, duke of, 65
Normans, 5, 44, 59, 62
Norreys, John, 2
Norris, Richard, 29
Norris, Sir William, of Speke (Lancashire), 156, 229, 237, 239
Norroy kings of arms, 53
Northampton, 125
Northamptonshire, 105
Northumberland, 65, 75, 76, 77
Northumberland, earl of, see Henry Percy
Northwich, 5, 97, 168, 184, 185, 196; hundred, 4, 23, 158
Norton priory/abbey, 23, 123, 198–9, 207–8, 211, 216, 234; prior of, 184. See also Thomas Birkenhead, William Merton
Nottingham, 167
Nottinghamshire, 29, 95, 106, 171, 228
Nowell, Lawrence (d. 1576), 60
Nun of Kent, see Barton, Elizabeth
Nuremberg (Germany), 58
Nuttall, Richard, 223

oath of 1434, 23
Odard, sword of, 53
office-holding, 14, 25, 73, 122, 143–61, 168, 178, 184, 188, 199–200, 212, 229, 242, 243; and litigation, 97; by Stanley family, 19, 169
Ogard, Alice, wife of Sir Andrew Ogard, 121
Ogard, Sir Andrew, 120, 121
Old Withington, 227
Orcharde of Syon, 35
Oriel College, Oxford, 37
Ormskirk (Lancashire), 176
Ormyshaw, Richard, 217
'Otwell', as Christian name, 50
outfangthief, 51–2
Over, 98
Overmarsh, 185
Owen, George, 246
Oxford, 35, 36
Oxford, earls of, see John de Vere
Oxfordshire, 105, 145, 192
Oxhey (Hertfordshire), 121

Packyngton, John, 29, 144–5
Page, Nicholas, 97
Paget, William, 159
Palmes, Guy, 92–3
papacy, 56
papal consistory, 200
Parfew, Robert, see Warton, Robert
Parker, Matthew, 58
parliament, Cheshire, 3, 4, 5, 44, 52, 67–8, 79, 242
parliament, English, 3, 7, 10, 11, 13, 14, 22, 43, 65, 72, 119–42; (1450), 3, 74, 104; (1497), 144; (1510), 144; (1539–40), 145, 149; (October 1553), 149; (1555), 236, 238, 239; Long Parliament, 7; Reformation Parliament, 115, 125–6; Tudor parliaments, 47
parliament, Irish, 3, 65, 99, 248
Parr, William, marquess of Northampton, 239
Parre, Margaret, 98
Paslew, John, 198
Pates, Richard, 117
Patmore, Henry, 234
Patryk, Richard, 107
Paulet, William, 204
Paunsfote, 193
Payling, Simon, 29
Pecche, Sir John, 175
Peckforton, 189